**INTEGRATING
INNOVATION IN
ARCHITECTURE**

This edition first published 2016
Copyright 2016 Ajla Aksamija
Published by John Wiley & Sons, Ltd

Registered office
John Wiley & Sons Ltd, The Atrium, Southern Gate, Chichester, West Sussex, PO19 8SQ, United Kingdom

For details of our global editorial offices, for customer services and for information about how to apply for permission to reuse the copyright material in this book please see our website at www.wiley.com.

All rights reserved. No part of this publication may be reproduced, stored in a retrieval system, or transmitted, in any form or by any means, electronic, mechanical, photocopying, recording or otherwise, except as permitted by the UK Copyright, Designs and Patents Act 1988, without the prior permission of the publisher.

Wiley publishes in a variety of print and electronic formats and by print-on-demand. Some material included with standard print versions of this book may not be included in e-books or in print-on-demand. If this book refers to media such as a CD or DVD that is not included in the version you purchased, you may download this material at http://booksupport.wiley.com. For more information about Wiley products, visit www.wiley.com.

Designations used by companies to distinguish their products are often claimed as trademarks. All brand names and product names used in this book are trade names, service marks, trademarks or registered trademarks of their respective owners. The publisher is not associated with any product or vendor mentioned in this book.

Limit of Liability/Disclaimer of Warranty: while the publisher and author have used their best efforts in preparing this book, they make no representations or warranties with respect to the accuracy or completeness of the contents of this book and specifically disclaim any implied warranties of merchantability or fitness for a particular purpose. It is sold on the understanding that the publisher is not engaged in rendering professional services and neither the publisher nor the author shall be liable for damages arising herefrom. If professional advice or other expert assistance is required, the services of a competent professional should be sought.

A catalogue record for this book is available from the British Library.

ISBN 978-1-119-16482-1 (hardback)
ISBN 978-1-119-16571-2 (ePDF)
ISBN 978-1-119-16481-4 (ePub)
ISBN 978-1-119-16480-7 (O-BK)

Executive Commissioning Editor: Helen Castle
Project Editor: Miriam Murphy
Assistant Editor: Calver Lezama

Page design by Emily Chicken
Cover design and page layouts by Karen Willcox, www.karenwillcox.com
Printed in Italy by Printer Trento Srl
Cover image © Synthesis Design + Architecture
Image page 250 © Rob Ley and Joshua G. Stein

AD SMART 04

INTEGRATING INNOVATION IN ARCHITECTURE

Design, Methods and Technology for Progressive Practice and Research

WILEY

Ajla Aksamija

CONTENTS

ACKNOWLEDGEMENTS 7

FOREWORD 9-11
by Phil Harrison

INTRODUCTION
INNOVATION IN ARCHITECTURE (WHAT, WHY AND HOW) 12-19
What is innovation? 13
Why innovate in architectural design? 16
How to innovate in architecture? 17

1 INNOVATIVE MATERIALS 20-59
Advances in concrete 23
Advances in glass 27
Advances in metals 37
Biomaterials 39
Composite materials 41
Electrochromics 45
Shape-memory alloys 45
Self-healing materials 47
Sensors and controls 48
Phase-change materials 49
Photovoltaics 51
Thermoelectrics 55
Conclusion: the impacts of advanced and smart materials on architectural design 57

2 INNOVATIONS IN COMPUTATIONAL DESIGN 60-127
Advances in computational design 63
Tools and methods 77
BIM in design 88
BIM in virtual construction 91
BIM in facility management 95
Environmental simulations and energy analysis 98
Structural analysis 101
CFD analysis 105
Digital fabrication and methods 111
Design to fabrication 121
Conclusion: the integration of advanced computational technologies with design and research 125

3 TECHNOLOGICAL INNOVATIONS 128-169
Advances in facade systems 131
Advances in HVAC systems 135
Advances in lighting 145
Building automation systems 151
Prefabrication and modular construction 156
Automation in construction 159
Robotics in construction 162
Smart and responsive buildings 163
Conclusion: the integration of advanced technologies in design and construction 167

4 INNOVATIONS IN THE DESIGN PROCESS AND ARCHITECTURAL PRACTICE 170-183
Motives and goals for innovation 171
Organisation and roles 172
Integration of research and design practice 174
Research methods for innovation 176
Financial factors and investments for innovation 177
Value of innovation 179
Innovations in project delivery 179
Risk management in innovative design practice 181
Conclusion: strategies for integrating innovation 183

5 BUILDING INTEGRATED INNOVATIONS AND METHODS (CASE STUDIES) 184-245
Center for Design Research, University of Kansas 187
Umwelt Arena 191
King Fahad National Library 199
Hanjie Wanda Square 205
Collaborative Life Sciences Building and Skourtes Tower 211
Shanghai Natural History Museum 219
The Yas Hotel 229
Health Sciences Education Building, Phoenix Biomedical Campus 233
Conclusion: lessons learned from case studies 243

FUTURE OUTLOOKS: CONCLUDING REMARKS 246-249

SELECT BIBLIOGRAPHY 250-253

APPENDIX: CASE STUDIES INDEX 254-259

INDEX 260-264

ACKNOWLEDGEMENTS

I would like to acknowledge all the valuable time, comments and feedback I have received, during the preparation and writing of this book from individuals, firms and organisations. They have worked closely with me, helping me to capture the essence of projects, design methods and approaches featured here in the case studies, projects, building systems and installations. I thank them all for their involvement, support and advice.

I would like to extend my gratitude to Phil Harrison for providing his perspective and for writing the foreword.

My research assistants, Yi Wang, Christopher Mansfield and Tom Forker deserve special recognition for their help.

I would also like to thank the Wiley editorial and production team, particularly Helen Castle, Calver Lezama and Miriam Murphy.

Lastly, I would like to acknowledge Zlatan, Nur and Iona Aksamija for their undivided love and support.

FOREWORD
TOWARDS A RESEARCH-BASED DESIGN PRACTICE

PHIL HARRISON

We are entering an age of serious design thinking.

The dominant modes of design over the last two centuries have been decoration, tectonics, theory, systematisation and intuition, among many others that have tended to be rooted in the past and the present. All have yielded beauty in various ways, and these foundational modes of thinking should and will remain part of modern practice, as designers embrace a richly layered approach to conceptualisation. But today, designers and their patrons are increasingly seeking proof that design will live up to expectations in the future. This yearning for predictability is pushing designers to balance their humanistic focus on what has been and what is, with a scientific rigour that attempts to establish what will be. This accelerating move towards fact-based predictive design thinking is revolutionising our creative process far beyond the limited aim of reducing risk, towards a new form of design practice that bristles with empirical discipline in balance with imagination.

Why? There are compelling economic, environmental and social reasons for this evolution. Economically, buildings simply cost more today than ever before, and building owners are demanding more from their capital investments. Environmentally, resource scarcity is similarly driving us all to do more with less. And socially, there is an increasing recognition that human performance and well-being are far more valuable than bricks and mortar. In all these, there is a growing awareness that design can answer these challenges. Design thinking is, in fact, the best answer to all these, because designers have the unique skill of using synthetic thinking to solve increasingly complex problems in simple and powerful ways.

But we have a problem. Modern design practice is not rooted in the kind of serious research-based thinking that is at the core of so many other innovative disciplines, such as medicine or engineering. To truly transform design practice to be stunningly innovative, we need to develop our own kind of intellectual rigour – a new type of design practice that is research-based and that is fundamentally conceived to yield breakthrough results.

This is an ambitious goal, and in my experience, this goal has been front of mind with many design educators and practitioners for at least the past decade. However, most have hesitated to move forward with meaningful action due to the uncertainty of the terrain of design research. What are the important research questions? How do we transform our profession, which is so rooted in history and intuition, and embrace a more scientific approach? How do we preserve what we love about the art of architecture with a new evidence-based approach; or, how do art and science mix for us?

How can the historically separate realms of the academy and the profession engage in research together?

Enter Ajla Aksamija and her book *Integrating Innovation in Architecture*. The following pages are at once a template, a primer and a call to action for serious research in architecture. The first step towards tackling any significant challenge is to simply understand it. The first three chapters of the book rigorously march through the various dimensions of architecture: materials, processes and technologies. Aksamija scans the global design market and reveals countless examples of innovative possibilities occurring all over the world. She succinctly explains each innovation and links each to relevant examples of their application, proving that these are not dreams but seriously useful and impactful innovations. This part of the book gives us the 'what', and anyone passionate about design should use the examples cited as an itinerary for their future travels. But Aksamija goes further in the second part of the book where she outlines the 'how' of research. I believe this part of the book is the most important, as it will provide practitioners with a prototype business strategy to develop their own research-based practice and the courage to do so.

Design practice is extremely difficult. Architects, interior designers, planners and landscape architects are historically less well compensated than other professional service providers. As such, our profession chronically skates on the edge of financial viability, even as the market grows increasingly demanding of our time and energy with more intense legal, regulatory, environmental and other pressures. In this predicament, it is understandably difficult for designers to find the energy to change their practices. Change is intimidating, but Aksamija's book helps break this down for us, and makes the prospect of change much less abstract. By explaining the 'what' and the 'how', she provides designers with an invaluable toolkit.

The key message of this book is action. The most important thing to do is to start something. By demystifying the challenge and breaking it down into smaller pieces, firms and design schools can find seeds of possibility and start incrementally. Aksamija's book title suggests that 'integrating' research into practice can be done as an evolution, not as a radical step. Our profession simply cannot afford to think about research in the manner of the pharmaceutical industry, for example. Instead, we can get there by reallocating current resources and establishing new degrees of rigour in our work. The evolution into research-based practice can be a subtle shift, but it needs to be a serious and purposeful one. Importantly, *diversity and transparency* will help our industry get further faster.

Here is what I mean by diversity: while Aksamija gives us a broad tableau of research possibilities, each designer, school and firm should craft their own research agendas that are more narrowly defined and have specific goals. Indeed, the possibilities are so broad and rich, there are virtually no limits to the work ahead of us, and so a diversified approach to investigation is the right model for the design industry. This idea is the opposite of a singularly focused 'moon shot' mentality; it is a divide and conquer approach. We should pursue many smaller goals because there are so many important areas of inquiry, and tackling smaller research problems will be inherently more economically feasible for us. But then we need to share what we learn. Diversity requires transparency. Unlike the pharmaceutical industry, we should not think about our research as a means to developing competitive advantage. Instead, we should take the leap of faith that sharing knowledge in a transparent approach will lead us to more innovation, more rapidly, and that this will ultimately make a stronger design industry in which we all can thrive.

But first, please read this excellent and important book, and please use it productively. I hope you enjoy it.

Phil Harrison, FAIA, LEED AP, is a Principal and Chief Executive Officer at Perkins+Will. He is responsible for the firm's strategic focus and business performance. He is directly involved with quality initiatives including design excellence, sustainability, research and technical delivery.

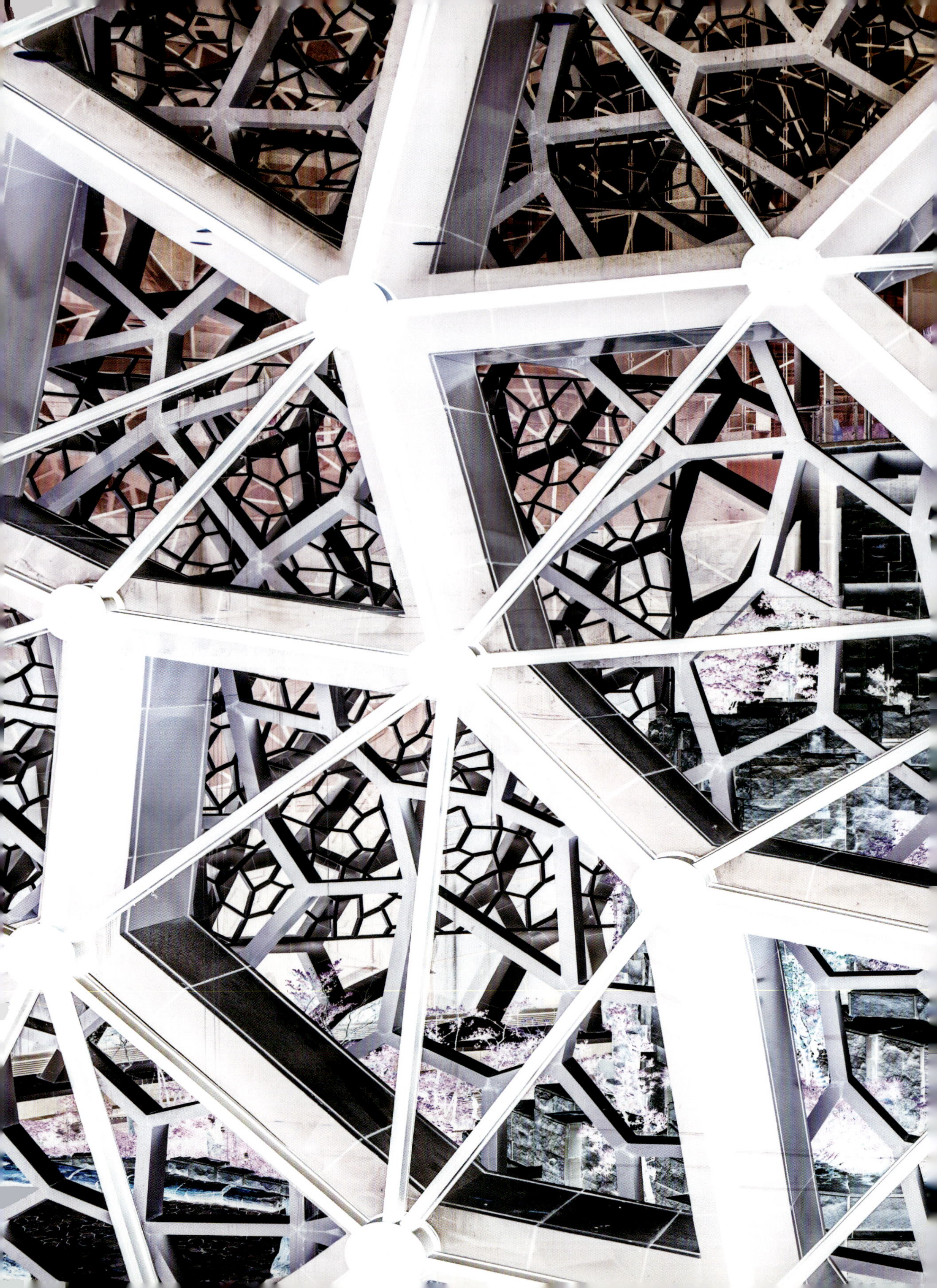

INTRODUCTION
INNOVATION IN ARCHITECTURE
(WHAT, WHY AND HOW)

Design professionals are currently faced with many challenges – rapid technological changes, the necessity to innovate and raise the bar in building performance, and a paradigm shift in architecture with the wider adoption of BIM-based design. There are a number of reasons why progressive practices must continuously invest in research and the implementation of advanced technologies, but the need to improve design processes and services is typically the overarching drive.

This book focuses on innovations in architecture, new materials and design methods, advances in computational design, innovations in building technologies and the integration of research with design. It also illustrates with case studies how these approaches have been implemented on actual architectural projects, and how design and technical innovations are used to improve building performance, as well as design practices in cutting-edge architectural and design firms. But first it is essential to discuss what innovation is, why it is necessary to innovate in architecture and how it relates to architectural design and practice.

WHAT IS INNOVATION?

The general definition of innovation is that it is the process of introducing changes to methods, services or products. These changes must be useful and meaningful, adding value to the established norms and contributing to our knowledge. Innovation and technological changes are complementary in nature, since innovation relies heavily on technological and scientific developments. For example, the diagram overleaf shows the use of the term 'innovation' in English language publications from the 1700s to today – it is evident that it coincides with major eras of technological developments, such as the Industrial Revolution and the Information Revolution. The last few decades have seen unprecedented social, technological and economic changes, and innovation is becoming critical to many fields including among others medicine, information technology, transport, engineering and design.

However, the concept of innovation in architectural design is not new – there are numerous examples throughout history where new ideas, design methods, materials and construction processes were introduced, resulting in new building typologies, design and construction methods. For example, the Romans introduced concrete and mastered the structural use of arches, resulting in monumental buildings and a style that significantly influenced

1

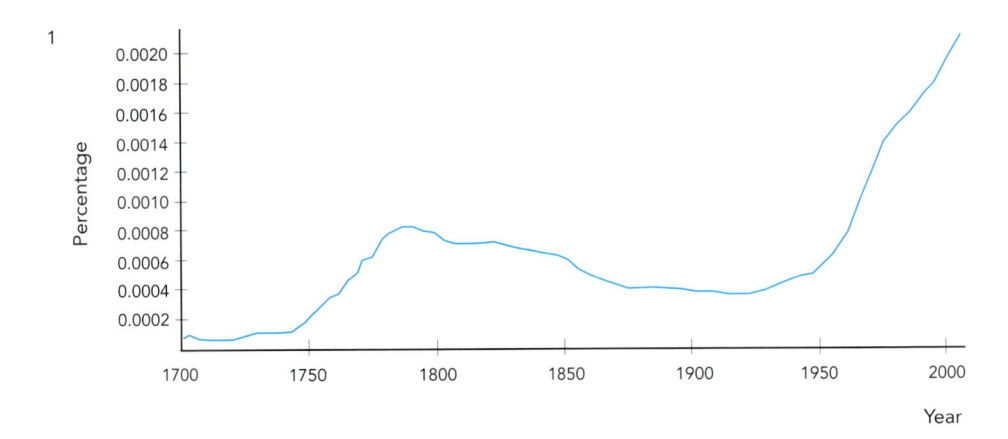

Line chart showing Percentage vs Year from 1700 to 2000. Values rise from ~0.0001 in 1700, peak around 0.0008 near 1790, decline slightly through 1900, then rise sharply to over 0.0020 by 2000.

2

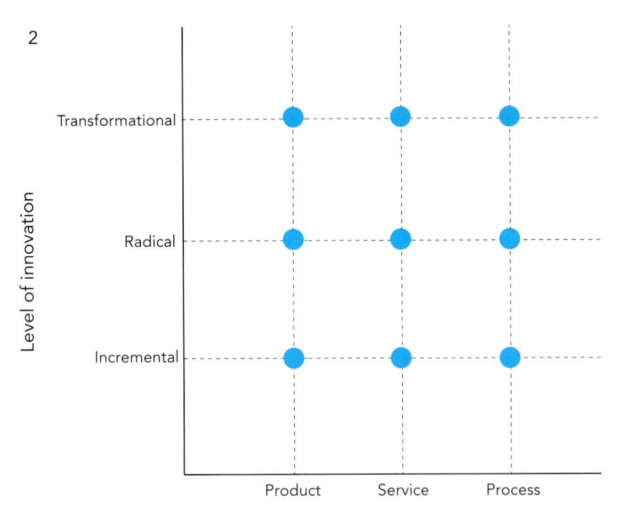 Level of innovation	Product	Service	Process
Transformational	●	●	●
Radical	●	●	●
Incremental	●	●	●

What is changed

3

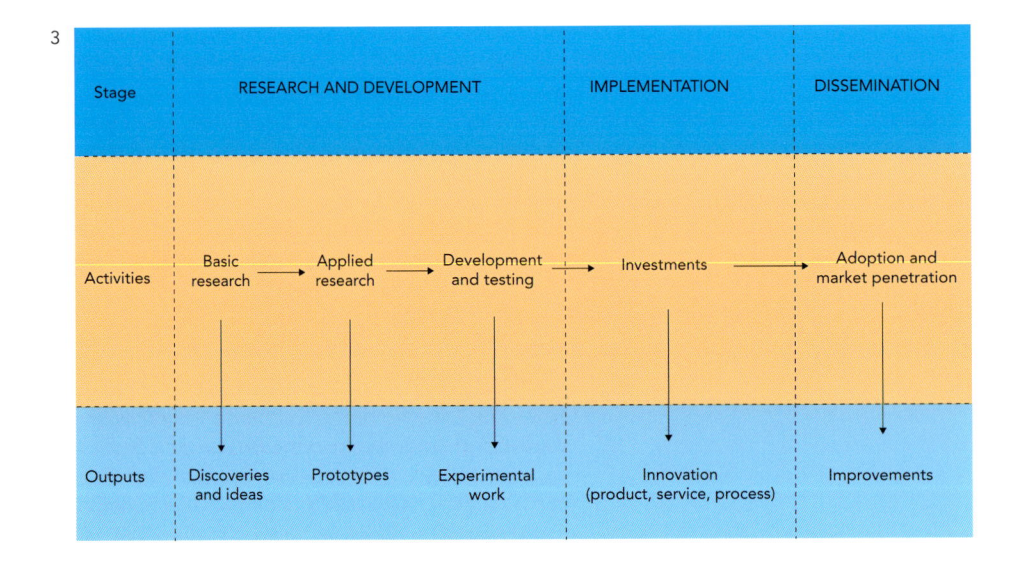

Stage	RESEARCH AND DEVELOPMENT			IMPLEMENTATION	DISSEMINATION
Activities	Basic research →	Applied research →	Development and testing →	Investments →	Adoption and market penetration
Outputs	Discoveries and ideas	Prototypes	Experimental work	Innovation (product, service, process)	Improvements

future architectural styles and form. The Gothic architectural style was developed as a direct result of innovations in structural form – pointed arches, ribbed vaulting and flying buttresses provided new methods for spanning large areas in stone and for building taller. The introduction of reinforced concrete in the late 19th century revolutionised architectural design and engineering. Steel skeleton frames and advances in vertical transportation through the invention of elevators initiated the development of tall buildings, which was also influenced by particular economic conditions. High density and rising costs of urban land in major cities led to the development of tall buildings as a building type, where the building footprint and site were minimised, and the capabilities of steel structural systems were exploited to provide a design solution for maximising the building area and return on investment. Moreover, the second half of the 20th century provided unprecedented developments in materials, building technologies and systems, computational methods for design, fabrication methods and mass production, and construction processes. For example, advances in facade systems and glass, as well as developments in mechanical systems, introduced a new typology of commercial office buildings in the 1950s and 1960s, which became symbols of the International Style across the globe.

Although the concept of innovation within the context of architectural design is not new, the deliberate use of the word 'innovation' in architecture has become widely popular over the last 15 years. It is difficult to determine the specific cause – such as the development of a certain technology – that influenced the adoption of this term to describe contemporary design and practice. The key underlining standpoint of this book is that multiple reasons and causes, including new building technologies and materials, advancements in building systems, the wider adoption of computational design techniques, the adoption of BIM as a paradigm shift in design, collaboration and construction, new design practices (including research and development) and economic impacts have all contributed to embracing innovation as a key component in contemporary design.

Architectural design, in the context of contemporary innovation, relies on the decision-making process, where an idea is transformed into an outcome: either a tangible product (ie, building) or intangible service (ie, design process). Regardless of the type, innovation must be useful and meaningful, and must create added value by applying new ideas. The diagram, which shows the relationships between aspects that can be changed (product, service and process) and the level of innovation (incremental, radical and transformational), indicates different types and levels of innovation. Within architectural design, the product is the building, physical space, material or object; service is the way that we interact with clients, constituents and building occupants; and process is the design process that is applied to create a building, space or a system. Therefore, all of these three categories can be changed and improved, and the level of innovation can vary from incremental to transformational.

1 The use of the term 'innovation' in English-language publications from the 1700s to today.
Unprecedented social, technological and economic changes within the last few decades, such as the Information Revolution, have resulted in the growing significance of innovation in many different fields, including architectural design.

2 Relationships between the levels of innovation and what can be changed.
In the context of architectural design, the product is the building, physical space or object; service is the way that we interact with clients, constituents and building occupants; and process refers to the design process. Incremental innovation is a small change that affects certain projects. Radical innovation has an impact on larger contexts (such as the development of new software), while transformational innovation creates a paradigm shift in architectural design and the profession.

3 Three stages of the innovation process: research and development, implementation and dissemination.
The outputs of specific stages, such as research and development, influence and direct activities of subsequent stages.

INTRODUCTION 14-15

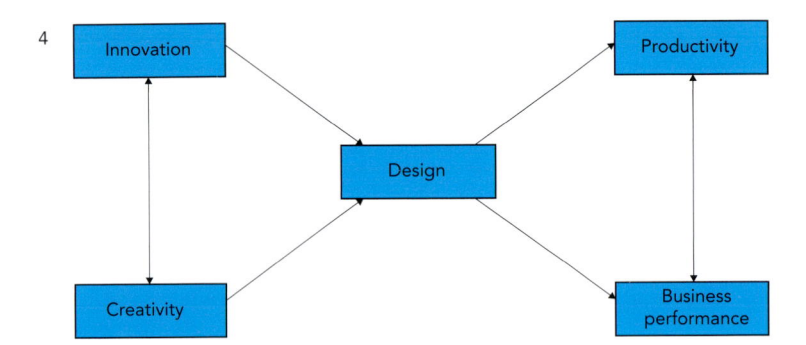

Incremental innovation is a small change that affects certain projects, such as the application of a novel material. Radical innovation has an impact on larger contexts, such as new computer software, or the improvement of a design process for a certain building type. Transformational innovation creates a paradigm shift in architectural design and the profession.

There are three stages that constitute the innovation process: research and development, commercialisation or implementation, and dissemination. During each stage, there are activities that require the input of knowledge, and the investment of time and resources. For example, research and development stages require basic research, applied research and development and testing. The outcomes include discoveries, new ideas, the development of new knowledge and the development of prototypes, testing and experimental work. The next stage constitutes implementation, and the last stage is dissemination and wider adoption. It is important to note that innovation is rarely a linear progression through the indicated stages, but rather specific outputs influence the activities of consequent stages.

WHY INNOVATE IN ARCHITECTURAL DESIGN?

An important question arises – why innovate in architectural design? What are the drivers for innovation in architectural design, and what is its value? Innovation helps organisations to progress and advance; it also affects efficiency, quality of work and improves design processes.

Innovation in architectural design requires the application of new design strategies and new project delivery methods. New design tools, materials, building technologies and construction techniques contribute to making buildings more responsive to the environment and their occupants. Innovative methods for collaboration, such as BIM, provide new ways for integrating design and construction. Project delivery innovations blur the traditional roles in design and construction and have an impact on business performance. Seeking innovation in architectural design encourages creative thinking, which helps architectural firms to adapt to changing market conditions and inner dynamics, ultimately affecting productivity and business performance.

4 Relationships between innovation, design and business performance.
Innovation in architecture has an impact on creativity and design processes, which in turn influence the productivity and business performance of a firm.

5 Relationships between the innovation and operation of architectural firms.
Architectural firms that embrace innovation should maintain a balance between innovation and operation, allowing new ideas and new market demands to influence meaningful changes to operation.

Changing markets and economics dictate development and opportunities in the architectural and construction industries, and entrepreneurial firms are able to respond to these changes and adapt their practices.

Beyond the economic and competitive advantages, innovation in architectural design also influences the outcomes of the design process and the built environment, so instituting social impacts and human well-being. Energy-efficient, responsive buildings that adapt to environmental changes and occupants are an emerging category of buildings that have the potential to change our future. Therefore, the value lies not only in organisational improvements, economic benefits and enhancements for individual firms, but in the broader benefits for society.

HOW TO INNOVATE IN ARCHITECTURE?

Organisations typically classify their activities under two broad categories – operation and innovation. Operations include all activities that provide an existing service to clients, while innovation consists of all activities that change operations and are focused on the future needs of the organisation, market and clients, as well as technological developments. In some cases, tension between the operating activities and innovation may exist, since established operations will be affected. Innovative organisations embrace this challenge and maintain a balance, allowing the results of innovation to have an impact on operation. The diagram below shows how architectural firms and organisations that embrace innovation should function. Operation and innovation should be linked, allowing the results of innovation to influence changes in operation.

The size of a firm dictates its operation, mainly in terms of the selection of clients, specialisation in specific building typologies and markets, types of design projects, as well as activities and roles in the design process. Small firms tend to focus on specific building types, such as residential, hospitality or commercial buildings, where the employees tend to be involved in all stages of the project and different roles are blurred between design, project management and technical delivery. Large firms typically

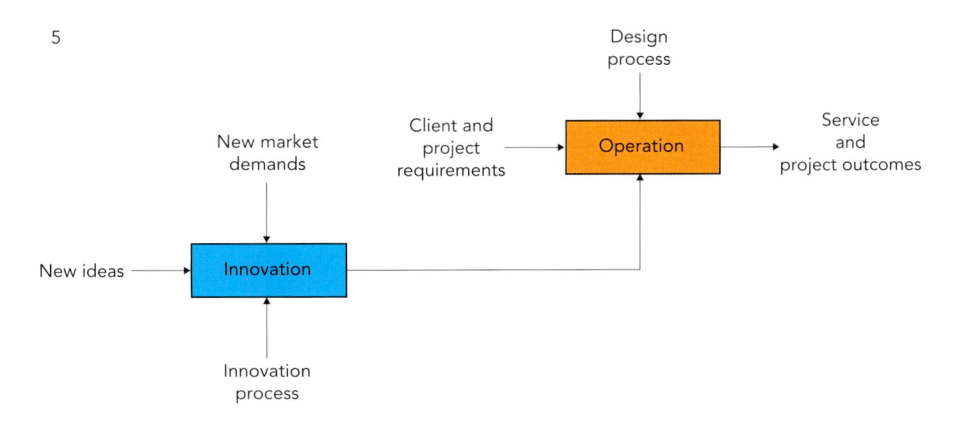

5

serve several market sectors and multiple building types, including healthcare, educational, academic, institutional, commercial and other building typologies. The roles of different employees are typically differentiated by the project stages, where design, project management and technical roles are distinguished and teams are organised by the market sector. However, innovative practices can be applied to any building type, and the firm's size is irrelevant in implementing innovative design approaches. New ideas, new market demands and innovative processes are applicable in all market sectors and drive innovation in all building types. The differences between small, medium and large firms in accepting and implementing innovation are mostly evident in the firms' operations. For example, larger firms may have more resources for research and development, where internal research teams are integrated with the design teams. Smaller firms may use different models for research, such as funding specific studies led by academic institutions or collaborating with research centres. Nevertheless, the size of the firm does not affect innovation, but rather its vision, motives and goals.

But, how to innovate in architecture? One of the most important aspects is that innovation requires integrated approaches, where design methods, technology and firm culture must coalesce to address issues and problems, and provide solutions that create value for the firm, client and society. Therefore, advanced materials and building technologies, design computation, innovative project delivery, BIM and construction techniques all play a role, as well as motives, the firm's organisation, research and development, and investments. An integrated model for innovation in architecture is shown in the following diagram overleaf, which demonstrates how these different factors influence innovation. The rest of this book discusses all of these factors in detail and provides guidelines for integrating innovation in architecture. Chapter 1 focuses on advances in materials: composite materials, responsive and smart materials, as well as energy-generating materials. Chapter 2 discusses innovations in computational design: tools and methods for successfully integrating computation with design and digital fabrication, the use of BIM for all stages of a building's life cycle, the use of simulations and performance-based analysis methods for environmental and structural investigations and processes for translating design to digital fabrication. Chapter 3 focuses on technological innovations: mainly innovative building technologies (facades, HVAC and lighting systems, and building automation); innovations in construction techniques (modular and prefabricated construction, automation of construction processes and robotics), as well as smart and responsive buildings. Chapter 4 presents guidelines for stimulating innovation in design practice: the integration of research and design, economic impacts and financial factors, innovations in project delivery and risk management in innovative design practices. Chapter 5 discusses specific case studies that illustrate methods for building-integrated innovations, including innovative materials and building technologies, responsive design, computational approaches, BIM and construction techniques. The concluding section of the

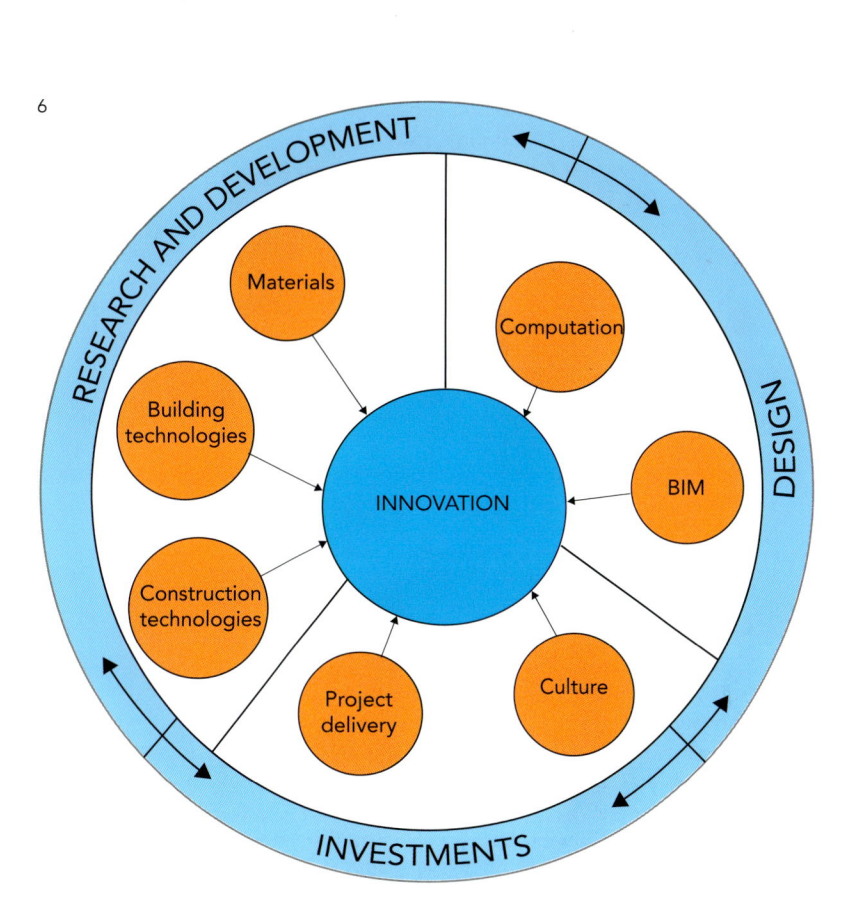

6 Model for integrating innovation in architecture.
Different factors – including advanced materials and building technologies, computational design, BIM, research and development innovations in project delivery and construction techniques – all play a role, besides the culture of the organisation.

book discusses future outlooks, and provides recommendations and steps that firms can take to integrate innovation into their operation and everyday activities.

We cannot exactly predict how cities will function in the future, how transport modes will work, or what types of new technologies will be discovered and developed. We cannot precisely predict how economic and societal changes will affect the human population in a long-term context, or how will our health be improved by new scientific discoveries and medical advances. But, we know that changes are imminent, and that architecture and the built environment will be affected. Contemporary practices that embrace technological, societal and economic changes, and establish innovation as a core value and design philosophy, are better equipped to face what the future will bring.

IMAGES
Opening image © James Steinkamp Photography; figures 1, 2, 3, 4, 5 and 6 © Ajla Aksamija

INTRODUCTION 18-19

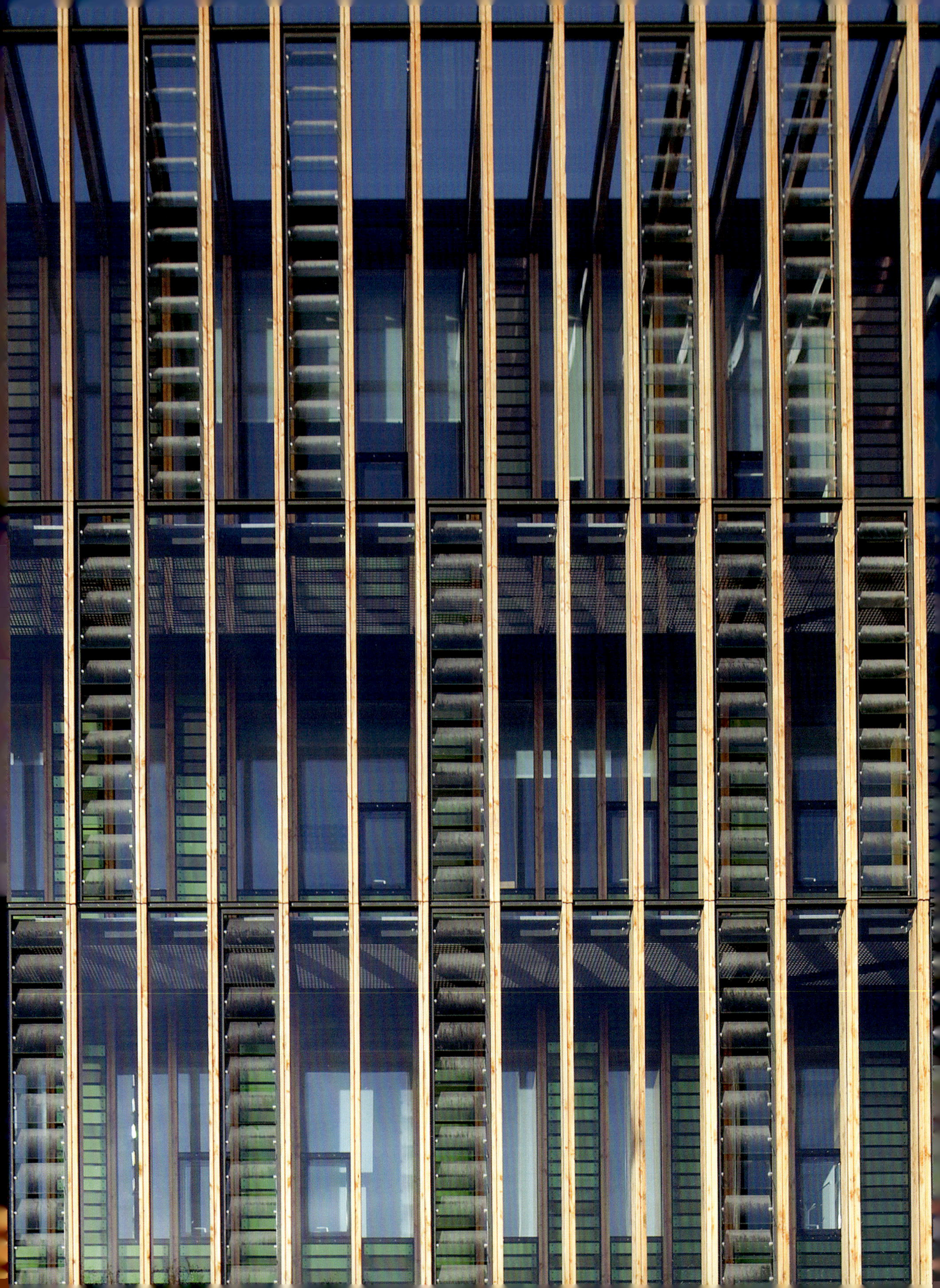

1 INNOVATIVE MATERIALS

Innovations in materials are influencing contemporary architectural practice. Today, the focus is primarily on new materials that exhibit enhanced properties. Therefore, advanced and composite materials, smart and responsive materials, and biologically inspired materials are gaining popularity in architectural design. Advanced materials are those that have enhanced properties (such as thermal performance, structural properties, durability and so on), and exhibit sensitivity to the environment in terms of production and use. Smart and responsive materials are those that exhibit properties that can be changed or altered, so that they act as sensors or actuators, responding to changes in the environment. These new emerging materials offer radical changes to the built environment in terms of energy usage, thermal behaviour, structural performance and aesthetics. This chapter provides an overview of emerging materials and discusses their use, performance, benefits and drawbacks.

Advances in physical sciences have led to a new understanding of changeable materials, particularly those compromising the acoustic, luminous and thermal environments of buildings. A smart structure can be defined as a non-biological physical structure that has a definite purpose, means and imperative to achieve that purpose, and a biological pattern of functioning. Smart materials are considered to be a subset, or components of smart structures, and act in such a way as to mimic the functioning of a biological or living organism and adapt to changing conditions in the environment. Smart materials can be classified into two general categories – materials that can sense and inherently respond to the changes in the environment, and materials that need control in a systematic manner in order to actuate based on a certain change. Different types of smart materials include piezoelectric, electrochromic, electrostrictive, magnetostrictive, electrorheological, shape-memory alloys and fibre-optic sensors. Piezoelectric materials exhibit significant material deformation in response to an applied electric field and produce dielectric polarisation in response to mechanical strains. Electrostrictive materials exhibit mechanical deformation when an electric field is applied. Magnetostrictive materials generate strains in response to an applied magnetic field. Electrorheological materials exhibit the 'ER response' or 'Winslow effect', which refers to a significant and reversible change in the

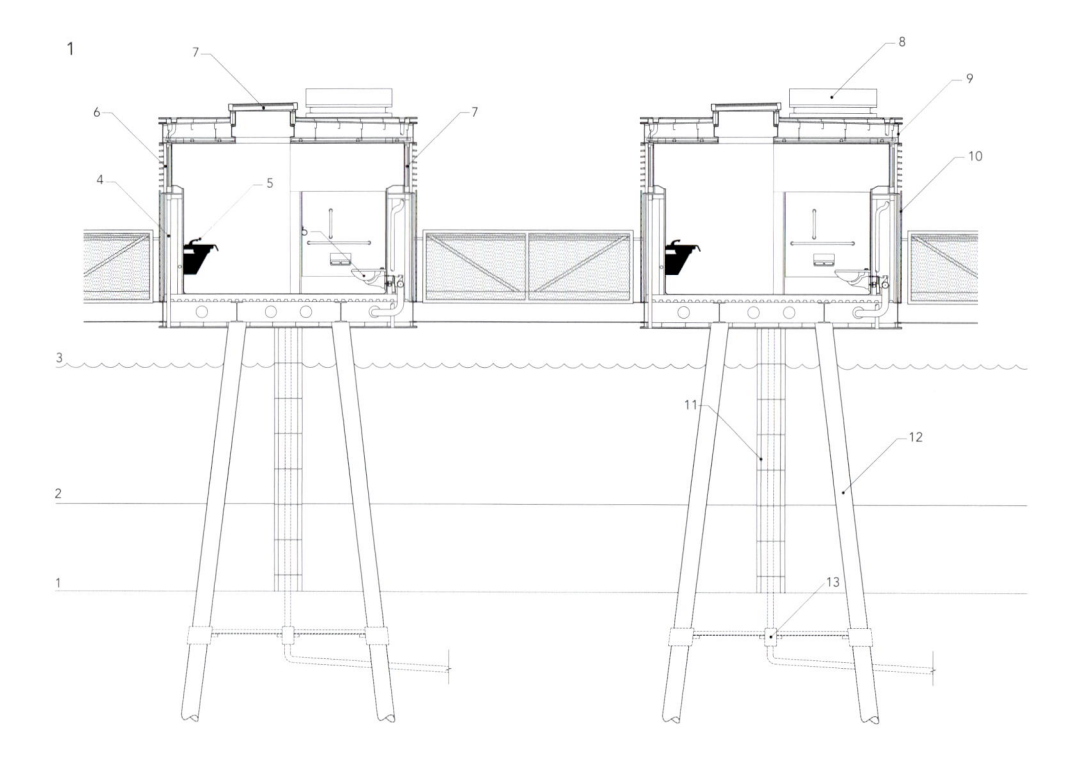

1 Garrison Architects, New York City Beach Restoration Modules, New York, USA, 2013.
The section shows building elements and systems. The modules are raised on concrete legs to withstand significant sea level rise.

1 Sand
2 Boardwalk
3 Advisory base flood elevation
4 Building envelope
5 Low flow plumbing fixtures
6 Operable windows
7 Skylights
8 Photovoltaics
9 Galvanised steel frame
10 Fibre-reinforced concrete cladding
11 Pre-stressed concrete pilings
12 Utility chase
13 Piping connectors

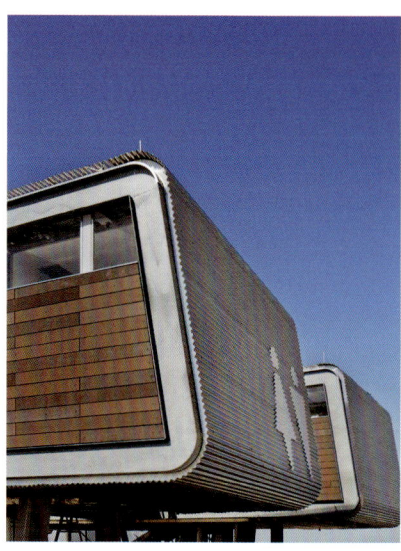

rheological behaviour of fluids subjected to an external applied electric field – low viscosity fluid converts into a solid substance. Shape-memory alloys are metal compounds that can sustain and recover large strains without undergoing plastic deformation under externally applied stress or thermal changes.

ADVANCES IN CONCRETE

Transforming the design and construction industries are new advances in concrete- and cement-based products. Among many new materials being used are superplasticising admixtures, high-strength mortars, self-compacting concrete and high-volume fly ash and slag concretes. A number of advances in new concrete technologies have been made in the past decade, including materials, recycling, mixture proportioning, durability and environmental quality. There are also diverse new methods and techniques in today's construction world, such as high-performance concrete (HPC) and fibre-reinforced concrete (FRC). Advanced composite materials have become popular in the construction industry for innovative building design solutions, including the strengthening and retrofitting of existing structures. The interface between different materials is a key issue of such design solutions, as the structural integrity relies on the bond between different materials. Knowledge about the durability of concrete/epoxy interfaces is becoming essential, as the use of these systems in applications such as fibre-reinforced plastic (FRP) strengthening and retrofitting of concrete structures is becoming increasingly popular.

Recycled materials are usually added to HPC, thereby reducing the need to dispose of them.[1] Some of the materials include fly ash (waste by-product from coal burning), ground-granulated blast-furnace slag and silica fume. But perhaps the biggest benefit of some of these other materials is the reduction in the need to use cement, also commonly referred to as Portland cement. The reduction in the production and use of cement has many beneficial aspects, including a decrease in the creation of carbon-dioxide emissions and energy consumption. In addition, fly ash and furnace slag have properties that improve the quality of the final concrete and the use of them is usually more cost-effective than cement.

Today's concrete technologies have produced new types of concrete that have lifespans measured in the hundreds of years rather than decades. When compared with standard concrete, new concretes have better corrosion resistance, equal or higher compressive and tensile strengths, higher fire resistance, and rapid curing and strength gain. In addition, the production and life cycle of these new concretes will reduce greenhouse gas emissions by as much as 90%.

Glass-fibre reinforced concrete (GFRC) is a new type of concrete with a much higher tensile and flexural (bending) strength than standard concrete.[2] This glass-fibre reinforced concrete is combined with pre-mixed dry components. It has higher density than standard concrete, and structural systems and building components need less material than conventional concrete for

2 (opposite below and below) Garrison Architects, New York City Beach Restoration Modules, New York, USA, 2013.
The beach modules incorporate GFRC panels as facade cladding materials.

3 Surface, colour and finishing textures of GFRC concrete.
A variety of finishing techniques and colours are possible for GFRC concrete facade cladding, so facades can have interesting, dynamic patterns.

4

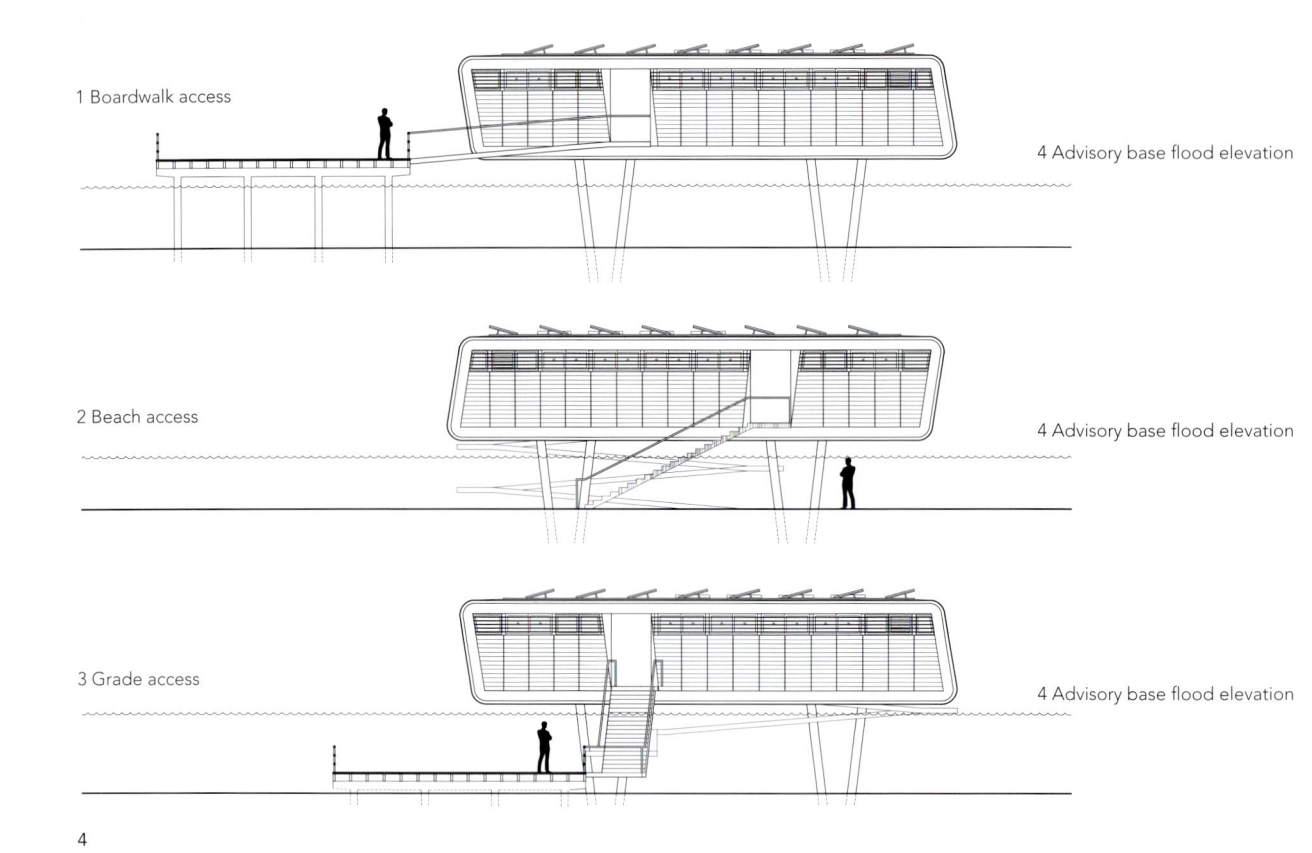

4 Garrison Architects, New York City Beach Restoration Modules, New York, USA, 2013. Elevations show facade treatment and indicate 500 year flood level.

5 Photocatalysis process for self-cleaning concrete.
The self-cleaning photocatalysis process for concrete consists of two steps: in the first step, UV light triggers an oxidation process on the titanium dioxide-coated surface, breaking down dirt and polluting substances; in the second (hydrophilic) stage, rain washes particles off the concrete surface.

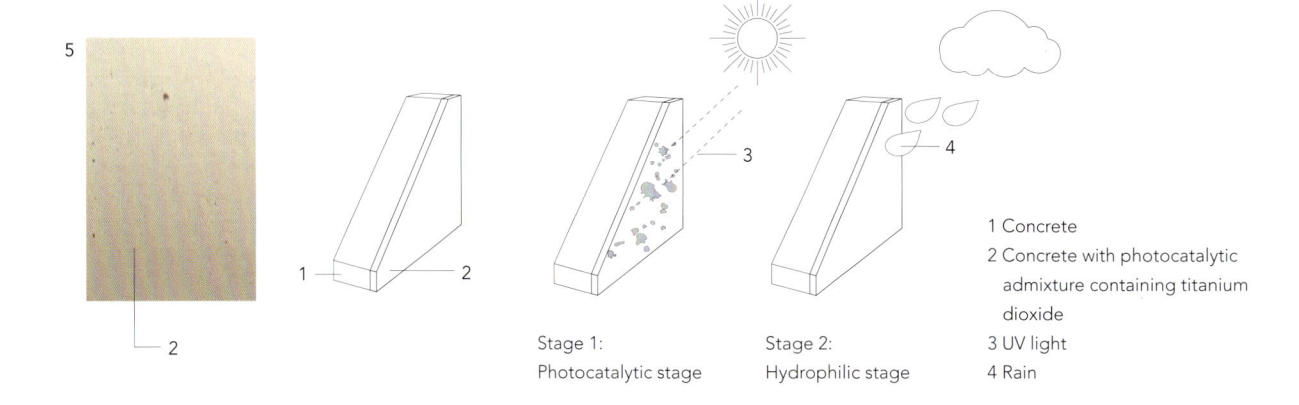

1 Concrete
2 Concrete with photocatalytic admixture containing titanium dioxide
3 UV light
4 Rain

Stage 1: Photocatalytic stage
Stage 2: Hydrophilic stage

structural stability. This high density gives GFRC concrete other properties, such as extremely high resistance to corrosion from chemicals. The higher strength also eliminates the need for steel rebars in structural designs. GFRC, or a variation with metallic fibres and/or superplasticisers, can be used to build extremely thin structural elements. Overall, structures built with GFRC will have much greater lifespans and require less maintenance. Special surface effects can be created with aggregates and a variety of finishing techniques. New York City's Beach Restoration Modules, designed by Garrison Architects, incorporate GFRC panels. These factory-assembled modules were designed following the devastating Hurricane Sandy that destroyed the coastline of New York City. The modules are mounted on concrete legs, raising the modules above the 500 year flood level, as shown in the sections and elevations. The modules, designed to withstand the next major ocean storm, rely on photovoltaics and a solar water-heating system.

Other advances include translucent concrete, which is created by adding optical fibres to the concrete admixtures. This is changing the perception of concrete as a primarily opaque mass. Applications to date have been mainly for interior and decorative use, partitions, and so on. Self-consolidating concrete is a special concrete mix that eliminates the need for mechanical consolidation and yields a smooth surface finish.[3] Insulated concrete form (ICF) walls are gaining popularity in the residential building sector. They consist of rigid thermal insulation that acts as a formwork and stays in place as a permanent substrate after concrete is poured. Since these systems are modular the benefits include rapid construction, improved thermal performance and energy savings.

Another low-tech innovation in concrete is the new concrete masonry unit (CMU) with varying surface geometry, as seen in the pictures opposite, which can be used to create an interesting pattern, form and facade geometry. The manufacturing process uses forms to create projections and voids within the exterior surface of the CMU, which when arranged in a typical wall can create a varied and dynamic facade.

New types of admixtures are also advancing properties of concrete. For example, a polymeric admixture that integrally waterproofs concrete is available and eliminates the need for external membranes. It also protects against corrosion of steel rebar reinforcement, and makes recycling easier after demolition. Self-repairing cement has been developed, which expands the longevity of concrete by reducing porosity. Additives that contain titanium dioxide can create self-cleaning effects, and cement with titanium dioxide (photocatalyst) is available for self-cleaning concrete. Photocatalysts are compounds that use the ultraviolet bands of sunlight to facilitate a chemical reaction. When exposed to sunlight, the titanium oxide triggers a strong oxidation process that converts noxious organic and inorganic substances into harmless compounds. The self-cleaning process involves two stages, as seen in the diagram on page 24. In the photocatalytic

6 Variable surfaces of CMU blocks.
Innovative manufacturing processes result in CMU blocks with assorted patterns, which can be used to create dynamic facade patterns.

7

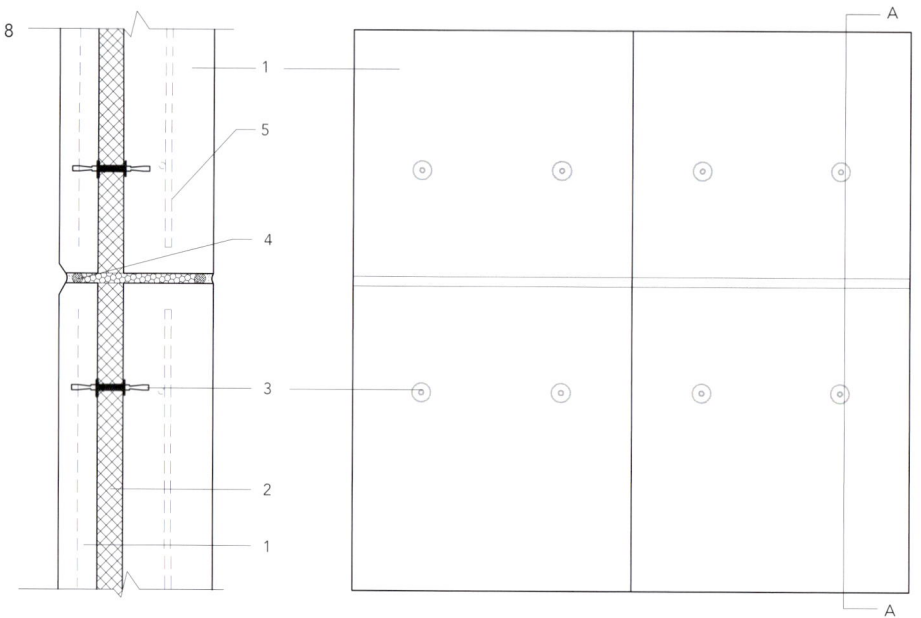

Section A-A

Partial elevation

1 Concrete
2 Insulation
3 Panel tie
4 Backer rod and caulk
5 Reinforcing

stage, organic dirt breaks down when concrete is exposed to sunlight. Next, in the hydrophilic stage, rain washes the dirt from the concrete by picking up the loose particles. This is an effective way of keeping concrete surfaces clean without high maintenance costs. Research has shown that self-cleaning materials with titanium dioxide also help to reduce air pollutants in dense urban areas.[4] The photograph here shows an academic building (School of Business Building, University at Albany, SUNY), designed by Perkins+Will, which incorporated titanium dioxide cement as an admixture for concrete facade cladding.

Improving the thermal performance of concrete materials and systems has been one of the drivers of innovations for this material type. New pre-engineered, sandwich wall systems that consist of high-strength fibre composite connectors, rigid insulation and concrete panels are available, as shown opposite in the building section. These systems can be applied to tilt-up, precast or cast-in-situ concrete panels and improve the thermal performance of building skins. For example, the University of Michigan Cardiovascular Center in Ann Arbor, by design firm Shepley Bulfinch, uses this concrete exterior wall system. The centre was designed to create an inclusive learning and healing environment for patients, visitors and medical staff.

Composite, cement-based facade cladding materials are available, which are specifically suited for rainscreen facade systems. These materials are lightweight, recyclable and can be manufactured in many different colours and textures. The Giant Interactive Group Corporate Headquarters in Shanghai, designed by Morphosis, uses this type of exterior cladding material. This office building is in a natural setting and blurs the distinction between the landscape and architecture. It contains three zones, one of them cantilevers over a lake. The building's envelope includes a rainscreen facade with cement composite cladding. Another application is the Hyllie Train Station in Malmö, designed by Metro Arkitekter. This new station includes cement composite panels as the roof cladding material.

ADVANCES IN GLASS

Although glass is durable and allows a percentage of sunlight to enter a building, it has very little resistance to heat flow. For glazed facades, the thermal and optical properties of the glazing units must be considered during the design. These properties include the heat transfer coefficient (U-value), solar heat gain coefficient (SHGC), the visual transmittance (Tv), and the light-to-solar-gain (LSG) ratio. The solar heat gain coefficient (SHGC) quantifies the amount of solar radiation transmitted through the glass. It is expressed as a number between 0 and 1, with 0 meaning that no radiation is admitted and 1 meaning that no radiation is blocked. Low-emissivity (low-e) coatings significantly reduce admitted solar radiation and can reduce SHGC for all types of insulated glazing units. Visual transmittance (Tv) is the amount of visible light energy that enters through the glass, expressed as a percentage from 0% to 100%. The higher the Tv of a glazing unit, the more visible light

7 Perkins+Will, School of Business Building, University at Albany, SUNY, New York, USA, 2013.
The concrete cladding facade incorporates a titanium dioxide cement admixture, which creates a self-cleaning exterior surface.

8 Concrete sandwich wall system.
This system consists of high-strength fibre composite connectors, rigid insulation and concrete panels. Thermal performance is improved, since continuous insulation is integrated within the system.

9 Shepley Bulfinch, University of Michigan Cardiovascular Center, Ann Arbor, MI, USA, 2007.
The concrete facade consists of concrete panels, fibre-composite connectors and insulation.

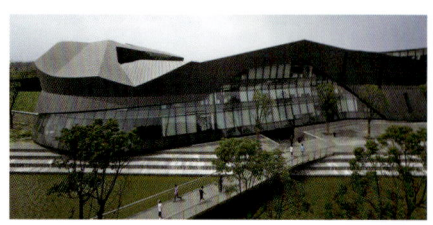

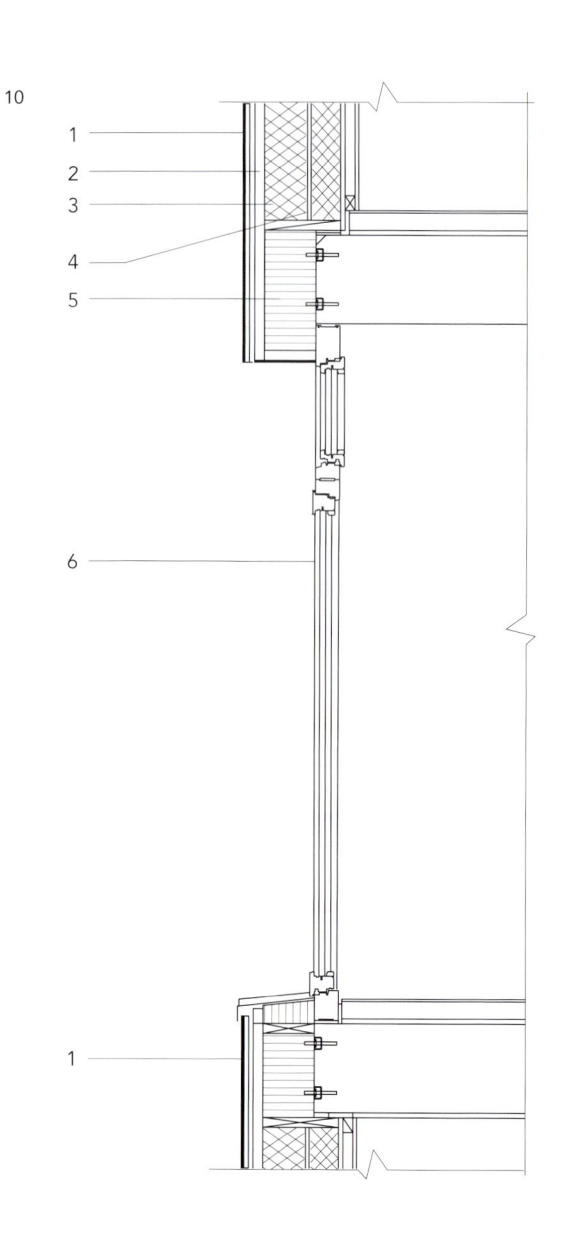

1 Cement concrete cladding
2 Air cavity
3 Insulation
4 Framing
5 Firesafing
6 Glazing

is admitted into the interior spaces. A high visual transmittance usually means a higher solar heat gain coefficient, so it is necessary to find a balance between allowing light into the building and blocking solar radiation.

During the past two decades, glazing technology has greatly changed. Research and development into types of glazing have created a new generation of materials that offer improved glass efficiency and performance. While this new generation of glazing materials quickly gained acceptance in the marketplace, the research and development of even more efficient technologies continues. Building performance simulations have shown that advanced glazing materials with spectrally selective coatings can reduce cooling requirements.[5] Spectrally selective glazing balances solar heat gain and visual transmittance. The light-to-solar-gain (LSG) is the ratio between the amount of light transmitted by the glass and the amount of absorbed solar heat gain, and spectrally selective glazing has an LSG of 1.25 or more. The LSG ratio is calculated by dividing the Tv by the SHGC for a specific glass product. Facades in colder climates benefit from lower LSG ratios, since some solar heat gain is beneficial for passive heating. Higher LSG ratios are appropriate for facades in warmer climates, to keep solar heat gain as low as possible.

Recent developments in fenestration products using new advances in building technology allow transparent, yet energy-efficient facades. Glazing units can be insulated using two, three or more layers of glass. The spaces between the glass layers can be filled with inert gases or aerogel insulation to lower the U-value of the unit. Low-e, reflective or ceramic frit coatings can be applied to the glass to reduce transmission of solar heat gain. The glass itself can be tinted with a colour. Interlayer films within laminated glass can also provide shading. New glass types are continually being introduced into the market to satisfy a variety of functional, security and aesthetic requirements.

Coatings can be applied to glass to improve its thermal and light transmission performance. Low-e coatings applied to the glass surface can block and reflect some daylight (making the glass look darker and more reflective). Through improvements in the formulation of the coating materials and their application processes, manufacturers are continually introducing better-performing, yet clearer, low-e glass. Because low-e coatings are susceptible to damage and require protection, they can only be applied to the inner surfaces of an insulating glass unit. Also, new types of coatings are being applied to create dynamic glass with changeable properties.

Electrochromic glass incorporates a film that changes its tint when electrical voltage is applied. For example, clear electrochromic glass can change to a dark tint. To return the glass to its transparent state, voltage is applied again. Darkening (and lightening) occurs from the edges, moving inward, and can take several minutes. This type of glass provides dynamic shading control for the building.

10 Rainscreen facade system with cement-based composite cladding material and glazing.
The section shows the application of cement-based composite cladding panels in a rainscreen facade system and other material components.

11 Morphosis, Giant Interactive Group Corporate Headquarters, Shanghai, China, 2010.
Cement composite panels are used as the cladding material for the rainscreen facade.

12 Metro Arkitekter, Hyllie Train Station, Malmö, Sweden, 2010.
Cement composite panels are used as the roof cladding material for this train station.

13 Metro Arkitekter, Hyllie Train Station, Malmö, Sweden, 2010.
Section and reflected ceiling plan showing location and components of the roofing system and placement of the cement composite panels.

14 Components and functionality of electrochromic glass.
The electrochromic coating is applied to the glass surface, which is transparent without an electric current. When voltage is applied, the electrochromic coating changes to tinted colour, so lowering the solar heat gain coefficient and visual transmittance of the glass. This type of glass can be used for shading, as well as dynamic glare control.

15 Studiotrope, Morgan Library, Colorado State University, Fort Collins, CO, USA, 2012.
Electrochromic glass is incorporated into the western facade to provide dynamic shading.

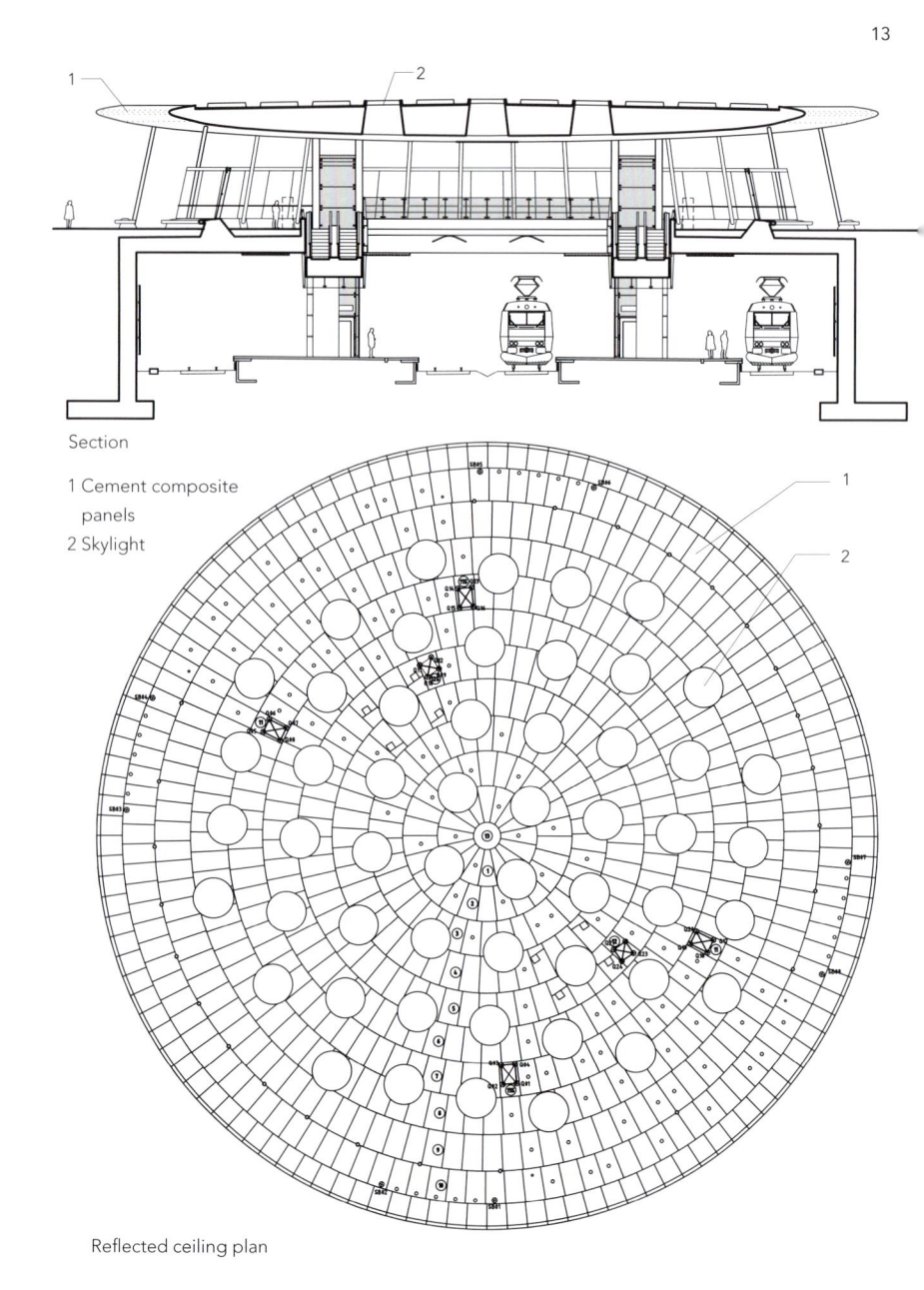

Section

1 Cement composite panels
2 Skylight

Reflected ceiling plan

Visual transmittance ranges from around 60% (for clear state) to 1% (tinted state), which is useful in controlling glare. The solar heat gain coefficient (SHGC) changes from 0.41 in the clear state to 0.09 in the tinted state. With this type of glass, the energy consumption of the building can be reduced despite the use of energy to change the tint of the glass. When used for shading applications, solar heat gain can be reduced. Morgan Library, Colorado State University in Fort Collins, designed by Studiotrope, uses this type of glass. The new addition to the library included an entry cube, which has western exposure. Electrochromic glass was used to mitigate harsh solar exposure along this orientation, while still providing views to the outside. The upper and lower floors are zoned separately, so that they can be controlled independently. Exterior light sensors are installed to allow automated control, but the glass can also be manually controlled. Another project that implemented electrochromic glass is the Cascade Meadow Wetlands and Environmental Science Center in Rochester, Minnesota, designed by LHB in conjunction with LKPB Engineers. This science centre includes a reception area, interactive exhibit spaces, classroom and meeting space, science laboratory, conference room and offices. The building site includes a restored wetland, a restored lake, outdoor learning spaces, native gardens and trails. Renewable energy systems are incorporated into the building and

14

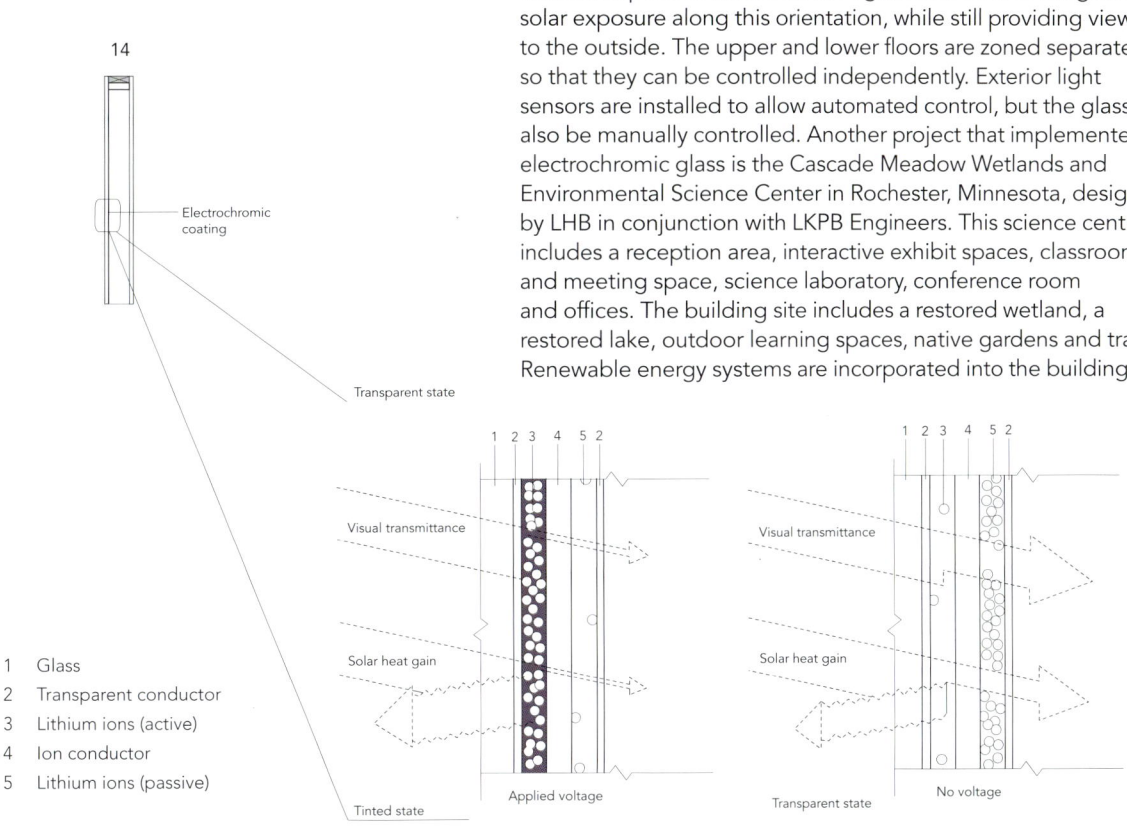

Electrochromic coating

Transparent state

1 Glass
2 Transparent conductor
3 Lithium ions (active)
4 Ion conductor
5 Lithium ions (passive)

Visual transmittance

Solar heat gain

Tinted state — Applied voltage

Transparent state — No voltage

15

1 INNOVATIVE MATERIALS 30-31

16

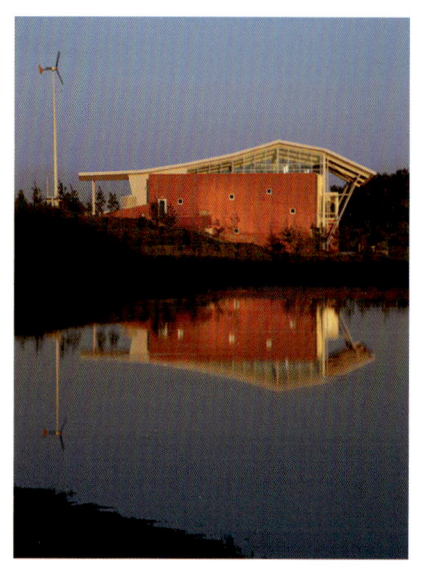

17

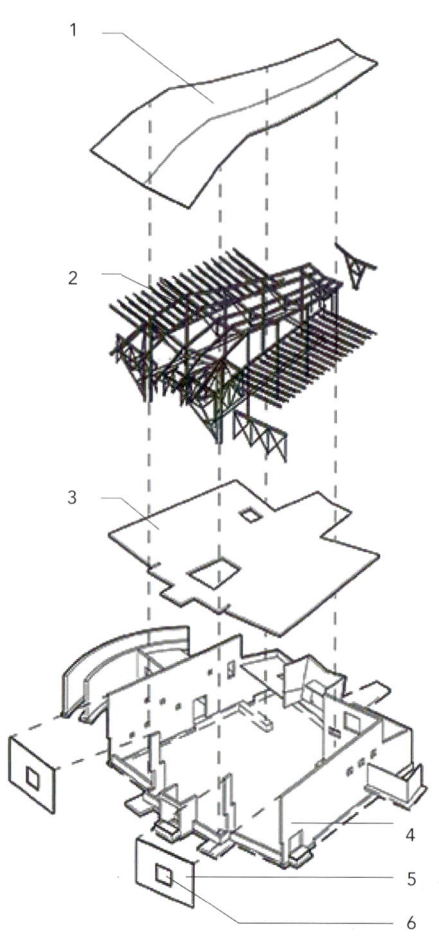

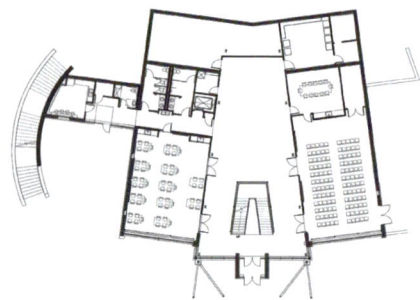

First-floor plan

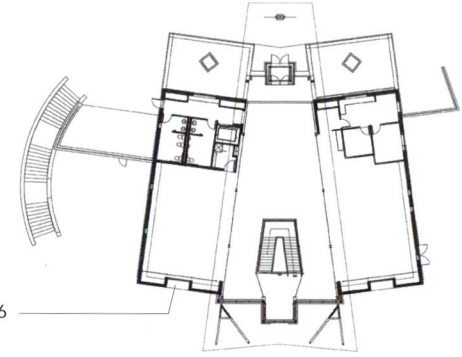

Second-floor plan

Axonometric

1 Folded-plate roof with SIPs
2 Structural steel exoskeleton
3 Precast plank floor system
4 Insulated concrete perimeter walls
5 SIP walls
6 Electrochromic glazing

16 LHB in conjunction with LKPB Engineers, Cascade Meadow Wetlands and Environmental Science Center, Rochester, MN, USA, 2011.
Electrochromic windows have been incorporated into the building's facade and dynamically shade the exhibition spaces.

17 LHB in conjunction with LKPB Engineers, Cascade Meadow Wetlands and Environmental Science Center, Rochester, MN, USA, 2011.
Axonometric view and floor plans demonstrating the different building systems and elements.

18 Functioning of suspended particle device (SPD) glass.
Without voltage SPD glass is translucent, but when voltage is applied it becomes transparent.

1 Glass
2 Transparent conductor
3 Suspension liquid/film
4 Suspended particle devices

site, including solar hot-water system, photovoltaics, and both horizontal and vertical axis wind turbines. A geothermal system is also integrated, and the building's energy use and renewable energy production are monitored by a building management system. Innovative materials are used throughout the building, including structural insulated panels (SIPs), insulated concrete forms (ICFs) and electrochromic glass for windows.

Photochromic glass changes transparency in response to light intensity. Photochromic materials have been used in eyewear that change from clear, in dim indoor light, to dark in a bright outdoor environment. Photochromic glass may be useful in conjunction with daylighting, allowing enough natural light to penetrate interior space while cutting out excess sunlight that creates glare. However, small units have been produced in volume as commercial products for the construction industry, but cost-effective, large, durable glazing products are not yet commercially available.

Thermochromic glass adapts to changing sunlight intensity, where a thermochromic layer in the glass changes transmission over a range of temperatures. If properly designed, thermochromic layers are minimally sensitive to changing outdoor or ambient temperatures, but respond to changing amounts of direct sunlight. The glass tints and blocks solar heat gain.

Suspended particle device (SPD) glass consists of a thin film of liquid crystals suspended in a transparent conductive material and laminated between two layers of glass. By applying voltage, the amount of light passing through the glass can be controlled. In the SPD's normal, non-electrified state, these liquid crystals are randomly arranged and light is scattered between the crystals to give the glass a translucent appearance. When voltage is applied, the crystal particles align, allowing light to pass through the material and make it transparent. SPD glass is typically used for privacy control in interior spaces, since the switch between translucent and transparent states is almost instantaneous. However, the effects on energy savings are not significant, and this technology is not recommended for exterior building applications, such as facades.

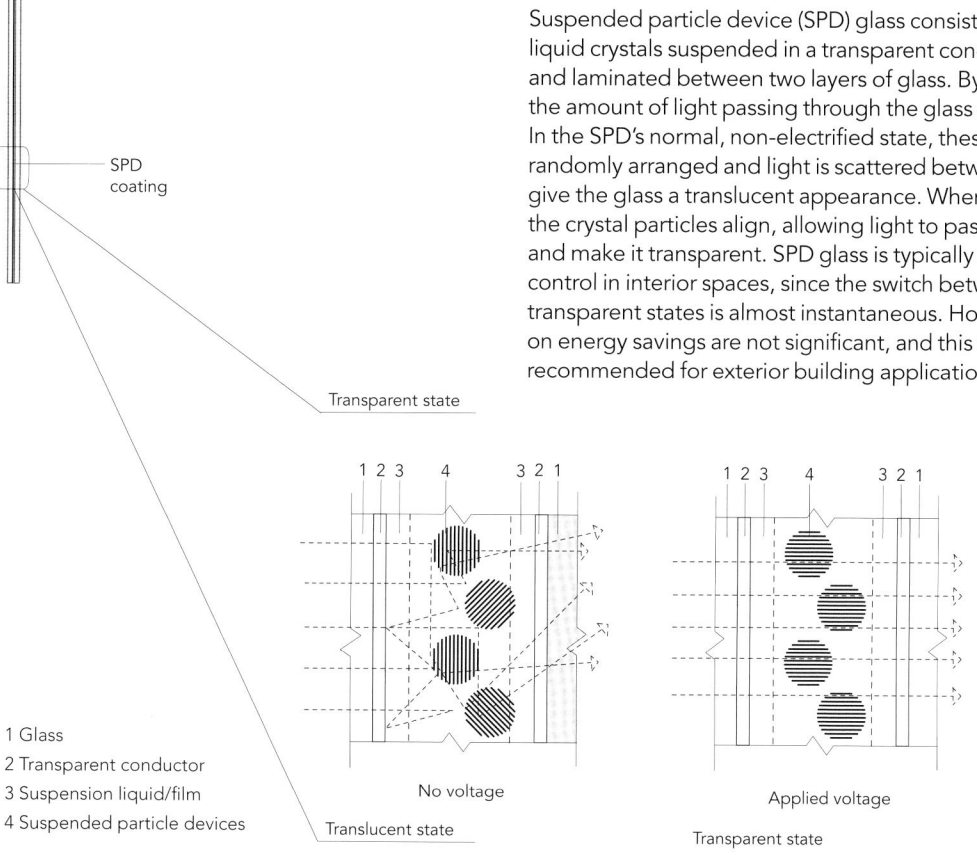

1 INNOVATIVE MATERIALS 32-33

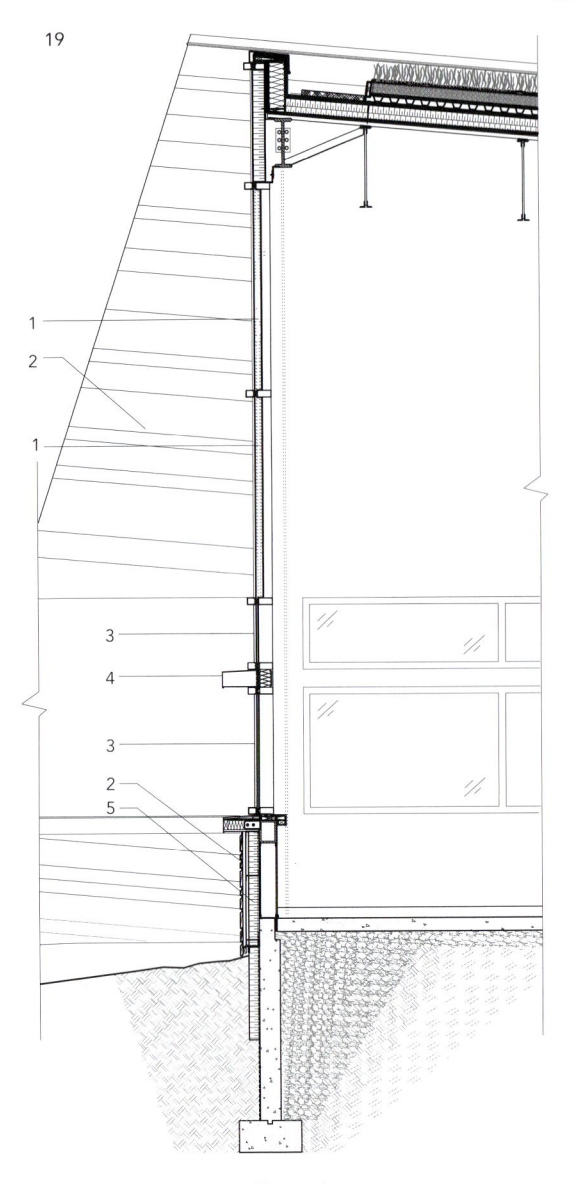

1 Light diffusing glazing
2 Wood cladding
3 Transparent glazing
4 Shading device
5 Insulation

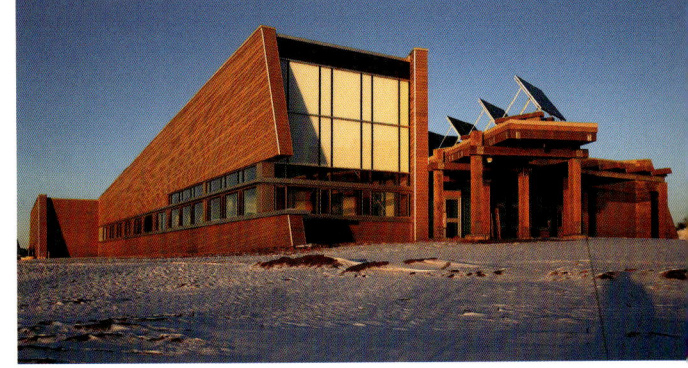

Vacuum-insulated glazing units provide improved thermal resistance compared with standard air- or gas-filled insulated glazing units. These units use a vacuum between two panes of glass to increase the assembly's thermal resistance. There is virtually no conduction or convection of heat between the two panes, since there is no gas to act as a medium for heat transfer. Vacuum-insulated glazing units can achieve U-values of less than 0.57 W/m^2-°K (0.10 Btu/hr-ft^2-°F). The vacuum between the two panes of glass places them under negative pressure, pulling them towards each other. To counteract this, a grid of spacers is placed between the panes. These spacers, or pillars, are made of material with low conductivity, and are positioned several inches from each other in both directions. Vacuum-insulated glazing units are typically thin, making them ideal where high-performance glazing needs to be installed in existing frames – a situation common for building retrofit projects.

Advanced glazing products specifically suited for daylighting applications are also available. These include products with light-diffusing interlayers, which can increase the amount of natural light and reduce the potential for glare. The Joggins Fossil Centre – designed by Architecture49 – is on the stretch of cliffs and beach along Nova Scotia's Bay of Fundy, which is a UNESCO World Heritage site. The interpretative centre exhibits examples of geological and scientific significance to this region, and a number of high-performance and sustainable design strategies were used to reduce energy consumption of the building. The facade incorporates advanced glazing with a light-diffusing interlayer and insulation, increasing available daylight within the interior space. Other notable design strategies that were used to improve the performance of this building include locally sourced and recycled materials, solar hot-water panels, heat pumps, photovoltaic panels and a wind turbine. A significant portion of the centre's energy needs is produced from renewable energy sources.

Commercial glazing products using aerogel inserts are a relatively new type of glazing material and have enhanced thermal properties. In some of these products, the aerogel is integrated with polycarbonate sheets to form a translucent cladding material. In others, silica aerogel in granular form fills the spaces

19 Architecture49, Joggins Fossil Centre, Nova Scotia, Canada, 2008.
Section showing the facade with integrated light-diffusing glazing.

20 Architecture49, Joggins Fossil Centre, Nova Scotia, Canada, 2008.
On Nova Scotia's Bay of Fundy coast, the building form corresponds to the shape of the cliffs.

21 (opposite below and below) Architecture49, Joggins Fossil Centre, Nova Scotia, Canada, 2008.
Exterior views showing the building facade treatment and placement of advanced, light-diffusing glazing.

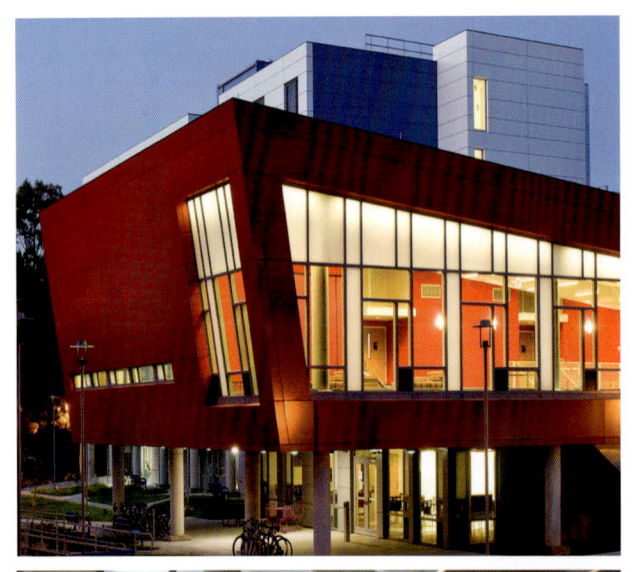

22 Goshow Architects, Nobel Halls, Stony Brook University, New York, USA, 2010. Aerogel glazing is incorporated into the building's facade. This improves the thermal performance of the building envelope, while balancing daylight and allowing views to the outside through clear vision glazing.

23 (below and opposite below) Interior applications of cellular aluminium foam. Interior applications of cellular aluminium foam range from interior panels and furniture to windows.

24 Types of cellular aluminium foam. Three cellular structures can be produced, depending on the size of cells (small, medium and large), sheets can also have various finishes.

24
Aluminium foam cellular types

Small cell

Medium cell

Large cell

Aluminium foam finish types

Normal

Open sided (one sided)

Open sided (two sided)

between the glass panes of insulating units or within the cavities of channel glass. Aerogels are synthetic solids that consist almost entirely of air. They have the lowest density among all known solids. Because of their low density, aerogels have extremely low thermal conductivity, so are ideal for applications where high thermal insulation is needed. Aerogel is a hydrophobic and non-combustible material with effective acoustic properties. The thermal resistance of aerogel-filled glazing – with U-values between 0.57 W/m^2-°K (0.10 Btu/hr-ft^2-°F) and 1.00 W/m^2-°K (0.18 Btu/hr-ft^2-°F) – is superior to standard insulating glazing units, which rarely achieve U-values less than 1.43 W/m^2-°K (0.25 Btu/hr-ft^2-°F). Silica aerogel is translucent, making it an excellent way to bring diffused daylight into interior spaces. On the other hand, its translucence makes it inappropriate for vision glass applications. Nobel Halls at Stony Brook University, New York, designed by Goshow Architects, is a hall of residence. The building envelope is highly insulated and includes aerogel glazing, which is combined with clear vision glazing. This design method allows views to the outside, while improving thermal performance and daylighting for the interior space.

ADVANCES IN METALS
Advances in the manufacturing processes of aluminium have resulted in the development of a new cellular aluminium foam material which can be produced as a continuously cast sheet. The manufacturing process consists of injecting air into molten aluminium, which contains a dispersion of ceramic particles. These particles stabilise the cells formed by the air. Three cellular structures can be produced, depending on the size of cells (small, medium and large). Aluminium foam sheets can also have varying textures, since continuous skin can be introduced to create a 'closed' cell arrangement, and removed to create an 'open' cell configuration. The aluminium foam sheets can be used in a variety of interior and exterior applications, including as facade cladding for rainscreen facades.

Weathering steel is a steel alloy that has a natural oxide coating which forms a protective layer for the steel surface and does not require painting. The finish of this material type has a natural patina, of reddish and brown hues. All low alloy steels have a tendency to rust in the presence of moisture and air, where the rust layer forms a protective layer for the steel surface. Specific alloying elements in weathering steel produce a stable rust layer that develops over time and protects this type of steel against corrosion. Although weathering steel has been available for several decades, the major disadvantages include a relatively slow oxidation process (since the weathering occurs in field after installation), and the possibility of staining adjoining elements if the detailing is not done properly. New advances in the manufacturing process have given rise to the development of pre-weathered steel materials produced by accelerating the natural weathering process in a controlled environment. This results in a pre-oxidised weathering steel that reduces the problems with staining. The Trinity River Audubon Center in Dallas, designed by architectural

25 Exterior applications of cellular aluminium foam.
Cellular aluminium foam used in facade applications.

26 Antoine Predock Architect PC, Trinity River Audubon Center, Dallas, TX, USA, 2008.
Pre-weathered steel cladding is used for the building's facade.

27 Aluminium composite panels.
These types of panels are available in a variety of colours and textures.

28 Patrick Arotcharen Agence d'Architecture, L'Office 64 de l'Habitat, Bayonne, Aquitaine, France, 2011.
Aluminium composite panels are used as one of the components for the building's facade. They are incorporated into a double-skin facade system along the south orientation, which consists of glass, wood-framing members and an internal layer of aluminium composite panels. On the north side, a single-skin facade system is used, where aluminium composite panels serve as cladding material.

firm Antoine Predock Architect PC, uses pre-weathered steel cladding for the building envelope. This building is within the largest urban forest in the United States and serves as an exhibition hall and education centre for environmental stewardship. The building includes a green roof, rainwater collection systems, energy-efficient systems and recycled materials.

Composite panels that integrate extremely thin aluminium sheets and a fire-resistant polyethylene core are suitable for facade applications. The aluminium sheets are thermo-bonded to the core, resulting in a highly durable material. This cladding material is lightweight, has the ability to form curves and comes in a variety of colours and textures. It is possible to use recycled aluminium. L'Office 64 de l'Habitat in Bayonne, France designed by Patrick Arotcharen Agence d'Architecture, integrates an intricate double-skin facade system along the south orientation, consisting of glass, wood-framing members and an internal layer of aluminium composite panels. The facade system also integrates operable windows, and aluminium composite panels are used as shading elements. The same type of material is used for the north facade too, where it is applied as a cladding material for the rainscreen facade system.

BIOMATERIALS
Biomaterials can be derived from nature or synthesised using different components and material sources, but their origin is based on a living structure. Biomaterials have been used mainly for medical applications and devices, but have recently been

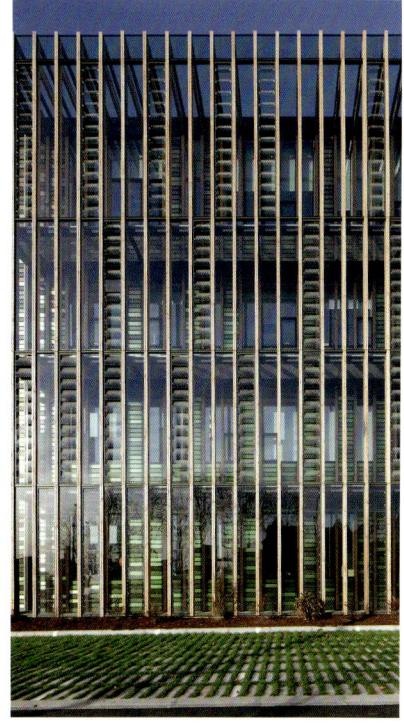

29

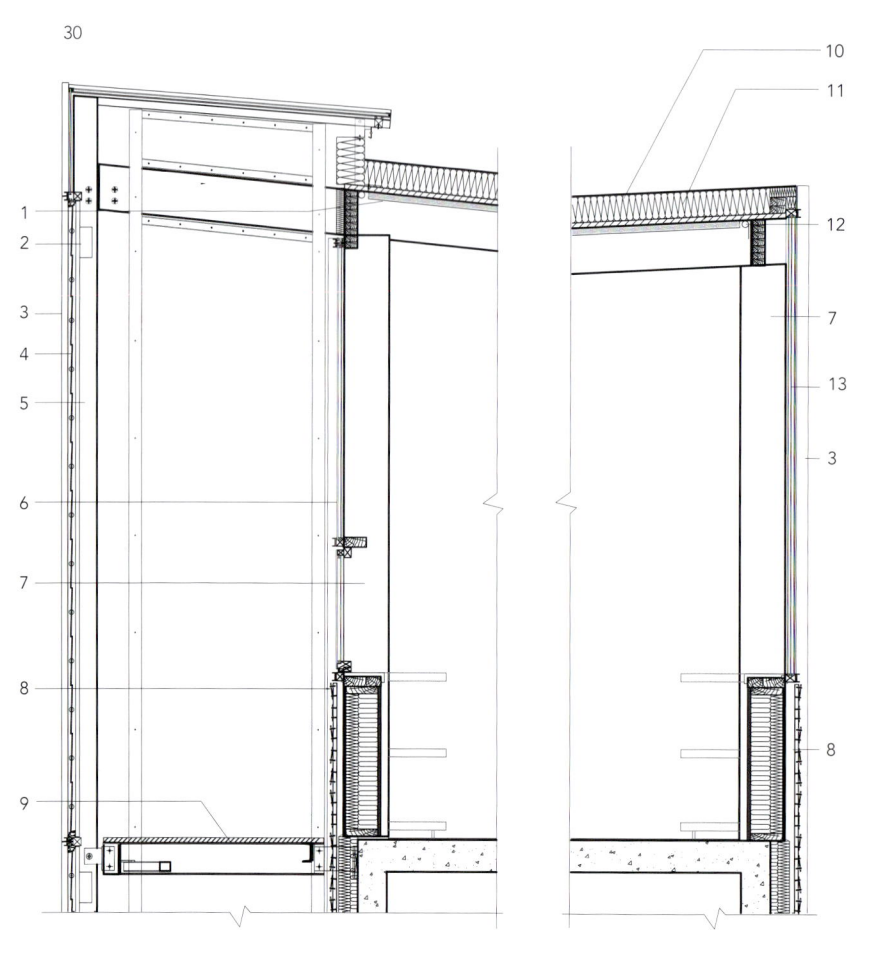

30

1 Acoustic boards
2 Motor for horizontal wood shades
3 Vertical wood components
4 Motorised horizontal wood shades
5 Secondary wood structure
6 Double glazing
7 Glulam column
8 Aluminium composite panels
9 Catwalk
10 Roof membrane
11 Insulation
12 Interior shade
13 Triple glazing

29 Patrick Arotcharen Agence d'Architecture, L'Office 64 de l'Habitat, Bayonne, Aquitaine, France, 2011.
South- and north-oriented facades showing the different applications of aluminium composite panels.

30 Patrick Arotcharen Agence d'Architecture, L'Office 64 de l'Habitat, Bayonne, Aquitaine, France, 2011.
Sections of the building's facades (double and single skin), indicating detailed components.

31 MAD Architects, Taichung Convention Center, Taiwan, proposal.
The design concept for this new convention centre integrates architecture and the landscape, creating mountain-like buildings to harmonise the relationship between nature and the built environment.

introduced to architectural and construction industries, primarily due to an interest in biomimicry and biomimetic design.[6,7] An interest in renewable raw materials in buildings and sustainable design strategies (improving air quality, human health and well-being), have been the drivers for research and development, and the application of biomaterials in architecture.

The proposal for a new convention centre in Taichung, Taiwan, by MAD Architects is an example of biomimetic architecture. The complex consists of a convention centre, retail, hotel and office towers, and services. The aerodynamic form was developed to optimise ventilation around the buildings and the public plazas. The design – a series of mountain-like buildings –integrates buildings and landscape. One of the driving goals for the design was the harmony between nature and the built form. The surface of the buildings is a lightweight pleated skin system, allowing natural ventilation and creating a 'breathable' facade. The exterior skin also integrates photovoltaic panels.

New developments in wood composites are allowing the unprecedented use of this natural, renewable material. For example, glued laminated timber (glulam) is comprised of layers of dimensioned timber, bonded with moisture-resistant structural adhesives. Therefore, structural members can be fabricated and used for columns, beams, arches and curved shapes for long spans. Connections can be made with bolts and steel plates.

Phenolic wood composites consist of high-pressure wood laminates and thermosetting resins. Cladding panels for rainscreen facades are available and can be manufactured in a variety of colours. The HEMA building in Oosterbeek, the Netherlands, designed by Strategie Architecten, is a commercial building that uses innovative phenolic wood composite cladding for the facade system. Based on a Dutch painting from the 19th century, the facade was designed in a collaboration between the design team and the artist Jan van IJzendoorn. The design team developed an intricate pattern of different colours, and phenolic wood cladding was used to create this effect. The east facade has flush cladding panels, while the south facade incorporates different sizes of overlapping panels, some of which are twisted outwards to create interesting shading effects.

COMPOSITE MATERIALS
Composite materials are materials that consist of two or more components – such as reinforced concrete – and have been used in architecture and construction for decades. The primary advantage of composite materials is that the strengths and benefits of two or more components are combined to create a better performing material – in the case of reinforced concrete, steel rebars are used to improve concrete's tensile strength and ductility. But recent developments in material science and engineering are creating new composite materials, combining polymers, resins, matrices and fibres with different substrates, such as concrete and cement-based materials, metals, fabrics and ceramics.

1 INNOVATIVE MATERIALS 40-41

32 MAD Architects, Taichung Convention Center, Taiwan, proposal.
Interior view of the convention centre, showing the lightweight pleated-skin system. It allows natural ventilation and creates a 'breathable' facade.

33 Glued laminated timber.
This composite material consists of wood and structural adhesives. Structural members, arches and curved shapes can be used for long spans.

34 Connections.
Connections for glued laminated timber.

35 Strategie Architecten, HEMA building, Oosterbeek, the Netherlands, 2009.
The elevations and facade technical detail show how phenolic wood cladding is used to create an intricate, colourful pattern on the building's facades.

36 Strategie Architecten, HEMA building, Oosterbeek, the Netherlands, 2009.
Flush phenolic wood cladding is used along the east facade and overlapping panels along the south facade.

35

East elevation

South elevation

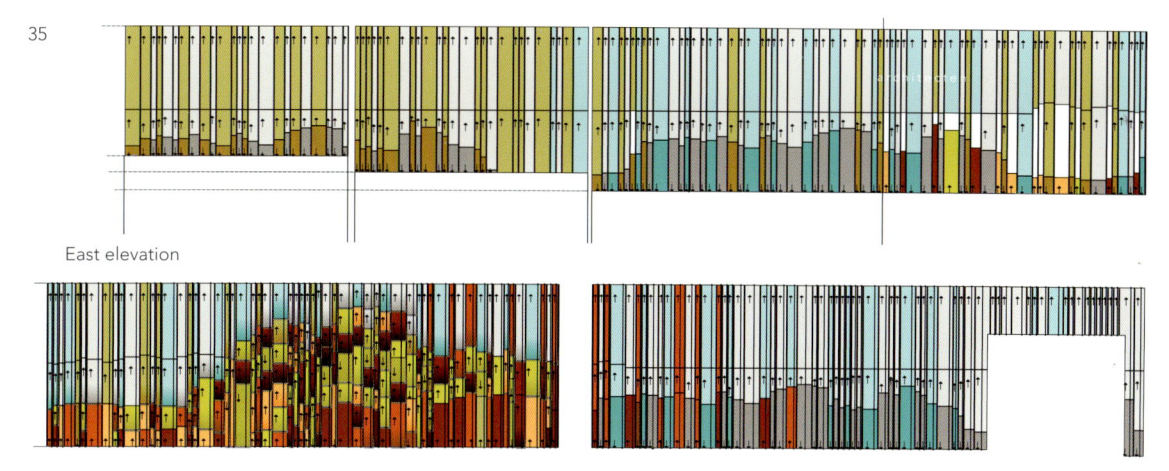

West elevation

1 Phenolic wood cladding
2 Air cavity
3 Support system for cladding
4 Insulation
5 Brick
6 Support wall

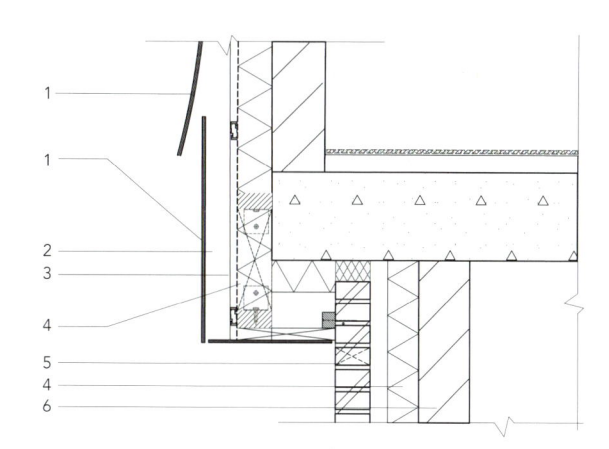

36

1 INNOVATIVE MATERIALS 42-43

37

38

1 Pavers
2 Concrete slab
3 Slate facade panels
4 Concrete wall
5 Fibre-cement cladding
6 Insulation
7 Glazing
8 Steel truss
9 Rainwater drainage

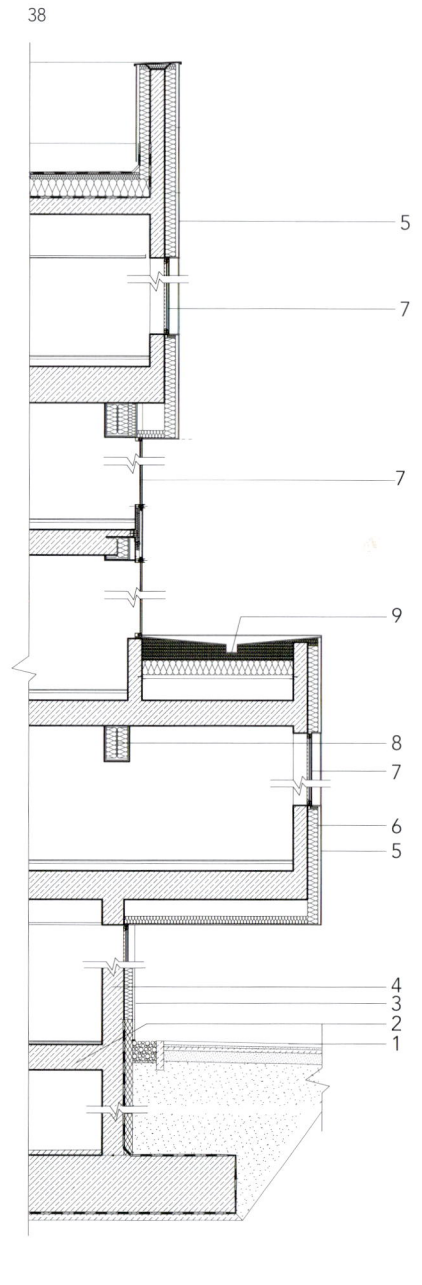

37 FAAB Architektura, PGE GiEK Corporate Headquarters, Bełchatów, Poland, 2013.
Fibre-cement composite panels are used for the building's facade system.

38 FAAB Architektura, PGE GiEK Corporate Headquarters, Bełchatów, Poland, 2013.
The section demonstrates the material components of the facade.

39 FAAB Architektura, PGE GiEK Corporate Headquarters, Bełchatów, Poland, 2013.
The terraced garden provides a green open space for the building's occupants.

40 Molecular change in shape-memory alloys.
Molecular change in shape-memory alloys (SMAs) is achieved by thermally induced transformations.

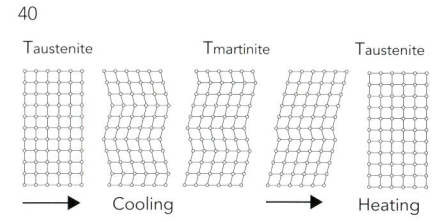

Fibre-cement composite panels – composed of cement, cellulose, mineral materials and reinforced with a fibre matrix – are available as a cladding material for facades. PGE GiEK Corporate Headquarters in Bełchatów, Poland, designed by FAAB Architektura, employs a fibre-cement composite cladding material. The office building is for one of the largest energy producers in Poland, and the building form and massing were inspired by energy production and distribution. Access to daylight was one of the driving forces for the building form, which features a narrow floor plan and an atrium. A terraced square and garden are included in the building, and a rainwater collection system is used for irrigation.

ELECTROCHROMICS

Electrochromic materials are characterised by an ability to change their optical properties reversibly, and persistently, when a voltage is applied across them. Electrochromic glass has been discussed in a previous section, advances in glass. Electrochromic glass controls sunlight to optimise daylight, outdoor views and comfort while preventing glare, fading and overheating. By letting sunlight in on cool days and blocking it on hot days, electrochromic windows can reduce energy demand.

SHAPE-MEMORY ALLOYS

Shape-memory alloys (SMAs) belong to a class of shape-memory materials that have the ability to 'memorise' or retain their previous form when subjected to certain stimulus, such as thermomechanical or magnetic variations. SMAs have attracted significant attention and interest in recent years in a broad range of applications, due to their unique and superior properties. This commercial development has been supported by fundamental and applied research studies.

Perhaps surprisingly, bendable eyeglass frames, medical stents for opening arteries that are implanted in a compressed form and then expand to the right size and shape when warmed by the body, tiny actuators that eject disks from laptop computers, small micro-valves and a variety of other devices, all share this common material technology. The transformable behaviour of these devices relies on a phenomenon called the 'shape-

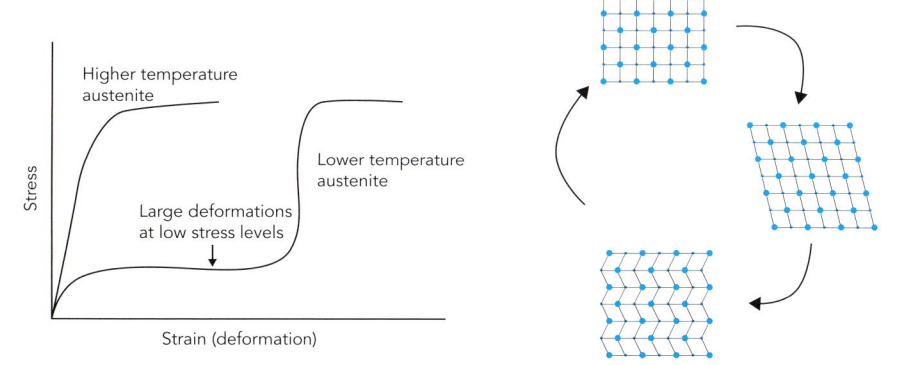

1 INNOVATIVE MATERIALS 44-45

1 Reef installation
2 Gallery enclosure
3 Fins
4 Wood support system
5 SMA wires and motors

42

Axonometric

Top view

Side view (fins)

Side view (support and SMA wires)

41

41 Rob Ley (Urbana) and Joshua Stein (Radical Craft), Reef, New York, USA, 2009.
This installation is a kinetic, responsive surface consisting of an aluminium frame, SMA wires (nitinol), fibre-reinforced composite fins and a control system. The fins rotate and change form as the SMA wires are heated with an electric current.

42 Rob Ley (Urbana) and Joshua Stein (Radical Craft), Reef, New York, USA, 2009.
Diagrams and illustrations showing different components of the installation.

43 Rob Ley (Urbana) and Joshua Stein (Radical Craft), Reef, New York, USA, 2009.
Components of the installation, showing the fibre-reinforced composite fins and SMA wires that are used as a primary mechanism for the kinetic changes.

44 Principle for self-healing materials.
Self-healing materials contain microcapsules filled with polymeric substances. If the material cracks, the microcapsules open and release polymeric substances that harden and repair the crack.

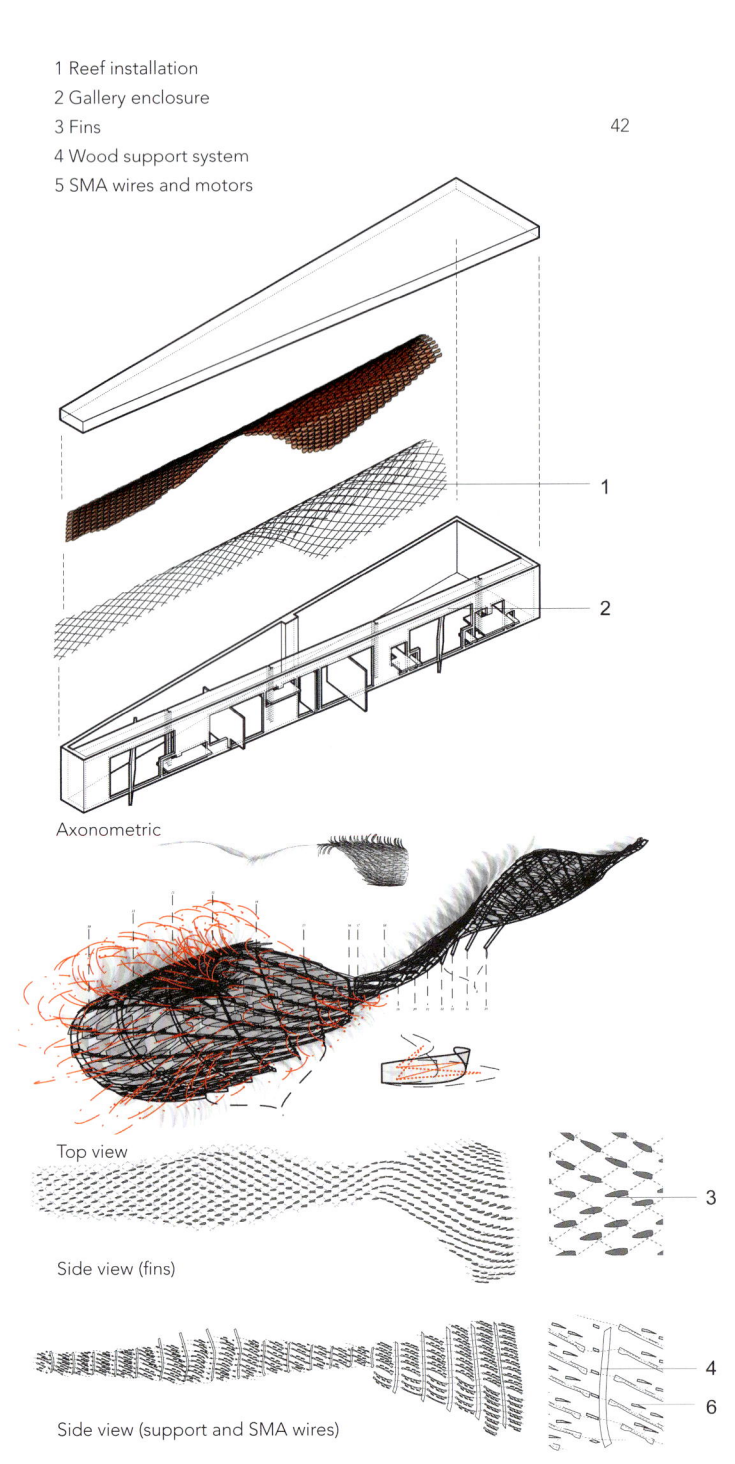

memory effect', which refers to the ability of a particular kind of alloy material to revert to, or remember, a previously memorised or pre-set shape. The characteristic derives from the phase-transformation characteristics of the material. A solid-state phase change (molecular rearrangement) occurs in the shape-memory alloy that is temperature-dependent and reversible. For example, the material can be shaped into one configuration at a high temperature, deformed dramatically while at a low temperature, and then reverted back to its original shape on the application of heat in any form, including electrical current. Diagram 40 indicates the process for thermally induced change in SMA materials.

Nickel-titanium (NiTi) alloys are commonly used in shape-memory applications, although many other kinds of alloys also exhibit shape-memory effects.[8] These alloys can exist in final product form in two different temperature-dependent crystalline states or phases. The primary and higher temperature phase is called the austenite state. The lower temperature phase is called the martensite state. The physical properties of the material in the austenite and martensite phases are different. The material in the austenite state is strong and hard, while it is soft and ductile in the martensite phase. The austenite crystal structure is a simple body-centred cubic structure, while martensite has a more complex rhombic structure. With respect to the stress–strain curve, the higher temperature austenite behaves similarly to most metals. The stress–strain curve of the lower-temperature martensitic structure, however, resembles an elastomer, since it has 'plateau' stress-deformation characteristics where large deformations can easily occur with little force.

Although SMA materials have been widely used in medical and aerospace applications, their application in architecture is still limited to installations and small-scale projects, mainly due to cost-prohibitive applications for larger, structural uses. Reef, a collaboration between Rob Ley (Urbana) and Joshua Stein (Radical Craft), incorporated SMAs within the responsive, kinetic installation. The installation consists of an aluminium frame, nitinol wires, fibre-reinforced composite fins and a control system. The length of nitinol wires changes when heated with an electric current, having an impact on the shape and form of 600 fins. The result is a kinetic, responsive surface that changes its shape.

SELF-HEALING MATERIALS
Self-healing materials are a subset of smart materials that have the ability to repair damage caused by mechanical or structural use over time. They are typically composite materials that contain microcapsules filled with polymeric substances. When the material cracks, the microcapsules open and seal up the crack. Recent research and development has focused on different types of self-healing materials, including concrete, paint and polymer-based composites.[9, 10, 11] Self-healing paint is especially interesting, because with this system tiny scratches can be automatically sealed. To achieve this, a highly elastic resin is used, which spreads itself out evenly over the surface and seals small cracks.

43

44

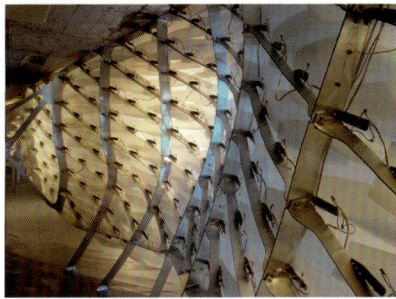

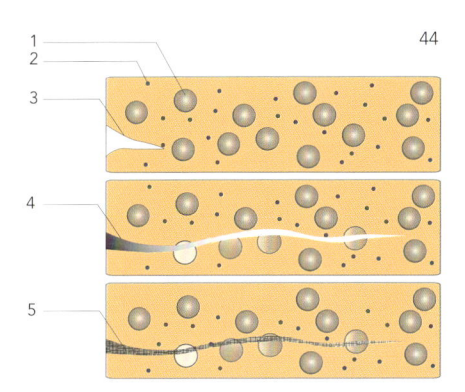

1 Microcapsule
2 Catalyst
3 Crack
4 Healing agent
5 Polymerised healing agent

The first production-line use of such a paint has recently been implemented, and in the near future its use is likely to be extended to scratch-prone items.

Research and development of self-healing concrete with calcite-precipitating bacteria is currently under way at TU Delft.[12] The principle behind this research is that certain types of bacteria produce calcium carbonate-based minerals which can be used to repair cracks in concrete. By embedding calcite-precipitating bacteria in concrete as an admixture, the researchers are working on determining the right conditions for the bacteria to produce as much calcite as possible, as well as the self-healing ability of bacterial concrete and how this is affected by different environmental conditions. This material was used for the First Aid Emergency Post in Galder, the Netherlands, designed by Frank Marcus. The concrete structure includes a protective layer of self-repairing concrete with bacteria, and the photograph below shows a self-healed crack.

SENSORS AND CONTROLS

Sensors and control systems are gaining popularity in architecture and construction. Sensing equipment, building management systems and controls that regulate the performance of building systems are increasingly being used, ranging from sensors for specific building elements (such as sensors and controls used for lighting fixtures), to specific systems (such as HVAC) or whole-building controls (building energy management software and controls).

There are many different types of sensors used in buildings. Lighting sensors include photodiode sensors or phototransistors, which allow lighting levels to be monitored and controlled. Thermal sensors include classic thermometers, thermocouples and thermistors, and are used to monitor thermal conditions in the environment. Humidity sensors are used to monitor humidity levels. Motion and occupancy sensors are used to detect the presence of building occupants, and are mainly integrated with lighting systems. There are also a variety of sensors that have been developed to detect the presence of different types of chemicals. These are used for environmental sensing, mainly for the detection of air pollutants.

Environmental sensors are used to test or measure changes in environmental conditions and include many types of sensors described above. A variety of sensor-based devices have been developed to initially assess and continuously monitor environmental conditions at different scales (element, building and urban scale).

A recently developed prototype for an exterior shading system (consisting of folding geometry and a movable track system) uses sensors, a control system and a mobile application to transform its form. This shading system has been developed by Sean McKeever (NBBJ), and uses occupancy sensors to detect building occupants.

45

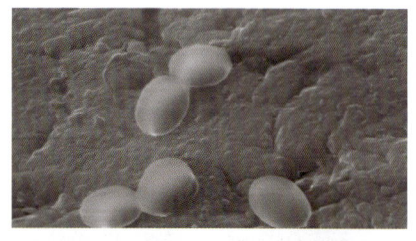

46

45 Microscopic view of self-repairing concrete.
Self-repairing concrete incorporates calcite-precipitating bacteria. The bacteria create minerals that repair cracks in concrete.

46 Frank Marcus, First Aid Emergency Post, Galder, the Netherlands, 2011.
The concrete structure includes a protective layer of self-healing concrete with calcite-precipitating bacteria.

47 Sean McKeever (NBBJ), exterior shading system prototype.
This prototype consists of folding geometry and a movable track system. Folding geometry, sensors, a control system and a mobile application are used to control the form of the shading system.

The shades open automatically if occupants are present, but can also be overridden by building occupants. Sensors for environmental conditions are integrated, specifically for measuring solar radiation and weather conditions, allowing the control of shading devices based on the exterior environment.

Control systems are an integral part of high-performing buildings. Building automation systems (BAS) are centralised, interlinked networks of sensors, hardware and software, which monitor and control building systems and performance. Mechanical, electrical and plumbing systems, lighting, power, security and vertical circulation (elevators and escalators) can be monitored and controlled via BAS. Although BAS have been around for decades, significant innovations have occurred with the introduction of digitised systems, wireless sensors and open communication protocols between different systems. Also, the improvement of energy efficiency and buildings' energy performance has demanded wider adoption of BAS and energy management systems. Monitoring, tracking and visualising energy usage in buildings allows improved operations and facility management. Smart and intelligent buildings rely on BAS, where the variety of sensors, controls and monitoring systems are integrated to detect environment conditions or respond and influence building operation.

PHASE-CHANGE MATERIALS
In principle, all materials that are able to reversibly change their state in response to external influences are classified as phase-change materials (PCM). Most of the known materials exhibit temperature-dependent phase changes. There are also other influences, such as chemical stimuli, which can trigger phase changes and these are often associated with changes in elasticity. In addition to the states of solid, liquid and gas, there are other, largely stable intermediate states, such as the colloidal state derived from gels.

In the architecture and construction industries, the term PCM has become generally applicable to materials and products that can be used as temperature regulating media, for example latent heat or latent cold storage media for the regulation of temperature. They have the ability to change their state from liquid to solid by crystallisation below an inherent material-dependent phase-change temperature, and to release a quantity of heat energy previously taken in and stored at a high temperature. The temperature of the material remains constant during the course of the phase change, from solid to liquid, and during the heat energy input.

These types of materials are solid at room temperature, but liquefy at higher temperatures, absorbing and storing heat in the process. PCMs are either organic (such as waxes) or inorganic (such as salts). When PCMs are incorporated into the building elements, they can absorb high exterior temperatures during the day and dissipate the heat at night.

1 INNOVATIVE MATERIALS 48-49

Different types of PCM materials used in architecture include paraffin and paraffin mixtures, salt hydrate and salt hydrate mixtures, and water. The melting point of paraffin mixtures depends on the particular paraffin used and any added constituents. The advantages of these mixtures are that they are widely available, can be made in large quantities and can be used over a relatively large temperature range, approximately -12°C (10°F) to 180°C (356°F) for many applications. The disadvantages are that they are highly combustible, change volume during phase change and are relatively expensive compared with other types of PCM materials. Salt hydrate mixtures are non-combustible and can be used over a relatively large temperature range, approximately -70°C (-94°F) to 120°C (248°F). They are relatively inexpensive compared with paraffin-based PCMs. Disadvantages include a tendency to supercool when used for cold storage, a tendency to segregate and promote corrosion, and also to change volume during phase change. Water mixtures can be used over a relatively large temperature range, approximately 40°C (104°F) to 100°C (212°F). They do not segregate, and are comparatively inexpensive compared with other types of PCMs. Disadvantages are relatively poor thermal conductivity compared with paraffin and salt hydrate PCMs and volume change during phase change.

Products such as triple-insulated glazing units (IGUs) with integrated PCM are commercially available. These IGUs consist of four layers of glass and three insulating gaps. A prismatic pane is placed within the outermost gap. Inert gas fills the two outer gaps, and a PCM encapsulated within transparent polycarbonate containers fills the inside gap. This type of IGU acts as a passive heat source. During the winter months, the prismatic pane allows low-angle sunlight to pass through the glass layers and heat up the PCM. This causes the PCM to liquefy and release heat to the interior. During the summer months, the prismatic pane acts as a barrier, reflecting high-angle solar rays back to the outside, allowing the PCM to stay in its solid form. Insulating properties of this type of glazing unit are very high, with U-values for commercial products of 0.48 W/m²-°K (0.08 Btu/hr-ft²-°F). Visual transmittance for a solid-state PCM is between 0% and 28%, with an SHGC as low as 0.17 and as high as 0.48. Liquid-state PCM has visual transmittance from 4% to 45%, with an SHGC as high as 0.48 and as low as 0.17. In either its solid or liquid state, a PCM makes the glazing unit translucent, so this material is not appropriate for applications where views to the outside are desired.

For thermal storage in buildings PCMs are applicable and can be integrated in Trombe walls, exterior walls, underfloor heating systems and ceiling boards. The benefits of using PCMs in Trombe wall applications are that PCMs require less space than mass walls and are lighter in weight. Applications for underfloor heating systems and ceiling applications have been investigated.

One of the first large-scale commercial applications of PCMs is the iCon Innovation Centre in Daventry, UK, designed by Consarc Architects. This is a new type of publicly funded building, aimed

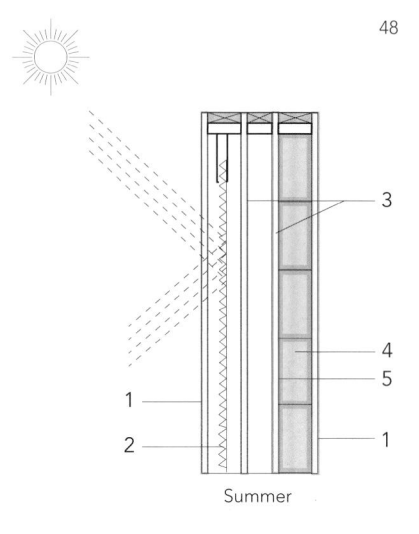

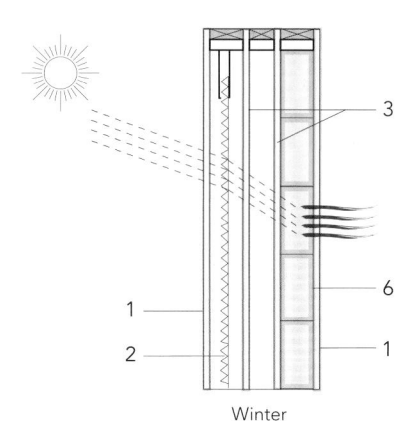

Summer

Winter

1 Tempered glass
2 Prismatic pane
3 Low-e glass
4 Solid PCM
5 PCM containers
6 Liquid PCM

actively to promote economic sustainability through the promotion of innovation networks. This high-performance building includes incubation units for start-up businesses, public exhibition space, conference facilities and a café. The building's structural system is composed of a timber-frame construction (glulam). Sustainable design strategies included a natural ventilation system, efficient heat recovery and PCMs to limit overheating. PCM panels have been introduced into interior spaces at soffit level to reduce interior temperature peaks, so improving thermal comfort levels and energy savings. The PCMs reduce the interior temperature by as much as 7°C (45°F), which decreases air-conditioning costs by 35% and heating costs by 15%. The PCM panels are sealed behind the plasterboard in walls and above ceiling panels, where they absorb ambient heat as the interior temperature rises at around 22°C (72°F), storing it until the temperature drops to around 18°C (64°F), and then releasing it back into the interior space. The building facade is constructed of wood and includes vertical shading fins to reduce solar heat gain. The central atrium of the building is covered by an Ethylene Tetrafluoroethylene (ETFE) skylight.

PHOTOVOLTAICS

Photovoltaics (PVs) are among the most commonly used active energy-generation systems for buildings. They convert sunlight into electricity and can be integrated into roof or facade applications. There are different types of PVs, but the most common differentiation is between thin films and solid cells. Thin films consist of interconnected solar cells which convert visible light into electricity, and can be applied to different building materials (glass, metals, ETFE and so on). Thin-film cells can be integrated into almost any surface, such as shading devices, spandrels, vision glass and roofing elements. Solid solar cell modules are integrated into panels and are commercially available in standard and custom shapes and sizes. These types of PV panels can be installed on roofs and building facades, and integrated with spandrel areas or shading devices. The performance and aesthetic appearance of PVs depend on their type, their size and their position relative to the sun's path.

There are also many different types of PVs, depending on the material structure and components. Monocrystalline silicon cells are uniform in colour and structure and are the most conventional type of cells used in PV modules. Their efficiency, measured as a percentage of solar energy converted into electric energy, is typically not larger than 25% under the best conditions. Polycrystalline silicon cells have a non-uniform surface structure and colour, with visible variations in the silicon structure. Polycrystalline cells generally have lower costs and lower efficiencies than monocrystalline cells. Amorphous silicon cells use hydrogenated amorphous silicon, with only a few microns of material needed to absorb the incident light. Since they can be deposited on both rigid and flexible substrates, thin films typically use this type of cell. Manufacturing costs for amorphous cells are relatively low, but their efficiencies are also low, typically no more than 7%. The advantage of amorphous thin films is that they work

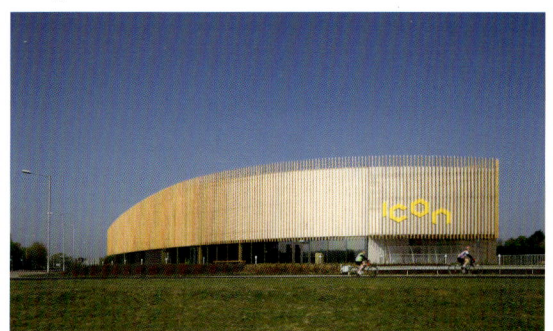

49

48 Insulated glazing unit with phase-change material (PCM) inserted.
During the winter months, the prismatic pane allows low-angle sunlight to pass through the glass layers and heat up the PCM. This causes the PCM to become liquid and release heat to the interior. During summer months, the prismatic pane acts as a barrier, reflecting high-angle solar rays back to the outside, allowing the PCM to stay in its solid form.

49 Consarc Architects, iCon Innovation Centre, Daventry, Northamptonshire, UK, 2011.
This new type of publicly funded building actively boosts economic sustainability through the promotion of innovation networks and sustainability.

50

51

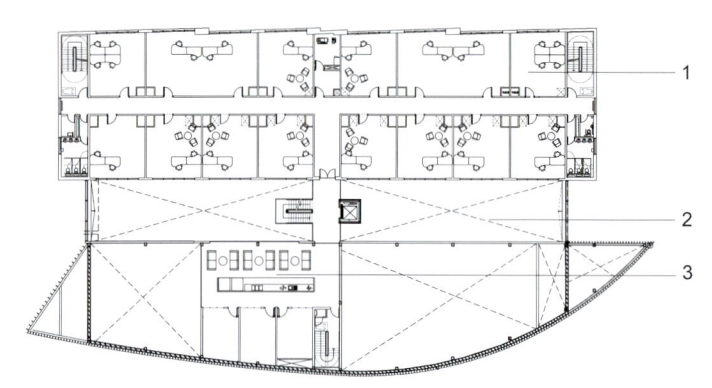

First-floor plan

1 Offices
2 Atrium
3 Lounge
4 Lighting
5 PCM incorporated into ceiling
6 HVAC distribution

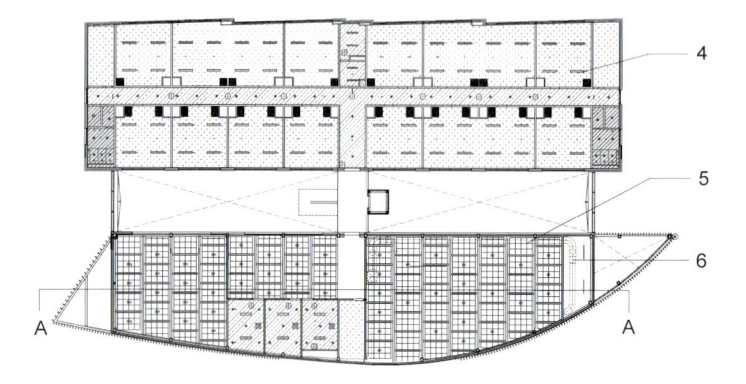

First-floor reflected ceiling plan

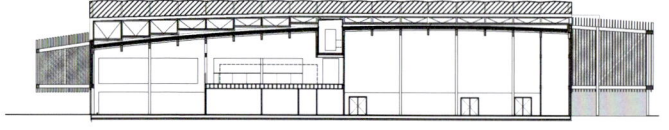

Section A-A

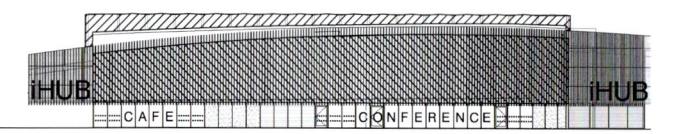

South elevation

50 Consarc Architects, iCon Innovation Centre, Daventry, Northamptonshire, UK, 2011.
Timber-frame construction was implemented, reducing embodied energy associated with the structural system.

51 Consarc Architects, iCon Innovation Centre, Daventry, Northamptonshire, UK, 2011.
Floor plan, reflected ceiling plan, section and elevation showing spatial arrangement, facade treatment and materials.

52 Consarc Architects, iCon Innovation Centre, Daventry, Northamptonshire, UK, 2011.
PCM panels are used within interior spaces, they are sealed behind the plasterboard in walls and above ceiling panels, where they absorb ambient heat as the interior temperature rises. This is released when the temperature drops. These panels help to improve thermal comfort levels and energy savings.

53 Types of PV glass.
Semitransparent PV glass uses amorphous silicon. It allows some daylight to penetrate into the interior space and provides views to the outside. Opaque PV glass uses solid PVs and is appropriate for spandrels and other non-vision areas of the facade.

52

53

Semitransparent PV glass

Opaque PV glass

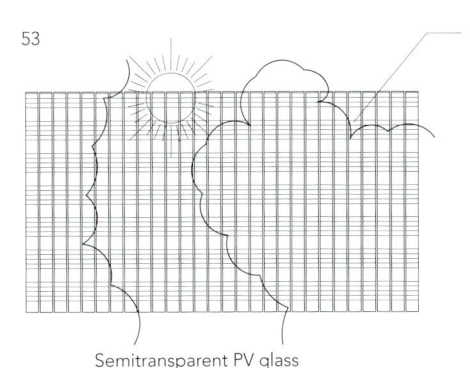

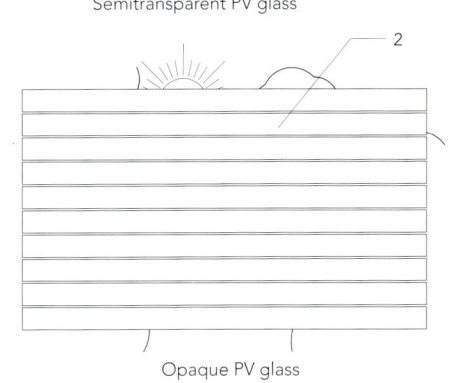

1 Amorphous thin-film PV cells
2 Crystalline PV cells

equally well in shaded areas as in direct sunlight. Monocrystalline and polycrystalline cells require direct sunlight to achieve their highest efficiencies. Their energy production is reduced if they are shaded, not oriented in the optimal way to receive the maximum amount of sunlight, or covered by snow, sand or dust.

Photovoltaic glass integrates crystalline solar cells or amorphous thin films, where the PV cells are integrated into laminated or double-glazed units and are applicable for building facade integration. There are two general types of PV glass: semitransparent and opaque. Semitransparent PV glass is similar to patterned ceramic frit, allowing some daylight to penetrate through the glass while giving occupants views to the outside. Opaque PV glass uses solid PVs, and is appropriate for spandrels and other non-vision areas of the facade.

The SwissTech Convention Center at the École Polytechnique Fédérale de Lausanne (EPFL) in Switzerland, designed by architects Richter Dahl Rocha & Associés, incorporates newly developed dye-synthesised PV panels within the western facade of the building. The building has become a new landmark for this institution, creating a clearly identifiable volume within the landscape. It is also connected to the newly designed student housing centre and a hotel, to the east of the convention centre. The metallic roof shell cantilevers over the interior and glazed facades, allowing maximum daylight for interior spaces. The building consists of a large auditorium for 3,000 people, a foyer and supporting spaces. The auditorium has been designed to allow subdivision into smaller spaces, which defined the building's form. Hydraulic platforms and rotating seat mounts allow the auditorium to be transformed into a multi-purpose room. Anodised aluminium diamond-shaped tiles are used for the building envelope. The west facade of the building integrates dye-sensitised solar cells, which is the first, large-scale commercial application of this type of PVs. These translucent panels are integrated as vertical shading devices, and create an interesting pattern through a variety of different colours. For these

54

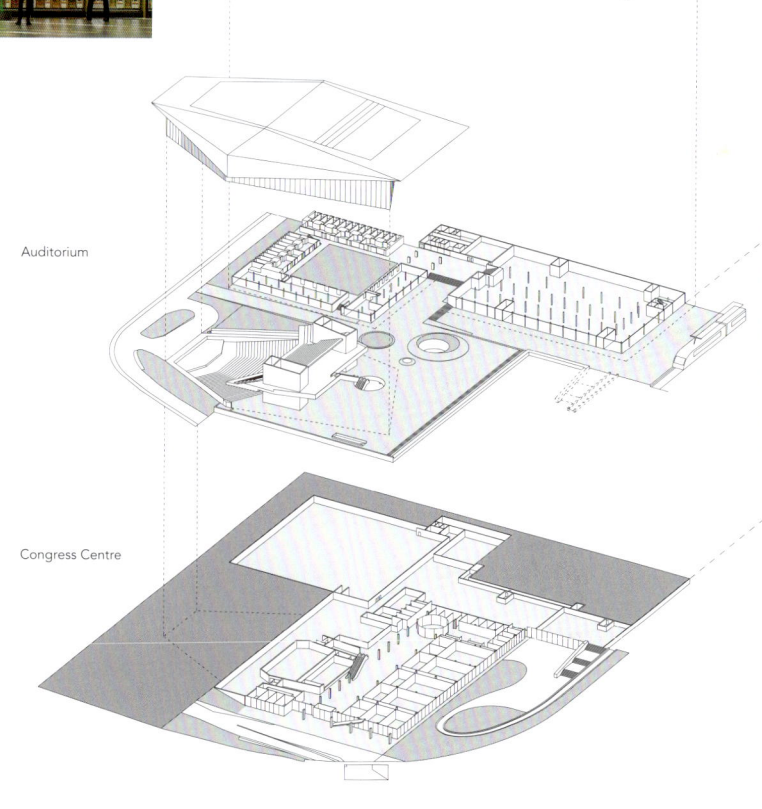

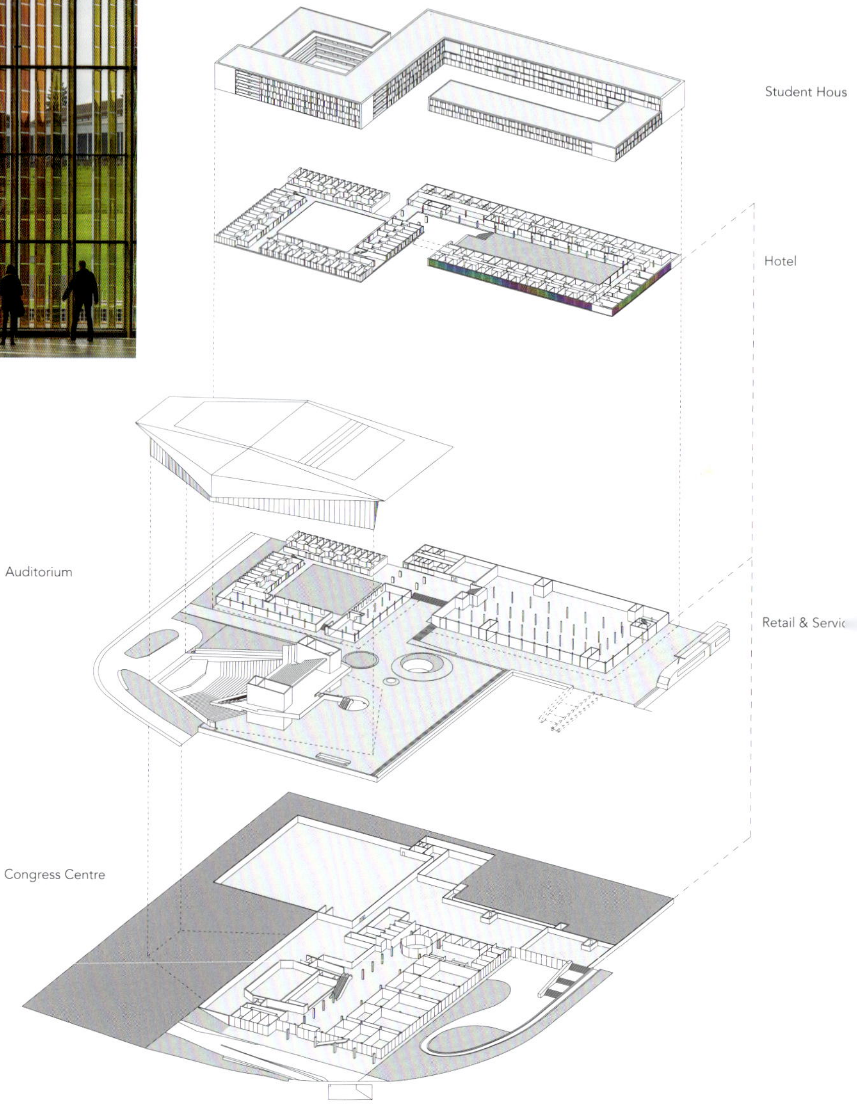

54 Richter Dahl Rocha & Associés, SwissTech Convention Center, École Polytechnique Fédérale de Lausanne (EPFL), Switzerland, 2014.
The building form and volume clearly identify this building as a landmark within the EPFL campus.

55 Richter Dahl Rocha & Associés, SwissTech Convention Center, École Polytechnique Fédérale de Lausanne (EPFL), Switzerland, 2014.
The axonometric shows different parts of the complex, and spatial organisation.

55

56

56 Richter Dahl Rocha & Associés, SwissTech Convention Center, École Polytechnique Fédérale de Lausanne (EPFL), Switzerland, 2014.
Dye-synthesised PV cells are used along the western facade creating an interesting pattern of colours.

57 Richter Dahl Rocha & Associés, SwissTech Convention Center, École Polytechnique Fédérale de Lausanne (EPFL), Switzerland, 2014.
The building form and volume were primarily influenced by the design of a large auditorium that can transform into multiple spaces with the use of movable partitions, hydraulic platforms and rotating seats.

57

types of solar cells, vertical orientation does not reduce energy output, and they produce 2,000 kWh of electricity per year.

The new headquarters building for Brussels Environment, the government authority overseeing environmental and habitat issues, demonstrates an innovative application of PVs. Designed by Dutch architects, cepezed, the building is in Brussels' largest urban renewal district. It has a compact volume with stepped receding floors, protected by a rounded and mainly transparent roof. The building includes a visitors' centre, an auditorium, multimedia library, conference centre, offices, laboratory and a central atrium. The facade incorporates triple-insulated glazing units with thermally broken framing, as well as automatic shading devices that respond to solar radiation. Natural ventilation is used throughout the building, along with a minimal amount of mechanical ventilation. A geoexchange system is incorporated, as well as a heat recovery system. The sloping roof and facade integrate 366 PVs, consisting of black monocrystalline solar cells, black foils, glass and black aluminium frame. All panels have identical dimensions, and 36 of them are curved. The total capacity of all the PV panels is 104,130 W, which outputs 87,000 kWh annually. The roof is covered by aluminium, therefore the seamless integration of the roofing, facade and PVs was achieved by precise detailing. Recessed gutters and black grates are incorporated for rainwater drainage. Brussels Environment is BREEAM-Excellent and PHPP (Passivhaus) certified.

THERMOELECTRICS

Thermoelectric materials exhibit thermoelectric effects, referring to phenomena where either a temperature difference creates an electric current, or electric potential creates a temperature difference. Thermoelectric modules are commercially available that consist of flat wafers, an array of miniature alloy junctions, connected electrically in series but operating thermally in parallel. When operating, the modules work as a heat pump, with a specific

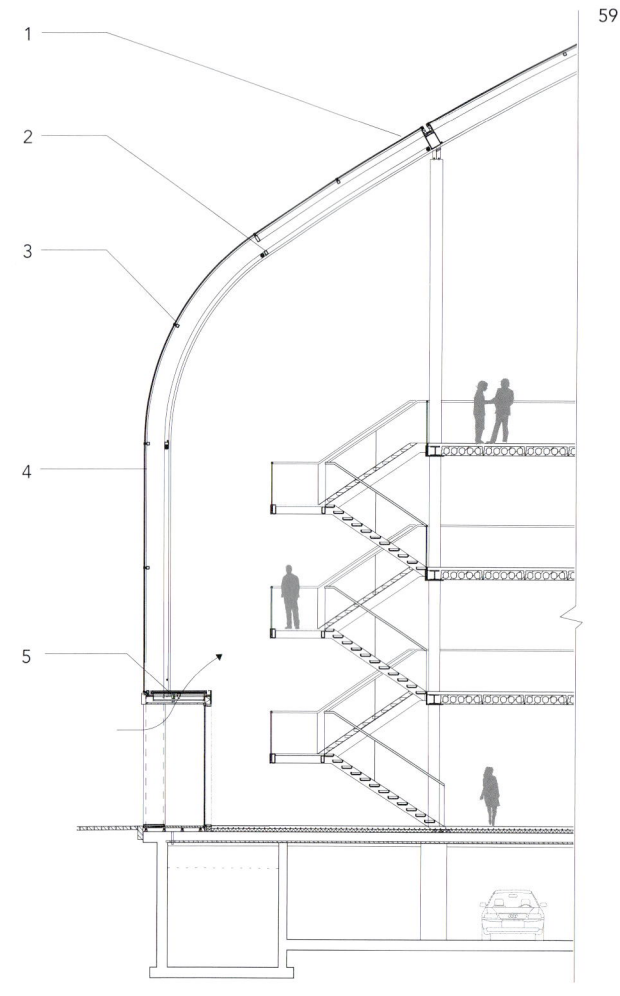

58

1 Skylight glazing
2 Interior shades
3 Framing
4 Glazing
5 Ventilation opening

59

Enlarged section

58 cepezed, Brussels Environment, Brussels, Belgium, 2014.
The building's compact form is protected by a rounded roof. The facade and roof are continuous and integrate black monocrystalline PV panels.

59 cepezed, Brussels Environment, Brussels, Belgium, 2014.
The enlarged section demonstrates the material components of the building envelope.

60 cepezed, Brussels Environment, Brussels, Belgium, 2014.
Plans, section and elevation showing spatial organisation, layout and building envelope treatment.

60

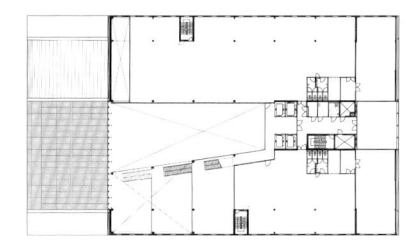

First-floor plan

Sixth-floor plan

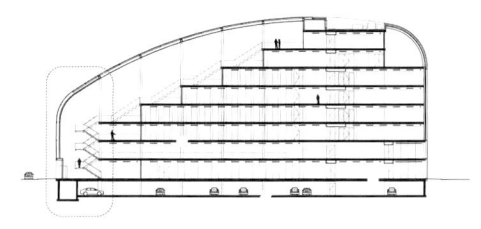

Section A-A

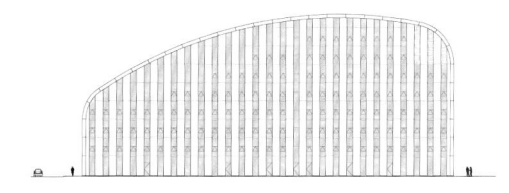

East elevation

amount of heat being transferred from one side of every junction to the other side of the module, thus yielding hot and cold sides. Alternatively, the temperature difference between the different sides of the module generates electricity.

Traditionally the efficiency of thermoelectric generation had been as low as 2%, restricting its applications within architectural and construction industries. Moreover, with the high cost of thermoelectric materials, commercialisation of this technology for large-scale architectural applications had been considered financially unfeasible. With the advent of nano-materials and structure synthesis techniques, recent years have seen an increased surge of interest in thermoelectric research and applications. Specifically, researchers are investigating new types of materials that would increase efficiency and energy production, including graphene and carbon nanotubes.[13, 14]

A novel application of thermoelectric modules has been explored, focusing on the integration of micro and nanoscale thermoelectric materials with window glass to generate electricity based on the temperature difference that exists between the exterior and interior environments.[15] The major challenge is that thermoelectric materials need to be integrated through the entire depth of glass to take advantage of the temperature differential between the exterior and interior environment. Conventional deposition techniques cannot achieve this thickness, so alternative fabrication techniques need to be developed. Current research focuses on milling micrometre-sized thermoelectric powders and then hot pressing into a mould to form thermoelectric modules that can be inserted into window glass. This fabrication technique needs further research and development to be widely adopted in the architecture and construction industries.

CONCLUSION: THE IMPACT OF ADVANCED AND SMART MATERIALS ON ARCHITECTURAL DESIGN
As we have seen in this chapter, numerous developments in materials are influencing how architects, engineers and other design professionals are envisioning better performing buildings and spaces, and how they are utilising advanced and smart materials to turn these ideas into built work. Advances in glass, concrete, metals and biomaterials are creating new classes of materials that have enhanced properties, such as improved structural performance, thermal properties, acoustic, optical and visual characteristics and environmental impact. Various types of composite materials are being developed and becoming increasingly used in the architectural and construction industries, since they combine two or more materials to enhance their properties and performance, such as polymers, resins, matrices and fibres with different substrates, with concrete and cement-based materials, metals, fabrics, ceramics, and so on. Smart materials adapt to changing conditions in the environment, and mimic the functioning of a biological or living organism. They can be classified into two general categories – materials that can sense and inherently respond to the changes in the

environment, and materials that need control, in a systematic manner, in order to be active based on a certain change. We have discussed different types of smart materials and their applications in architecture and design. These types of materials are initiating new typologies in architecture – smart and intelligent buildings that can react to changes in the environment and operation, and adjust their functionalities accordingly. The main barriers for the implementation of advanced and smart materials in architectural design are lack of long-term performance data and their higher costs. New, cost-effective manufacturing processes and economies of scale are influencing economic impacts. For example, the cost of electrochromic glass has drastically reduced over the last five years due to the development of new manufacturing techniques and higher demand. The increased number of applications, as well as performance monitoring and continued research, will address the lack of performance data for these innovative materials. The future of architectural design is highly dependent on the advancements in materials, improved and new products and the development of new classes of materials.

REFERENCES
1 Suneel N Vanikar, 'The Advances and Barriers in Application of New Concrete Technology', *Proceedings of the International Workshop on Sustainable Development and Concrete Technology*, Beijing, China, 2004, pp 25–33.
2 P Kumar Mehta and Paulo JM Monteiro, *Concrete: Microstructure, Properties, and Materials*, McGraw-Hill (New York), 2013.
3 Zongjin Li, *Advanced Concrete Technology*, Wiley (Hoboken, NJ), 2011.
4 Anne Chabas, Tiziana Lombardo, Hélène Cachier, Marie Hélène Pertuisot, K Oikonomou, Rino Falcone, Marco Verità and Franco Geotti-Bianchini, 'Behaviour of Self-Cleaning Glass in Urban Atmosphere', *Building and Environment*, Vol 43, No 12, 2008, pp 2124–31.
5 Ajla Aksamija, *Sustainable Facades: Design Methods for High-Performance Building Envelopes*, Wiley (Hoboken, NJ), 2013.
6 Michael Pawlyn, *Biomimicry in Architecture*, RIBA Publishing (London), 2011.
7 Ilaria Mazzoleni, *Architecture Follows Nature: Biomimetic Principles for Innovative Design*, CRC Press (Boca Raton, FL), 2013.
8 D Michelle Addington and Daniel Schodek, *Smart Materials and Technologies: For the Architecture and Design Professions*, Architectural Press (Oxford), 2005.
9 Marta Roig Flores, Simone Moscato, Pedro Serna Ros, and Liberato Ferrara, 'Self-Healing Capability of Concrete with Crystalline Admixtures in Different Environments', *Construction and Building Materials*, Vol 86, 2015, pp 1–11.
10 Tamás Szabó, Lívia Molnár-Nagy, János Bognár, Lajos Nyikos, Judit Telegdi, 'Self-Healing Microcapsules and Slow Release Microspheres in Paints', *Progress in Organic*

Coatings, Vol 72, No 1–2, 2011, pp 52–7.
11 Santiago J Garcia and Hartmut R Fischer, 'Self-Healing Polymer Systems: Properties, Synthesis and Applications', in Maria Rosa Aguilar and Julio San Román (eds), *Smart Polymers and their Applications*, Woodhead Publishing (Oxford), 2014.
12 Henk M Jonkers, Arjan Thijssen, Gerard Muyzer, Oguzhan Copuroglu and Erik Schlangen, 'Application of Bacteria as Self-Healing Agent for the Development of Sustainable Concrete', *Ecological Engineering*, Vol 36, No 2, 2010, pp 230–5.
13 Zlatan Aksamija and Irena Knezevic, 'Thermal Transport in Large-Area Polycrystalline Graphene', *Physical Review B*, Vol 90, No 3, 2014, pp 035419–27.
14 Myung-Ho Bae, Zuanyi Li, Zlatan Aksamija, Pierre N Martin, Feng Xiong, Zhun-Yong Ong, Irena Knezevic and Eric Pop, 'Ballistic to Diffusive Crossover of Heat Flow in Graphene Ribbons', *Nature Communications*, Vol 4, 2013, p 1734.
15 Salman B Inayat, Kelly R Rader and Muhammad M Hussain, 'Nano-Manufacturing of Thermoelectric Nanomaterials ($Bi_{0.4}Sb_{1.6}Te_3$/ $Bi_{1.75}Te_{3.25}$) and Their Integration into Window Glasses for Thermoelectricity Generation', *Energy Technology*, Vol 2, No 3, 2014, pp 292–329.

IMAGES
Opening Image © Mathieu Choiselat – Biarritz; figures 1 and 4 © Garrison Architects; figures 3, 5, 8, 10, 14, 18, 27, 40, 44, 48 and 53 © Ajla Aksamija; figure 2 © Andrew Rugge / archphoto; figure 6 © Loom, Ralph Nelson with Don Vu; figure 7 © Halkin Mason Photography; figure 9 © Richard Mandelkorn; figure 11 © Roland Halbe; figures 12 and 13 © Metro Arkitekter, Claes Janson, Carl Kylberg; figure 15 © Kevin Eilbeck Photography, Courtesy of Sage Glass; figure 16 © Dana Wheelock; figure 17 © LHB, Inc.; figures 19, 20 and 21 © Architecture49; figure 22 © Goshow Architects; figures 23, 24 and 25 © ALUSION TM; figure 26 © Tim Hursley; figures 28 and 29 © Mathieu Choiselat - Biarritz; figure 30 © Arotcharen Architects; figures 31 and 32 © MAD Architects; figures 33 and 34 © IGNISTERRA S. A./ Gianni Vercellino; figures 35 and 36 © Strategie Architecten Oosterbeek NL; figures 37 and 39 © FAAB Architektura, photo by Bartlomiej Senkowski; figure 38 © FAAB Architektura; figures 41, 42 and 43 © Rob Ley and Joshua G. Stein; figures 45 and 46 © Delft University of Technology; figure 47 © Sean McKeever / NBBJ; figures 49, 50, 51 and 52 © Consarc Architects; figures 54, 55, 56 and 57 © Fernando Guerra | FG+SG architectural photography; figures 58 and 61 © cepezed / photo Leon van Woerkom; figures 59 and 60 © cepezed

61 cepezed, Brussels Environment, Brussels, Belgium, 2014.
The sloping roof and facade seamlessly integrate PV panels.

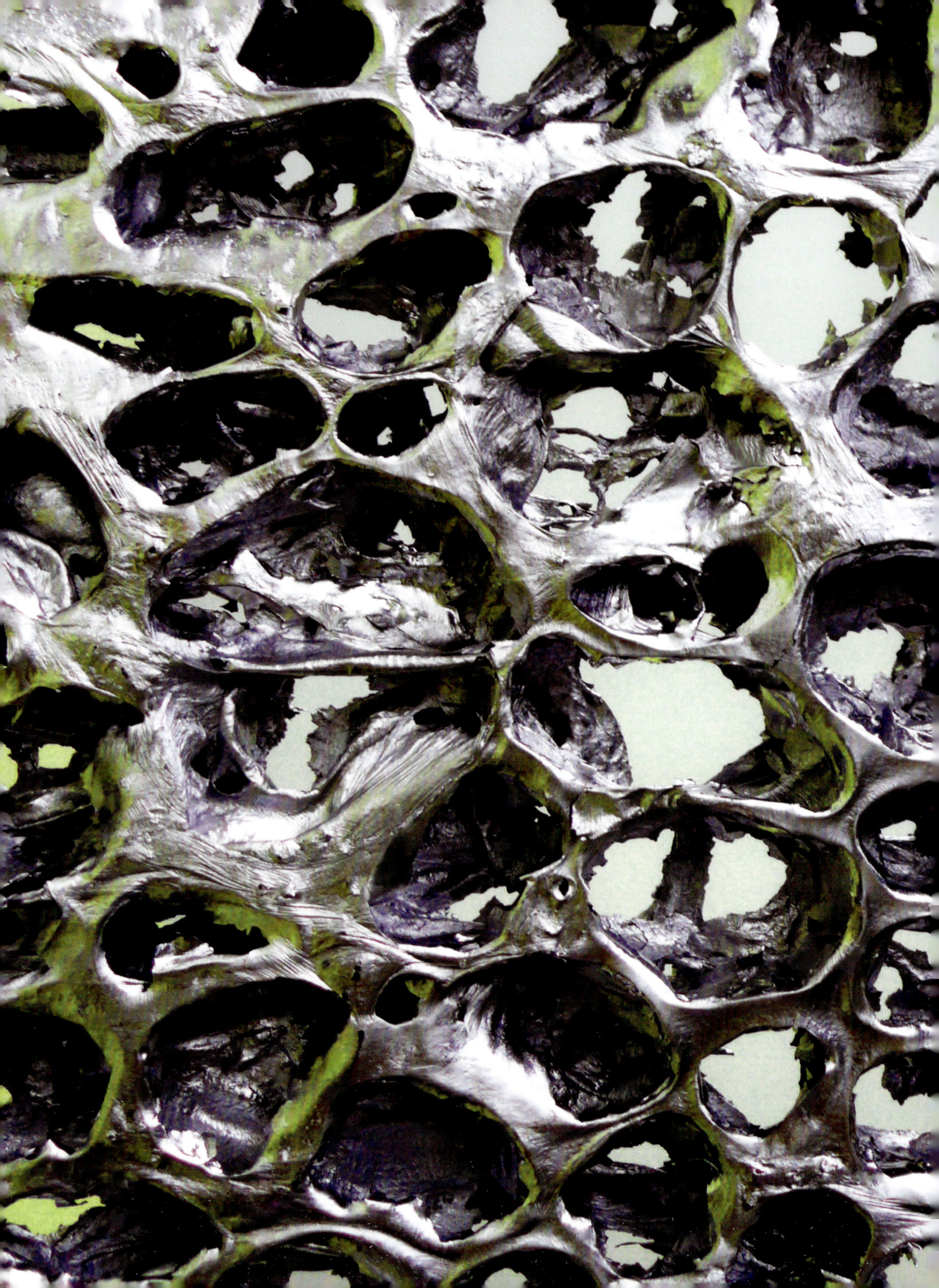

2 INNOVATIONS IN COMPUTATIONAL DESIGN

Innovations and developments in information technology and computation are causing unprecedented changes in architectural design and construction: transforming design processes and procedures, delivery methods, fabrication and construction methods. Computational, performance-based design; building information modelling (BIM); simulations and virtual construction; digital fabrication, all are creating a paradigm shift in architecture and these changes will transform contemporary practice.

The application of computation in architectural design is a consequence of advances in software development that have enhanced digital tools for design disciplines, as well as design procedures. Algorithmic and generative design, parametric design methods and scripting techniques are increasingly being used to aid the design process. Algorithms can be used to solve, organise and execute design problems with increased visual and organisational complexity. There is still the necessity for a certain level of programming knowledge in this process. Access to the code, and controlling flexibility within the code, is vital. Generative software programs and applications have made the coding interface as user-friendly as possible, enabling the architect/designer to manipulate and control these algorithms during the design process. At the very least, these applications provide an environment that integrates both the architect/designer with the programmer/algorithm specialist and gives each of them access to the three-dimensional design representation. These new methods of utilising digital tools for design can be more challenging in comparison to the traditional 3D modelling software applications, but they allow advanced form exploration.

As rapid developments in digital technologies continue to make computers and computing essential in today's professional world, architectural practices must embrace new technologies and design approaches. A paradigm shift in architectural design has been initiated and we are currently entering a new era in architecture. It must be noted that the paradigm shift not only influences the outcomes and products of architectural design (building forms, geometries and volumes), but also the design processes and services, including building information modelling (BIM), integration of simulation tools and performance analysis procedures, digital fabrication, and so on. Therefore, the computational design paradigm is not only evident in the end products and building with complex geometries, but also it is

1

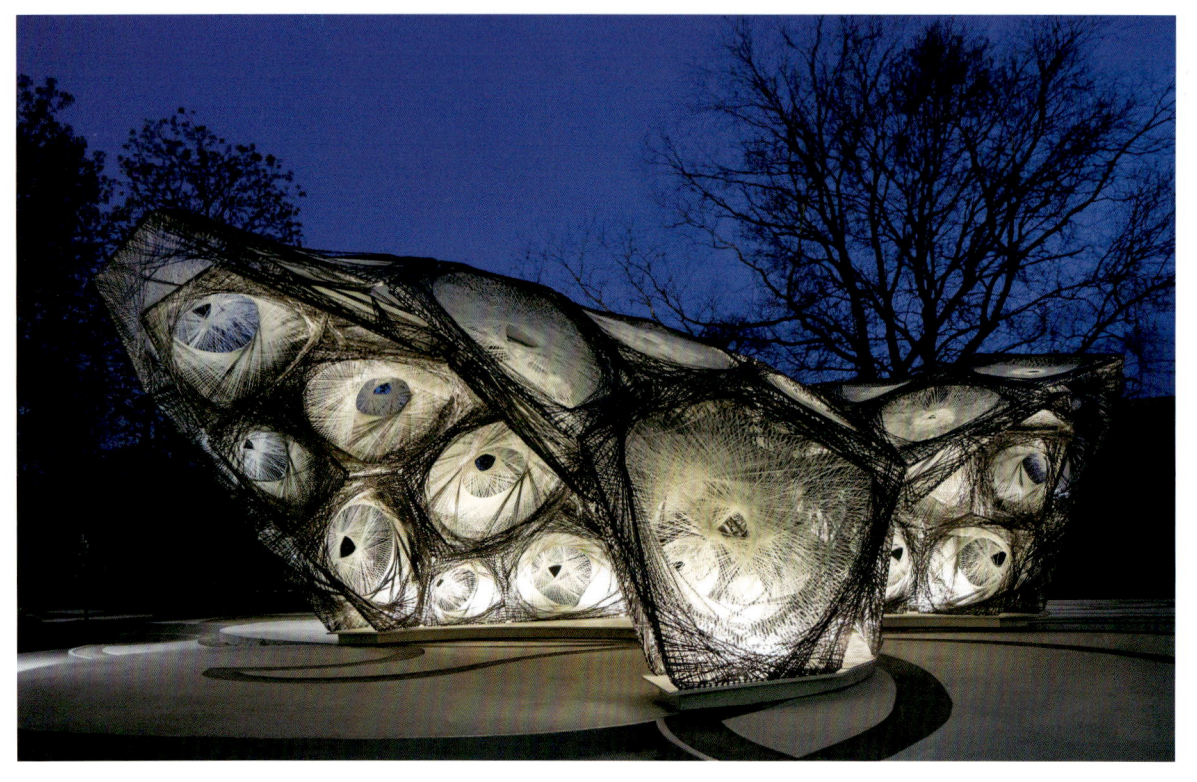

1 ICD/ITKE Research Pavilion 2013–2014, ICD/ITKE University of Stuttgart, Stuttgart, Germany, 2014.
The completed research pavilion showcases innovations in materials, computational design methods and digital fabrication.

2 ICD/ITKE Research Pavilion 2013–2014, ICD/ITKE University of Stuttgart, Stuttgart, Germany, 2014.
The design and digital fabrication process indicating relationships between biomimicry, computational design and robotic fabrication.

implicitly embedded in all projects and buildings that rely on the use of advanced digital technologies, BIM, simulations and modelling or digital fabrication.

ADVANCES IN COMPUTATIONAL DESIGN

What exactly constitutes parametric modelling? These processes and tools are relatively new to the architectural community and are based on the concept of rules, constraints, features and associations between parameters and objects in the model, such as geometry. The rules and constraints, usually consisting of mathematical formulae, data values or numbers, can be used to control the properties of the model or an object in a model, such as geometry, shape, size, and so on. The underlying driver for parametric design is to be able quickly to adapt the characteristics of a model component based on a certain rule, without having to recreate the entire model for each design iteration. The rules, or numeric values, may represent structural loads, environmental data (such as solar radiation, solar angles, wind velocity), or simply a change in dimensions. The benefits of parametric tools in practice have been acclaimed, but also acknowledged as increasing the complexity and time required for certain design tasks.[1]

Parametric design offers some advantages over traditional modelling methods, since it allows the adaptation of an object through the use of rules and constraints or 'parameters' to influence an object's properties. They enable the adaptation of

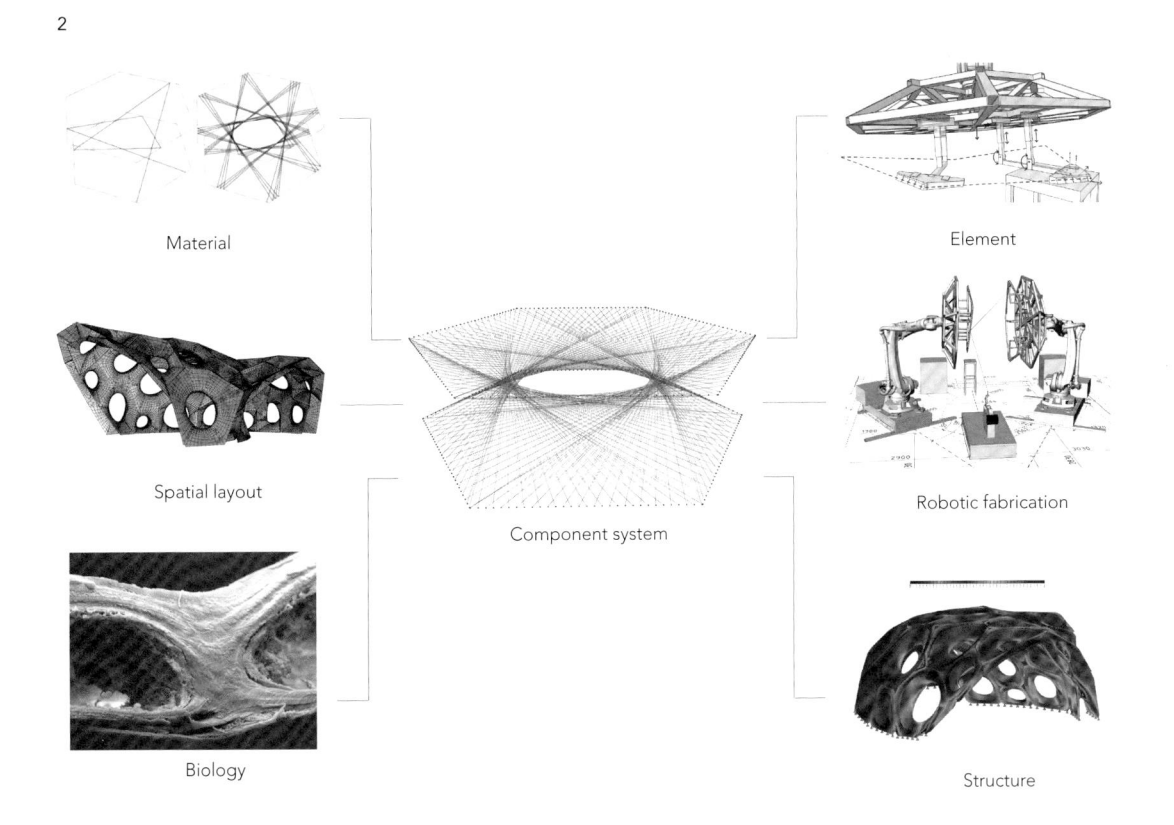

Material

Spatial layout

Biology

Component system

Element

Robotic fabrication

Structure

3

— Diameter to structural depth ratio
— Minimum edge length
— Minimum angle
— Non-planarity
— Maximum component size

— Stress response
— Moment response

4

1 Assembled frame
2 Space frame
3 Mobile robot base
4 Resin bath
5 Fibre spool

model geometry based on rules or data values, eliminating the need to recreate the model for every design change. In essence, the benefits of parametric design are:

- Parametric modelling utilises the manipulation and adaptation of an object's properties based on rules and data values.
- Multiple design options and design iterations can be created by modifying object attributes and properties (such as dimensions or shape) without recreating the entire model.
- Analytical data, developed in response to environmental constraints or other types of logic-based control, can be used to derive geometry.

There are also limitations to parametric design. For example, these design techniques require the use of advanced computational tools that need investment and time. In some instances, this design method also requires customisation of software applications for implementation. But more importantly, the logic behind the architectural design process must be understood in order to be implemented in the parametric design.

The Institute for Computational Design (ICD) at the University of Stuttgart has been exploring computational design and computer-aided manufacturing processes in architecture. In collaboration with the Institute of Building Structures and Structural Design (ITKE), the ICD has been exploring an integrated approach for computational design: the use of simulations, and digital fabrication techniques for lightweight structures. The ICD/ITKE Research Pavilion 2013–2014 consists of a glass and carbon-fibre composite material and is the result of a research project that investigated biomimicry supported by computational design, composite materials and robotic fabrication. Natural systems produce highly complex structures that integrate different functional properties, and this research project aimed to investigate how computational design and fabrication can be integrated to design and construct a small pavilion based on biomimetic design principles. The structure consists of a double-layer fibre composite material, which reduces the required formwork and allows significant freedom in geometric expression. During the design process, the multidisciplinary team investigated biological systems – particularly protective beetles' shells – and their geometric morphologies. Simulations and structural analysis of various shells were undertaken to understand structural capabilities and properties. The results indicated that a double-layer structure that is connected by curved support elements creates a robust support system, which was translated into an architectural prototype that relies on a similar structural system composed of a composite material. The composite material consisted of glass and carbon fibres and a polymer matrix, and exhibited anisotropic characteristics. This allowed for locally differentiated material properties based on the placement of fibres. Conventional fabrication methods for fibre composite

3 ICD/ITKE Research Pavilion 2013–2014, ICD/ITKE University of Stuttgart, Stuttgart, Germany, 2014.
Structural analysis using the finite element method (FEM) and computational design approach.

4 ICD/ITKE Research Pavilion 2013–2014, ICD/ITKE University of Stuttgart, Stuttgart, Germany, 2014.
Digital/robotic fabrication utilised two six-axis industrial robots, which wound fibres between two reconfigurable steel-frame elements.

5 ICD/ITKE Research Pavilion 2013–2014, ICD/ITKE University of Stuttgart, Stuttgart, Germany, 2014. The fibres were initially linearly tensioned between the frames, and then wrapped on top of the initial layer to form a double-curved surface.

6 ICD/ITKE Research Pavilion 2013–2014, ICD/ITKE University of Stuttgart, Stuttgart, Germany, 2014.
Different modules were created by varying the geometry of the frame, as well as the sequence and orientation of the fibre.

7 ICD/ITKE Research Pavilion 2013–2014, ICD/ITKE University of Stuttgart, Stuttgart, Germany, 2014.
The form and geometry resemble a biological form, and the pavilion showcases the innovative application of composite materials and robotic fabrication.

systems require moulds to define form. But, a robotic coreless, winding fabrication method was developed for this prototype structure, which used two six-axis industrial robots to wind fibres between two reconfigurable steel-framed elements. The frames defined the edges of each module, but the final geometry was defined through the interaction of assembled fibres. The fibres were initially linearly tensioned between the frames, and then wrapped on top of the initial layer to form a double-curved surface. The final prototype consisted of 36 elements that had a specific layout of fibres, resulting in an efficient load-bearing system. The biggest element had a 2.6 m (8.5 ft) diameter and weighed 24 kg (53 lbs). The completed installation covered an area of 50 m^2 (540 ft^2) and weighed 593 kg (1,300 lbs).

The Eskenazi Hospital parking structure art facade in Indianapolis – named 'May/September' due to its changing and variable character – was designed by Rob Ley Studio. This is an example of computational design where the computation is embedded in the design process to find a solution for a specific design goal, rather than explicitly being manifested in the geometry and form. The project started with the intention of challenging the typical notion of the parking structure as an ordinary infrastructural building type to transform the new parking structure for the Eskenazi Hospital into an inviting, aesthetically pleasing building. The solution was to design a dynamic facade that provides a unique visual experience for observers, depending on their position and perspective. The facade consists of 7,000 angled metal panels of two different colours, yellow and blue, where the angle of each panel is varied to create this dynamic effect. Pedestrians and slow-moving vehicles within close proximity experience a noticeable shift in colour and transparency of the facade, while faster moving cars experience a faster, gradient change in colour. The facade design was based on a two-dimensional image construction and tectonic considerations. The complex arrangement of patterns was developed, considering digital image manipulation and

8 (below and opposite) Rob Ley Studio, Eskenazi Hospital parking structure art facade ('May/September'), Indianapolis, IN, USA, 2014.
The facade has variable character and changes colour and transparency as you move within the site.

9 Rob Ley Studio, Eskenazi Hospital parking structure art facade ('May/September'), Indianapolis, IN, USA, 2014.
Computational design approaches were used to develop the facade pattern and transparency.

10 Rob Ley Studio, Eskenazi Hospital parking structure art facade ('May/September'), Indianapolis, IN, USA, 2014.
Primary colours (yellow and blue) were used for the metal panels, which vary in angle relative to the vertical axis and create an interesting, dynamic facade effect.

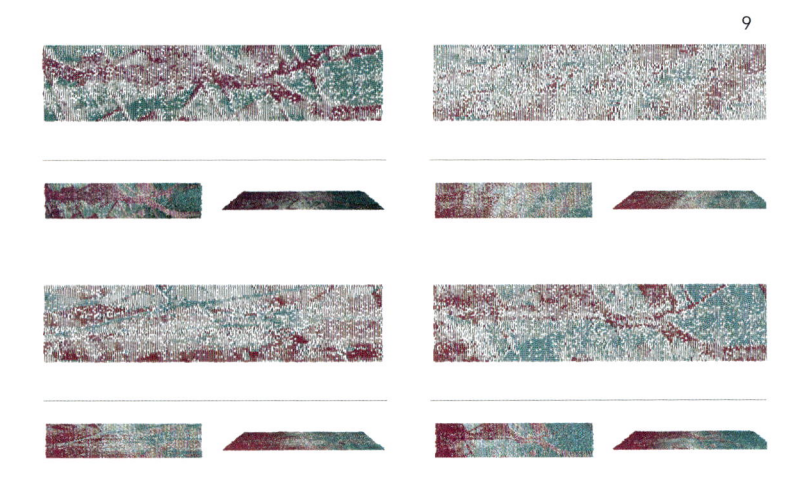

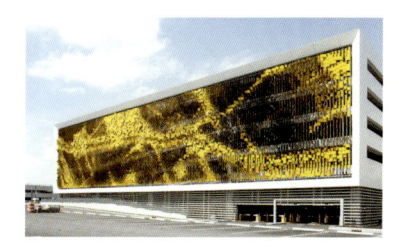

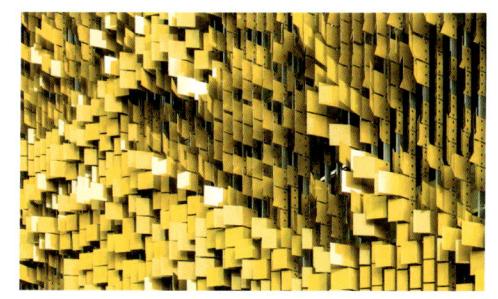

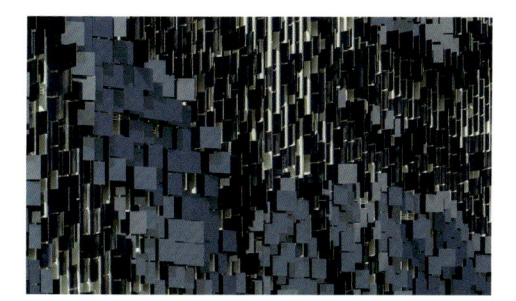

reproduction techniques. Computational design approaches investigated different patterns, textures, positioning of the panels and the respective angles. The design team also used custom software applications to create the final effect, implementing three basic typologies of patterns, with three different-sized subsets and mirroring, to produce a palette of 18 unique patterns. These components, as well as the yellow and blue binary colour scheme, produced a complex facade system.

Designed by Trahan Architects, the Louisiana State Museum and Sports Hall of Fame, in Natchitoches on the banks of the Cane River Lake, is a new museum dedicated to Louisiana's sports teams' memorabilia. The building's innovative entrance, circulation and the central atrium space are defined by a free-form cast stone system. The design was driven by the interrelationship between sports and history, past and future, container and contained. The building's programme includes exhibition spaces, educational and supporting spaces. These flow both physically and visually, and the internal organisation is an extension of the existing urban circulation. The building's exterior is simple, clad with copper panels, and integrates horizontal louvres that control light, views and ventilation. The flowing interior was inspired by river geomorphology and the way that water carves and sculpts the land. The atrium is clad with white cast stone panels, which flow into the galleries. The circulation path ends at the upper level, and provides a veranda that overlooks the city square. Computational design methods were extensively used during the design of this building. BIM and 3D modelling software, and model-based coordination, were used throughout the process. The motivation for using model-based coordination was grounded in the inability to represent complex geometry properly using traditional methods, where the translation of complex geometries into 2D representation would be inefficient and prone to errors and misinterpretations. Therefore, model-based design, fabrication and construction coordination provided the means to design and construct this complex building, and to bridge the gap between visual representation and building technology. Among other design and construction aspects the model was used to investigate design issues, perform structural analysis, track progress, examine prototypes, plan installation and construction and visualise construction sequencing.

The cast stone surface of the atrium and interior circulation consists of 1,100 panels that weigh about 700 tons. Each panel was created as a unique component, having a different size and shape from all other panels. The pattern was created digitally, and it was essential that all panels be properly assembled. The original BIM design model was used to panelise surfaces in five sequences, in order to develop the structural geometry of the supporting steel frame, the geometry of panels and the panel connections. The panels are supported by a steel space frame, which is in turn supported by the ground-floor slab and the second-floor framing. Movement connections were required for almost all panels due to structural deflection. Structural analysis was performed using a 3D structural

11

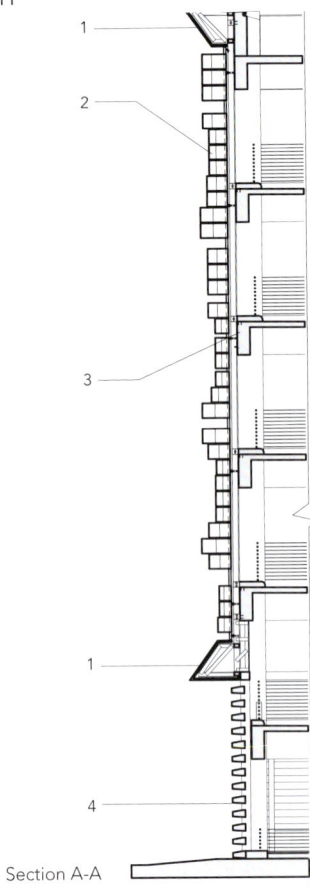

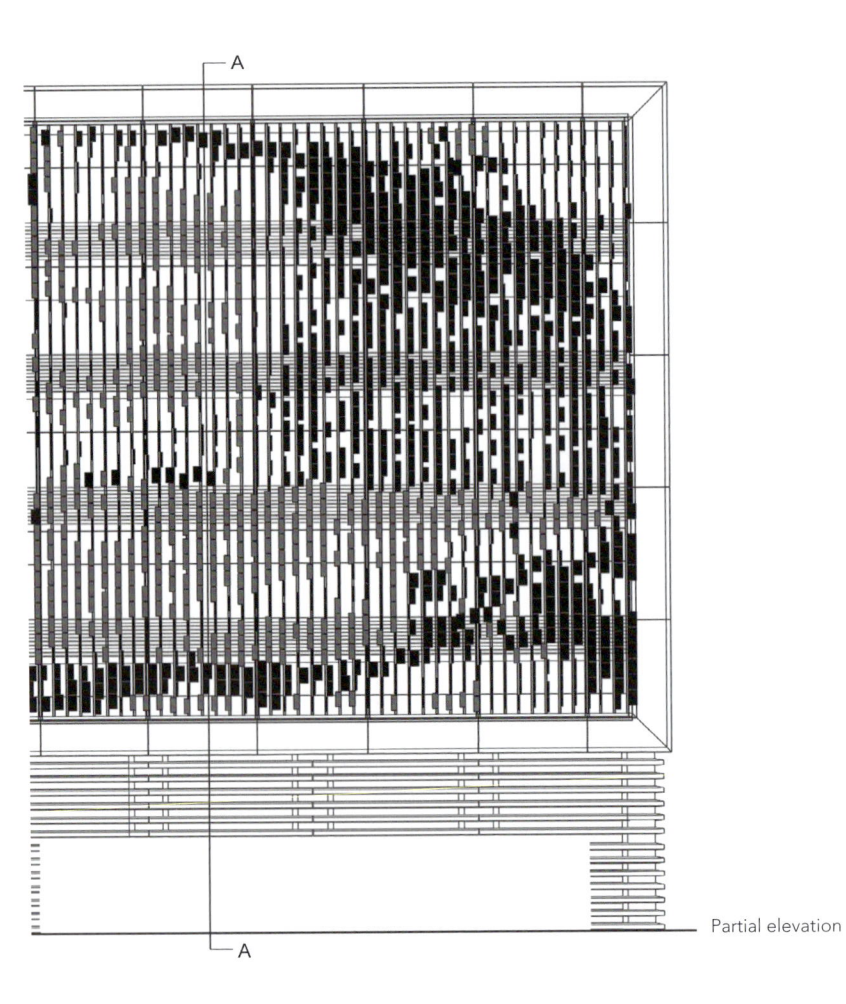

Section A-A

Partial elevation

11 Rob Ley Studio, Eskenazi Hospital parking structure art facade ('May/September'), Indianapolis, IN, USA, 2014. Partial elevation and section showing material components and assembly.

1 Aluminium fascia
2 Anodised aluminium panels
3 Concrete structure
4 Aluminium louvres

12

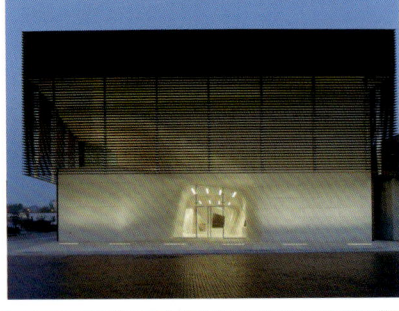

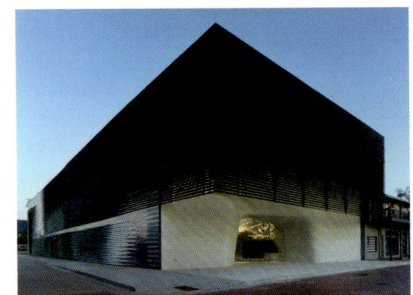

13 Angles

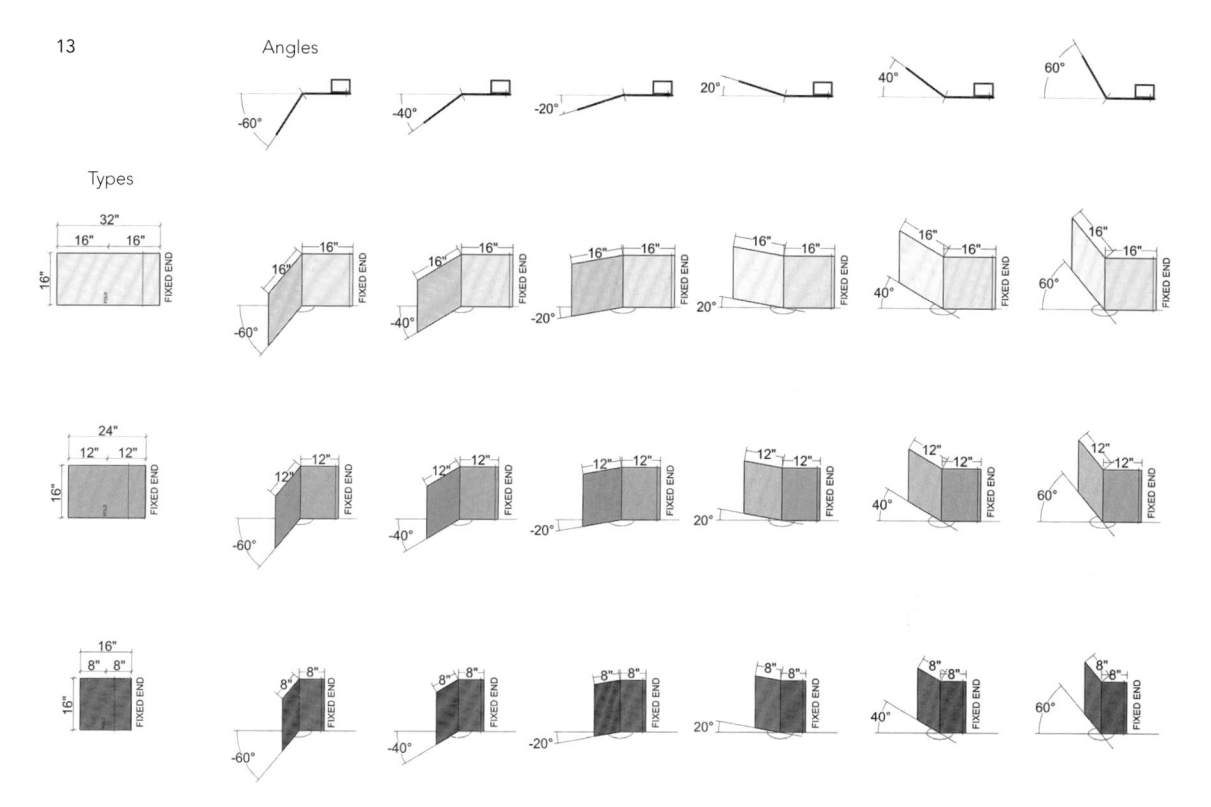

Types

12 Trahan Architects, Louisiana State Museum and Sports Hall of Fame, Natchitoches, USA, 2013.
The building's innovative entrance, circulation and the central atrium space is defined by a free-form cast stone system.

13 Rob Ley Studio, Eskenazi Hospital parking structure art facade ('May/September'), Indianapolis, IN, USA, 2014.
The facade components include three basic typologies of patterns, with three different-sized subsets mirroring, to produce a palette of 18 unique patterns.

analysis program and results were used to modify local structural elements, providing more support for heavier loads and lighter elements for under-stressed components, to reduce the weight of the structural systems. A steel detailing software application was used to generate shop drawings, and construction sequencing was digitally conducted using BIM to locate steel elements and stone panels during construction.

Metropol Parasol is a redevelopment project for the Plaza de la Encarnación in Seville, Spain, designed by J Mayer H Architects. The project includes an archaeological museum, a farmers' market, bars and restaurants, skywalk and a panorama terrace. The timber structure, designed using computational design, unifies these different aspects of the programme and provides an iconic landmark for the urban centre of Seville. Sitting within the dense fabric of the medieval inner city, Metropol Parasol animates the plaza and creates a contemporary landmark.

Parametric modelling was used during the design process to develop a design language and pattern for the wood structures. The code was generated through scripting and applied to the design at different scales, including the structural expression of the parasols, the plaza surface, water features, street furniture and green spaces. The end result is a highly complex form that expresses parametric generation. The wood composite structure, consisting of a waffle grid system of interlocking composite timber components and steel connectors, was used to create

14 Trahan Architects, Louisiana State Museum and Sports Hall of Fame, Natchitoches, USA, 2013.
Copper panels and horizontal louvres are used for the building facade.

15 Trahan Architects, Louisiana State Museum and Sports Hall of Fame, Natchitoches, USA, 2013.
The design of the interior atrium and circulation was inspired by river geomorphology. The atrium is clad with white cast stone panels, which flow into the galleries.

2 INNOVATIONS IN COMPUTATIONAL DESIGN

16

First-floor reflected ceiling plan

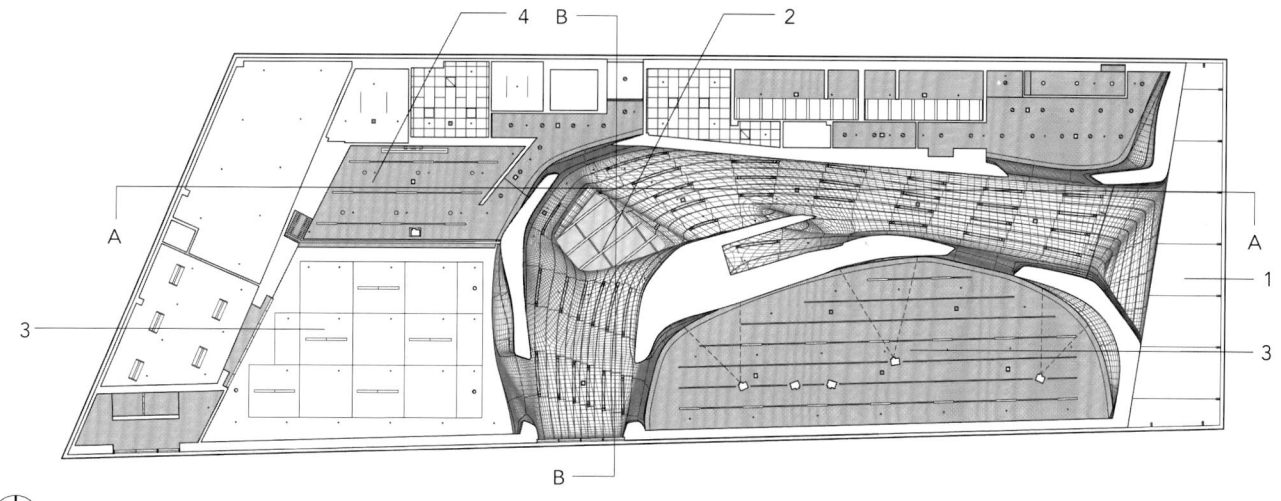

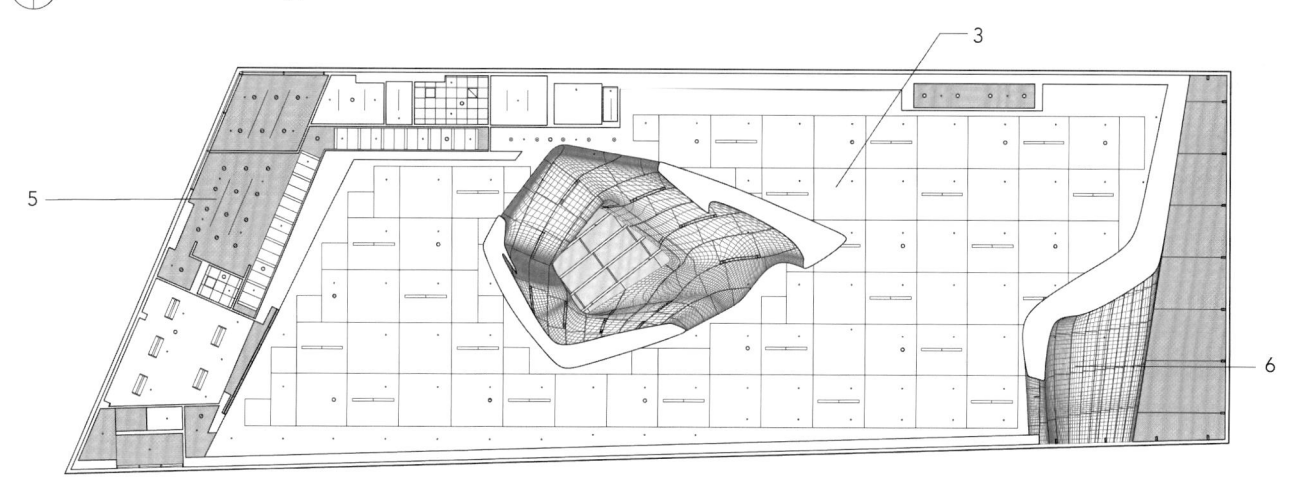

Second-floor reflected ceiling plan

1 Porch
2 Foyer
3 Gallery
4 Classroom
5 Offices
6 Veranda

16 Trahan Architects, Louisiana State Museum and Sports Hall of Fame, Natchitoches, USA, 2013.
The circulation path ends at the upper level and provides a veranda that overlooks the city square.

17 Trahan Architects, Louisiana State Museum and Sports Hall of Fame, Natchitoches, USA, 2013.
Reflected ceiling plans show relationships between the interior free-flowing space and exterior rigid, rectangular contours.

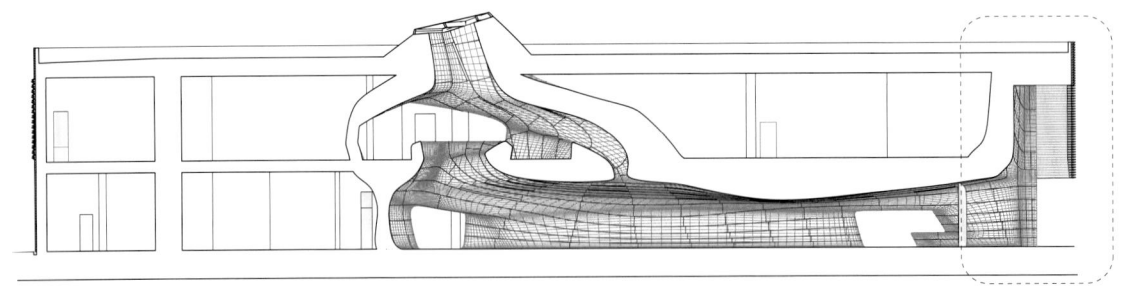

Section A-A

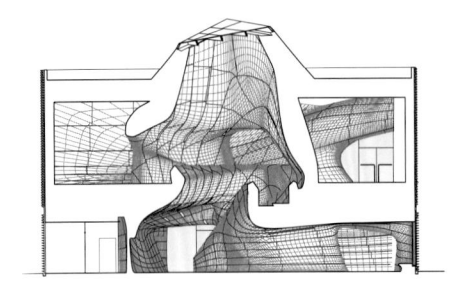

Section B-B

18 Trahan Architects, Louisiana State Museum and Sports Hall of Fame, Natchitoches, USA, 2013.
Building sections showing the form, structure and flow of interior spaces.

1 Copper horizontal shading
2 Exterior stone panels
3 Interior stone panels
4 Steel beam
5 Surface support steel
6 Glazing
7 Concrete slab

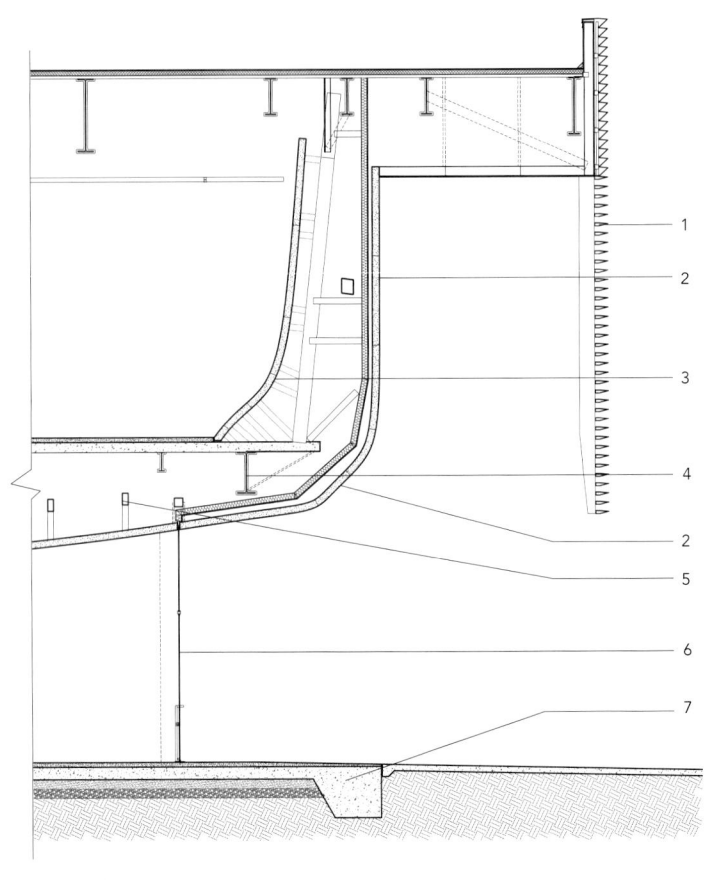

Enlarged section

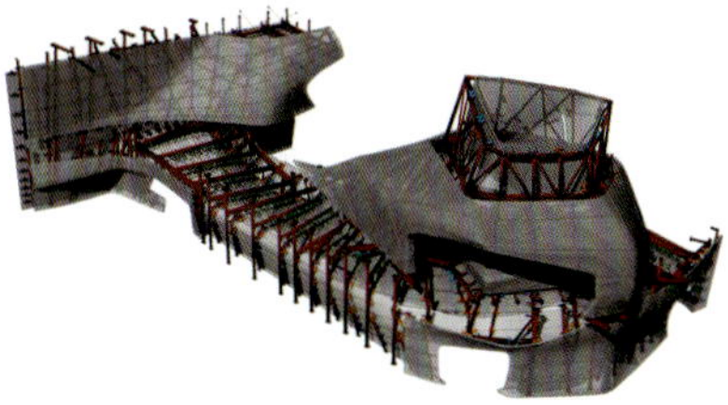

19

19 Trahan Architects, Louisiana State Museum and Sports Hall of Fame, Natchitoches, USA, 2013.
Model-based coordination was used throughout the design and construction process to allow proper representation of the complex geometry, elements, construction sequencing and fabrication.

20 Trahan Architects, Louisiana State Museum and Sports Hall of Fame, Natchitoches, USA, 2013.
A BIM model was used to panelise surfaces in five sequences in order to develop the structural geometry of the supporting steel frame and the geometry of panels and panel connections.

20

a three-dimensional load-bearing system for the parasols. The supporting structural system consists of steel and concrete, and cylindrical concrete cores enveloped in wood sheathing, which contain elevators and vertical services.

Precise shaping, sizing and structural optimisation was necessary for this project. The computational design process was fundamental, and started with form generation and parametric modelling by the design team. Then, comprehensive BIM was developed, which was also used for structural calculations. Since an iterative process was used for structural analysis in order to investigate different loading scenarios and the sizing of individual elements, a partially automated calculation method was developed that allowed seamless interaction between the finite element method (FEM) structural analysis model and the structural verification spreadsheet. Therefore, the thickness of each timber member and the number and weight of connections were automatically calculated and added to the BIM model to be shared with fabricators. A CAD/CAM system was used during fabrication and CNC milling for cutting and milling timber structural members.

TOOLS AND METHODS
Computer-aided architectural design (CAAD) relies on many different software programs and platforms. Historically, early computer-aided design (CAD) programs were introduced in the 1970s as 2D drafting programs that translated manual drafting into computer-based systems. Although today this notion seems very outdated, especially with the wider adoption of BIM and model-based design and construction, early CAD platforms revolutionised some aspects of design, including the automated generation of construction documents layout and the ability to standardise

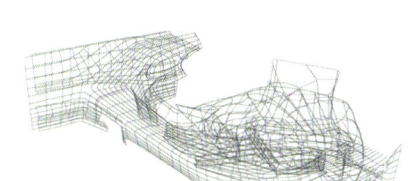

Joints

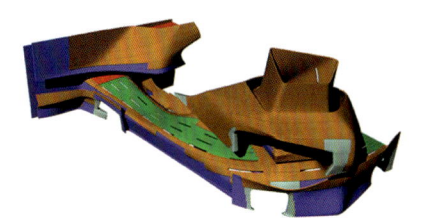

Panels

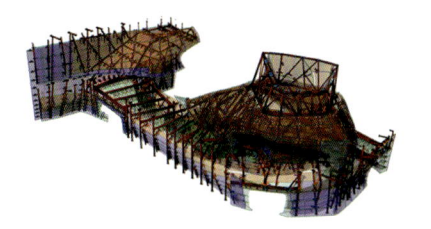

Surface support steel

Panel connections

Integrated systems

Full structure

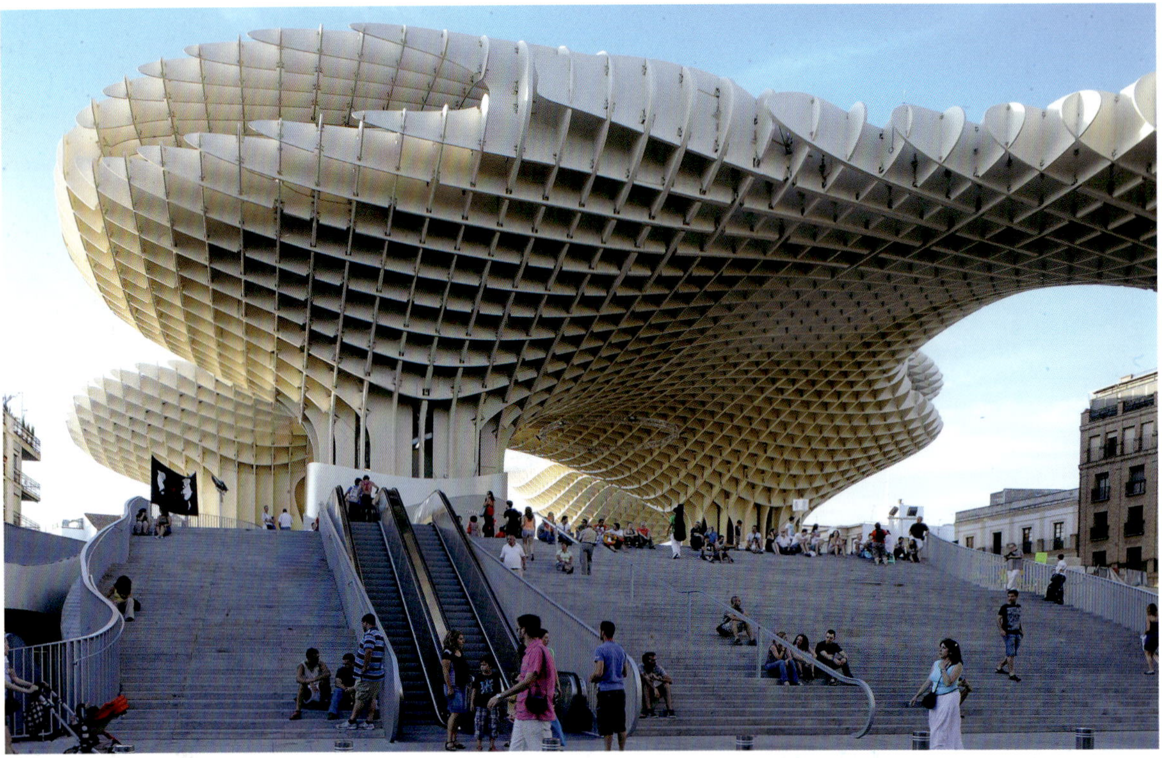

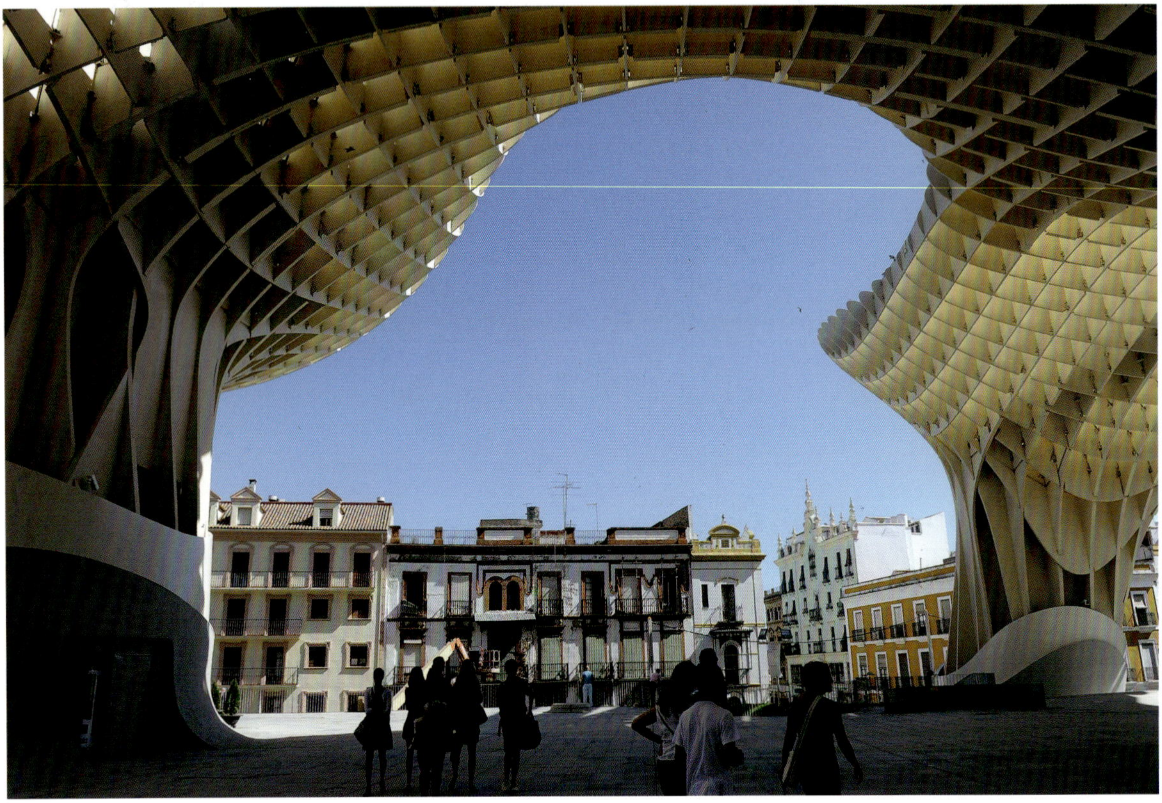

21 J Mayer H Architects, Metropol Parasol, Plaza de la Encarnación, Seville, Spain, 2011. The timber structure, designed using computational design, unifies different aspects of the programme and provides an iconic landmark for the urban centre of Seville.

22 J Mayer H Architects, Metropol Parasol, Plaza de la Encarnación, Seville, Spain, 2011. Parametric modelling was used during the design process to develop the design language and pattern for the timber structures.

Plan

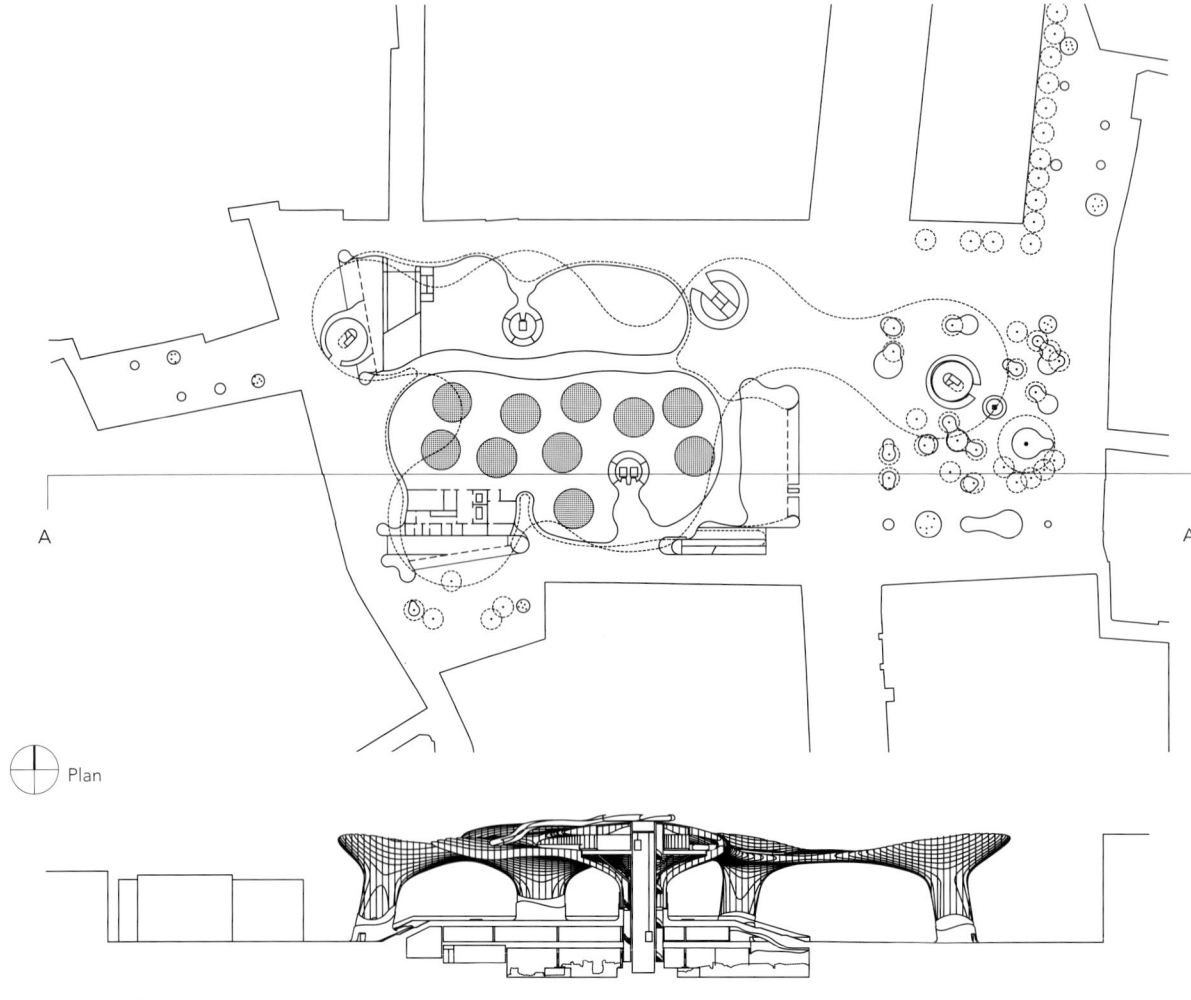

Section A-A

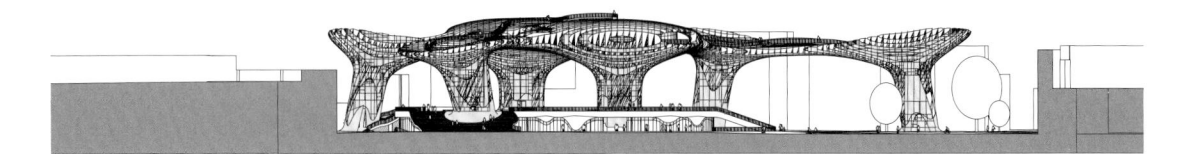

South elevation

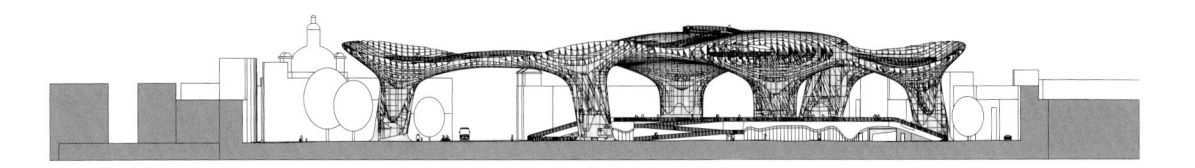

North elevation

graphics, representations and so on. Starting in the 1990s, model-based design procedures and BIM created a paradigm shift in architectural design, transforming computational design from 2D drafting into a 3D model-based design process. Also, increased interest in energy efficiency, high-performance design, structural optimisation and building science resulted in the wider availability and development of modelling and simulation software programs to aid design decision-making. Now CAAD terminology has been adopted to represent a broad range of software applications that can be used for architectural design, analysis, project management, clash detection, fabrication and construction.

The purpose of this book is not to provide a comprehensive list of all available CAAD software applications, but it is necessary to provide a classification and brief overview of widely used software applications. Table 1 lists five different categories of CAAD software applications (CAD and 3D modelling, BIM, visualisation, parametric design/form generation and simulation tools), as well as specific platforms. CAD and 3D modelling applications are

Table 1 Categories of computer-aided architectural design (CAAD) software applications and widely adopted software programs.

CAD and 3D modelling	BIM	Visualisation	Parametric design/form generation	Simulation tools
Allplan	ArchiCAD	Atlantis	CATIA	bSol
AutoCAD	Digital Project	Flamingo	Dynamo	DAYSIM
Blender	Microstation		Generative Components	DesignBuilder
Bricscad	Revit	LightWave	Grasshopper	Ecotect
Caddie	Vectorworks	LuxRender	Maya	ENERGIEplanner
CINEMA 4D		Maxwell Render	SolidWorks	eQuest
DDS-CAD		mental ray	3ds Max	EnergyPlus
form Z		POV-Ray		IDA ICE
Google SketchUp		RenderMan		IES VE
Houdini		RenderWorks		SAP200
IntelliPlus Architecturals		VRenderZone		Radiance
Rhinoceros 3D		V-Ray		THERM
Spirit		YafaRay		WUFI

23 J Mayer H Architects, Metropol Parasol, Plaza de la Encarnación, Seville, Spain, 2011.
The plan, section and elevations show different components and spatial organisation.

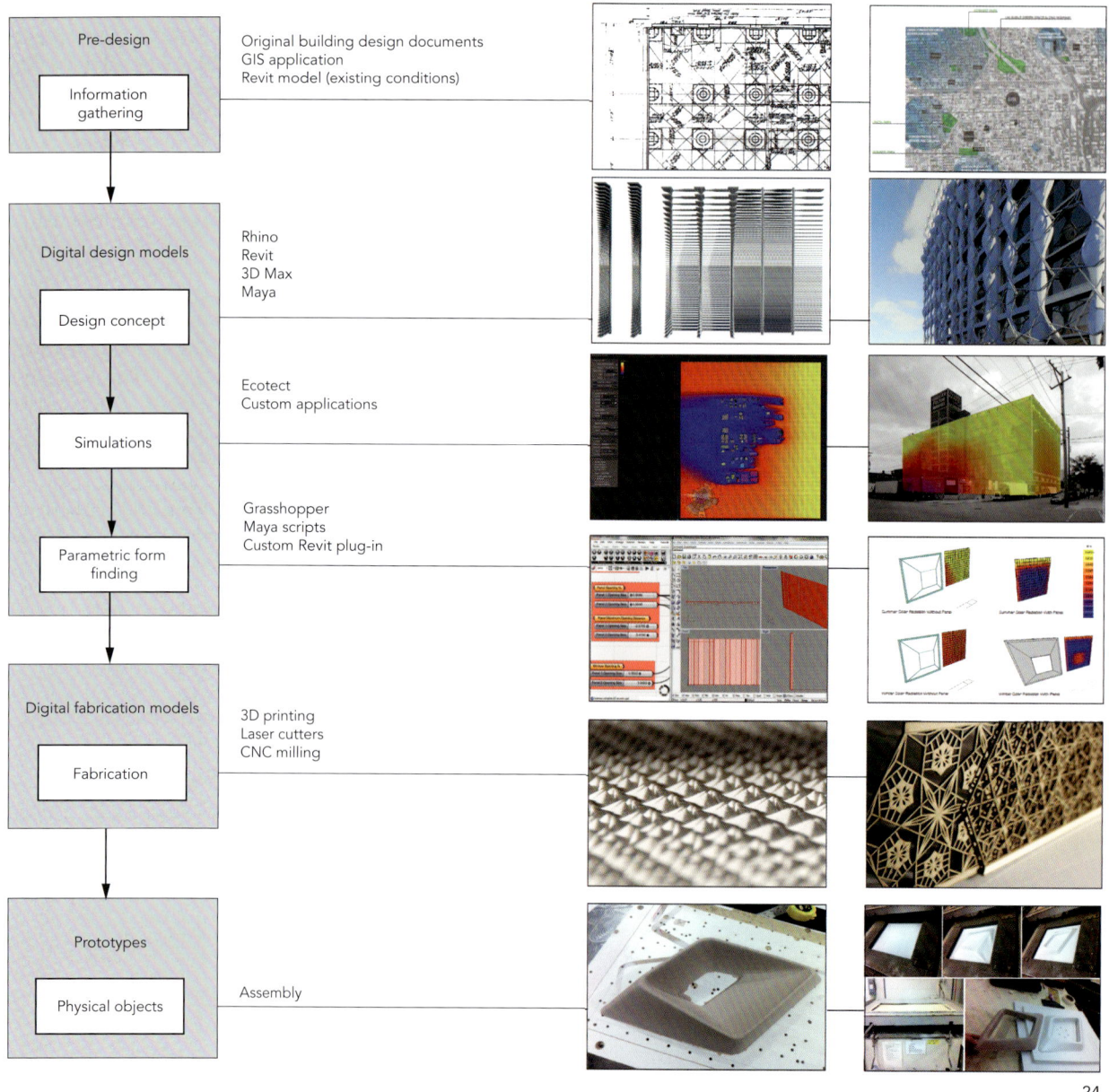

Process	Authoring software/production method		
Pre-design Information gathering	Original building design documents GIS application Revit model (existing conditions)		
Digital design models Design concept	Rhino Revit 3D Max Maya		
Simulations	Ecotect Custom applications		
Parametric form finding	Grasshopper Maya scripts Custom Revit plug-in		
Digital fabrication models Fabrication	3D printing Laser cutters CNC milling		
Prototypes Physical objects	Assembly		

24 Perkins+Will and the University of Cincinnati, research project, 2012.
The digital design and production process included distinct design and fabrication phases, and relied on different software applications. Data exchange was performed between 3D modelling, BIM, parametric design and building performance analysis tools.

used for modelling and design representation. BIM applications are used for model-based design and construction. Visualisation applications are used for rendering, while parametric design/form generation are used for parametric design capabilities. Both visualisation engines and some parametric tools are interoperable and are used by 3D modelling applications (for example, Grasshopper™ is a plug-in for Rhino3D®, while V-Ray can be used as a rendering engine for Rhino3D). Simulation applications are used for different types of performance analysis, such as structural analysis (SAP2000®), energy modelling (EnergyPlus™, eQuest®, IDA ICE, IES VE and so on), daylight simulations (DAYSIM and Radiance) and thermal analysis (THERM and WUFI®).

All CAAD and CAD systems employ a database with geometric and other properties of objects; they all have graphic user interfaces to manipulate visual representations, and all are used to assemble or analyse designs from standard and non-standard components. There are two differences between CAAD and CAD systems: first, CAAD systems have an explicit object database of building parts and construction knowledge and, second, they explicitly support the creation of architectural objects. Parametric, algorithmic and scripting techniques allow the modification of objects in a non-traditional way, since the users can modify their properties using programming, without directly changing the model-based view of the objects. BIM is the process of generating and managing building data during its life cycle, and it relies on the use of 3D, real-time, dynamic modelling software applications for building design and construction. BIM includes building geometry, spatial relationships and properties and quantities of building components. It allows the digital representation of the building process besides the exchange of building and design information in a digital format. Parametric modelling in BIM applications can be achieved by programming or scripting parametric objects. For example, Geometric Descriptive Language (GDL) is used in ArchiCAD BIM software and objects are defined using this programming language. Users have the ability to manipulate the properties of objects by modifying parameters through GDL. Dynamo™ is a plug-in for Revit® that allows the parametric control and algorithmic editing of BIM elements.

Interoperability and successful data exchange with different software applications are crucial. Architectural design and construction do not rely on only one software application and typically, many different types of tools are used for: design exploration, form finding, preparation of architectural and construction documents, analysis and simulation, fabrication and manufacturing and construction. Seamless transfer between different software applications is necessary, as well as exchange through a common set for file formats. The buildingSMART initiative, led by the International Alliance for Interoperability, has been developing a standard protocol for data exchange and information sharing between different software applications. Industry Foundation Classes (IFC) are the result of this effort, a data model in a neutral and open specification format not controlled

25

25 Perkins+Will and the University of Cincinnati, research project, 2012.
Existing conditions for the adaptive reuse of a building, used in collaborative research to explore the integration between computational design, performance-based methods and digital fabrication.

by a single software-developing company. It is an object-oriented file format that can facilitate interoperability within the building industry and is commonly used in BIM applications.

To illustrate integration between computational design, performance-based methods and digital fabrication, the following case study reviews collaborative research between Perkins+Will and the University of Cincinnati.[2] The objectives of the study were to investigate parametric design methods, building performance analysis, simulations and fabrication, and to design and fabricate building facade components for an adaptive reuse project. The goals were: to investigate the integration of performance analysis and computational design methods to drive design decisions, the use of parametric modelling tools to explore building skin design, and the fabrication and prototyping methods to test constructability, material choices and form. The building was a 10-storey cold-storage facility constructed during the 1910s in Chicago, being redesigned into a commercial premises.

The digital production processes used allowed for distinct design and fabrication phases. Initially, information about the site and its characteristics was compiled and assembled from geographic information system (GIS) applications, as well as existing building conditions from the original construction documents and BIM model. Different software programs were used to develop design concepts, such as Revit®, Maya®, Rhino3D and 3ds Max. During the design phase, simulation and performance analysis tools were introduced, such as Ecotect™ and custom applications. Results of the analysis process, including solar radiation along the different facade orientations, were used to drive design decisions and design optimal facade solutions. Parametric modelling tools, such as Grasshopper, Maya scripts and a customised plug-in for Revit, were used to size and position building skin components, and determine appropriate forms and geometry based on analysis results. The design phase required the use of simulations and parametric modelling techniques in the creation of forms and components based on performance data. The digital fabrication phase introduced different techniques, including laser cutting, CNC milling and 3D printing, which allowed design solutions to be physically studied and examined. The end results were physical prototypes of the building-skin components.

Building performance has historically been considered an evaluative process. As such, the traditional design typically uses analysis and simulation tools at set destination points in a linear design process. However, performance-driven design processes provide the computational means to design solutions at any stage, but preferably from the very beginning of a design to maximise the potential of an integrated design/performance feedback. The non-linear parametric model associations, connected to the input from analysis and simulation software, can provide a design feedback loop between geometry and performance/environmental data. In this relationship, parametric geometry associated with analytical data can represent building massing, envelope/wall system shading

26 Perkins+Will and the University of Cincinnati, research project, 2012. Performance results (solar radiation data for different facade orientations obtained from Ecotect) were used for parametric modelling applications (Grasshopper and Rhinoceros 3D) as inputs for the parametric control of model elements.

North West South East

Solar radiation data from Ecotect

Grasshopper script

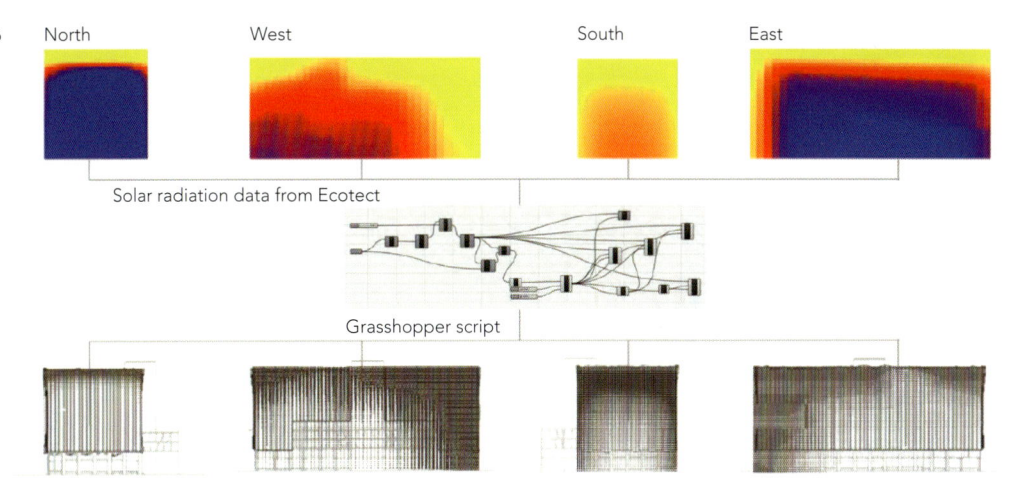

Parametric control of building facade components in Rhinoceros 3D

components, or bay spacing in a column grid tied to an external envelope/skin module. In a performance-driven design approach, the performance results can become the input for parametric control of geometric model elements. The core of a performance-driven design process can be environmental performance data, based on simulated physical conditions, used directly as an input to the parametric building model. The data can be transferred to the model via a spreadsheet, or by a software application plug-in, to drive element/component optimisation in the model.

Computer-aided manufacturing (CAM) tools have also yielded a significant leap for designers, providing new digital fabrication means of exploring material limits and form. By combining parametric design tools with rapid prototyping techniques in the design process, architects have powerful real-time capabilities to generate multiple design options, iterate conceptual approaches and end with scaled artefacts to study, review and critique the design solutions. Digitally generated design solutions were used for digital fabrication, such as 3D printing, CNC milling or laser-cutting methods. Part of the challenge when using digital fabrication in the design process is the ability to realise the conceptual idea within the size limitations and allowances of the current fabrication tools. For example, one of the challenges is how to break down complex forms – generated from the performance-driven design process – as simplified components that can be realised by fabrication and assembling. This can be solved by the slicing and tessellation method where a complex form is divided into a large quantity of two-dimensional contours or patterns, which are fabricated individually and assembled to construct the original form.

The workflow from performance data, such as solar radiation, to the pattern of the building skin, to the fabrication stage, provided many interesting approaches for building-skin designs.

27

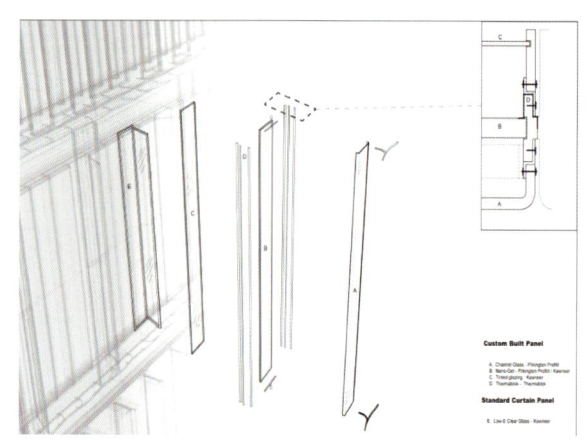

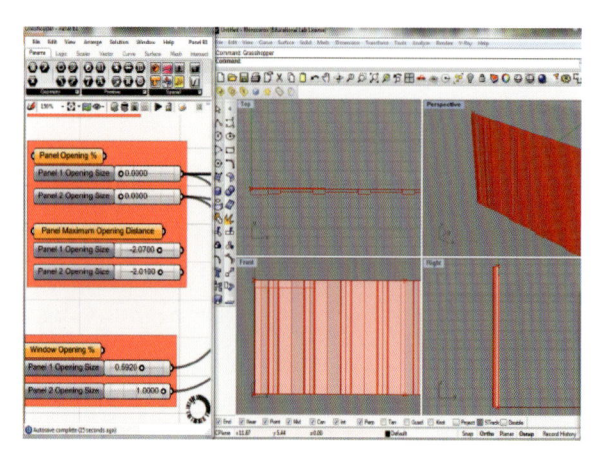

27 Perkins+Will and the University of Cincinnati, research project, 2012. The design scenario for adaptable building skin components, responding to daily or seasonal environmental changes. The facade consists of a standard curtain wall with low-e clear glazing and secondary movable panels, which would be able to close and open depending on changes in the environmental conditions. Parametric modelling and environmental performance data were used to determine the size and geometry of facade components.

28 Perkins+Will and the University of Cincinnati, research project, 2012. A design scenario that includes three-dimensional shading elements. Parametric modelling and environmental performance data were used to determine the shape and size of facade GFRP components, which vary in response to solar radiation along the different facade orientations.

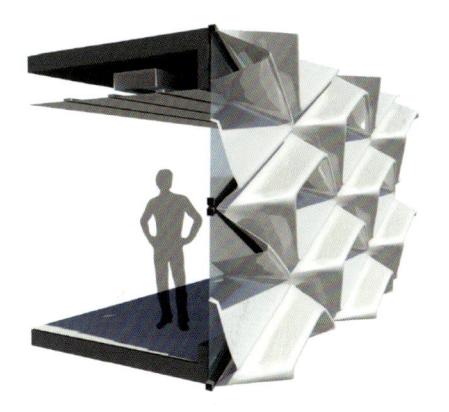

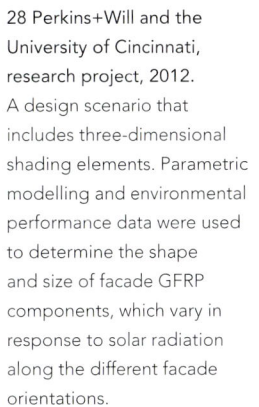

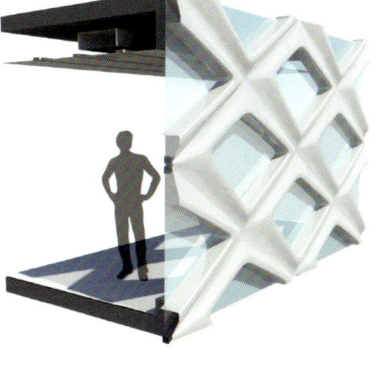

29 Perkins+Will and the University of Cincinnati, research project, 2012. The digital fabrication process included CNC milling to create moulds for shading elements. Low-fidelity prototypes were constructed from the vacuum moulding process with a plastic material.

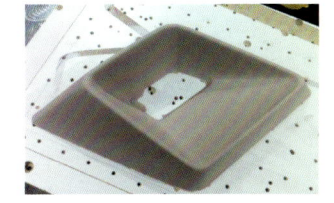

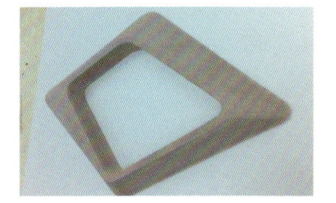

2 INNOVATIONS IN COMPUTATIONAL DESIGN 86–87

For example, one design scenario focused on adaptable building-skin components that could respond to daily or seasonal environmental changes. The design solution consisted of a standard curtain wall with low-e clear glazing and secondary movable panels, which would be able to open and close depending on changes in the environmental conditions. The movable panels consist of channel glass with aerogel insulation and a track system attached to the building's primary facade. Another design scenario included a system where the geometry of three-dimensional shading elements was varied in response to solar radiation along the different facade orientations. Dimensions, depth and the percentage of glazing were varied to reduce solar heat gain for critical areas of the facade with the highest solar exposure, while balancing access to daylight. Parametric tools were used to size and position shading elements, which would be constructed from glass-fibre reinforced polymer (GFRP) material. Early study models were executed using 3D powder printing. The digital fabrication process for this design solution used CNC milling to create moulds for the shading elements, and low-fidelity prototypes were constructed from the vacuum moulding process with a plastic material.

BIM IN DESIGN
Building information modelling (BIM) is currently one of the major paradigm shifts in the building industry, where the primary elements of change are:

- The representation of building elements as data-rich 3D objects, rather than as a combination of 2D orthogonal diagrams.
- The use of an interdisciplinary, comprehensive, building model as the source for derived 'views', rather than a collection of 'drawings' that is used to infer a 3D design.

The common database of information BIM provides about a building, includes its geometry and attributes. It is an integrated, comprehensive building model that stores the information contained in traditional building documents, such as drawings, specifications and construction details, as well as additional 3D information and metadata in a database. The goal of BIM is to provide a common structure for information sharing that can be used by all agents in the design process and construction. It virtually simulates design and construction, and provides groundwork for collaborative design, since all relevant information, such as spatial organisation, building components and building systems – mechanical, electrical, plumbing, HVAC – can be incorporated into building descriptions.

The visualisation of design in three-dimensional space is one of the advantages of BIM; however, this is not the only capability and the integrative nature of the contents must be emphasised. BIM can be used for simulations, building performance predictions and environmental analysis, for example, where the data contained in the BIM is used for daylight studies, energy analysis, solar access studies, and so on. BIM is based on the premise of designing and delivering a building resulting from intelligent 3D objects, such as virtual walls that are characterised by their material formulation and cost, heating units that display maintenance information and windows that can automatically report their insulation value for sustainability certification. The applications of BIM continually expand: scheduling, estimating, clash detection and digital fabrication. As described above, the latter manufacturing focus has played a leading role in the formal departure from mass production by offering a parameterised syntax through which unique and often geometrically complex components can be designed and built within the realm of economic reality. BIM has come a long way to provide detailed information that allows for custom components to be designed, fabricated and erected to fit into a precise building assembly.

In contemporary architectural practice BIM is changing the design methods being used and the ways in which architectural documentation is prepared. Since BIM is equivalent to the virtual representation of buildings, rich in information of a relational nature, it allows an intelligent, model-based process for designing buildings where building elements, systems, schedules and specifications are stored within a single database, and can be shared among stakeholders.[3] Traditional architectural design documentation (floor plans, sections, elevations, details) is only a single view of an integrated model and this BIM characteristic is revolutionising architectural practice.

Four decades ago BIM first emerged with the conception of a 'Building Product Model' in a research-oriented context.[4,5] However, its adoption within the building industry gained momentum slowly, mostly due to the lack of robust software applications and computing power necessary for representing and documenting complex architectural design. Only in the early 2000s did advances in computer technologies and the development of robust software programs allow BIM to be widely adopted. Within the last decade, BIM has become a paradigm shift in architectural design and practice, having an impact on the way that buildings are designed and changing the way that architectural documents are prepared.[6]

The evolution of BIM to be an integral part of design activities today has given the acronym a dual meaning that is often used interchangeably as both a noun: Building Information Model(s), the deliverable or deliverable-generator, as well as a verb: Building Information Modelling, a process. The goal of BIM is to provide a common structure for information sharing that can be used by all agents in the design process and construction, as well as for facility management after a building is constructed and occupied. Information that resembles traditional architectural documentation includes specific views of common information, design and construction and provides groundwork for collaborative design, since all the relevant information – such as spatial organisation, building components, building systems, materials and schedules – is incorporated into building descriptions. Beyond visualisation, BIMs are used to review constructability issues, where the construction team is able to analyse design decisions in the early stages of the process and provide responses to the design team. Information about the site – such as existing conditions, infrastructure systems and utilities – can be included in BIM and analysed. The construction schedule can be integrated with the building model to visualise the sequencing of construction activities, also referred to as '4D' modelling, since the time dimension is included. Cost estimation is another dimension, commonly referred to as '5D'. Materials and components are analysed and directly linked to cost databases to produce financial information that can assist in design decisions related to economic factors. Construction documentation is automatically generated and updated when changes are made to the model.

Given the variance in possibilities and in an effort to define a common language for what and how much design information is to be included in each model (the 'I' in BIM), industry guidelines are available that define the level of completeness.[7] This concept is defined as Level of Development (LOD) and consists of five clearly distinguished tiers:

- LOD 100: overall building massing indicative of area, height, volume, location and orientation may be modelled in three dimensions or represented by other data.
- LOD 200: model elements are modelled as generalised systems or assemblies with approximate quantities, size, shape, location and orientation.
- LOD 300: model elements are modelled as specific assemblies accurate in terms of quantity, size, shape, location and orientation. Non-geometric information may also be included.
- LOD 400: model elements are modelled as specific assemblies that are accurate in terms of size, shape, location, quantity and orientation with complete fabrication, assembly and detailing information. Non-geometric information may also be included.
- LOD 500: model elements are modelled as constructed assemblies actual and accurate in terms of size, shape, location, quantity and orientation. Non-geometric information may also be included.

It is very important, however, to find the correct balance for conveying the design intent and providing the correct level of information. Typically, architectural BIM should not be modelled above the LOD 300 level. Fabrication models are developed at LOD 400, while as-built models are at the LOD 500 level. Information sharing is possible with BIM: the different stakeholders contribute to developing it as a repository for all the data produced for, or required, to operate a building. Integrated practice and project delivery allows this to happen, and BIM as a design tool lies in the centre of an integrated design process.

It must be stated that BIM does not necessarily have to be used in integrated project delivery (IPD) – it can also be used in the traditional design–bid–build project delivery. But the true potential and real benefits are achieved when BIM and IPD are implemented – the technology enables the process, and helps design professionals to achieve their ultimate goals to design and deliver high-performing buildings.[8] Since all key stakeholders are involved in the IPD process – including owners, designers, contractors, subcontractors and facility managers – information sharing, visualisation, code compliance, analysis of design performance, constructability, quality assurance and quality control, construction planning and ultimately facility management are all enabled with BIM. The diagram below shows the relationships between different types of design methods (linear, sequential and concurrent) and technology – the incorporation of BIM with IPD results in concurrent design methods, where all stakeholders are involved in the design from the beginning and are actively participating in the design process. BIM, as a technology and process, facilitates easier information exchange among the different stakeholders, while IPD, as a contractual method, allows concurrent design to happen.

BIM IN VIRTUAL CONSTRUCTION

The use of BIM for construction offers many benefits compared with traditional construction methods, including virtual coordination, construction planning and monitoring, model-based design and construction, immersive visualisation to communicate complex coordination among different stakeholders, and the possibility of including modular and prefabricated building elements. Prior to the start of construction, the primary benefit of BIM is that it allows virtual coordination among different stakeholders and trades, and the ability to capture and communicate design intent digitally. Schedule and cost integration are also key benefits for using BIM for construction, as well as construction planning, quantity take-offs and material planning. During construction, BIM can be used to determine model-driven layout in the field, which reduces reworking and increases accuracy. The reduction of physical errors and construction mistakes is the principal benefit of using BIM during construction. Moreover, model-driven prefabrication is also beneficial, since it reduces

30 Diagram showing the relationships between different types of design methods (linear, sequential and concurrent), technology and project delivery.
BIM, as a technology and process, facilitates easier information exchange between the different stakeholders while integrated project delivery (IPD), as a contractual method, allows concurrent design to happen.

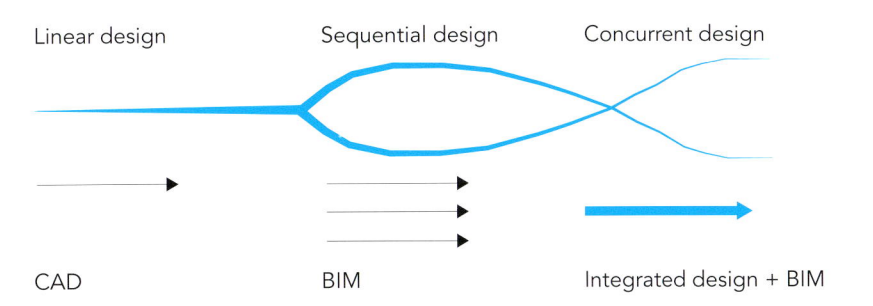

Linear design   Sequential design   Concurrent design

CAD   BIM   Integrated design + BIM

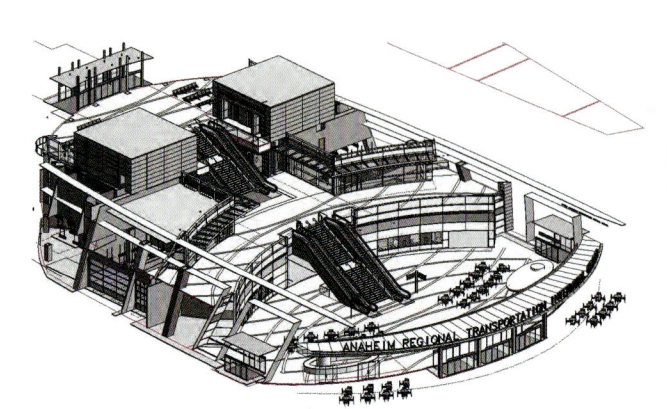

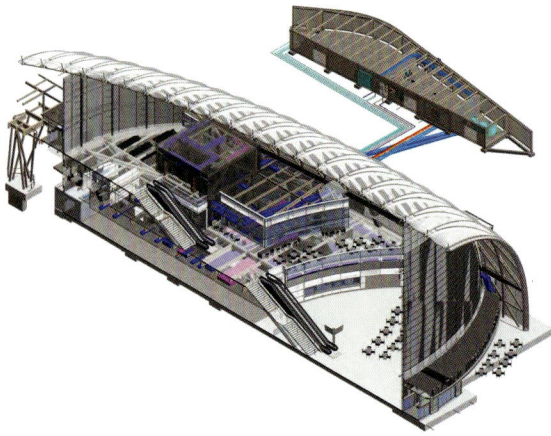

31

32

31 HOK, Anaheim Regional Transportation Intermodal Center (ARTIC), Anaheim, CA, USA, 2014.
This facility is a transportation gateway to Orange County. Innovative materials, computational design techniques, BIM and model-based coordination were used during the design and construction.

32 HOK, Anaheim Regional Transportation Intermodal Center (ARTIC), Anaheim, CA, USA, 2014.
The use of BIM was crucial during design and construction, due to the complex form, geometry and innovative design that needed to be translated into the built form.

costs and schedule time. Building trades – including structural, mechanical, electrical and plumbing – employ model-based prefabrication to increase productivity and provide more controlled environments for the manufacture of building components and elements, which are then assembled on-site.

Virtual reality (VR) uses computer-generated simulations of a 3D image or environment, which can be interacted with using digital technologies. VR technology has been used in 3D graphics, video games, scientific visualisation, medical research and education as well as design. In architecture and construction, it is a useful method to simulate and visualise project designs, construction plans and schedules, design and analysis of construction equipment and so on. Visualisation and interactive navigation of the construction process are possible using VR. There are two types of VR technologies – desktop VR and immersive VR. For example, virtual construction using BIM can be used as a project management tool to assist decision-making in the construction planning process. These methods link BIM with construction activities and schedules, allowing time to be assigned as the fourth dimension to BIM. This enables visualisation of the material movement and installation of construction components.

The Anaheim Regional Transportation Intermodal Center (ARTIC) in Anaheim, California, was designed by HOK. The building is a transportation gateway to Orange County, and serves a population of more than three million people across 34 cities in the area. It includes retail spaces, restaurants, ticketing and waiting areas, as well as community uses. The building envelope consists of translucent ETFE cushions which enclose a grandiose hall. The use of BIM was crucial during the design and construction of this facility, due to its complex form, geometry and innovative design that needed to be translated into the built form. Different software tools were used, such as Rhino3D®, Revit® and CATIA, as well as preconstruction clash detection software, energy modelling and performance analysis, and structural analysis software. The greatest benefit of BIM implementation was coordination efficiency achieved during design and construction. BIM standards were developed for the design phase through a BIM planning process, which specified exactly how the primary models were to be divided, who would be responsible for modelling and developing certain parts of the design, what the communication protocol would be and how information would be exchanged. The primary models were divided into site, bridge, architectural, structural, mechanical, electrical and plumbing (MEP), enclosure and geometry systems. BIM was used for design authoring, design review and coordination, energy analysis, computational fluid dynamics (CFD) analysis, environmental simulation, structural analysis, cost estimation, clash detection, space planning and construction sequencing. The roles of the different stakeholders were as follows: 1) the architects authored the design model for coordination; 2) the structural and MEP engineers authored the designed models and reviewed the coordination model; 3) the building enclosure engineers authored the design model, the geometry model and reviewed

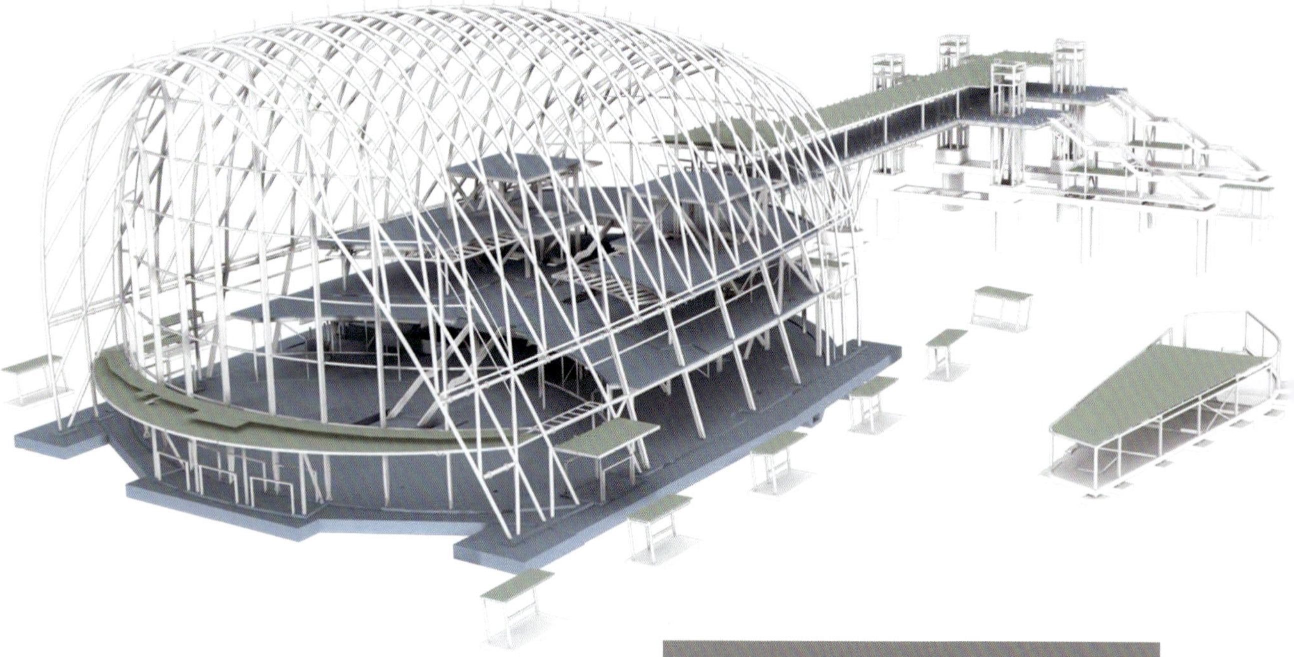

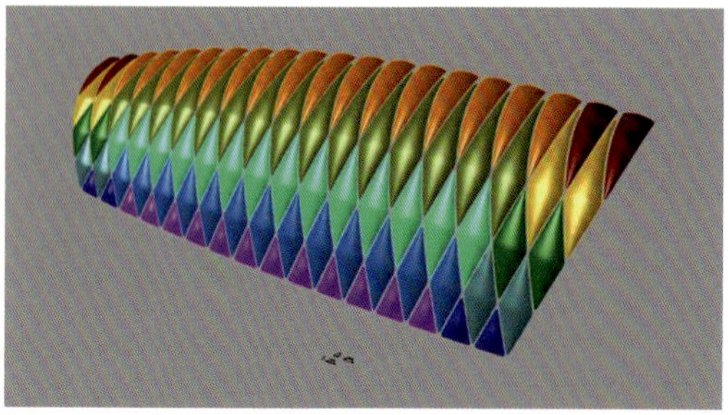

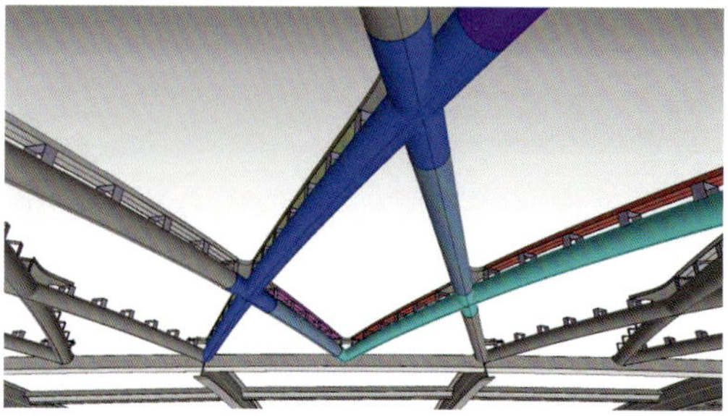

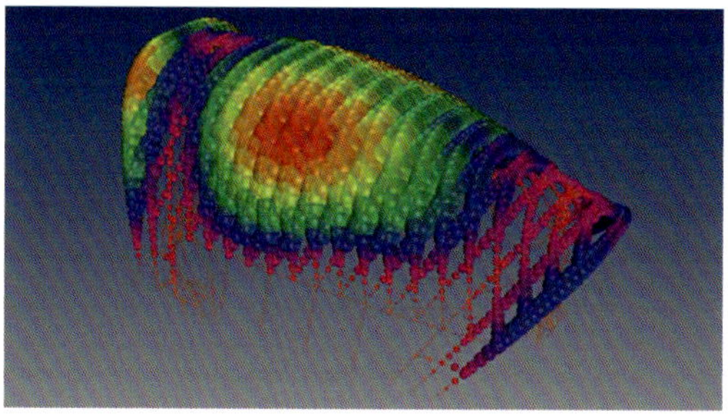

the coordination model; 4) the construction manager facilitated BIM coordination and performed model-based estimating; and 5) the plumbing/HVAC/electrical/steel/curtain-wall subcontractors authored the coordination and fabrication models respectively. Each team appointed a BIM coordinator to manage the process for their respective discipline. The design team designated a 3D process for construction quality assurance.

The ARTIC shell structure consists of a diagonal grid of steel arches forming a complex diagrid envelope. The shell geometry was developed in collaboration between the architect and the structural engineer. The structural analysis model in SAP2000 was used to analyse the structural system to predict its responses and to determine internal forces, stresses and deformations. Non-linear buckling analyses were performed to verify the buckling stability of the structure as a whole. Parametric modelling, through custom scripting, was used to automate the modelling and form exploration. This allowed multiple design iterations without sacrificing the time needed for manual modelling.

The BIM model was very significant to the general contractor and subcontractors. Due to the complexities of the project, it would be impossible to coordinate locations of different building elements without a model. The fabrication of the structural steel was designed with complex compound curves, and the model was necessary for the fabrication. CNC fabrication was used for structural elements. Construction sequencing and geometry coordination were used for design control, and interoperability of all components associated with the complex shell form was coded into a 3D model that was reduced to the simplest geometric elements, points and arcs. This was used to convey exact design dimensions to all stakeholders. BIM was used for 3D coordination, visualisation, cost estimation, fabrication, clash detection, construction sequencing, field coordination, procurement and as-built documentation.

BIM IN FACILITY MANAGEMENT

A building's entire life cycle is encompassed by BIM, including facility management. It offers a new method for the management of buildings, building systems and physical assets within the buildings. Traditionally, facility management has relied on 2D drawings, specifications and operation manuals for different systems, where often it was necessary to modify as-built construction documents to make them useful for this stage of a building's life cycle. BIM, on the other hand, provides a unified database of all building components and allows all types of information to be stored within the application or in an external database (including specifications, user manuals and so on). Tracking various types of information, performing area calculations, tracking building usage and occupancy, locating equipment objects and their specifications is possible with BIM. The benefits of using BIM for facility management include faster and more effective management and access to information, as well as a centralised repository of data necessary for the building operation.

33 HOK, Anaheim Regional Transportation Intermodal Center (ARTIC), Anaheim, CA, USA, 2014.
The building envelope consists of a complex diagrid structure and ETFE cushions. The shell geometry was developed in a collaboration between the architect and the structural engineer, and structural analysis was used to determine internal forces, stresses and deformations.

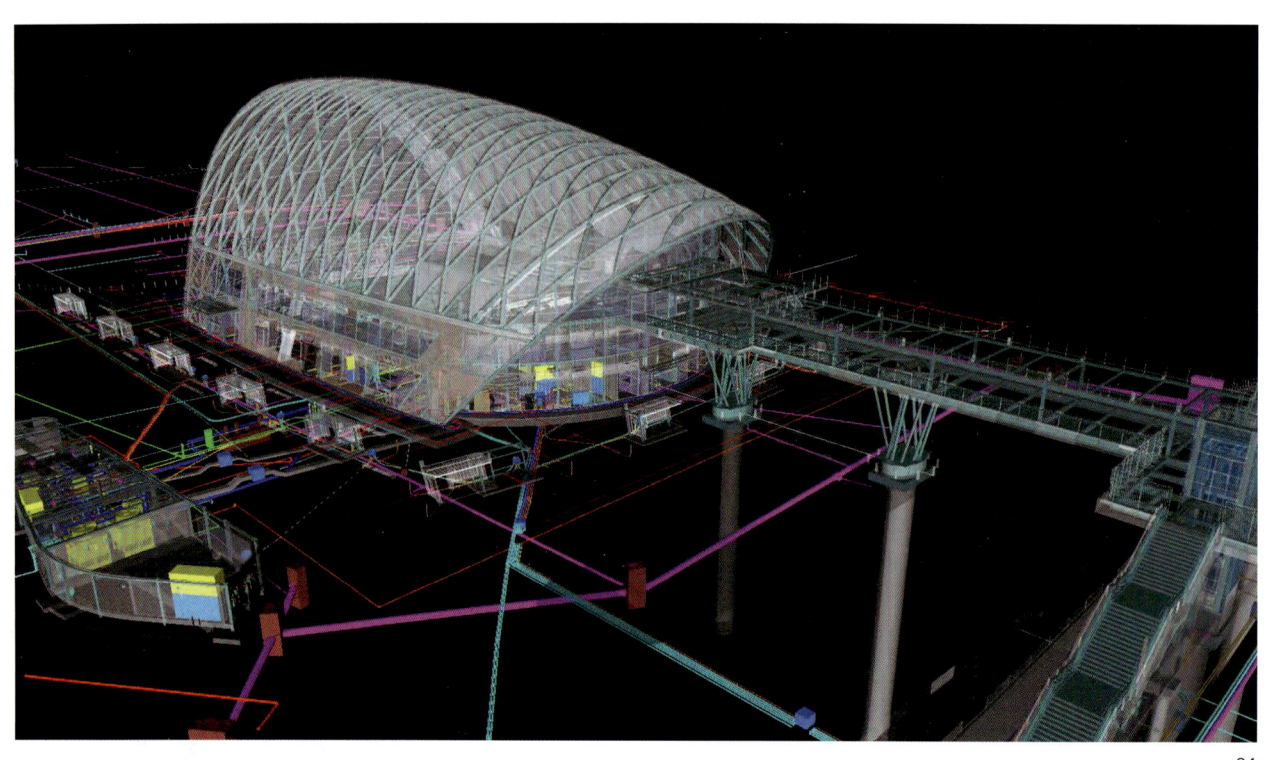

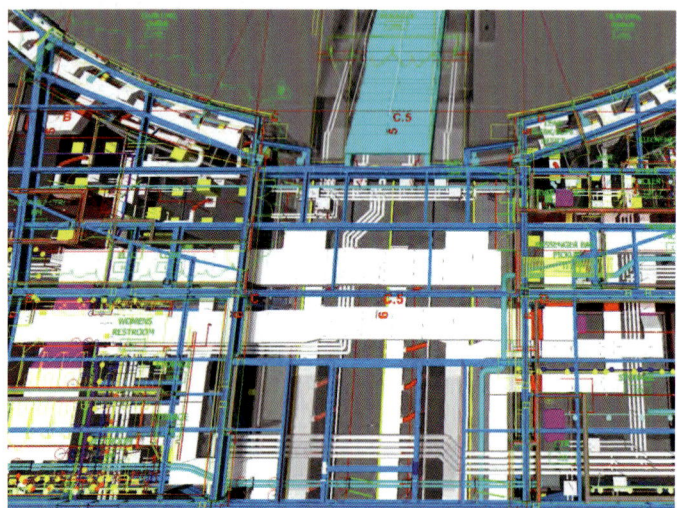

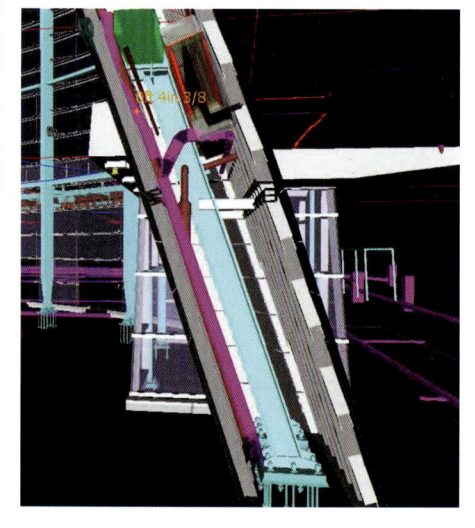

34 HOK, Anaheim Regional Transportation Intermodal Center (ARTIC), Anaheim, CA, USA, 2014.
The BIM construction model was essential, due to the complex form and geometry of the ARTIC. Fabrication of structural steel with complex curves, as well as positioning and coordination of different building elements during construction, relied on model-based coordination and fabrication.

35

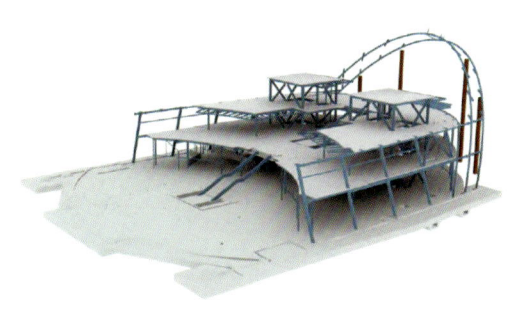

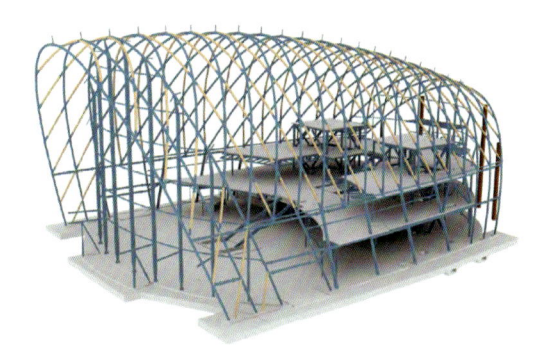

35 HOK, Anaheim Regional Transportation Intermodal Center (ARTIC), Anaheim, CA, USA, 2014.
Construction sequencing was used for the ARTIC.

The emerging software technologies offer web-based access and management of BIM, using a 3D immersive environment for navigation, scheduling, maintenance and operation.

ENVIRONMENTAL SIMULATIONS AND ENERGY ANALYSIS
Environmental simulations and building performance and energy analysis are an integral part of the design process for energy-efficient and high-performance buildings, since they help in investigating design options and assess the environmental and energy impacts of design decisions.[9] Energy-efficient buildings aim to reduce the overall energy consumption necessary for their operation. High-performance buildings are designed to improve the overall building performance, besides energy usage, such as improving occupants' thermal, visual and acoustic comfort. A performance-based design method should be used to evaluate and optimise building performance, which relies on different analysis cycles that must be integrated into the design process. This performance-based design method challenges the traditional design paradigm. A performance-based design method has the ability to estimate the impact of a design solution since: 1) performance measures are investigated with actual quantifiable data and not rules-of-thumb; 2) it uses detailed building models to simulate, analyse and predict behaviour of the system; and 3) it can produce an evaluation of multiple design alternatives.

The simulations and performance analysis tools can be grouped into BIM-based or non-BIM-based software programs and there are a variety of simulation tools. A recently conducted survey investigated the use of building performance tools in architectural practice, particularly comparing the following simulation programs: Ecotect, HEED, Energy 10, DesignBuilder, eQuest, DOE-2, Green Building Studio, IES VE, EnergyPlus™ and EnergyPlus-SketchUp Plugin (OpenStudio®).[10] The survey ranked the utilisation of tools and investigated the requirements for potential future improvements of these applications. Findings show that Ecotect is currently most widely used, followed by eQuest, EnergyPlus-SketchUp and EnergyPlus, IES VE, Energy 10, Design Builder, DOE-2, HEED and Green Building Studio. The survey also revealed that different tools tend to be used for different stages of the design process; the 'lightweight' tools are used in conceptual and schematic stages of the design, whereas more detailed, complex software programs are used during design development. However, compatibility with BIM-based design software is limited to a few applications, mainly Green Building Studio, Ecotect and IES VE. Efforts to integrate building performance analysis capabilities directly within BIM-design modelling software programs are currently under way. For example, Revit 2016 includes energy analysis capabilities within this application, mainly by allowing the creation of analytical models using building elements in this authoring tool and cloud-based energy modelling simulation through Green Building Studio directly in Revit. Also, the recently launched EcoDesigner STAR allows energy analysis capabilities within ArchiCAD. However, it is essential that these tools are validated against more robust energy-modelling and performance-analysis applications, and that documentation is developed that outlines the benefits, drawbacks and any limitations, and a comparison made of results obtained from these applications with other established modelling software programs.

Best practices for data exchange between BIM and environmental analysis software depend on the analysis objectives and what type of data is needed. For example, for the determination of building massing that minimises solar exposure or incident solar exposure on the facade, geometric properties of the building massing or component under analysis (for example, part of the facade with shading devices) are sufficient, as developed in the LOD 100 model. For other types of studies, such as daylight or thermal analysis, enriched information about interior spatial organisation, material properties and properties of shading surfaces is needed. Therefore information stored in 'design' BIM needs to be exported as 'analysis' BIM.[11] There are specific data schemes that have been developed to facilitate the transfer of building properties stored in BIM to analysis tools, such as Green Building XML (gbXML). However, different BIM-based energy analysis programs currently have different gbXML supporting capabilities.[12] The basic structure of gbXML consists of elements such as rooms, walls, floors, ceilings, shading surfaces and windows, which inherit properties embedded in the model (actual numeric values) and transfer to analysis applications. These basic parameters can be embedded in the model from the earliest stages of the design process (LOD 100), and developed in LOD 200 to investigate the effects of different design scenarios.

There are also ongoing efforts to streamline the data exchange between BIM design authoring software applications and energy performance analysis tools through IFCs.[13] However, the current state of the art in software implementations and building-performance analyses is inadequate to fully support this.[14] The automated data exchange between commonly used software applications for design and performance analysis using IFCs still remains a goal, but is currently not widely implemented in practice.

Exploratory Hall, at the main campus of the George Mason University in Fairfax, Virginia, was designed by Perkins+Will. Extensive building performance simulations and energy analysis were performed during the design to inform decision-making. The building complex consists of an addition that connects two existing academic science buildings, and the complete renovation of one of those buildings. The heart of the addition is an atrium that knits together the internal circulation of all three structures. Shading strategies, daylight levels and solar exposure for various building orientations and components were investigated during the design as well as design methods for improving the performance of facades. The different analyses were conducted during the schematic and design development phases.

The original BIM design documentation was used to create all analysis models and the data exchange was mainly performed

36 Perkins+Will, Exploratory Hall, George Mason University, Fairfax, VA, USA, 2013. The complex consists of a new addition and the renovation of an academic research building. Extensive building performance simulations and energy analysis were performed during the design to inform decision-making.

through the gbXML format. The analysis tools that were used to study the design effects on building performance included Ecotect (for site context, shading and solar exposure studies); Radiance (for daylight simulations and glare analysis, where the model geometry was exported from Ecotect); and Green Building Studio and EnergyPlus (for energy modelling). The authorising BIM design tool was Revit. The design team incorporated the necessary design characteristics and information to streamline the data exchange between BIM design and analysis software applications using gbXML. Close collaboration between the design and building performance analysis teams was necessary to determine the analysis objectives, and different design scenarios of interest that were to be investigated. The iterative design-analysis process ensured that the analysis results were used effectively to modify building design attributes in relation to their simulated performance. Also, proper modelling methods and the LOD necessary for streamlined information exchange between design and analysis applications heavily depended on the close working relationship between the design and analysis team.

Shadow analysis was performed for the entire site. Overall site context, surrounding buildings and daily shadow ranges for selected dates were investigated. Gradient intensity indicates the amount of time that the building surfaces spend in the shade. Detailed shading analysis was performed to understand the effects of surrounding buildings and solar access for various building orientations, and solar exposure analysis studies were performed for critical facades (east, west and south). The selection of shading devices depends on the building orientation. The results shown below compare average solar exposure for the west facade without and with vertical shading devices (aluminium screen mesh with 60% transparency). In this case, this facade was modelled at LOD 200, including curtain-wall components, mullions, glass and shading devices. These vertical shading elements significantly reduce solar heat gain, also the optimal orientation angle was investigated to further decrease solar heat gain. The design of the shading devices was changed based on this analysis.

Daylight analysis was conducted to investigate the effects of shading devices on the availability of natural light in the interior of the building. Daylight levels in the corridor are shown overleaf (plan view, contour lines indicate approximately 90 lux or 10 fc change in values), which are sufficient for this circulation space. Three-dimensional daylight distribution within this space is also shown. Based on the results of these simulations, it was concluded that the shading devices along the west facade effectively block solar radiation without negatively affecting the availability of natural light.

STRUCTURAL ANALYSIS
Computational tools are being implemented increasingly for structural analysis and design. Free-formed and complex structures require a new understanding of engineering and redefine the role of the engineer in the design process. The meshing of the

37 Perkins+Will, Exploratory Hall, George Mason University, Fairfax, VA, USA, 2013. The atrium within the Exploratory Hall connects the new addition and the renovated academic science complex.

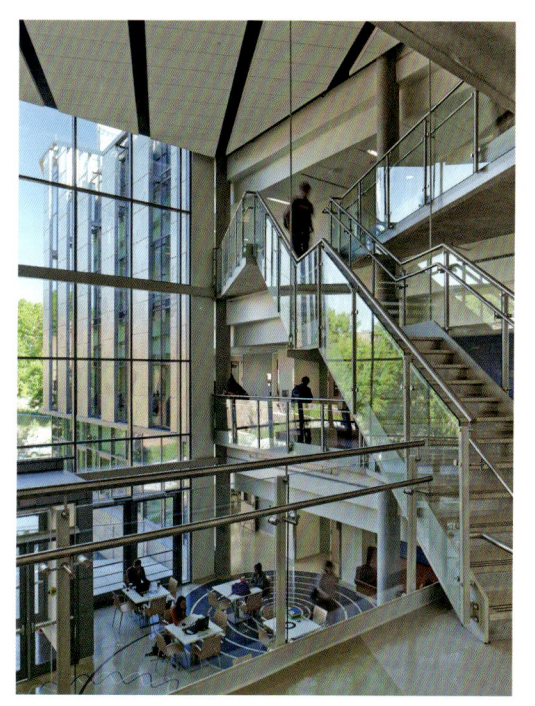

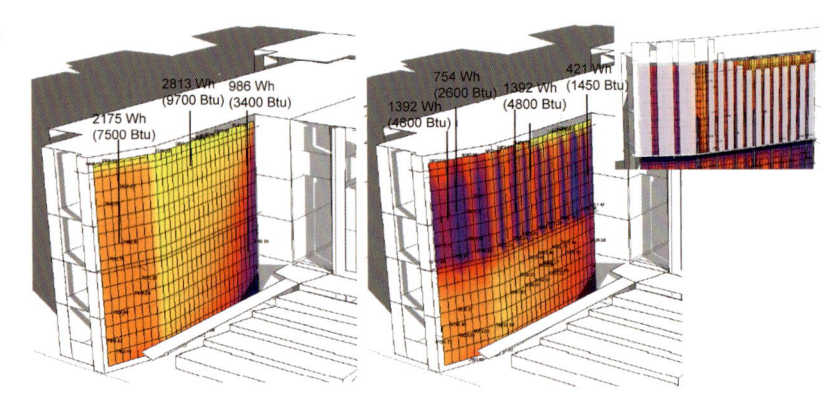

38 Perkins+Will, Exploratory Hall, George Mason University, Fairfax, VA, USA, 2013. Site context and shadow analysis for specific dates.

39 Perkins+Will, Exploratory Hall, George Mason University, Fairfax, VA, USA, 2013. Daylight levels in the corridor (plan view).

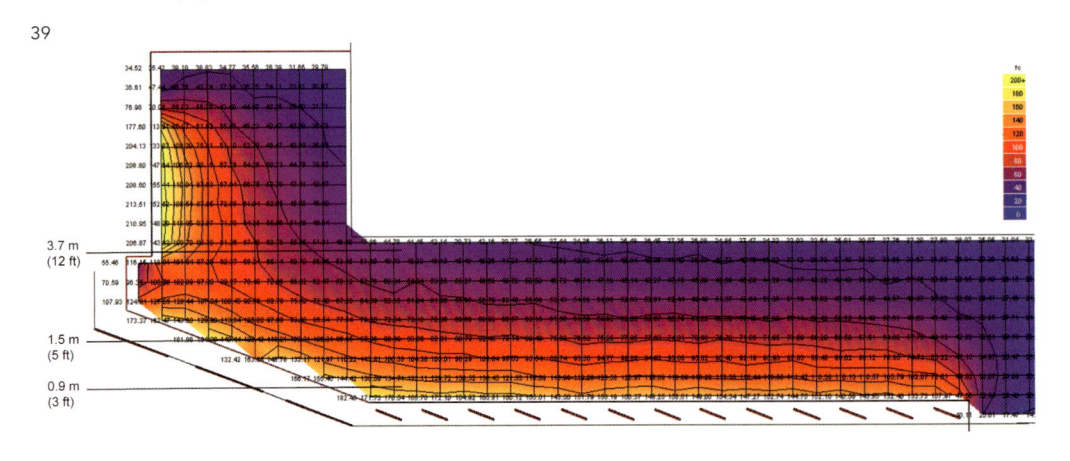

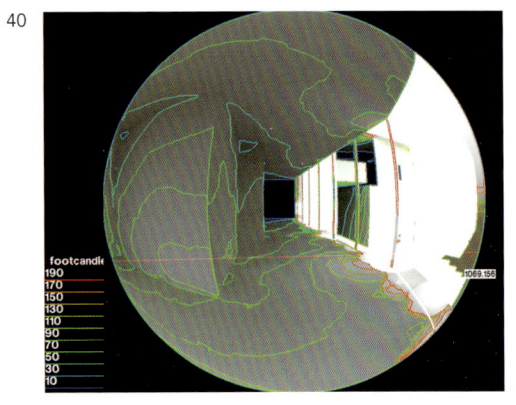

40 Perkins+Will, Exploratory Hall, George Mason University, Fairfax, VA, USA, 2013. Daylight levels in the corridor (3D view).

41 Perkins+Will, Exploratory Hall, George Mason University, Fairfax, VA, USA, 2013. Comparison of solar exposure for the west facade (without and with vertical shading elements).

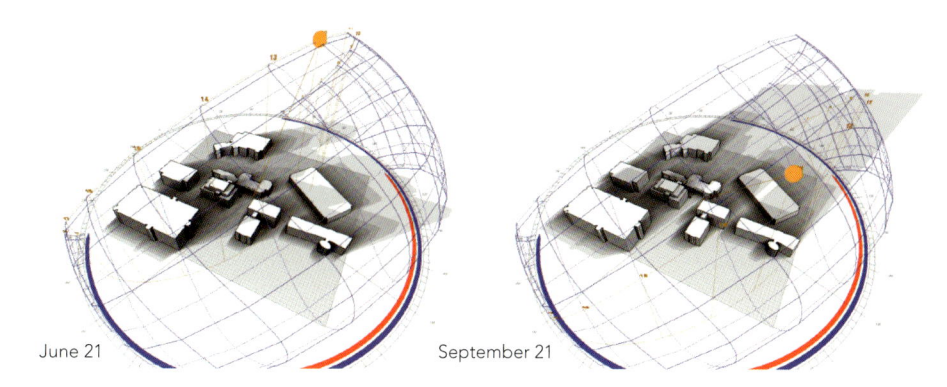

June 21

September 21

structural grid, in particular, is a new design direction that requires new tools and procedures. Previously, in grid-shell design, the optimisation of the geometry and the construction sequence were usually the goals for structural design and analysis. Reducing the weight of the structure, integration with architecture and building systems, as well as determining the sizes of different structural members were usually the objectives of structural analysis. These are still among the primary goals of structural engineering. However, current technological advancements are making complex shapes and geometries plausible, and the integration of structural design and analysis from the beginning of the design process is necessary. These types of complex forms require a continuous process of engineering from inception to construction. Computational structural analysis assists in optimising the shape and geometry, the mapping of load-bearing elements on 3D geometry and the design and analysis of the structural system and members. Also, computational tools can be used to transfer this information to production and manufacturing.

Heydar Aliyev Centre in Baku, Azerbaijan, designed by Zaha Hadid Architects, is an example where the integration of architecture, structural design and analysis, fabrication, and coordination between the different stakeholders, made the complex architectural form and geometry a reality. A large public plaza provides an open space and unifies the building and the landscape. The programme for this cultural centre included three main components: a convention centre with a 1,200 seat auditorium, a museum and an eight-storey library. These programmatic elements merge and appear as a continuous architectural form, but function separately in the interior, sharing only service areas and communal spaces, including cafeterias, meeting rooms, bars, restaurants and other supporting services. The integration of architectural and structural design, and the coordination among architects, engineers and fabricators, were critical during the design and construction of this building. The location is subject to high wind loads and lies within a seismic zone, which created challenges for the design team. The free-form structure was developed from the architectural design concept of modifying a single surface to embrace different functional requirements. The objective was to create a large unobstructed

42

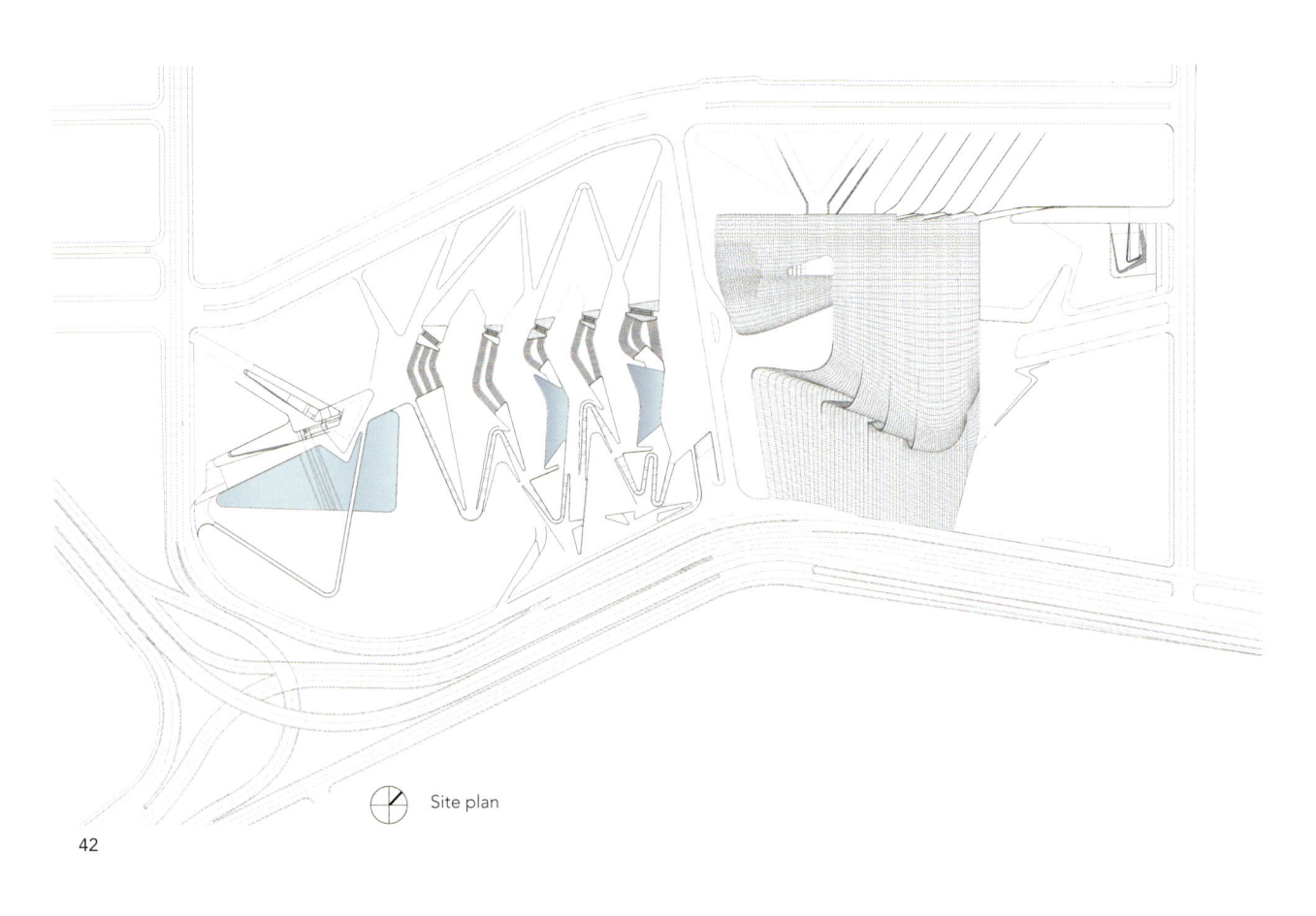

⊕ Site plan

43

and flowing interior, so vertical structural elements were integrated into the building envelope to provide column-free space. The structure consists of a concrete system and a space frame with a single movement joint.

The surface geometry driven by complex architectural form dictated the need to pursue unconventional structural solutions. The foundation system consists of piled rafts. The structural designers used parametric tools to analyse variances in form and structure under different loading conditions. The space frame consists of trusses that are 150 m (492 ft) long, and up to 70 m (230 ft) high at 9 m (30 ft) intervals. The curving form of the building required circular geometry for the trusses, where each individual truss had a slightly different circular form. Fixed and sliding supports were added to the trusses to minimise seismic stresses and thermal movement. The library consists of an eight-storey concrete structure with vertical cores providing lateral stability. The building envelope has lightweight GFRC panels, individually moulded to form curved shapes. The topographical analysis of the roof showing the location and size of different panels is shown overleaf. The thickness of the GFRC panels varies between 8 and 13 mm (0.3 and 0.5 in), and three general categories were used: flat-planar, single and double curvature. Flat panels were fabricated through extrusion, while curved panels were moulded. CNC milling was used during the fabrication of panels to create moulds which were used to cast curved panels. Computational modelling was essential during the design and fabrication of the building envelope, since 15,000 unique individual panels and supporting metal tubes were used in the design. Also, GFRC panels were used for the plaza to create a continuous form. Numerous studies were carried out on the surface geometry to rationalise and panelise the form while maintaining the continuity of the building and landscape, and a seamless transition between different elements. Coordination and communication among architects, engineers, fabricators and contractors as well as advanced computational design and fabrication techniques were essential to realise a building of such complexity.

CFD ANALYSIS
The understanding of natural phenomena in relation to buildings, and in particular internal and external airflow, is becoming increasingly important to architectural design. Computational fluid dynamics (CFD) analysis can play an important role in building design, since it can be used to provide simulations of airflow, pressure, temperature and similar parameters that are important to building performance. Generally, the process involved in conducting CFD analyses is relatively complex and requires a certain level of skill to carry out an accurate analysis.

As a tool CFD is used intensively for evaluating the indoor environment of a building and its interaction with the building envelope, and for analysing the outdoor environment surrounding the building, such as wind flows and patterns, wind loading and stresses on the building, as well as the urban scale. CFD has also

42 Zaha Hadid Architects, Heydar Aliyev Centre, Baku, Azerbaijan, 2012.
Site plan, showing the relationship between the building and the public plaza.

43 Zaha Hadid Architects, Heydar Aliyev Centre, Baku, Azerbaijan, 2012.
The integration of architecture, structural design and analysis and fabrication, as well as coordination among different stakeholders, was essential during the design and construction.

First-floor plan

Topographical analysis of roof

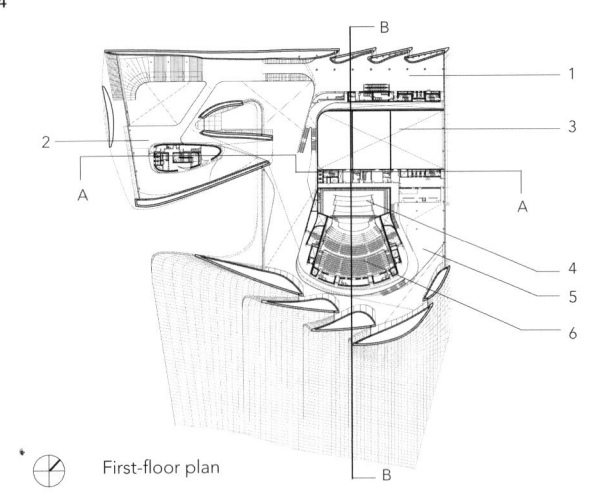

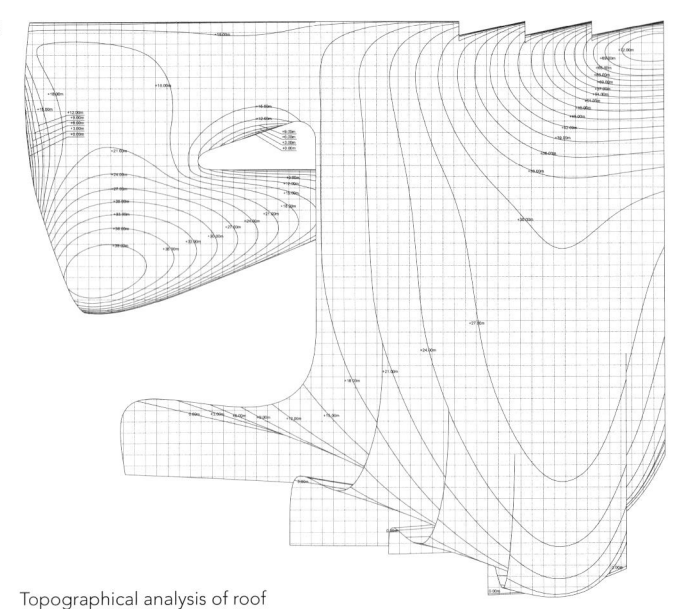

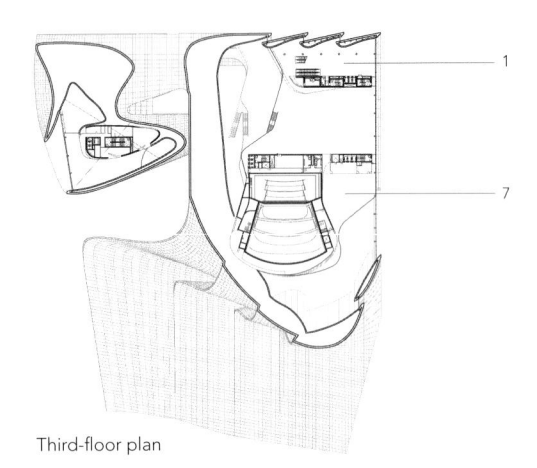

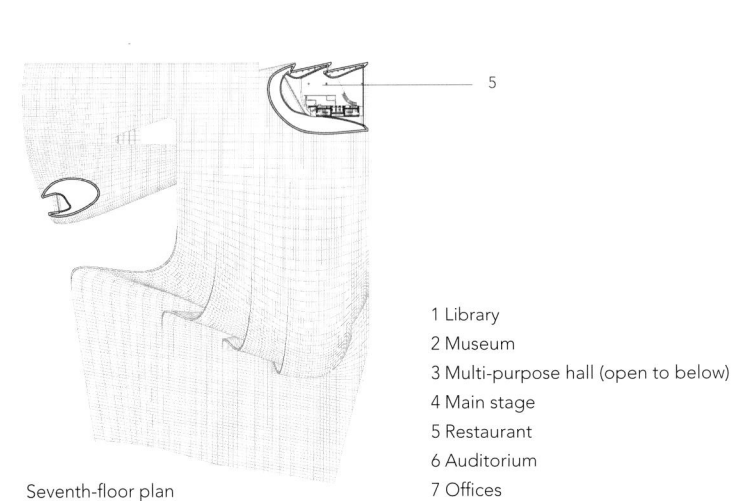

Third-floor plan

Seventh-floor plan

1 Library
2 Museum
3 Multi-purpose hall (open to below)
4 Main stage
5 Restaurant
6 Auditorium
7 Offices

44 Zaha Hadid Architects, Heydar Aliyev Centre, Baku, Azerbaijan, 2012.
Floor plans, showing the relationship between the main programmatic elements (auditorium, museum and library).

45 Zaha Hadid Architects, Heydar Aliyev Centre, Baku, Azerbaijan, 2012.
Topographical analysis of the roof, showing locations and sizes of GFRC panels. Flat-planar, single- and double-curvature panels were used, where flat panels were fabricated through extrusion and curved panels were moulded. CNC milling was used to create moulds. Computational modelling was essential during the design and fabrication of the building envelope as 15,000 unique individual panels and supporting metal tubes were used in the design.

46 Zaha Hadid Architects, Heydar Aliyev Centre, Baku, Azerbaijan, 2012.
Elevations and sections, showing the structural system that consists of concrete and a space frame.

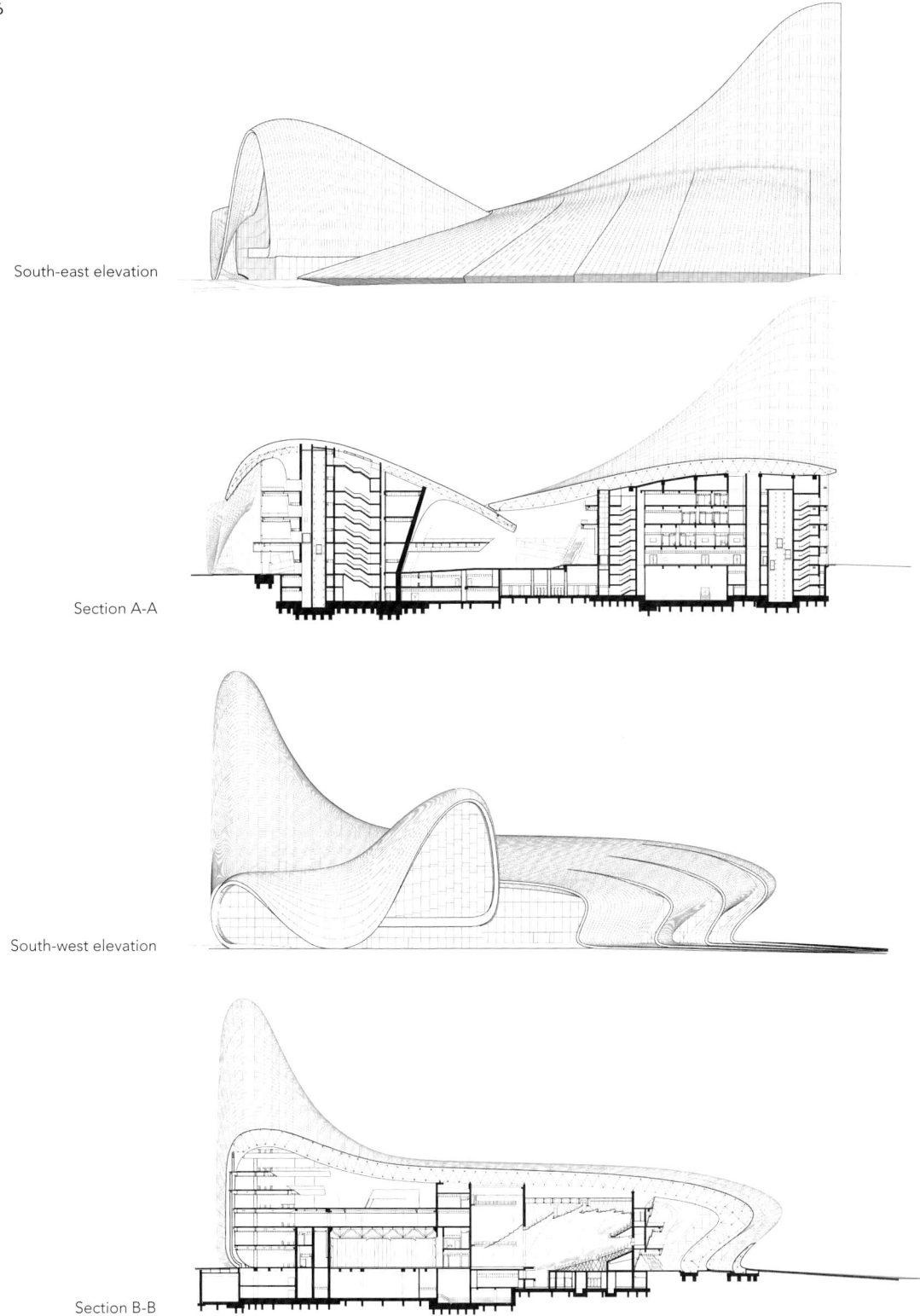

46

South-east elevation

Section A-A

South-west elevation

Section B-B

2 INNOVATIONS IN COMPUTATIONAL DESIGN 106-107

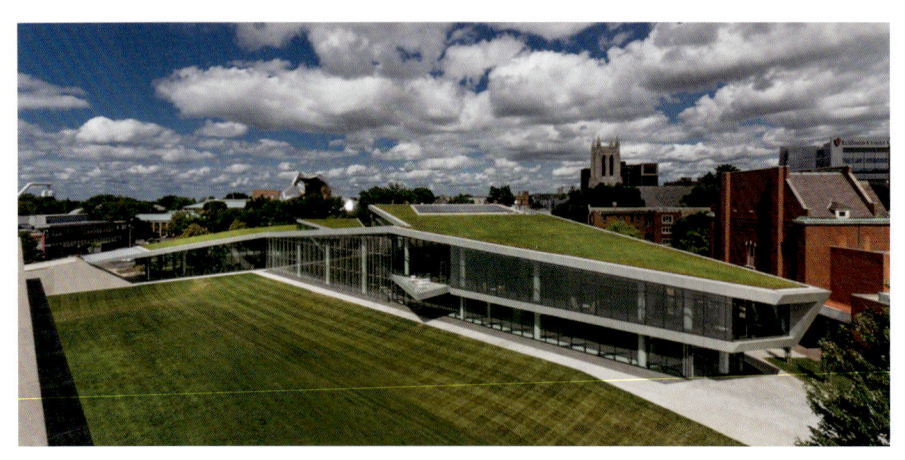

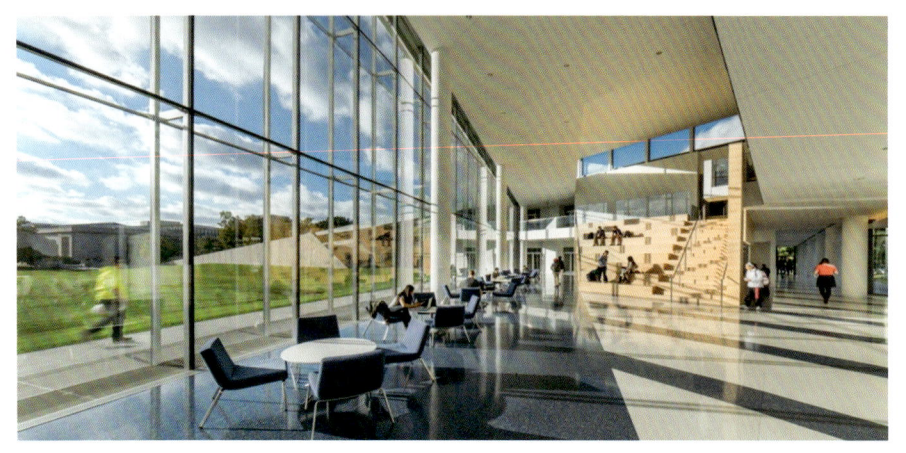

47 Perkins+Will, Case Western Reserve University, Tinkham Veale University Center, Cleveland, OH, USA, 2014.
View of the double skin, west-facing facade of the new student centre, which overlooks a green open space.

been applied to test proposed natural ventilation, mixed-mode ventilation and HVAC systems in buildings, which involves the prediction of air temperature, velocity and relative humidity, among other parameters.

Compared with traditional wind-tunnel testing, CFD analysis offers some advantages since it can generate full-scale simulations as opposed to scale models and provides data more extensive than that measured in a laboratory setting. Also, results of CFD analysis can be visualised clearly and analysed. On the other hand, CFD does have some drawbacks. Understanding CFD simulation tools and procedures – not to mention extensive knowledge of fluid mechanics – is required to evaluate CFD results. Moreover, CFD analysis software, such as Fluent, STAR-CCM+® or IES VE, is complex and requires specific expertise for conducting these types of simulations.

Case Western Reserve University, Tinkham Veale University Center in Cleveland, Ohio, designed by Perkins+Will, used CFD analysis during the design of a double-skin glazed facade system.[15] The building is a student centre, and the west-facing double-skin facade overlooks green open space. Several options for this facade were explored during design to control solar heat gain and glare, including fixed external shading elements, internal shades, electrochromic glass and a double-skin facade system. Initially, energy modelling was conducted to investigate different design options and their effect on energy consumption using EnergyPlus modelling software. It was selected due to its high level of accuracy, ability to simulate multiple facade design options and double-skin facade ventilation effects. Simulations were performed to understand the peak energy demand. Results indicated that the double-skin facade would be the best choice for energy savings, since it provides a buffer between the interior and exterior environment. This chosen facade design option would also integrate interior shades within the air cavity to limit solar heat gain. The configuration of the glazing for each plane of the double skin was investigated to optimise facade

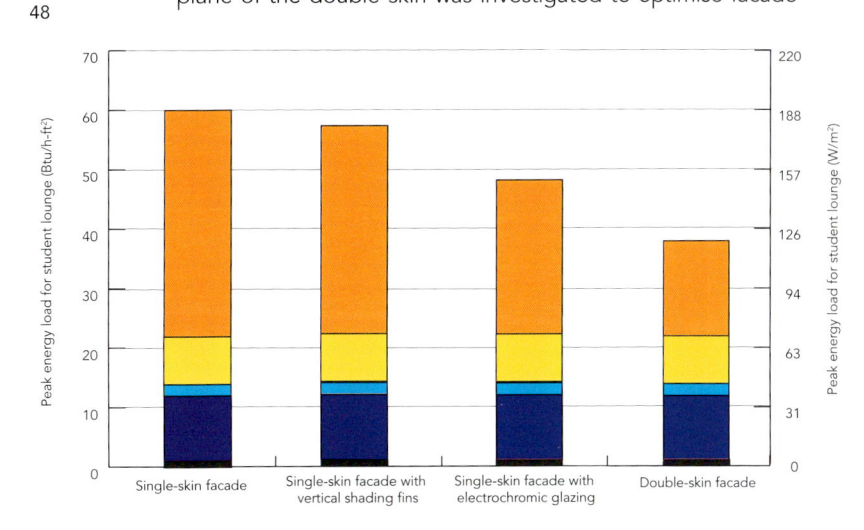

48 Perkins+Will, Case Western Reserve University, Tinkham Veale University Center, Cleveland, OH, USA, 2014.
Energy modelling was conducted to investigate different facade design options and their effect on energy consumption. The results indicated that the double-skin facade would be the best choice for energy savings, since it provides a buffer between the interior and exterior environment.

- Infiltration
- People
- Equipment
- Lighting
- Solar heat gain

49

50

Natural ventilation

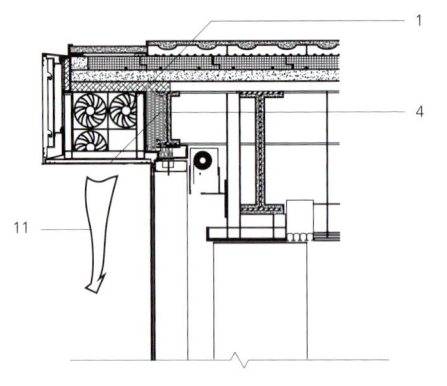

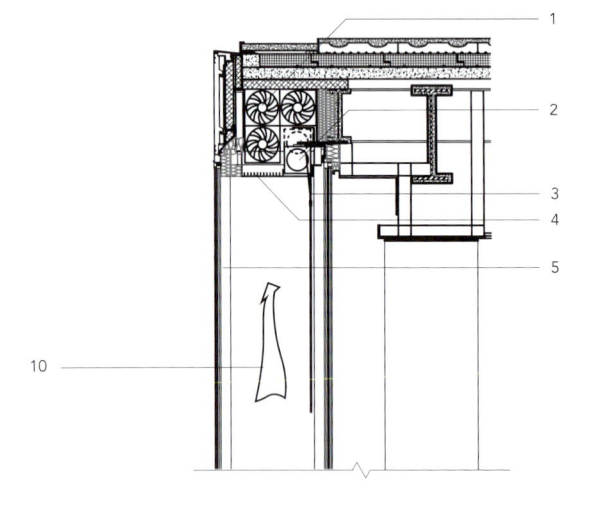

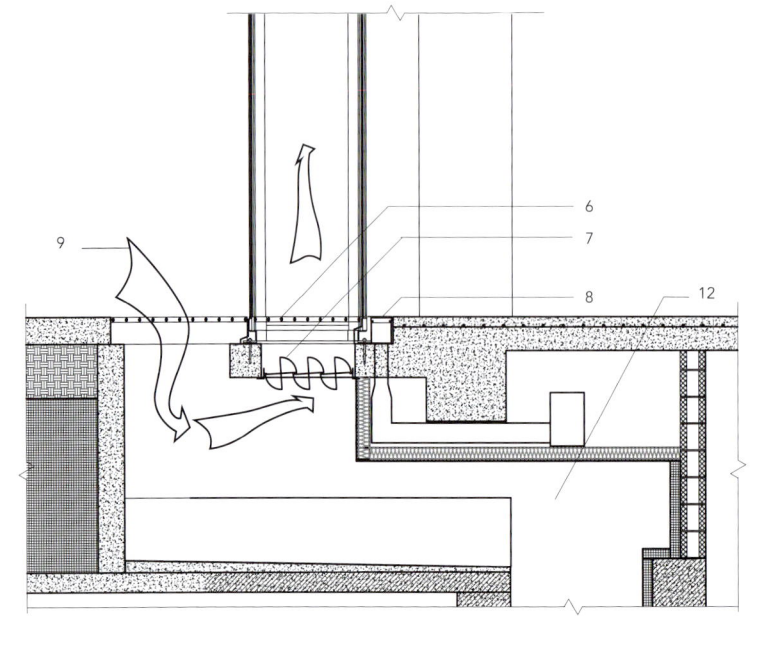

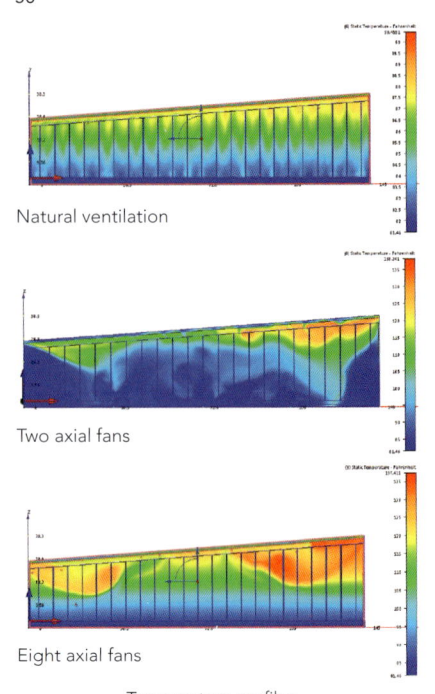

Two axial fans

Eight axial fans

Temperature profiles

1   Axial fans
2   Roller shade housing
3   Roller shade with guide wire
4   Continuous Aluminium bar grille
5   Curtain-wall system
6   Stainless-steel cross bars at the bottom
7   Automated dampers
8   Continuous linear floor grille
9   Air intake during summer to ventilate the double-skin cavity
10 Ventilated air to go through the axial fan and exit the building
11 Air ventilated out
12 Air intake for an existing underground garage

49 Perkins+Will, Case Western Reserve University, Tinkham Veale University Center, Cleveland, OH, USA, 2014.
Section of the west facade, showing components of the double-skin facade system and ventilation. The dampers at the bottom of the cavity open during summer and warm weather and axial fans pull the air through the cavity to prevent the accumulation of excessively warm air.

performance. The general configuration can be categorised as a 'buffer system', which is an effective method to control thermal gain and loss, as well as glare in cooling-dominated climates. The operational scheme was developed to respond to outside air conditions and to control direct solar gains. Therefore, during summer and warm seasons (when sensors indicate that the temperature at the top of air cavity has reached 35°C or 95°F), the dampers at the bottom of the cavity open and axial fans at the top pull the air through the cavity to prevent the accumulation of excessively warm air. When the temperature drops, as measured by the sensors, the dampers close and the fans stop. During winter and in cold weather, the dampers remain shut and the fans do not operate, trapping warm air in the cavity and improving the thermal performance of the facade.

The design and engineering team also engaged in extensive study and exploration of the airflow through the double-skin cavity to guide the configuration of ventilation components, which was conducted using CFD analysis. Understanding the nature of the airflow and the operational modes was crucial in developing the design. Thirteen design alternatives were investigated, varying the position, number and size of the axial fans and lower dampers, as well as natural ventilation. The methodology for the CFD analysis included modelling the worst-case scenario, representing the highest summer heat gain for the facade. Results from the energy model in EnergyPlus were used to determine those values, since it could estimate conditions when the highest airflow through the cavity would be needed. The baseline case considered an idealised version of a naturally ventilated double-skin facade with intake and exhaust running continuously along the bottom and top of the cavity. However, this facade configuration was not possible for the design, since it included a metal wrap around the facade, which would not allow unrestricted openings. The next step was to investigate configurations with multiple fan-based ventilation schemes. The results of the CFD analysis showed that a design scheme with two large fans exhausting from either side of the cavity would reach a high temperature at the upper portion of the facade (60°C or 140°F), and extremely fast and turbulent airflow would occur within the cavity, which could damage the shades. One of the options was a design that consisted of eight fans at the top of the cavity, three on each side and two in the centre of the facade. The results of the CFD analysis indicated lower temperature profiles, while also minimising turbulence and air velocity in the cavity. The CFD analysis helped the design team to develop a facade configuration that would optimise thermal and airflow performance of the double-skin facade.

DIGITAL FABRICATION AND METHODS
Computer-aided manufacturing (CAM) and digital fabrication are increasingly being used for design prototyping, prefabrication and modular construction. These methods are also useful for testing constructability, material properties, form and geometric properties. By combining computational design tools with rapid prototyping techniques in the design process, designers

51

Natural ventilation

Two axial fans

Eight axial fans

Airflow profiles

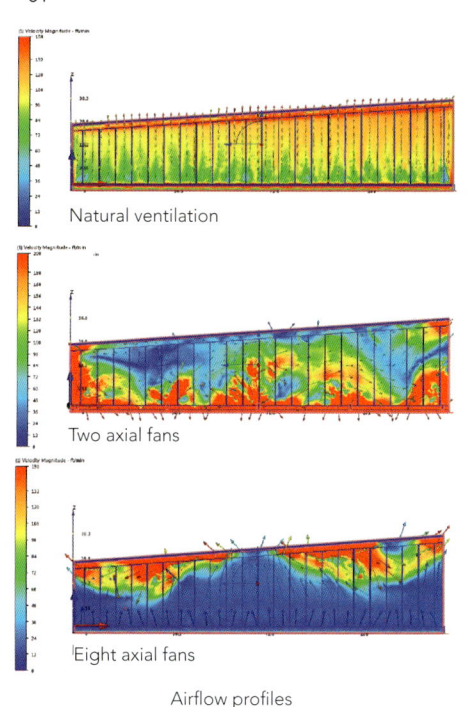

50 Perkins+Will, Case Western Reserve University, Tinkham Veale University Center, Cleveland, OH, USA, 2014.
The results of CFD analysis, showing the temperature profiles for three design scenarios – natural ventilation, two large axial fans and eight smaller fans – for the air cavity of the double-skin facade. The design scenario with two large fans exhausting from either side of the cavity would reach a high temperature at the upper portion of the facade, while eight fans would result in a lower temperature profile.

51 Perkins+Will, Case Western Reserve University, Tinkham Veale University Center, Cleveland, OH, USA, 2014.
The results of CFD analysis showing airflow profiles for three design scenarios within the air cavity of the double-skin facade. Extremely fast and turbulent airflow would occur for the design scenario with two large fans. The design scenario with eight fans would minimise turbulence and air velocity in the cavity.

and architects have real-time capabilities to generate multiple design options, iterate design approaches and end with scaled artefacts to study, review and critique the design solutions. Other CAM tools have also yielded a significant leap for designers, providing new digital fabrication means of exploring material limits and form. By combining parametric design tools with rapid prototyping techniques in the design process, designers and architects have powerful real-time capabilities to generate multiple design options, iterate conceptual approaches and end with scaled artefacts to study, review and critique the design solutions. Part of the challenge, when using digital fabrication in the design process, is the ability to realise the conceptual idea within size limitations and allowances of the current fabrication tools. For example, one of the challenges is how to break down complex forms as simplified components that can be realised by fabrication and assembling. This can be solved by the slicing and tessellation method, where a complex form is divided into a large quantity of two-dimensional contours or patterns, which are fabricated individually and assembled to construct the original form.

Digital fabrication is changing the way of designing and producing architectural objects. The diversity of accessible fabrication processes – such as laser cutting, 3D printing, computer-numeric controlled (CNC) milling and robotic construction – enable the production of components in a variety of forms and materials. Decreasing costs of digital fabrication tools and a growing number of fabrication services have increased the use of these technologies in architectural design. A number of case studies previously discussed in this book have illustrated how digital technologies and fabrication are creating a paradigm shift in architecture, specifically allowing complex forms and geometries to be realised and constructed.

For human–computer interaction digital fabrication has a number of implications. By increasing the audience for computational design and digital manufacturing, it generates a need for new software tools with intuitive and specialised interfaces. The ability to design architectural artefacts using computational design methods, analyse and simulate their behaviours, optimise design performance, share files digitally, and fabricate through a model-based design and construction is currently creating a paradigm shift in architecture and construction, and has the potential to revolutionise these fields.

The classification of digital fabrication methods can be grouped into three general categories: additive, subtractive and formative. Additive methods include 3D printing, such as 3D extrusion, where a material is deposited and solidifies based on thermal or chemical stimuli. A digital model is needed which defines the geometry of an object or component to be printed, and the finished artefacts are solid. Subtractive techniques – such as CNC milling or laser cutting – remove parts of a material to form a shape or an object. Within the formative category, techniques such as robotic construction are used to form objects and components, and also depend on the digital model of an artefact to be constructed. Some of these methods are suitable for planar and 2D fabrication, such as laser cutting and CNC milling, while others are suitable for 3D fabrication, for instance, 3D printing and robotic construction.

Fabrication methods based on additive principles construct materials in layers, such as 3D printing. 3D printing is based on depositing successive layers of material through computational control, where a 3D model is used as a data source to determine the shape, size and layering patterns. Objects of almost any shape and geometry can be created. There are different techniques and material types for 3D printing. For example, extrusion uses fused deposition modelling to deposit diverse types of polymers, rubber, clay and ceramics, or robocasting for ceramics, metal alloys and composites. Wire-feed 3D printing uses electron beam free-form fabrication for different types of metal alloys. Granular 3D printing uses various types of melting techniques for ceramics, metal alloys, stainless steel and aluminium. Plaster-based 3D printing uses inkjet-head 3D printing, which is often used for rapid prototyping and model making, while laminated 3D printing can be used for paper, metal foil, plastic film, and so on. These digital fabrication methods currently have size limitations for architectural use, since the largest 3D printer can produce an object with a diameter of only 1.2 m (4 ft) and up to 3 m (10 ft) in height.

The commonly applied subtractive method for digital fabrication is cutting. There is a range of particular cutting techniques, but they all enable the production of flat components using a cutting head that follows the instructions provided by the digital design model and input parameters to make shaped elements from sheet materials. The material and cutting head move along two axes in relation to each other. The cutting techniques are often limited by the thickness of materials being cut. Laser, plasma arc and water-jet technologies are used for cutting. Other subtractive methods rely on removing a material from an existing solid volume, so creating specified features and components. Milling or routing processes are typically used for these operations. Two-axis milling machines operate by having the rotating drill move along two axes (X and Y), subtracting 2D patterns of a material. Three-axis machines enable the drill to also move in a third direction (Z), allowing volumetric subtraction of a material. Complex forms use four- and five-axis machines, since they allow rotating drills to revolve.

Formative fabrication processes use mechanical forces to shape or deform a material into the required shape. Heat or steam is typically used in such processes. Also, robotic construction is often used for formative fabrication processes. The basic strategy for digital fabrication in current architectural practice typically relies on the decomposition of complex forms and shapes into segments that can be easily fabricated. Decomposition techniques and applicable methods for fabrication largely depend on the project scope, size, form, geometry and material. These two aspects are interrelated and should be considered for any project.

52

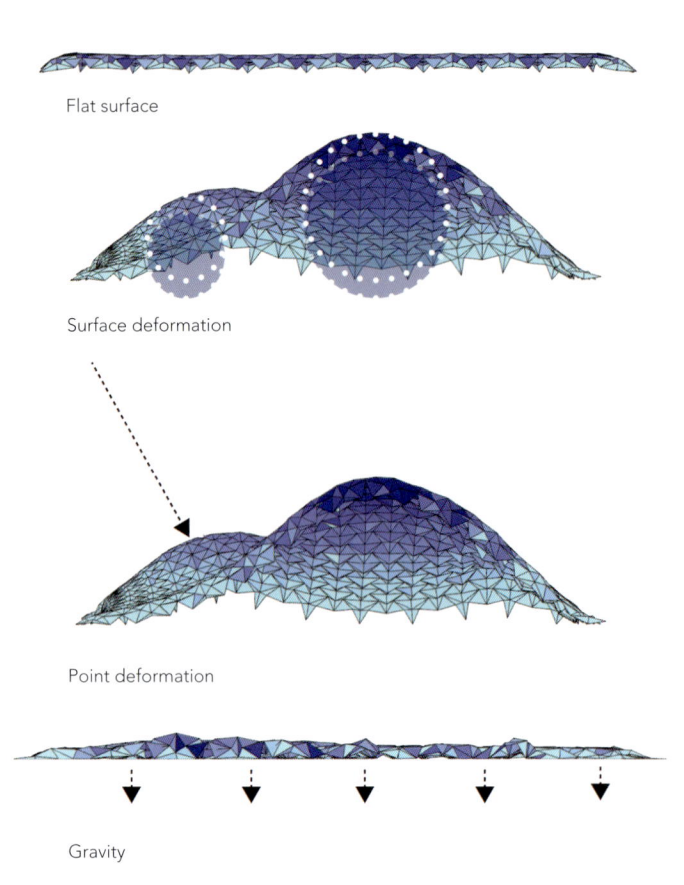

Flat surface

Surface deformation

Point deformation

Gravity

53

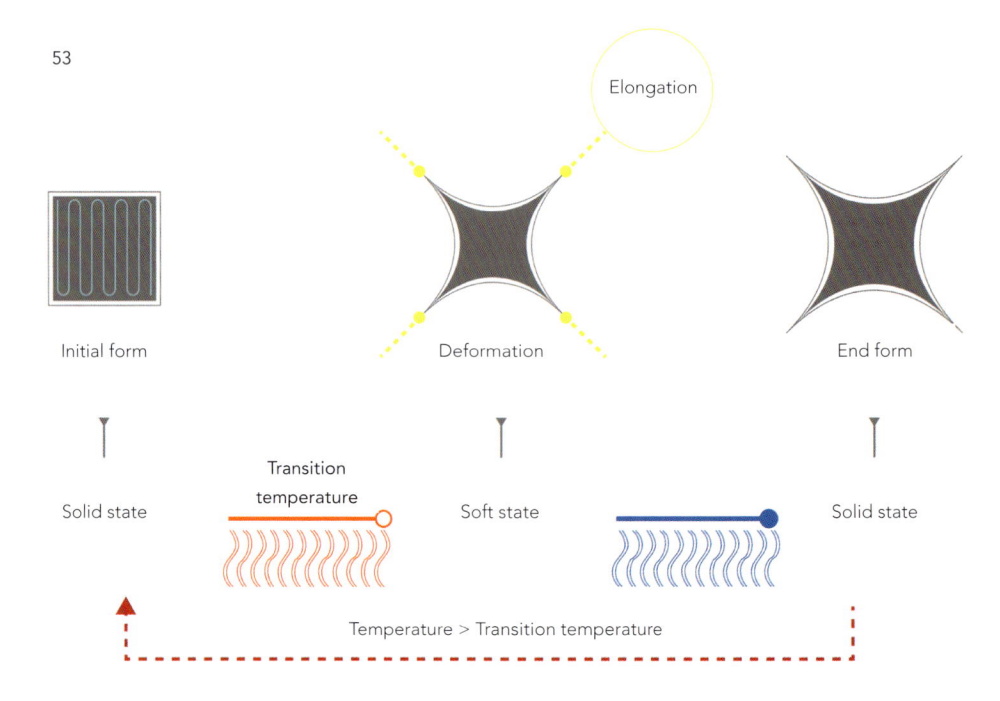

Elongation

Initial form — Deformation — End form

Solid state — Transition temperature — Soft state — Solid state

Temperature > Transition temperature

52 The Institute for Advanced Architecture of Catalonia, Translated Geometries, 2014. This research project investigated computational design methods, smart materials and digital fabrication to form responsive building elements. Shape-memory polymers (SMP) were used, these can undergo geometrical transformation when exposed to heat, retain the new shape upon cooling, and revert to the original shape when a heat source is applied.

53 The Institute for Advanced Architecture of Catalonia, Translated Geometries, 2014. Form and geometry design were developed using computational design tools, where the initial flat mesh was transformed into a 3D shape, and deformed simulating pulling forces.

A research project conducted by the Institute for Advanced Architecture of Catalonia –Translated Geometries – investigated computational design techniques, smart materials and digital fabrication to form responsive building elements. The objective was to develop a prototype that can change depending on spatial or environmental needs. Shape-memory polymers (SMP) were used, which can reach a soft and flexible state when exposed to heat of around 60 to 70°C (140 to 158°F), at which point they can undergo geometrical deformations. Upon reheating, the SMP reverts to its original state. Rhino3D®, Grasshopper™ and the Kangaroo plug-in were used to determine the tessellated triangulated pattern, which resembles origami. The initial flat mesh was input into the Kangaroo, then point forces and anchor points were selected to transform the mesh into a 3D shape. Then, the second deformation was achieved by simulating pulling forces, and the simulation was set up so that the joints would be in the 'soft' heated state, and upon cooling they would hold the desired shape. The prototypes were digitally fabricated using SMP, acrylic, plywood, fabric and a polymer composite. The components were laser cut using a MultiCam. Laser-cut acrylic wedges were heat formed over a mould and all components were assembled manually. The wiring for SMP consisted of heat and electricity wires. The end result was a working prototype that demonstrated the integration of emerging technologies, smart materials, computational design and digital fabrication.

Gantenbein Vineyard facade in Fläsch, Switzerland, was designed by Gramazio Kohler Architects using computational design approaches and was digitally fabricated. The building was designed by Bearth & Deplazes Architects, and Gramazio Kohler Architects were invited to design a non-standard brick facade when the building was already under construction. The initial design proposed a simple concrete skeleton with a brick infill, where the bricks are offset so that light can penetrate the interior through the gaps between the bricks. The design concept for the facade was developed based on the wine production process – the concrete frame was interpreted as a container to be filled with abstract, oversized grapes of varying sizes. This was simulated using computational tools, until the desired form and geometry was found, representing a closely packed container of spherical forms. This was transferred, as a digital image, to the facade design to determine the rotation of individual bricks. The wall elements were manufactured in a research facility at ETH Zurich, transported to the construction site and installed using a crane. Robotic fabrication was used to lay each of the 20,000 bricks precisely according to programmed parameters, at the desired angle and specifically prescribed intervals. In order to accelerate the manufacturing process, an automated procedure was developed for applying the two-component bonding agent to the bricks. Since each brick has a different rotation angle and a different and unique overlap with the bricks directly below and above, a manufacturing method was established in which four parallel bonding agent paths were applied to each brick at pre-defined intervals to the central axis of the wall. The testing

54

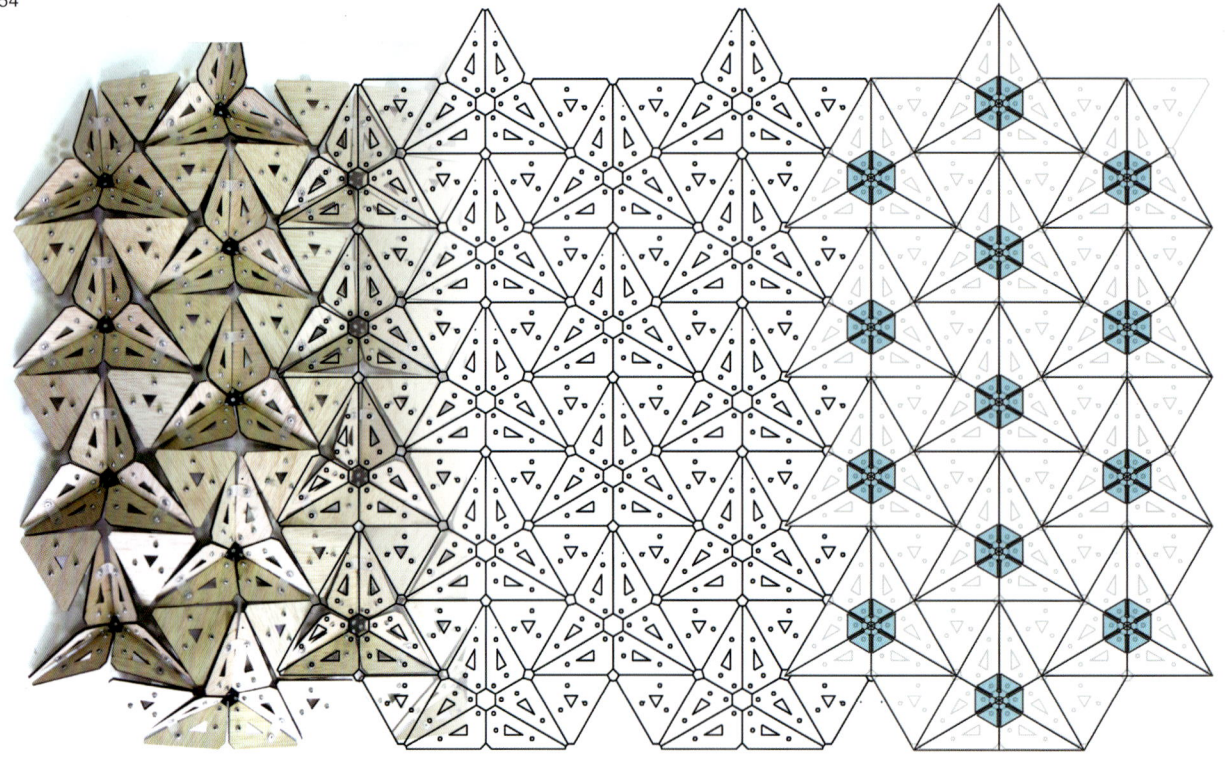

SMP placed along hexagonal nodes

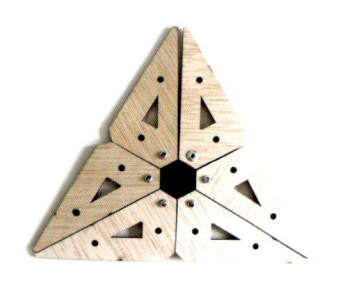

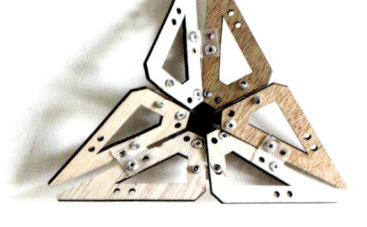

Open position   Semi-open position   Closed position

54 The Institute for Advanced Architecture of Catalonia, Translated Geometries, 2014. The prototypes were laser cut using SMP, acrylic, plywood, fabric and a polymer composite and manually assembled. SMP was placed along the hexagonal nodes, which can control the movement of individual elements.

55 The Institute for Advanced Architecture of Catalonia, Translated Geometries, 2014. The end result is a responsive prototype that can open and close depending on the environmental stimuli. SMP components react to applied heat, upon which they change the shape of the overall prototype by opening or closing individual elements.

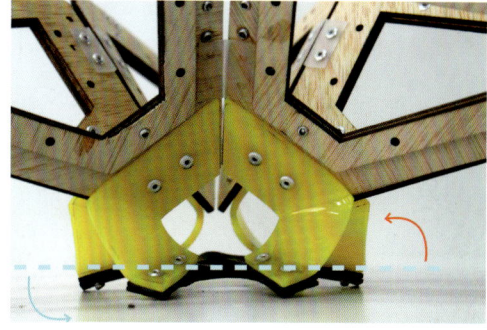

Open position

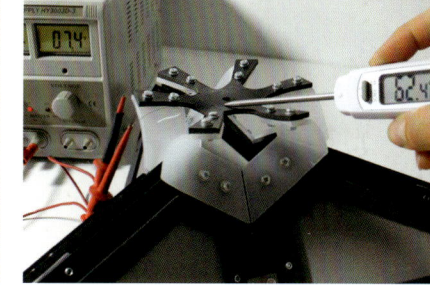

Closed position

SMP component

Testing

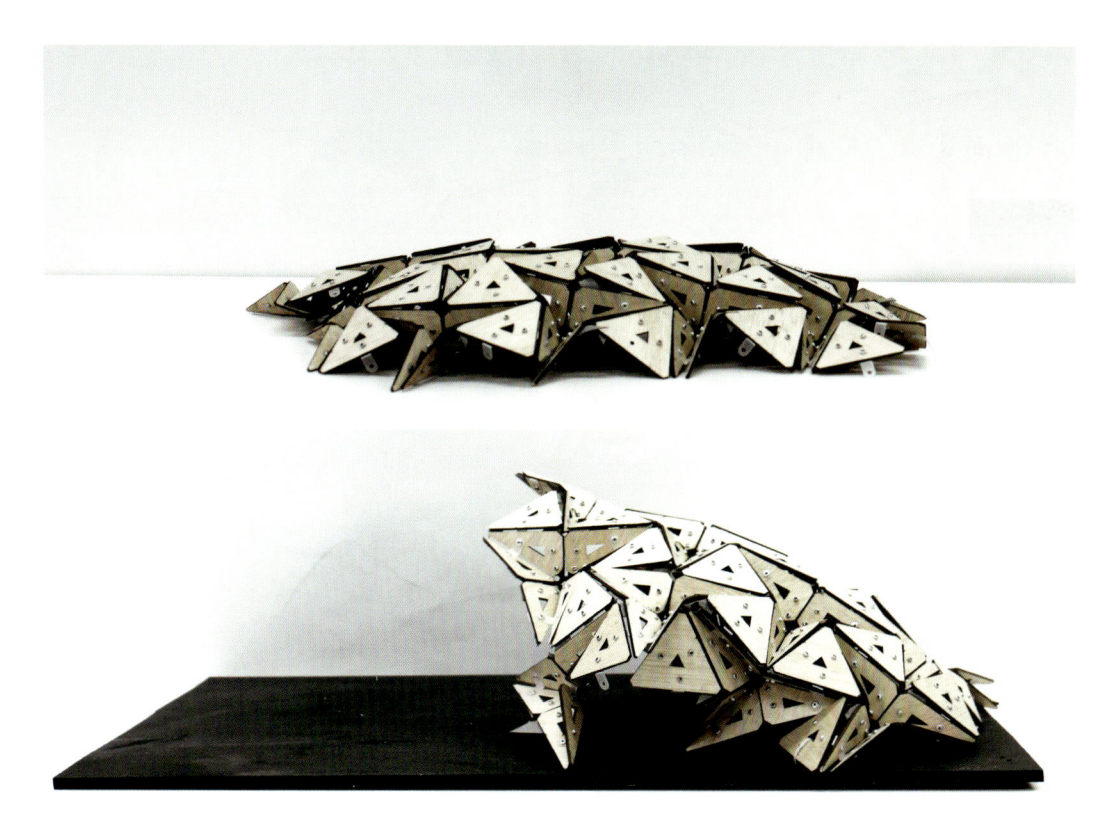

56

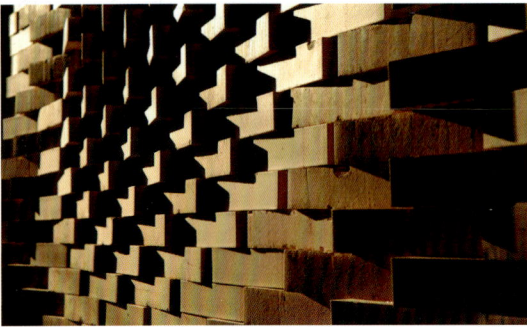

57

56 Gramazio Kohler Architects, Gantenbein Vineyard facade, Fläsch, Switzerland, 2006. The design concept was developed based on the wine production process – the concrete frame was interpreted as a container to be filled with abstract, oversized grapes of varying sizes. This was simulated using computational tools until the desired form and geometry were found, representing a closely packed container of spherical configurations.

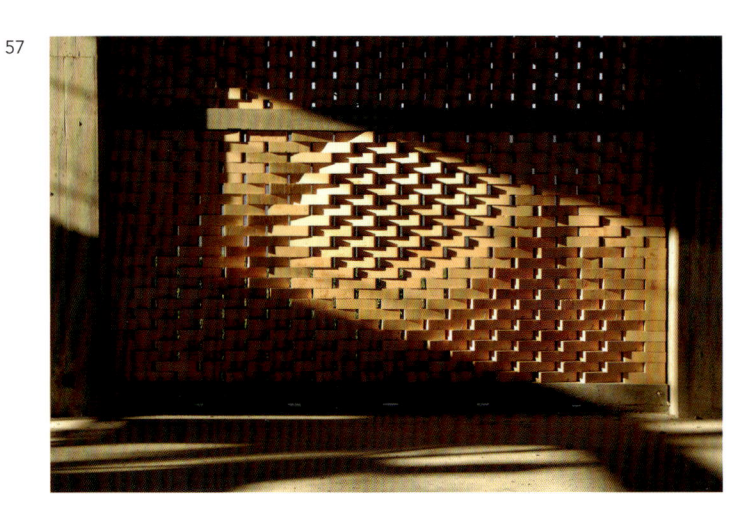

57 Gramazio Kohler Architects, Gantenbein Vineyard facade, Fläsch, Switzerland, 2006. The facade appears as solid and dynamic with a pattern of round forms. Individual bricks are used to create spherical forms, and allow light and air to penetrate the interior space.

58 Gramazio Kohler Architects, Gantenbein Vineyard facade, Fläsch, Switzerland, 2006 The wall elements were manufactured using robotic fabrication at a research facility, transported to the site as prefabricated, modular units, and assembled to form the facade. Robotic fabrication was used to lay each one of the 20,000 bricks precisely according to programmed parameters, at the desired angle and specifically prescribed intervals. A bonding agent was used to hold the bricks in place.

59 UNStudio, Theatre de Stoep, Spijkenisse, the Netherlands, 2014.
The building form resembles a flower.

revealed that the bonding agent was very effective, and that the reinforcement typically required for conventional prefabricated walls was unnecessary. Each wall was designed and constructed to achieve the desired light and air permeability, while creating a pattern that covers the entire building facade. The facade appears as solid and dynamic, where the soft, round forms are composed of individual bricks that allow light and air to penetrate the interior space.

DESIGN TO FABRICATION
Digital design and fabrication, as it has been presented in this chapter, is transforming contemporary architectural design and offering unprecedented opportunities for direct linkage between the design, manufacturing and construction phases of the building's life cycle. Model-based design and fabrication are automating the manufacturing processes, where building elements and components can be directly fabricated from the design models, brought to the site and erected to form the building as a whole. Traditionally, architects and designers have relied on shop drawings, which are created by fabricators based on the construction documents and specify all components for certain building elements, such as dimensions, shapes, material specifications, and so on. The number of shop drawings on any project may exceed the number of construction drawings and require significant lengths of time to be prepared, reviewed and approved. BIM can contain information necessary for fabrication, eliminating the need to produce shop drawings. The design information from BIM can be exported for detailing and fabrication, saving time and resources. Also, this technique produces higher quality results, since it eliminates the discrepancies between the design and fabrication documentation. However, it is imperative that design information is accurate, coordinated and consistent, therefore coordination and communication among architects and designers, engineers, fabricators and contractors is essential. The uses for model-based design and fabrication include sheet-metal fabrication, structural-steel fabrication, pipe cutting, prototyping for design, panel design and fabrication, and so on.

The benefits of model-based design and fabrication are: 1) improved quality of information; 2) increased fabrication productivity; 3) reduced time necessary for fabrication and construction; 4) minimised tolerances; and 5) reduced dependency on 2D drawings. The necessary resources for enabling model-based design and fabrication include design-authoring software, machine-readable data for fabrication, and digital fabrication software and equipment. The typical workflow includes the creation of a design model, the extraction of digital information for fabrication, the creation of fabrication models, the translation of information about components to be manufactured to fabrication equipment, and the actual manufacturing.

Theatre de Stoep in Spijkenisse, the Netherlands, designed by UNStudio, is a new theatre in the centre of the city. The building

60

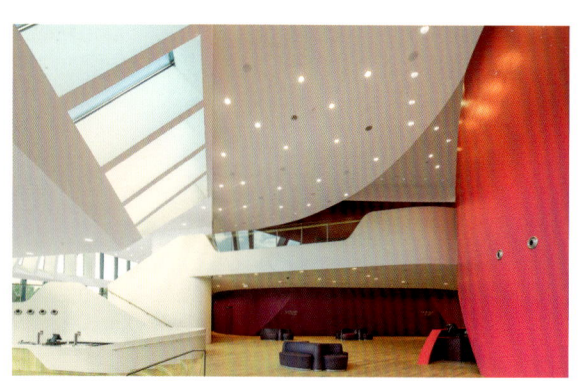

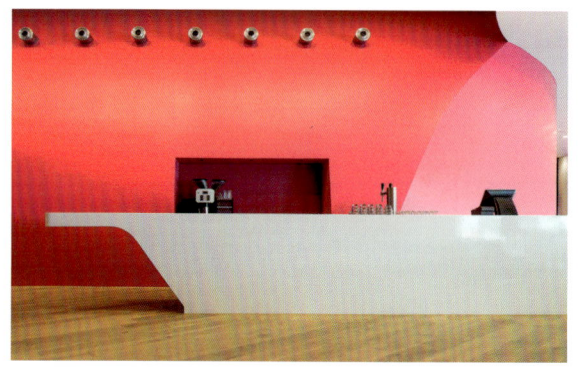

61

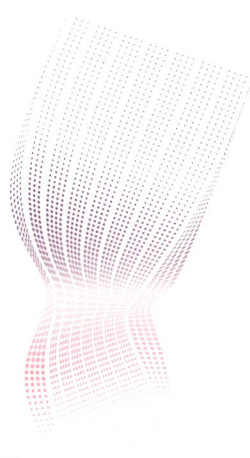

Parametric pattern on the roof

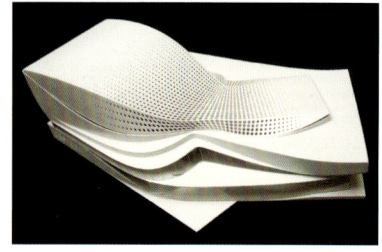

3D printed model

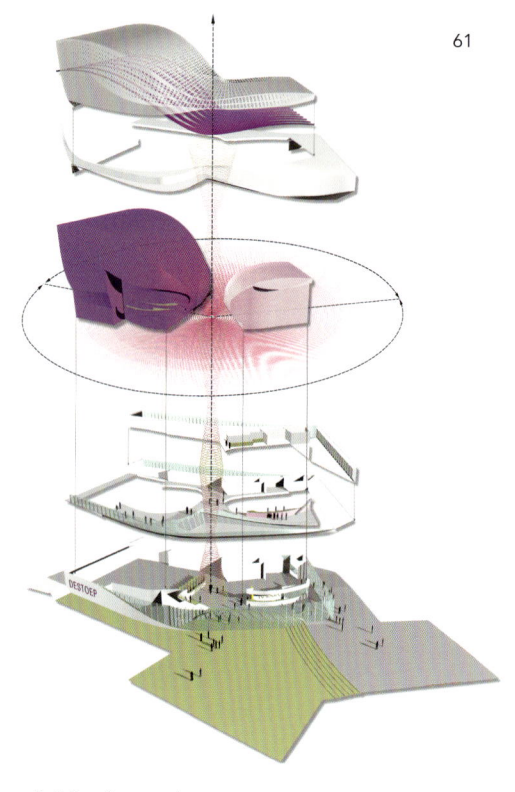

Building form and components

60 UNStudio, Theatre de Stoep, Spijkenisse, the Netherlands, 2014.
The central column-free atrium forms an important social space and is the vital point in the social functioning of the theatre. The programme includes larger and smaller auditoria, several linked atria, a café and a restaurant, dressing rooms, multifunctional rooms and offices.

61 UNStudio, Theatre de Stoep, Spijkenisse, the Netherlands, 2014.
A perforated, curved roof was developed using parametric modelling tools, and the position of the openings that provide natural ventilation and daylight was generated using computational design. LED lights are incorporated into the building envelope, providing lighting effects for the curved roof.

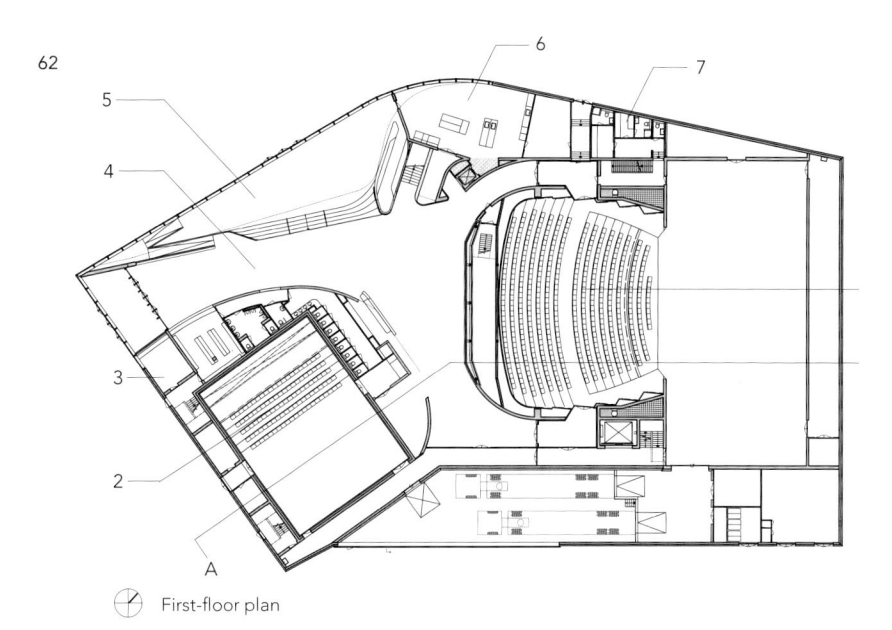

First-floor plan

62 UNStudio, Theatre de Stoep, Spijkenisse, the Netherlands, 2014.
Floor plans showing spatial organisation and layout.

1 Large auditorium
2 Small auditorium
3 Ticket office
4 Foyer
5 Cafe
6 Kitchen
7 Dressing rooms
8 Large auditorium balcony
9 Small auditorium balcony
10 Meeting space
11 Installations

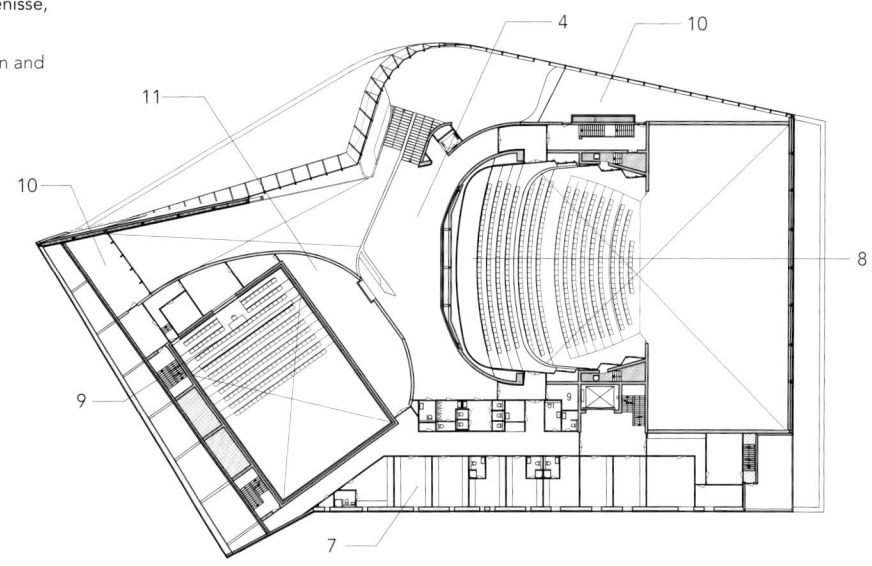

Second-floor plan

2 INNOVATIONS IN COMPUTATIONAL DESIGN 122-123

63

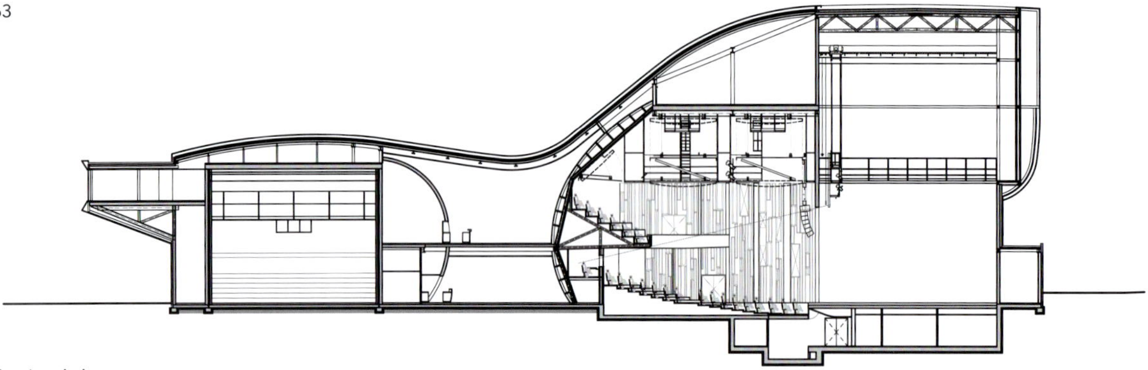

Section A-A

64

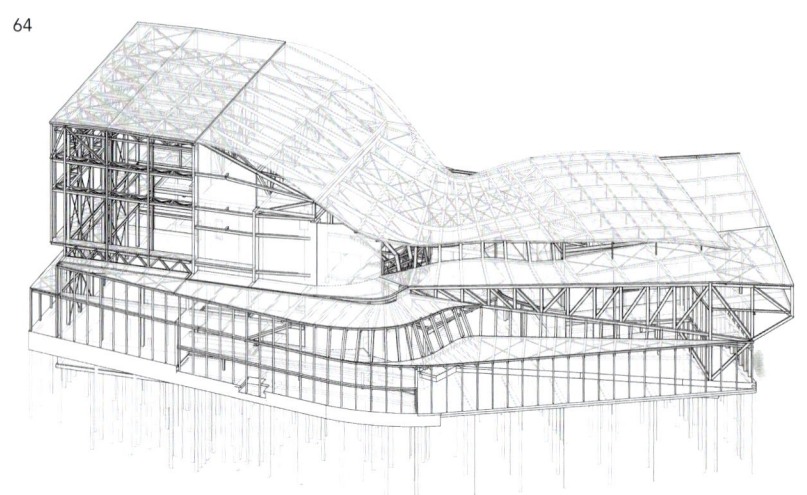

Structural components in BIM

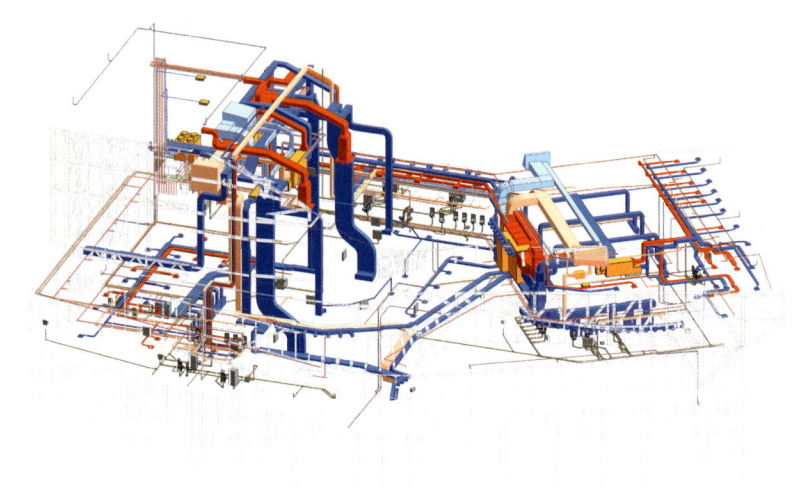

MEP components in BIM

63 UNStudio, Theatre de Stoep, Spijkenisse, the Netherlands, 2014.
Section showing building components and structure.

64 UNStudio, Theatre de Stoep, Spijkenisse, the Netherlands, 2014.
BIM model, showing structural and MEP components. A well-developed model was crucial for the fabrication and construction of this building, and all design and construction team members were involved in the development of the model.

65 UNStudio, Theatre de Stoep, Spijkenisse, the Netherlands, 2014.
The construction process showing different stages in the assembly.

programme includes larger and smaller auditoria, several linked atria, a café and a restaurant, dressing rooms, multifunctional rooms and offices. The building form resembles a flower, with free-flowing interior space and a central atrium without columns. The central atrium forms an important social space and is the vital point in the social functioning of the theatre. A perforated, curved roof was developed using parametric modelling tools and the positions of the openings that provide natural ventilation and daylight were generated using computational design.

A close working relationship between the architects, engineers, fabricators and contractors was essential for this project. During the early stages of design, BIM was developed by the architectural team that contained mostly architectural design information. After the contractor was chosen for the project, this model was translated into a fully developed BIM that contained all the necessary information for fabrication and construction. Clash detection was performed before construction began to investigate all three-dimensional details, as well as constructability. The team utilised a reverse engineering method, where subcontractors, suppliers and fabricators were involved in the design process to ensure repetition, control of details and integration of all building systems. Also, BIM was used to reduce the change orders during construction, minimise changes and costs. During the design and execution of the project, nearly 70 different companies and stakeholders collaborated on developing BIM, translating this information for fabrication and construction. The owner also played a crucial role during the design, and as-built BIM was requested for the maintenance and facility management.

CONCLUSION: THE INTEGRATION OF ADVANCED COMPUTATIONAL TECHNOLOGIES WITH DESIGN AND RESEARCH

Computational design methods, BIM, simulations and modelling, and digital fabrication are currently transforming the architectural and construction industries, where performance-oriented, model-based design, fabrication and construction are offering unprecedented advantages, compared with traditional design and construction techniques. As we have seen in this chapter, contemporary practice is being influenced by parametric modelling, BIM used for all stages of the building's life cycle, enhanced decision-making supported by performance analysis and simulation tools, improved collaboration and coordination, as well as virtual reality. Various software applications and tools can significantly improve design processes. Moreover, research-based design requires the use and implementation of advanced computational methods, especially simulation and modelling tools, for testing and evaluating design options and strategies. The presented case studies illustrate various research and design applications, and how advanced computational techniques have been implemented to test and evaluate materials and their properties, structural behaviour, energy-efficiency measures, coordination between different building systems, construction sequencing and digital fabrication. Innovative practices and research organisations rely on these advanced computational methods and should embrace digital technologies since they can improve the design and delivery of projects, coordination, collaboration and decision-making. It should be noted that specific software applications and tools change (and improve) over time, or become obsolete as new digital technologies are introduced. However, the paradigm shift has been initiated, and there is no going back. Innovative firms and organisations should be agile and create a culture that embraces new digital technologies and experimentation, without dreading the changes that might be caused by the implementation of these technologies. The changes and adaptations are the essential and necessary parts of innovation.

REFERENCES
1 Robert Aish and Robert Woodbury, 'Multi-Level Interaction in Parametric Design', *Lecture Notes in Computer Science,* Vol 3638, 2005, pp 151–62.
2 Ajla Aksamija, Todd Snapp, Michael Hodge and Michael Tang, 'Re-Skinning: Performance-Based Design and Fabrication of Building Facade Components – Design Computing, Analytics and Prototyping', *Perkins+Will Research Journal,* Vol 4, No 1, 2012, pp 15–28.
3 Ajla Aksamija, 'Information Modeling in Architectural Design: Collaborative Environment for Decision-Making Process', *Design Principles and Practices: An International Journal,* Vol 2, No 2, 2008, pp 79–88.
4 Charles M Eastman, *Building Product Models: Computer Environments Supporting Design and Construction,* CRC Press (Boca Raton, FL), 1999.
5 Charles M Eastman, Paul Teicholz, Rafael Sacks and Kathleen Liston, *BIM Handbook: A Guide to Building Information Modelling for Owners, Managers, Designers, Engineers and Contractors,* John Wiley & Sons (Hoboken, NJ), 2008.
6 Richard Garber, *BIM Design: Realising the Creative Potential of Building Information Modelling,* John Wiley & Sons (Chichester), UK, 2014.
7 American Institute of Architects, AIA Document E202: *The American Institute of Architects Building Information Modeling Protocol Exhibit,* 2008.
8 Randy Deutsch, *BIM and Integrated Design: Strategies for Architectural Practice,* John Wiley & Sons (Hoboken, NJ), 2011.
9 Ajla Aksamija, 'Analysis and Computation: Sustainable Design in Practice', *Design Principles and Practices: An International* Journal, Vol 4, No 4, 2010, pp 291–314.
10 Shady Attia, Liliana Beltrán, André De Herde and Jan Hensen, 'Architect Friendly: A Comparison of Ten Different Building Performance Simulation Tools', *Proceedings of IBPSA '09 Building Simulation Conference,* The International Building Performance Simulation Association, (Glasgow), 2009, pp 204–11.
11 Ajla Aksamija, 'BIM-Based Building Performance

Analysis in Architectural Practice: When, Why and How', in Ahmed Z Khan and Karen Allacker (eds), *Architecture and Sustainability: Critical Perspectives for Integrated Design*, , Sint-Lucas Architecture Press (Brussels), 2015, pp 221–30.

12 Hyeun Jun Moon, Min Seok Choi, Sa Kyum Kim and Seung Ho Ryu, 'Case Studies for the Evaluation of Interoperability between a BIM Based Architectural Model and Building Performance Analysis Programs', *Proceedings of IBPSA '11 Building Simulation Conference,* The International Building Performance Simulation Association (Sydney), 2011, pp 1521–6.

13 Robert Hitchcock and Justin Wong, 'Transforming IFC Architectural View BIMS for Energy Simulation: 2011', *Proceedings of IBPSA '11 Building Simulation Conference,* The International Building Performance Simulation Association (Sydney), 2011, pp 1089–95.

14 Arno Schlueter and Frank Thesseling, 'Building Information Model Based Energy/Exergy Performance Assessment in Early Design Stages', *Automation in Construction*, Vol 18, No 2, 2009, pp 153–63.

15 Mark Walsh, Christopher Augustyn and Matthew Brugman, 'Holding the Sun at Bay: A Study in the Development of the Double-Skin Facade for the Case Western Reserve University Tinkham Veale University Center', *Perkins+Will Research Journal*, Vol 5, No 2, 2013, pp 18–40.

IMAGES

Opening image © ALUSION TM; figures 1, 2, 3, 4, 5, 6 and 7 © ICD/ITKE University of Stuttgart; figures 8 and 10 © Rob Ley Studio/Photography by Serge Hoeltschi; figures 9, 11 and 13 © Rob Ley Studio; figures 12, 14, 15 and 16 © Trahan Architects/Photo Tim Hursley; figures 17 and 18 © Trahan Architects; figures 19 and 20 © Trahan Architects/CASE and Method Design; figures 21 and 22 © J. Mayer H. Architects/Nikkol Rot for Holcim; figure 23 © J. Mayer H. Architects; table 1 © Ajla Aksamija; figures 24, 25, 26, 27, 28, 29, 38, 39, 40 and 41 © Ajla Aksamija; figures 31, 32, 33, 34 and 35 © HOK; figures 36 and 37 ©Alan Karchmer; figure 43 © Iwan Baan; figures 42, 44, 45 and 46 Courtesy of Zaha Hadid Architects; figure 47 © James Steinkamp Photography; figures 48, 49, 50 and 51 © Perkins+Will; figures 52, 53, 54 and 55 © Institute for Advanced Architecture of Catalonia; figures 56, 57 and 58 © Gramazio & Kohler, ETH Zurich; figures 59 and 60 UNStudio © Jan Paul Mioulet; figures 61, 62 and 63 © UNStudio; figure 64 UNStudio © ARUP; figure 65 UNStudio © Roel van Deursen

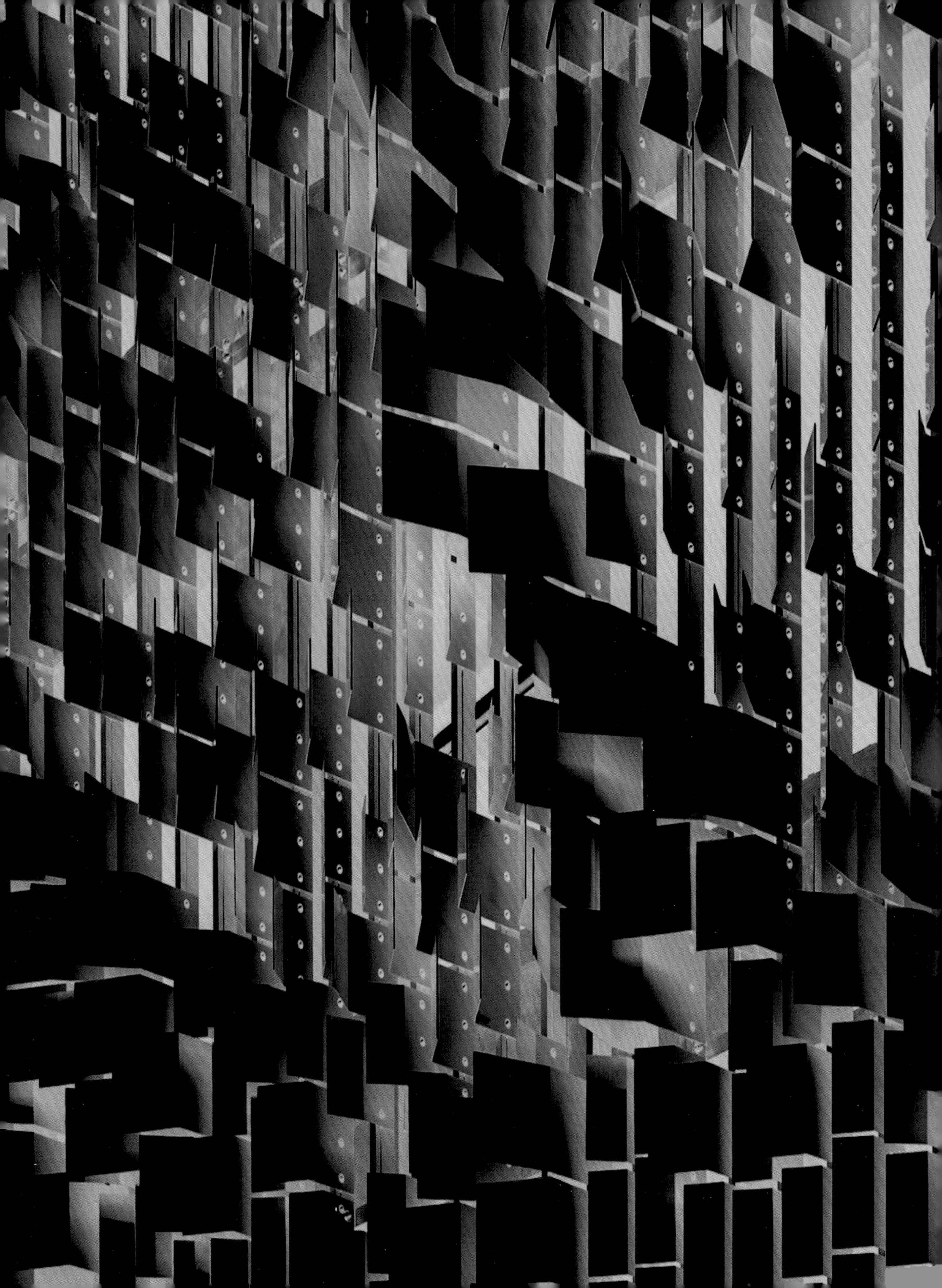

3 TECHNOLOGICAL INNOVATIONS

Technological innovations – such as advanced building technologies, construction techniques and smart and responsive buildings – are influencing contemporary architectural design. Throughout history, technological innovations have changed the course of architectural practice and have caused new building types, forms and systems to develop. High-rise buildings, for example, have been made possible by the invention of elevators, advances in structural systems and fire protection. Raised floors for ventilation and wiring, originally developed for computer rooms and other equipment-oriented spaces, are now commonly used in a variety of buildings. Today, the emphasis is mainly on innovative technologies and building systems that can be used to create energy-efficient, high-performance, responsive and intelligent buildings.

This chapter introduces advances in facades, HVAC and lighting systems, building automation systems (BAS), sensors and controls, and discusses how these systems are influencing the design and performance of innovative buildings, and the implementation in various case studies. Energy-efficiency measures and resilient design are demanding new design approaches and methods that improve building performance and energy consumption, since buildings are the largest energy consumers in the world. Environmental challenges and climate change require that we rethink the design and operation of the built environment, and that we create buildings and cities that have a positive impact on our environment.

The chapter also introduces advances in construction techniques, primarily prefabrication and modular construction, automation and robotics used for fabrication, and the installation and assembly of building components and buildings. Increased complexity of buildings and economic factors are requiring new methods for fabrication, manufacture and assembly, and designers, engineers, fabricators and contractors must work collaboratively to find new solutions and methods to meet these challenges. The last part of the chapter discusses smart and responsive buildings: an emerging type that relies on sensors and controls to respond to changes in environmental conditions, occupancy patterns, energy consumption and so on, and modifies the buildings' operation and functioning. The future of architecture and the built environment depends on these advanced building technologies

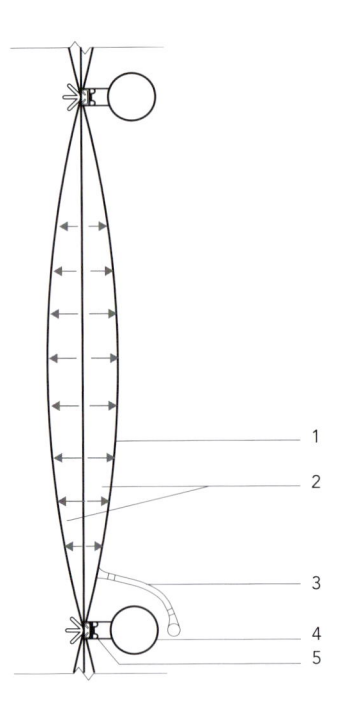

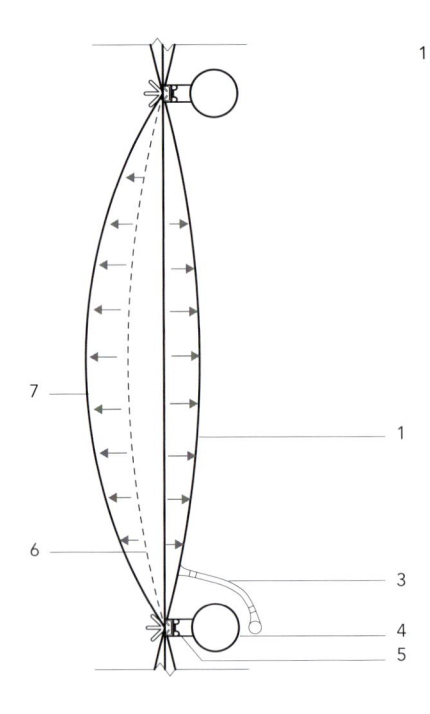

1	Triple-ply ETFE cushion
2	Air
3	Air-pressure pump
4	Tubular support structure
5	Cushion restraint
6	Inital position of ETFE cushion
7	Changed position by varying air pressure

1 Components of the ETFE facade system.
ETFE cushions consist of two- or three-ply sheets and are filled with air. They are maintained by pumps at a constant air pressure, relative to wind loads.

2 Prototype of a self-contained ETFE module with integrated thin film PV and light-emitting diodes (LEDs).
This prototype shows components of a module that are able to generate electricity and power the integrated lighting system.

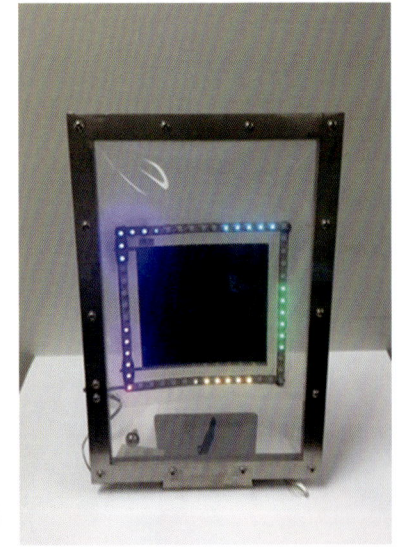

and construction techniques, and innovative practices and research organisations are adopting and implementing them for various types of buildings, installations and applications.

ADVANCES IN FACADE SYSTEMS

Recent developments in facade technology are following three general trends.[1] The first is in small-scale technology: coatings, thin films, advanced glazing technologies and advanced materials developed to improve facade performance at the micro-level. The second is towards large-scale innovations, such as double-skin facades. The third trend is the increased integration of energy-generation components into the building skin. With each of these trends, the functional performance goals are the same: separating the indoor and outdoor environments, mitigating adverse external environmental effects, and maintaining internal occupant comfort conditions with minimum energy consumption.

ETFE (ethylene tetrafluoroethylene) is a Teflon®-coated fluoropolymer material blown or extruded to form large, durable sheets. ETFE is resistant to degradation by ultraviolet (UV) light and atmospheric pollution. To address different use conditions, it can be manufactured as single-ply sheets or double- or triple-ply air-filled 'cushions'. ETFE is low-maintenance, recyclable, and, when compared with glass, extremely lightweight. As a single-sheet material, ETFE has very poor thermal and acoustic performance and should not be used in facade applications. However, in the double- and triple-ply configurations it has excellent thermal properties, since the air trapped between the layers acts as an insulator. The air-filled cushions are maintained by pumps at a constant air pressure, relative to wind loads, letting the skin adjust in response to the varying loads. ETFE is not a fabric and cannot be used as a self-supporting tensile structure. Instead, the pressurised air holds the cushions intact. A secondary structure, usually consisting of aluminium extrusions, steel rods or steel cables is needed to support the cushions.

ETFE is a combustible material; however, its flammability is inherently low because of the presence of fluorine in its chemical structures. This makes the ETFE material self-extinguishing. It does not block exterior sound well, since it is composed of very thin membranes. Impact noise, such as heavy rain striking the surface, is transferred to the interior. For some building occupancies, such as recreational facilities, pools or atria, this may not be a problem. However, in libraries, museums, and other spaces where acoustics are important, this can be a concern. Nets or meshes placed over the external surface of ETFE cushions can be used acoustically to dampen the impact noise.

A current project is under way which aims to develop a self-contained ETFE module with integrated thin-film PV and light-emitting diodes (LEDs) with flexible integrated circuits. This module would be able to harvest solar energy, produce electricity for the building's use and integrate lighting effects. The project, named ETFE-MFM, is being conducted by ITMA Materials

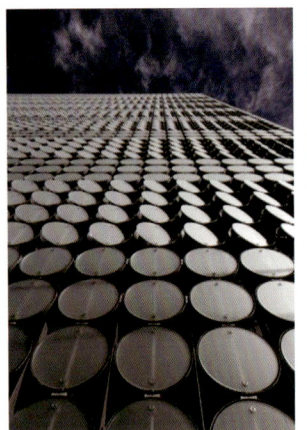

3

3 Sean Godsell Architects, the Royal Melbourne Institute of Technology (RMIT) Design Hub, Melbourne, Australia, 2012. This academic building incorporates an innovative double-skin facade. The outer layer of the double skin consists of more than 16,000 individually mounted translucent glass discs, repeated on all four building orientations.

4 Sean Godsell Architects, the Royal Melbourne Institute of Technology (RMIT) Design Hub, Melbourne, Australia, 2012. Partial elevation and plan showing the components of the double-skin facade. The outer skin consists of 774 panels and each panel contains 21 sandblasted glass discs, positioned in three vertical columns, where the top three discs are fixed and the bottom four are operable.

5 Sean Godsell Architects, the Royal Melbourne Institute of Technology (RMIT) Design Hub, Melbourne, Australia, 2012. Detailed plan of the operable disk, consisting of sandblasted glass. The discs can rotate between 5 and 80°.

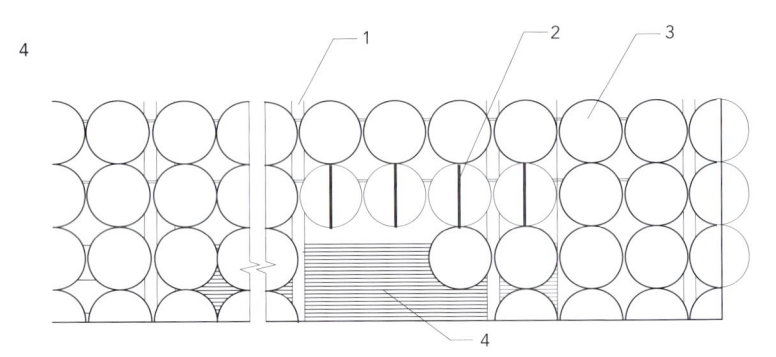

4

Partial elevation

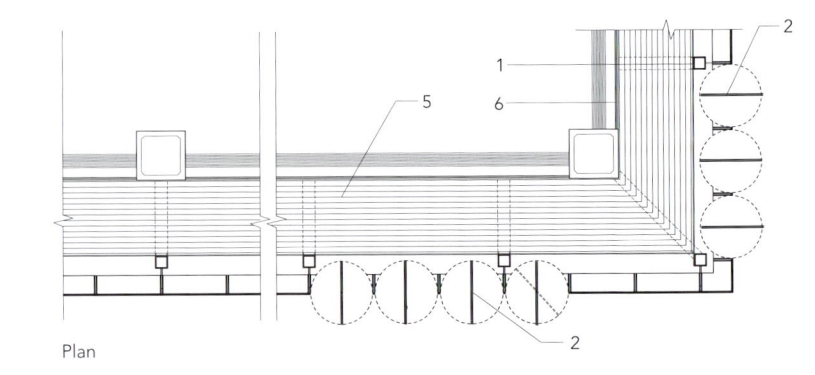

Plan

1 Vertical support
2 Rotated disk
3 Operable disk
4 Louvres
5 Catwalk
6 Curtain wall

Table 1 Comparison of commercially available emerging facade glazing material with standard high-performance products.

Material	Solar control	Insulation	Daylight	Glare control	Maintenance	View to exterior	Availability
Aerogel insulation within insulated glazing unit	0	+	+	+	0	-	0
Vacuum-insulated glazing unit	0	+	0	0	0	0	-
Electrochromic glass	+	0	0	+	0	0	0
Self-cleaning glass	0	0	0	0	+	+	0
PCM in insulated glazing unit	+	+	0	+	0	-	+
PV glass (semitransparent)	+	0	0	+	0	-	0

Legend: + Improved performance   0 Similar   – Lower performance

Technology, Acciona Infrastructure, Greenovate! Europe, Belectric, Taiyo Europe and Cener – the National Renewable Energy Center of Spain. There are prototypes available, which demonstrate material components and characteristics.

Emerging facade glazing and cladding materials have been extensively discussed in Chapter 1. For example, electrochromic glass, aerogel insulation, vacuum insulated glazing units, phase-change material (PCM) integrated glazing units and PV glass can all be used for facade glazing. Table 1 compares the properties of these advanced materials in relation to thermal performance, daylight and glare, maintenance, views and availability.

Double-skin glazed facades are fundamentally different from conventional single-skin facades, since they consist of distinct exterior and interior glazed-wall systems, separated by a ventilated air cavity. The cavity creates a thermal buffer between the interior and exterior environments. The air cavity can be ventilated by natural convection caused by warm air naturally rising, by mechanical devices or by a hybrid mode that combines the two methods. In some double-skin facade designs the air cavity is interrupted vertically or horizontally (or both) by solid or perforated partitions. Selection of the type of the glazing, the width and partitioning of the air cavity and the ventilation mode depends on climate, building orientation and design requirements. Double-skin facades are classified according to the ways the air cavity is partitioned (the facade type), the ventilation mode (natural, mechanical and hybrid), and the airflow pattern. These three variables can be combined in numerous ways for a wide variety of design possibilities.

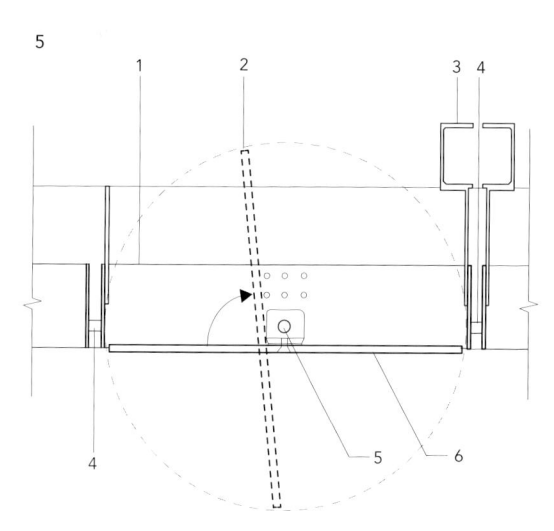

Detailed plan of an operable disk

1 Galvanised steel drum
2 Rotated disk
3 Vertical support
4 Welded connection between drums
5 Vertical rod for rotating disks
6 Operable disk

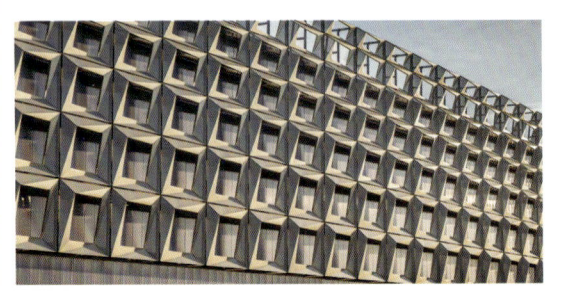

6

Basic double-skin facade types include:

- Box window facades, which have horizontal partitions at each floor level, as well as vertical partitions between windows. Each air cavity is typically ventilated naturally.
- Corridor facades, which have uninterrupted horizontal air cavities for each floor level but are physically partitioned at the floor levels. All three ventilation modes are possible.
- Shaft-box facades, which are similar to corridor facades, but use vertical shafts for natural stack-effect ventilation. Hybrid-mode ventilation is often used for this facade type.
- Multistorey facades, which have uninterrupted air cavities the full height and width of the facade. All three ventilation modes can be used.

Smart building skins, programmable surfaces, responsive facades and interactive building envelopes are active research areas in architectural design.[2] Technical advances allow architects and designers to create buildings as new types of interfaces and responsive elements, and it is possible to design building facades that respond to environmental changes and stimuli.

The Royal Melbourne Institute of Technology (RMIT) Design Hub was designed by Sean Godsell Architects. It is enclosed with a double-skin facade, the outer layer of which consists of more than 16,000 individually mounted translucent glass discs, repeated on all four building orientations. Selected groupings of the discs automatically rotate around a vertical axis in response to solar radiation. The outer facade of the double skin consists of 774 panels, and each panel contains 21 sandblasted glass discs positioned into three vertical columns, where the top three discs are fixed and the bottom four are operable. The panels are supported by a steel frame, and the air-cavity depth between the exterior and interior skins is 1 m (3 ft). The discs can rotate between 5 and 80°, and the movement is controlled by actuators. The west, east and north facades contain the movable discs. The interior facade consists of a curtain wall, with double argon-filled insulated glazing units.

The Multifunctional Sports Hall in Cluj-Napoca, Romania, designed by architects Dico si Tiganas, is a new facility for sports, training and cultural events. Conceived as part of a larger sports complex that includes Cluj Arena, a new soccer and athletics stadium, this facility includes the main hall, seating for 7,300 people, and supporting programmatic elements that can be used for sport activities and concerts. The building envelope consists of two layers which reflect and transmit light to the interior spaces. The outer layer is composed of parametrically distorted rectangular forms consisting of perforated steel plates. The inner layer is partially translucent and partially transparent, and made of channelled glass.

ADVANCES IN HVAC SYSTEMS
Conventional HVAC systems combine heating, ventilation and air conditioning into a single system, delivered by the building's

6 Dico si Tiganas, Multifunctional Sports Hall, Cluj-Napoca, Romania, 2014. This building is a new facility for sports, training and cultural events. The building facade consists of two layers: the outer layer is composed of parametrically distorted, perforated steel plates; the inner layer is partially translucent and partially transparent, consisting of channelled glass.

7

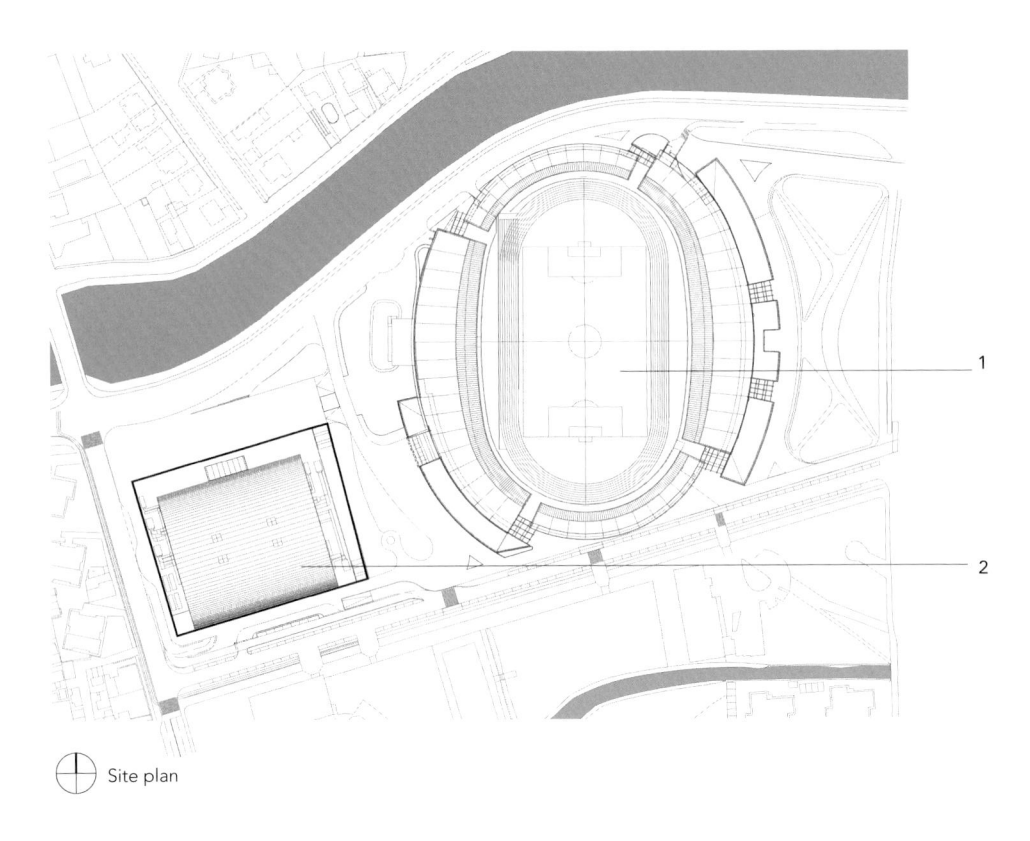

7 Dico si Tiganas, Multifunctional Sports Hall, Cluj-Napoca, Romania, 2014. Site plan showing the building as part of a larger sports complex, which includes Cluj Arena, a new soccer and athletics stadium. The floor plans show components of the Multifunctional Sports Hall, including the main hall, seating for 7,300 people, and supporting programmatic elements that can be used for sport activities and concerts.

1 Cluj Arena
2 Multifunctional Sports Hall
3 Main hall
4 Seating
5 Services
6 Circulation

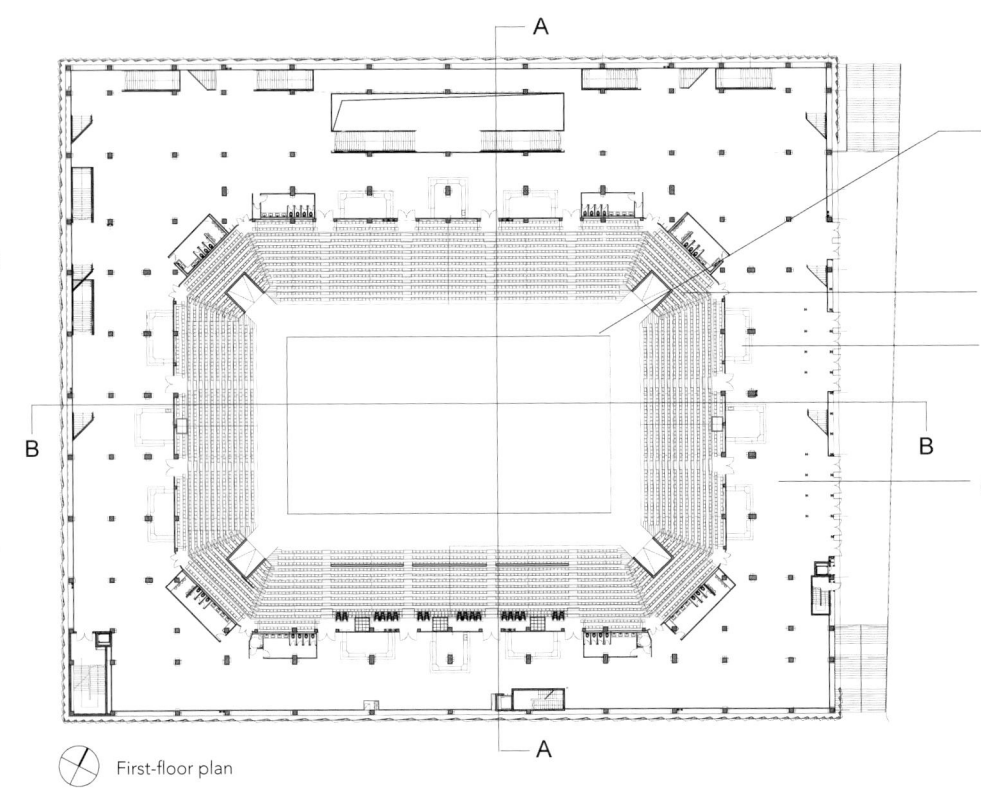

Site plan

First-floor plan

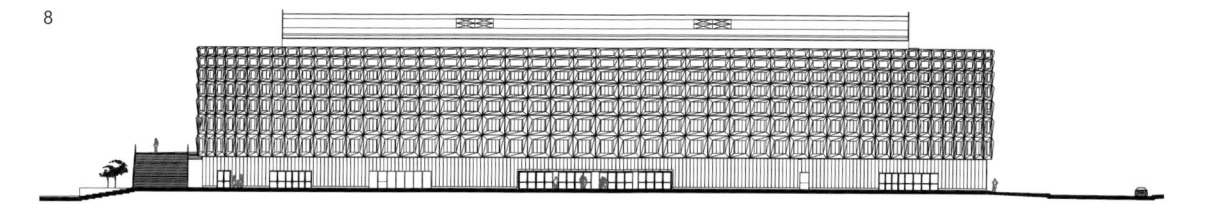

North elevation

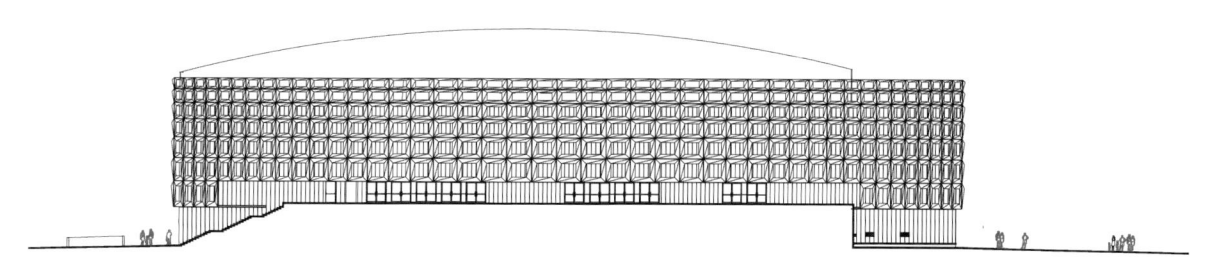

East elevation

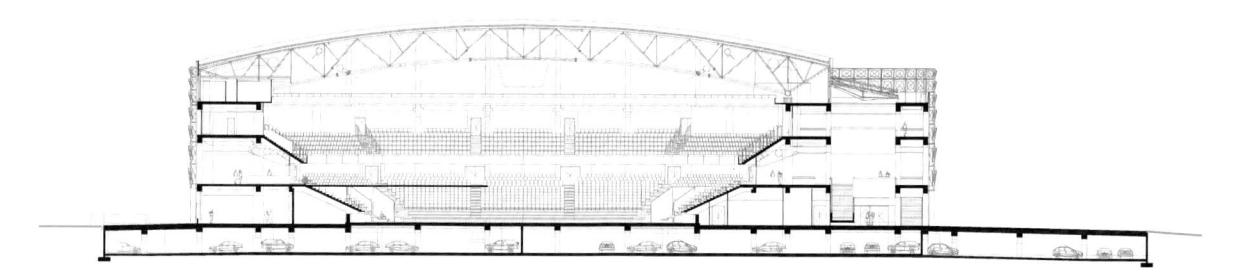

Section A-A

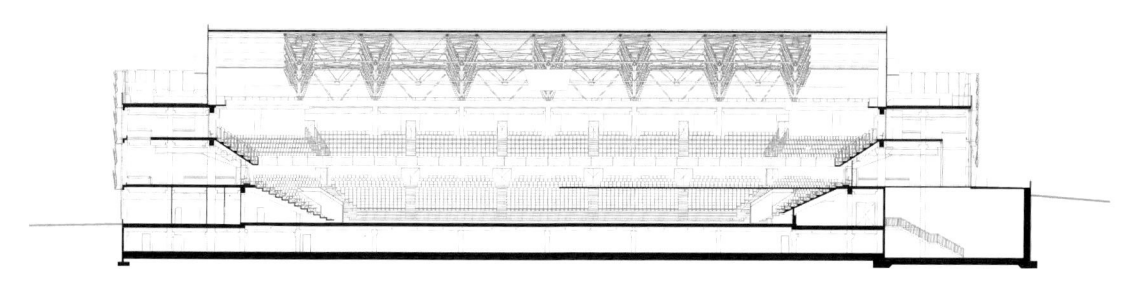

Section B-B

8 Dico si Tiganas, Multifunctional Sports Hall,
Cluj-Napoca, Romania, 2014.
Elevations and sections indicate the building
facade treatment and structural system.

9 Snøhetta, James B Hunt Jr Library, North Carolina State University, Raleigh, NC, USA, 2013.
Exterior images showing the facade treatment and building form.

central fan and air distribution network. Typically, a mixture of outdoor air for ventilation along with cool or warm air for temperature control are delivered to different zones of the building. Currently, this is changing with the emerging trend in advanced HVAC systems being the decoupling of ventilation and heating, directed by the need to design and operate buildings using less energy. The primary energy savings associated with decoupling the systems are the result of a reduction in fan energy. For example, a dedicated outdoor air system (DOAS) may provide the minimum ventilation component required by the building codes, and the DOAS handling unit provides heated and dehumidified air for ventilation, which can be coupled with some form of heat recovery. A DOAS system typically provides 20% less air than variable air volume (VAV) systems, and heating and cooling requirements for the interior spaces are met through a water-based system. Water has a much higher capacity for energy transfer than air, so the amount of energy required to deliver the heating and cooling is drastically reduced. DOAS systems also require smaller ductwork, since reduced air quantity does not require the same amount of ductwork as VAV systems.

A second type of decoupled system can be classified as a hybrid model. For example, active chilled beams can deliver ventilation, heating and cooling, where the inducted air supplied by the chilled beams provides most of the heating and cooling, while the air-handling unit provides ventilation. Chilled beams are an emerging type of HVAC system, which consist of a fin-and-tube heat exchanger, contained in a housing and suspended from the ceiling. Chilled water passes through the tubes and as warm air from the spaces rises towards the ceiling, the air surrounding the chilled beam is cooled and descends towards the floor. This creates a convective air motion and cools the interior space without the use of a fan. Active chilled beams also contain an integral air supply, which induces air from the space through a cooling coil. This allows an active chilled beam to provide more cooling capacity than a passive chilled beam. The primary air system must maintain the dew point of the interior space below the surface temperature of chilled beams to avoid condensation on the coil. It is possible to install chilled beams with integrated humidity sensors that monitor the humidity levels and control the operation of the chilled beams.

Radiant systems are another type of HVAC system that have advantages over traditional VAV systems. Hydronic radiant systems use water as the primary source for providing cooling and heating, and can be installed within the floor slab and ceilings. The system uses pipes and tubing embedded in concrete, and uses the thermal inertia of the slab or ceiling to reduce peak loads. The advantages of hydronic radiant systems over traditional VAV systems include higher energy efficiency, improved thermal comfort and a reduction in the amount of ductwork. Radiant panels that can be installed on ceilings or wall surfaces are also commercially available. Radiant systems can be combined with underfloor air distribution (UFAD) systems. UFAD systems use plenums between the floor slab and a raised access floor system

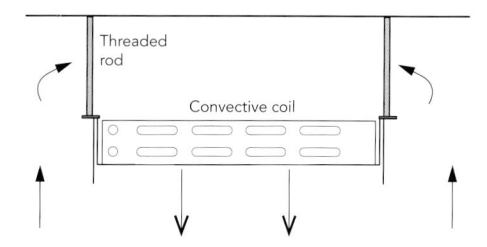

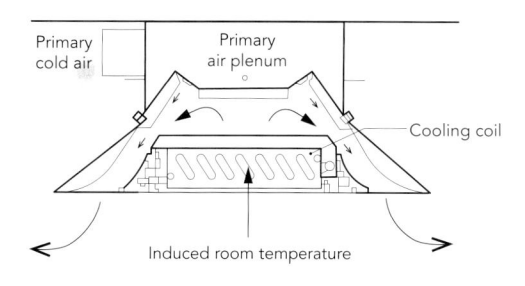

10 Diagrams showing the components of passive and active chilled beams.
Passive chilled beams consist of a heat exchanger and cooling coils. Chilled water passes through the coils and cools the surrounding air through convective air motion. Active chilled beams also contain an integral air supply, which induces air from the space through cooling coils.

3 TECHNOLOGICAL INNOVATIONS 138–139

First-floor plan

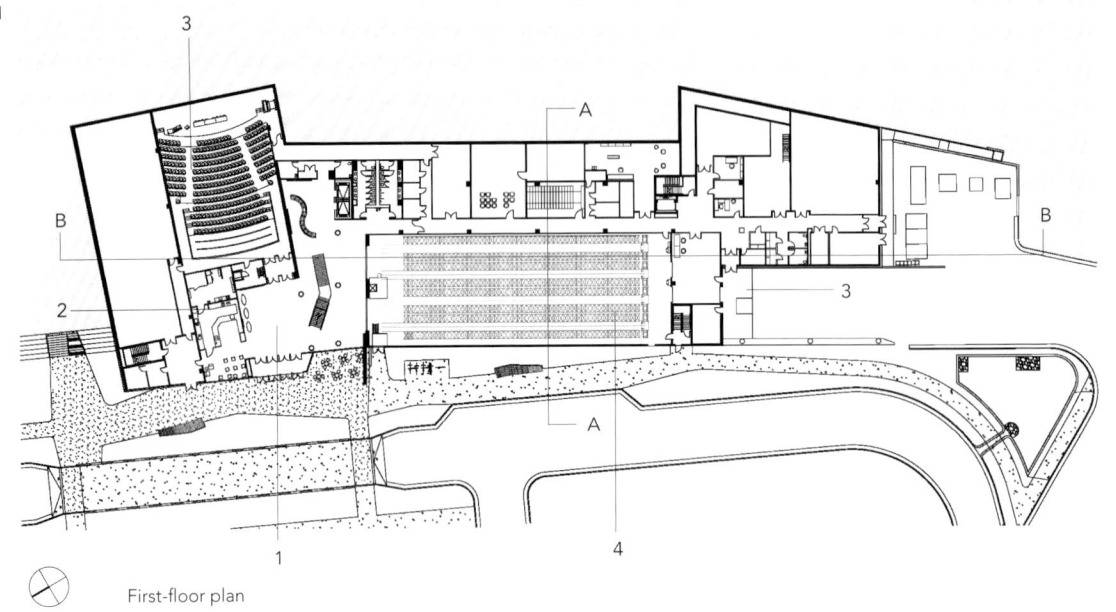

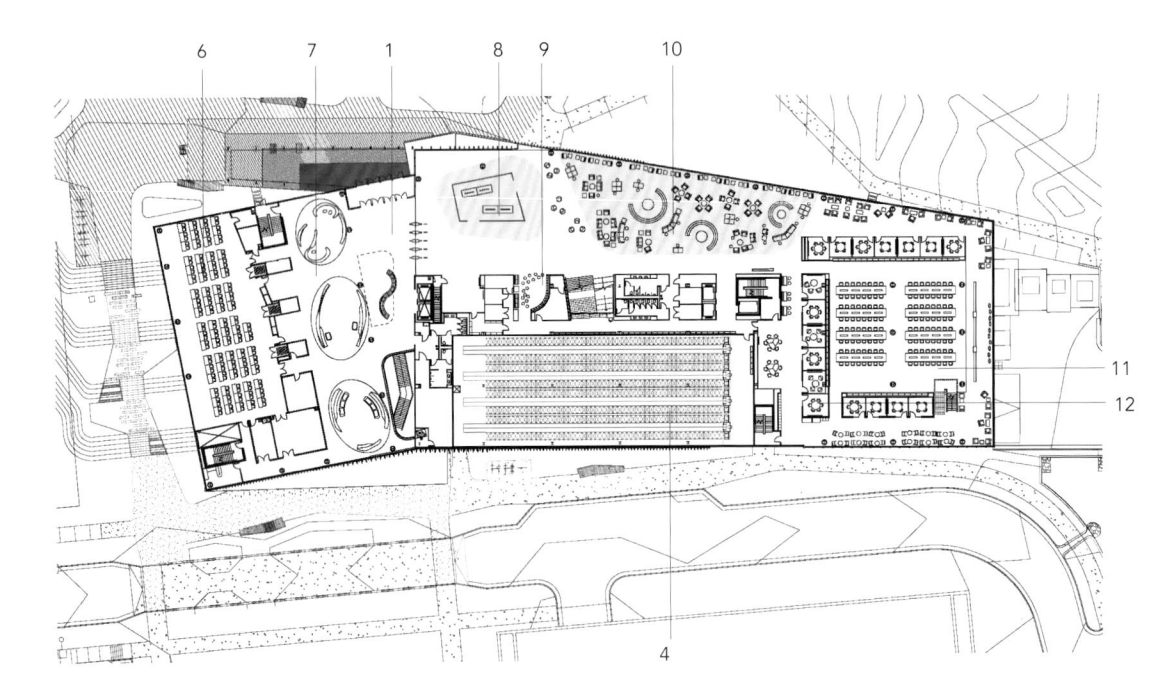

Second-floor plan

1 Lobby
2 Cafe
3 Auditorium
4 Robotic automated book delivery
5 Loading
6 Multi-purpose room
7 Gallery
8 Technology showcase
9 Immersion theatre
10 Reading lounge
11 Quiet reading room
12 Group study rooms

to supply conditioned air directly to the occupied zone. The advantages over traditional overhead systems include improved indoor air quality, thermal comfort and energy efficiency. Radiant systems can also be coupled with a geoexchange system which uses a ground source heat pump to transfer heat to or from the ground. Geoexchange systems use earth as a heat source or heat sink, and take advantage of the ground's relatively constant temperatures. There are two basic types – open and closed loop systems. Also, the systems differ based on the location and distribution of piping, where vertical systems consist of tall, vertical pipes that are 15 to 120 m (50 to 400 ft) deep. Horizontal systems are composed of pipes that run horizontally below the frost line at a depth of 1 to over 2 m (3 to 7 ft), but require a larger site than vertical systems.

The James B Hunt Jr Library, on the Centennial campus of the North Carolina State University in Raleigh, was designed by the practice Snøhetta. The building is a new library that includes forward-thinking learning environments, digital and visualisation laboratories, open and study spaces and supporting elements. The building floor plan is generally open, with stairs connecting different floors. The building also incorporates an innovative three-storey robotic automated book-retrieval system, which is capable of holding two million volumes with minimal space requirements. Visualisation and digital fabrication laboratories provide spaces for experimental research and teaching, as well as rapid prototyping and modelling. The building's facade includes an external aluminium shading system and fritted glass to reduce solar heat gain.

The building's HVAC system consists of a DOAS system with active chilled beams and radiant panels, which provide both cooling and heating. A dedicated air handler was provided for the auditorium, since it has a separate operation schedule. Demand control ventilation strategies were used to reduce the outside airflow. The lighting system includes occupancy and daylighting sensors which reduce lighting loads but also minimise internal gains associated with lighting fixtures. Different zones were incorporated into the building that allowed airflow reduction based on occupancy. CFD analysis was utilised during the design to investigate the operation of the chilled radiant system, especially in terms of modifying operating temperatures during occupied and unoccupied times. The use of chilled beams and radiant panels in the ceilings reduced the size and required capacity of the mechanical spaces, as well as the ductwork.

The NASA Sustainability Base, in Moffett Field, California – designed by William McDonough + Partners (design architect) and AECOM (architect of record) – was intended to be a net energy positive building. The building's energy demand was minimised by applying sustainable design methods, such as narrow floor plates to capitalise on daylight, energy-efficient HVAC that includes a geoexchange system and a radiant heating and cooling system, use of natural ventilation, an efficient lighting

11 Snøhetta, James B Hunt Jr Library, North Carolina State University, Raleigh, USA, 2013. Floor plans showing the building programme, which includes a library, learning environments, digital and visualisation laboratories, open and study spaces and a robotic automated book-retrieval system.

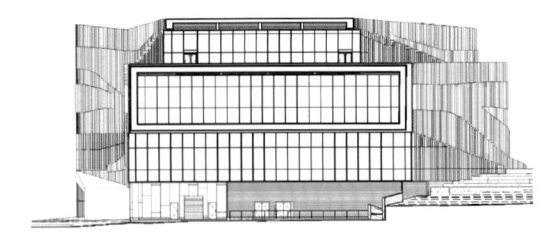

South elevation

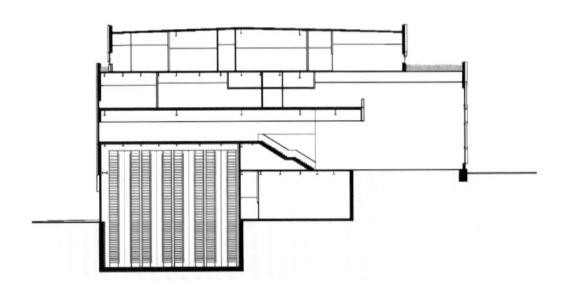

Section A-A

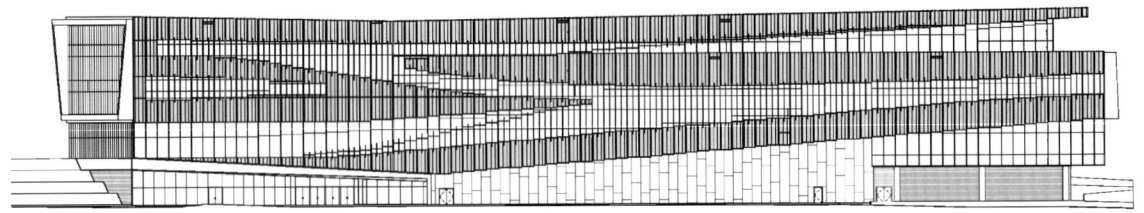

West elevation

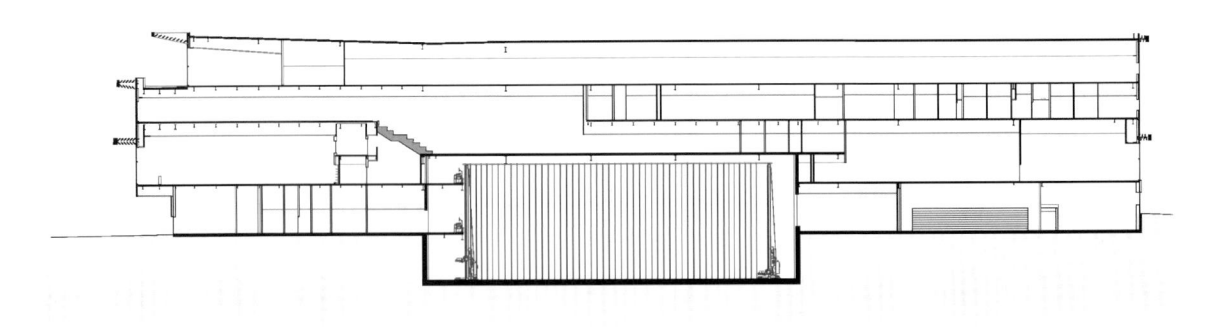

Section B-B

12 Snøhetta, James B Hunt Jr Library, North Carolina State University, Raleigh, USA, 2013. Sections and elevations demonstrate the building facade treatment, the vertical arrangement of spaces and the robotic book-retrieval system.

13 Snøhetta, James B Hunt Jr Library, North Carolina State University, Raleigh, USA, 2013. Active chilled beams and radiant panels, to provide both heating and cooling, were incorporated. The radiant panels are integrated into the ceiling. The building interior is inviting, open and fosters collaboration and interaction.

14

system and a building automation system. Several renewable energy systems were incorporated, including PV panels, fuel cells and off-site renewable power. There are 430 roof-installed PV panels – organised into 24 strings – which generate 30% of the building's electricity. Thin-film PV modules are also integrated into the horizontal overhangs, providing shade for the building's facade and generating electricity. The net positive energy is mainly achieved through fuel cells that convert natural gas and generate more electricity than the peak demand of the building. The building's two wings are separated by a courtyard to maximise natural ventilation from prevailing winds. Smart, automated windows, window shades and intelligent lighting were incorporated. The structural system consists of an exoskeleton which provides seismic stability and maximises the usable interior space. An intelligent, adaptive control system is used to optimise building operations, fault detection, maintenance and occupant comfort. The building includes more than 2,000 sensors that collect data for analysis, modelling, prediction, failure anticipation and anomaly detection.

The HVAC system combines passive techniques (a hydronic geoexchange system) and active (heat exchangers and radiant ceiling panels) to optimise energy use. The geoexchange system consists of four ground-source heat pumps, and 106 well bores with a vertical configuration. Radiant cooling panels are installed on the ceiling and use 40% less energy than typical VAV systems. Radiant heating panels are installed along the interior walls. Natural ventilation with automated windows is used to flush the air during evening hours.

As demonstrated with the previous case study, the integration of all building systems, including HVAC, lighting and the building envelope is crucial. Intelligent control of HVAC equipment and integration with all building systems is key to improving the energy efficiency of buildings.

ADVANCES IN LIGHTING
Lighting accounts for 15 to 20% of the energy usage in commercial buildings. Over the last several decades, the primary driver for research, development and technological innovations in lighting systems has been the search for more energy-efficient lighting fixtures and systems. Developments and advancements in light-emitting diode (LED) technology are currently the most promising energy-efficient solutions for lighting systems. The development of high brightness LEDs is the result of optimisation of the packaging of the diodes, since LEDs used for illumination need to be driven at higher power densities. The first high-power LEDs were manufactured from red materials, unsuitable for building applications. High-power LEDs made from blue and green materials have been developed over the last two decades, and have a much better lighting output which can be used for lighting systems in buildings. Commercial products that use high-brightness LEDs for lighting fixtures are now available and gaining popularity in the building industry as they are much more energy

14 William McDonough + Partners and AECOM, NASA Sustainability Base, Moffett Field, California, USA, 2012.
Exterior views showing the building form, exoskeletal structure and building envelope design.

15 William McDonough + Partners and AECOM, NASA Sustainability Base, Moffett Field, California, USA, 2012.
Sustainable design strategies included maximum use of daylight, a geoexchange system, a radiant heating and cooling system, natural ventilation, an efficient lighting system, a building automation system and several renewable energy sources.

16 William McDonough + Partners and AECOM, NASA Sustainability Base, Moffett Field, California, USA, 2012.
Floor plans showing the building form and spatial organisation. The building's two wings are separated by a courtyard to maximise natural ventilation.

17 William McDonough + Partners and AECOM, NASA Sustainability Base, Moffett Field, California, USA, 2012.
Radiant cooling panels are installed on the ceiling of the NASA Sustainability Base.

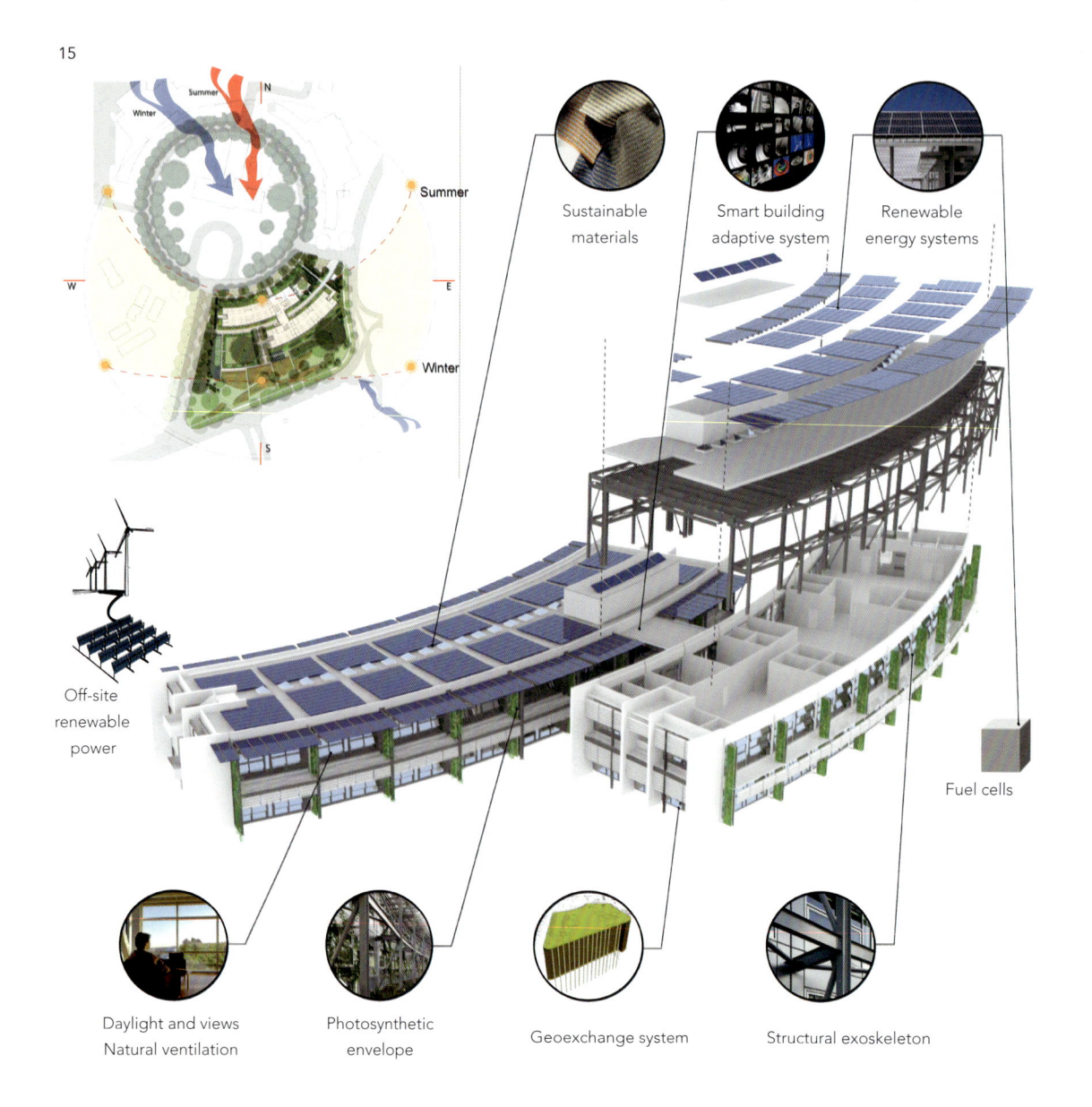

15

Sustainable materials

Smart building adaptive system

Renewable energy systems

Off-site renewable power

Fuel cells

Daylight and views
Natural ventilation

Photosynthetic envelope

Geoexchange system

Structural exoskeleton

16

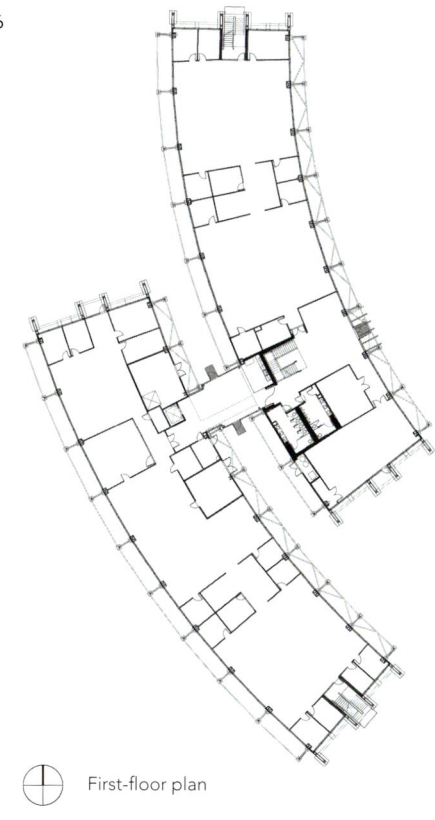

First-floor plan

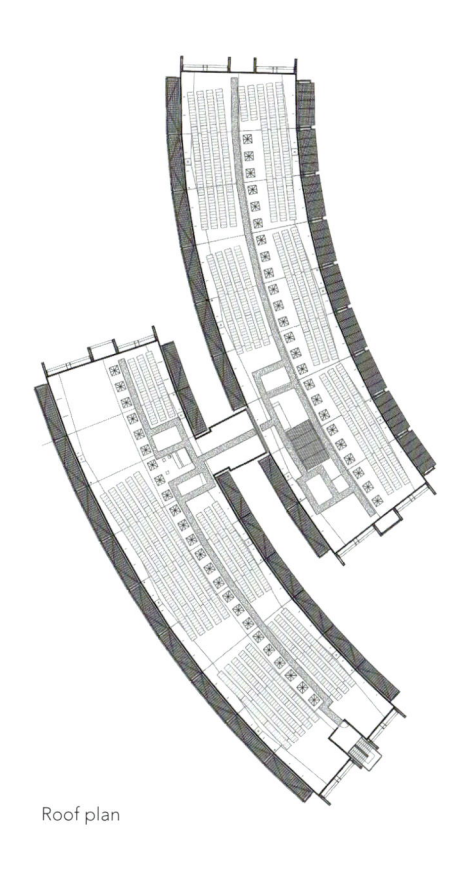

Roof plan

17

3 TECHNOLOGICAL INNOVATIONS 146-147

18 Synthesis Design + Architecture, The Groove, Bangkok, Thailand, 2013.
This building incorporates LED lighting in the facade to create a unique identity within the urban form.

efficient than traditional incandescent and fluorescent fixtures, and have significantly longer lives. LEDs are also increasingly being used in facade applications to produce 'media' facades.

The Groove is an expansion of the existing CentralWorld shopping centre in Bangkok, Thailand, designed by Synthesis Design + Architecture. The building includes enclosed retail spaces, restaurants and bars and a protected courtyard. Given the project's unique position, facing a busy road, the facade and roof create a graphic identity for the building while acting as a veil that reveals and conceals views. The primary driver of the programmatic organisation and design concept was the continuous flow of pedestrian and vehicular traffic. The facade incorporates continuous horizontal lines that change height to accommodate openings for restaurants and retail spaces, as well as terraces. The facade consists of a back-lit aluminium panel system with spherical openings, incorporating lighting and graphics. A dynamic LED backlighting system creates a unique facade glow effect during the night.

Various lighting control technologies have been developed for increased energy efficiency, including daylight harvesting, occupancy sensing, dimming, and so on. These technologies differ greatly in their input parameters, their control method, control algorithm, cost of installation, complexity of commissioning and so forth. Each of the control schemes has a unique set of factors that will affect its performance in terms of energy savings, and inevitably user acceptance.

Daylight harvesting is the most energy-efficient control strategy for spaces in perimeter zones where significant daylight is available. Dimming controls should be integrated with daylight harvesting, since lighting fixtures within perimeter zones may include photosensors, which measure available daylight and adjust the artificial lighting levels accordingly. Occupancy sensors dim or turn off the lights in a zone after the space has been vacant for a certain length of time and are the most common control strategy for lighting. Occupancy sensors employ motion-sensing techniques to detect the presence of occupants in a given range within the space. There are different types of sensors that can be employed, including passive infrared, ultrasonic, acoustic and microwave sensors. The potential lighting energy savings are estimated to be up to 50% when a proper combination of control strategies is effectively implemented. The emerging technologies in lighting control include wireless sensor and actuator networks – which have the potential to measure illuminance levels through wireless photosensors and control lighting systems – and occupancy detection using imaging.

San Mamés Stadium in Bilbao, Spain, designed by IDOM-ACXT, is a new sports complex and includes a soccer stadium, seating for 53,500 people, a museum, retail spaces and restaurants, meeting spaces and a swimming pool. The building is at the end of the expansion district of Bilbao, and its form and volume provide a

19 Synthesis Design + Architecture, The Groove, Bangkok, Thailand, 2013.
The building includes enclosed retail spaces, restaurants and bars and a protected courtyard.

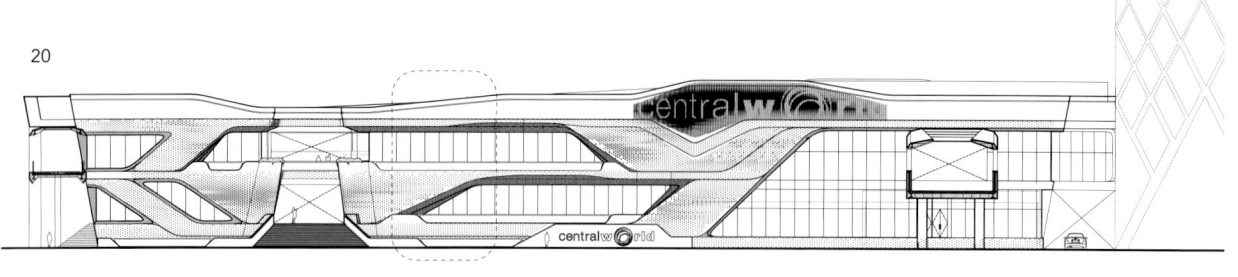

South elevation

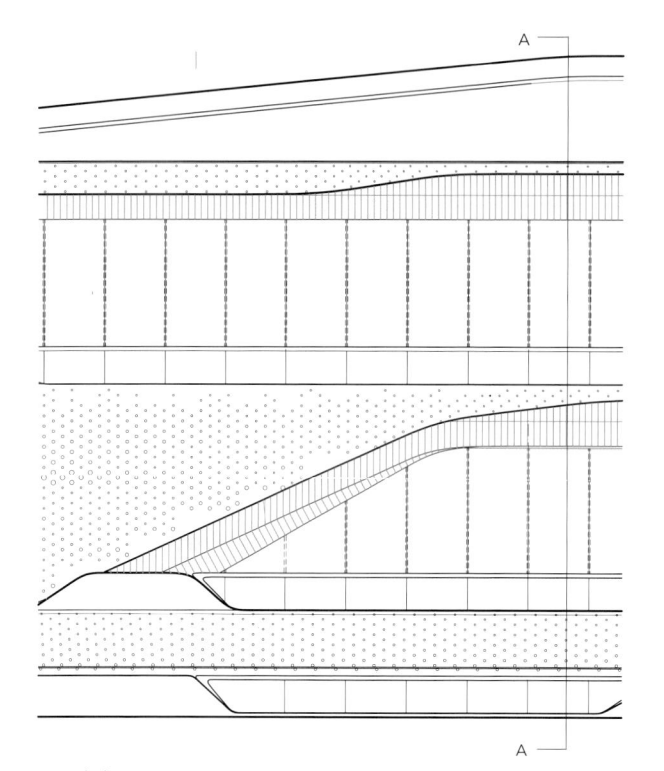

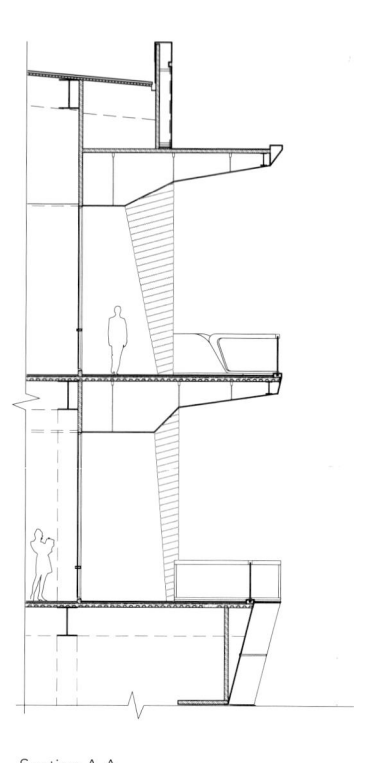

Partial elevation

Section A-A

20 Synthesis Design + Architecture, The Groove, Bangkok, Thailand, 2013.
South elevation, enlarged elevation and section of the facade system.

21 Synthesis Design + Architecture, The Groove, Bangkok, Thailand, 2013.
The building envelope creates a graphic identity for the building. The facade system incorporates continuous horizontal lines that change height to accommodate openings for restaurants, retail spaces and terraces.

22 Synthesis Design + Architecture, The Groove, Bangkok, Thailand, 2013.
The facade system consists of a back-lit aluminium panel system with spherical openings and incorporates LED lighting and graphics.

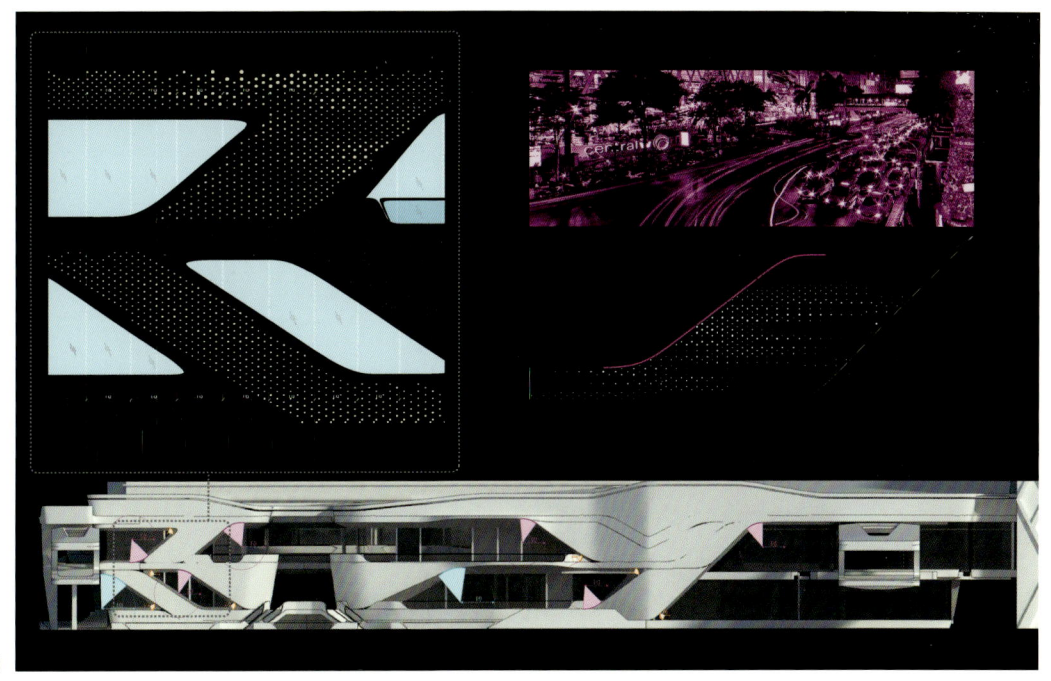

21

22

distinctive visual landmark while respecting the rest of the existing urban fabric. The building facade is composed of twisted ETFE elements, which integrate the dynamic lighting system with LED lights. The system consists of 2,500 vertical ETFE elements mounted on the facade, these are 5 m (17 ft) high and twisted at 90°. Each element is illuminated by 17 individually controlled LED elements positioned at different angles to prevent direct views. A total of 42,500 LED lights illuminate the facade, creating lighting effects and displaying media content. Lighting control systems are employed to control the lighting sequence and displayed media. The roof is formed of radial metal trusses – oriented towards the centre of the stadium – covered by white ETFE cushions that provide protection and shade the seating area.

BUILDING AUTOMATION SYSTEMS

Building automation systems (BAS) are designed to monitor building systems and components – such as HVAC, lighting and dynamic facade components – and can provide automatic control of various building systems and the interior environment when coupled with control systems. With the recent advancement in computer technologies, digital communications and controls, BAS have drastically improved and developed. Smart buildings typically use BAS for the integrated monitoring and control of assorted building elements, including HVAC maintenance and services, lighting controls, fire detection and alarms, indoor air-quality monitoring, energy supply and load management, environmental controls, security and access control.

One of the emerging approaches for the intelligent control of buildings is the integration of BAS, energy management and BIM

23 ACXT-IDOM, San Mamés Stadium, Bilbao, Spain, 2014.
The new sports complex creates a striking landmark for Bilbao.

23

24 IDOM-ACXT, San Mamés Stadium, Bilbao, Spain, 2014.
The sports complex includes a soccer stadium, seating for 53,500 people, a museum, retail spaces and restaurants, meeting spaces and a swimming pool.

25 IDOM-ACXT, San Mamés Stadium, Bilbao, Spain, 2014.
Section through the urban fabric showing the relationship between San Mamés Stadium and the surrounding urban fabric. The stadium's form and volume provide a distinctive visual urban landmark that respects the height of the neighbouring buildings.

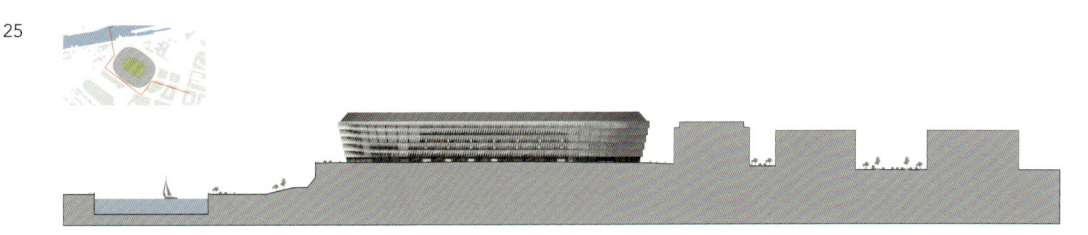

Section through the urban fabric

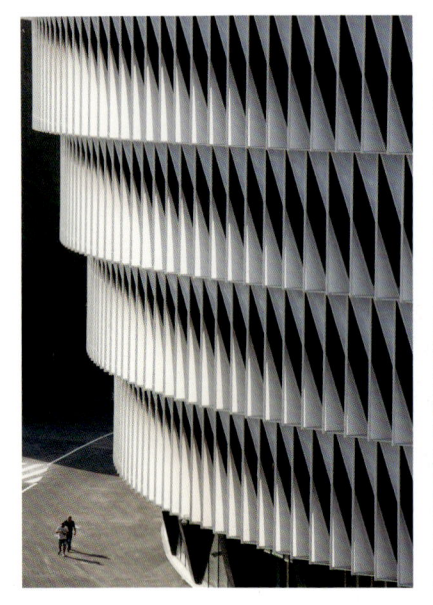

26 IDOM-ACXT, San Mamés Stadium, Bilbao, Spain, 2014.
The building facade consists of twisted ETFE elements, with an integrated LED dynamic lighting system. The system consists of 2,500 vertical ETFE elements mounted on the facade and 42,500 LED lights.

27

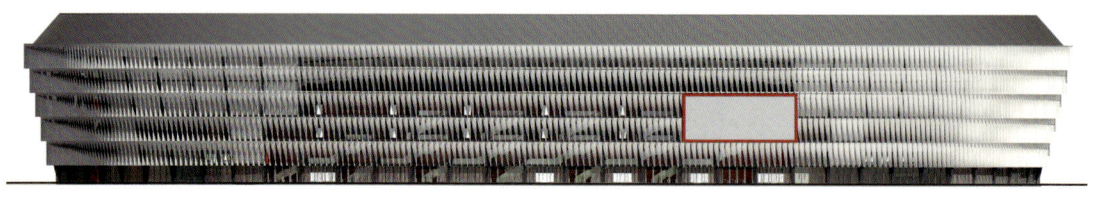

North elevation

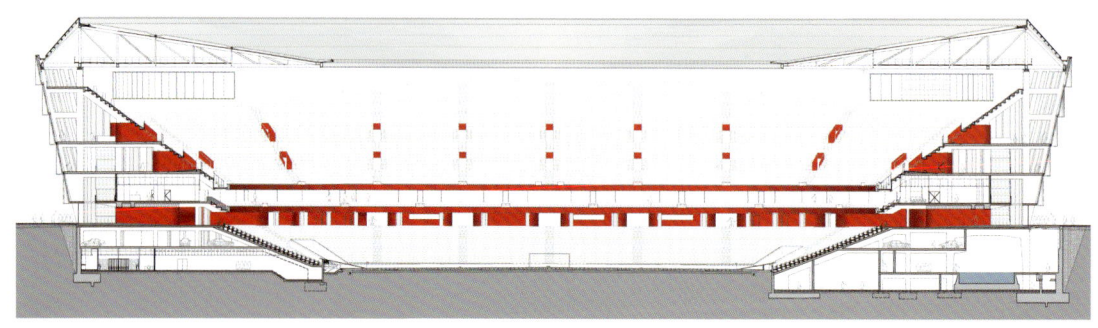

Section

28

27 IDOM-ACXT, San Mamés Stadium, Bilbao, Spain, 2014.
Elevation and section showing building envelope treatment, structure and vertical spatial arrangement.

28 IDOM-ACXT, San Mamés Stadium, Bilbao, Spain, 2014.
Dynamic lighting and media content is displayed on the facade, regulated by an advanced control system.

3 TECHNOLOGICAL INNOVATIONS 154-155

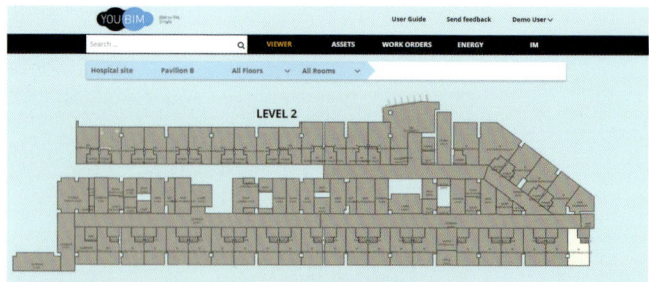

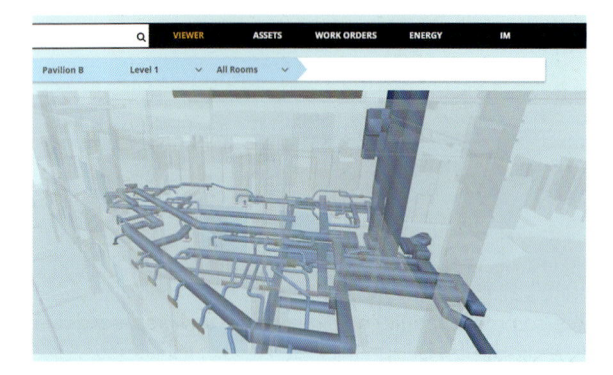

during the building operation. Building performance aspects that can be monitored within BIM may include space allocations, asset management, work orders, energy-efficiency metrics and security. This requires the integration of computerised maintenance management systems, electronic document management systems, energy management systems and BAS. Using BIM with the behavioural model of the building for predictive modelling is an emerging area of research and development currently being investigated. With this approach, what-if scenarios could be analysed to simulate a building's performance under various conditions, or how energy systems will work under different configurations. Also, with the integration of sensing technologies (occupancy and environmental sensors) and BIM-based visualisation, energy consumption can be controlled in an effective way.

PREFABRICATION AND MODULAR CONSTRUCTION
Technological advances in construction methods are influencing the design, delivery, manufacture, assembly and formation of buildings. Since building construction relies on the assemblage of a large number of components and subassemblies, it is a site-intense process that requires careful coordination, planning, quality control and execution. The degree of industrialisation measures the level of industrialisation adoption in construction, and is composed of five degrees: prefabrication, mechanisation, automation, robotics and reproduction.[3] Prefabrication is a manufacturing process that takes place in a specialised facility off-site, where different materials are joined to form a component part of the final installation. Mechanisation refers to any process where machinery is used to ease the workload of the construction

29 BIM for facility management and building controls interface.
BIM can be used for facility management to visualise the spaces, control building elements and systems, manage energy usage and improve building operation.

workers. Automation relies on the tools and machines to fully take over the tasks performed by the construction workers. Robotics depends on robots to perform a variety of construction tasks. Reproduction constitutes future construction methods that are still in research and development, which are capable of simplifying the manufacturing and assembly processes and repetitious production, such as 3D printing.

In modular construction, the major parts of a building are produced in a factory setting, and then assembled at the site. The benefits of modular construction include increased speed of construction, economy in manufacture and improved quality control.[4] Modular construction has primarily been used for mid-rise and low-rise buildings, but also has the potential to be implemented for high-rise construction. Modular pieces may include cores, infills, exterior wall panels, interior pods, and so on. Modular construction and open-building principles can be used to achieve flexibility in planning, space organisation and the interchange of components and construction.

In terms of building types, modular construction has been used on a variety of commercial buildings, healthcare facilities, academic buildings and manufacturing facilities. Modular construction is most often used for the building structure, MEP systems and exterior walls, and it improves project schedules, reduces costs and budgets, improves construction site safety and reduces construction waste.

Healthcare buildings are well suited for modular construction, since the interior layout of hospital rooms allows for efficient use of modularisation. Texas Health Harris Methodist Hospital Alliance in Fort Worth, designed by Perkins+Will, is an example of modular construction for healthcare facilities. This four-storey hospital adjoins a two-storey medical office building and was designed to accommodate two additional floors vertically for future expansions. The hospital building utilised the integrated project delivery (IPD) method and was one of the first hospital buildings in the United States delivered under the multiparty contractual agreement. Therefore, the owner, design team and contractor collaborated from the earliest stages of the design process. The key elements of the IPD process include intense team collaboration, focus on long-term-value, integrated design and construction innovation, and early inclusion of major trades and subcontractors. For this project, the two main goals were to implement the IPD process and to maximise the use of prefabrication.

During the design, BIM was used by all project members for design, coordination, information exchange and collaboration. Early input from the contractor and subcontractors fundamentally changed the process, since the focus shifted from the creation of construction documents to implementation, prefabrication, planning and assembly. The most challenging application of prefabrication was the multi-trade prefabrication of the racks in the hospital corridors. The racks combine the work of multiple

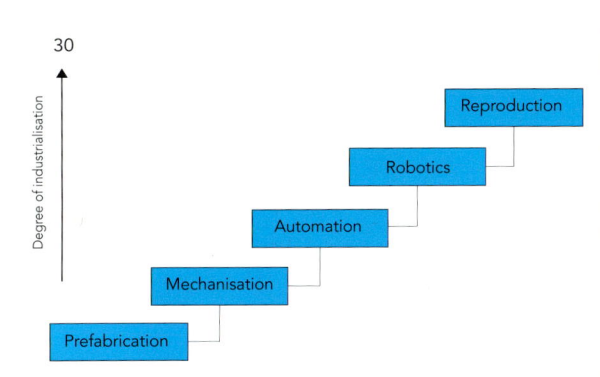

30 Diagram showing the degree of industrialisation in construction.
Five different levels (prefabrication, mechanisation, automation, robotics and reproduction) constitute industrialisation in the construction processes. Currently, the first four levels are implemented, while future research and development should focus on methods for increasing reproduction.

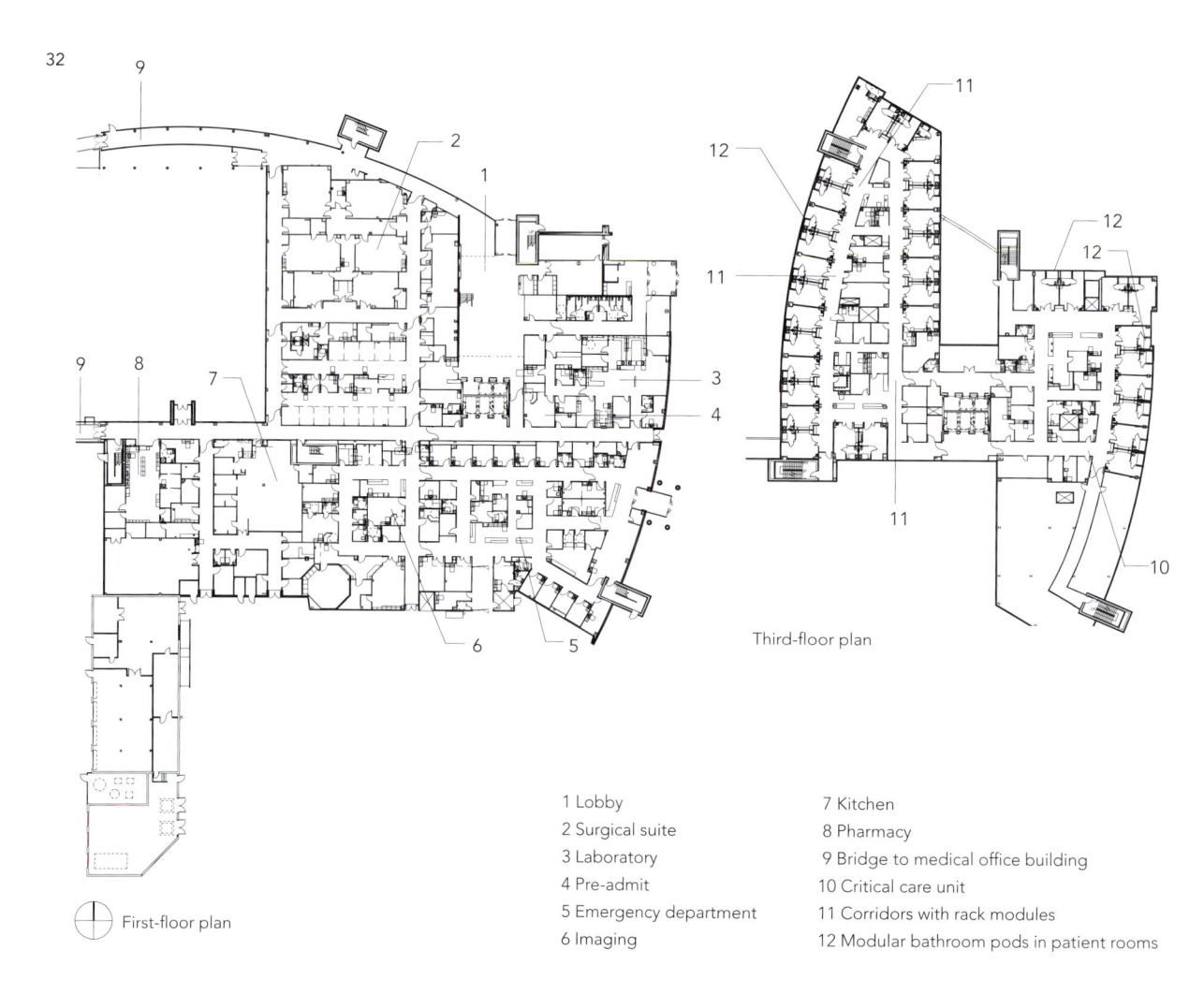

31

32

First-floor plan

Third-floor plan

1 Lobby
2 Surgical suite
3 Laboratory
4 Pre-admit
5 Emergency department
6 Imaging
7 Kitchen
8 Pharmacy
9 Bridge to medical office building
10 Critical care unit
11 Corridors with rack modules
12 Modular bathroom pods in patient rooms

trades, since they include ductwork, medical gas mains, hot-water supply and return for heating, domestic water piping, electrical conduits, communication system pathways and low-voltage systems. The production process included the development of a BIM model for the areas where the racks would be installed, fabrication of different parts and assemblage in a shop, with all the trades collaboratively coordinating the assembly. Since each rack weighs more than 1,000 kg (2,200 lbs), special lifts were developed to position the racks in place. Other prefabricated components included bathroom modules and headwalls for the patient rooms. These modular components improved the efficiency and quality of the construction and had an impact on the design, since spatial organisation and planning for prefabrication needed to occur from the initial stages of the design. The benefits for the project included schedule and cost savings, higher quality of construction and enhanced construction safety. Economic impacts included 35% cost savings for overhead racks, 25% on duct banks, 20% on wall assemblies, and significant savings for bathroom modules and patient room headwalls.

AUTOMATION IN CONSTRUCTION

Efficient automation of building production and construction has an enormous potential to transform current construction techniques. Use of BIM, prefabrication and model-based fabrication have been discussed in detail, but automated construction processes can be exploited for improved scheduling and sequencing, material tracking, assembly, and so on. The earliest research and development efforts relating to automated construction methods were initiated in the late 1970s, primarily in Japan. Over the last three decades, automated construction techniques have advanced and become more common.[5] However, there is still a lot of potential for the wider adoption of automated systems in construction.

There are four major categories of automated systems in construction: material manipulators, placing and finishing systems, remote controlled and sensing systems, and integrated automation systems. Material manipulators have been developed as a solution for placing oversized heavy equipment and components within the construction site. They are generally guided manually, but automated guided vehicles have been adapted for use on construction projects, since they provide the autonomous transportation of building components to the appropriate location on site. Placing and finishing systems improve the quality of construction and safety, and have been used for a variety of building components. For example, automated trowelling machines have been used for concrete levelling and finishing. Remote-controlled and sensing systems allow remote visualisation and control of construction machinery, and often combine GPS systems, tracking, stereoscopic images, lasers, virtual reality and various types of sensors and controls.[6] For example, radio-frequency identification (RFID) sensors can be used to track and monitor the progress of construction, to track the materials and equipment, and to provide visualisation for component status tracking.

31 Perkins+Will, Texas Health Harris Methodist Hospital Alliance, Fort Worth, USA, 2012.
This building is an example of modular construction for healthcare facilities.

32 Perkins+Will, Texas Health Harris Methodist Hospital Alliance, Fort Worth, USA, 2012.
Floor plans showing the building organisation, spatial layout and the location of prefabricated elements (prefabricated corridor rack modules and bathroom pods in patient rooms).

33

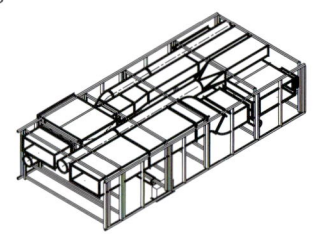

Ductwork

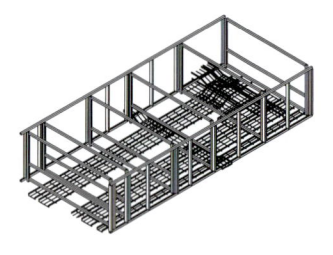

Containment

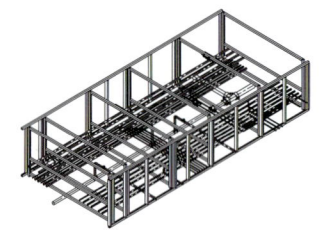

Pipework

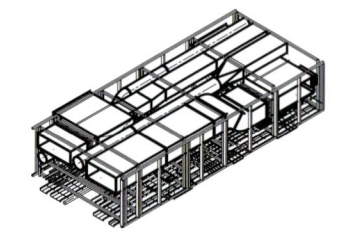

All services

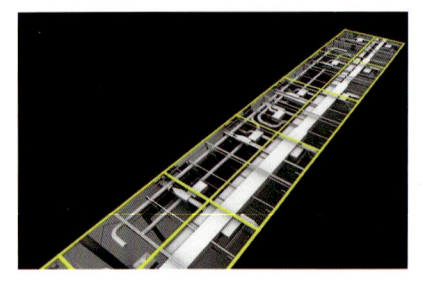

34

33 Perkins+Will, Texas Health Harris Methodist Hospital Alliance, Fort Worth, USA, 2012. Corridor rack modules contain all ductwork, medical gas mains, hot-water supply and return for heating, domestic water piping, electrical conduits, communication system pathways and low-voltage systems.

34 Perkins+Will, Texas Health Harris Methodist Hospital Alliance, Fort Worth, USA, 2012. Prefabrication and assembly of corridor rack modules.

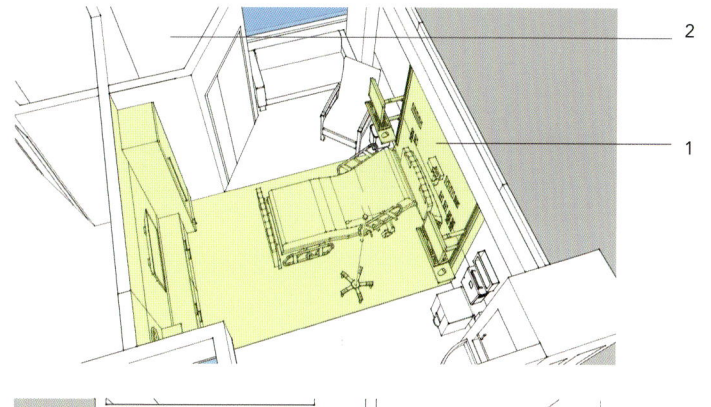

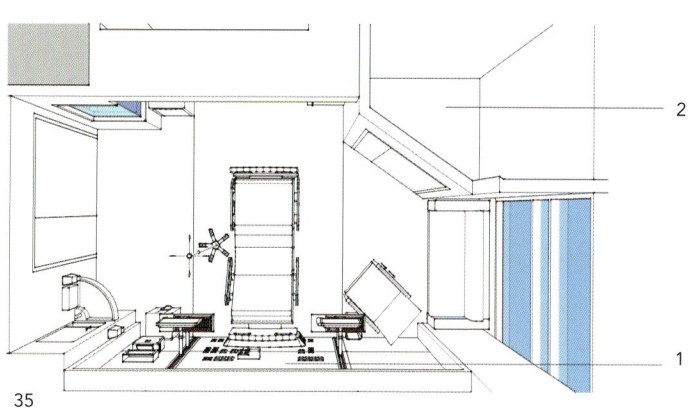

1 Prefabricated head wall
2 Prefabricated bathroom pod

35 Perkins+Will, Texas Health Harris Methodist Hospital Alliance, Fort Worth, USA, 2012. Diagram indicating location of prefabricated elements in patient rooms.

36 Perkins+Will, Texas Health Harris Methodist Hospital Alliance, Fort Worth, USA, 2012. Prefabricated bathroom pods, transportation and installation.

37 Perkins+Will, Texas Health Harris Methodist Hospital Alliance, Fort Worth, USA, 2012. Interior view of a patient room.

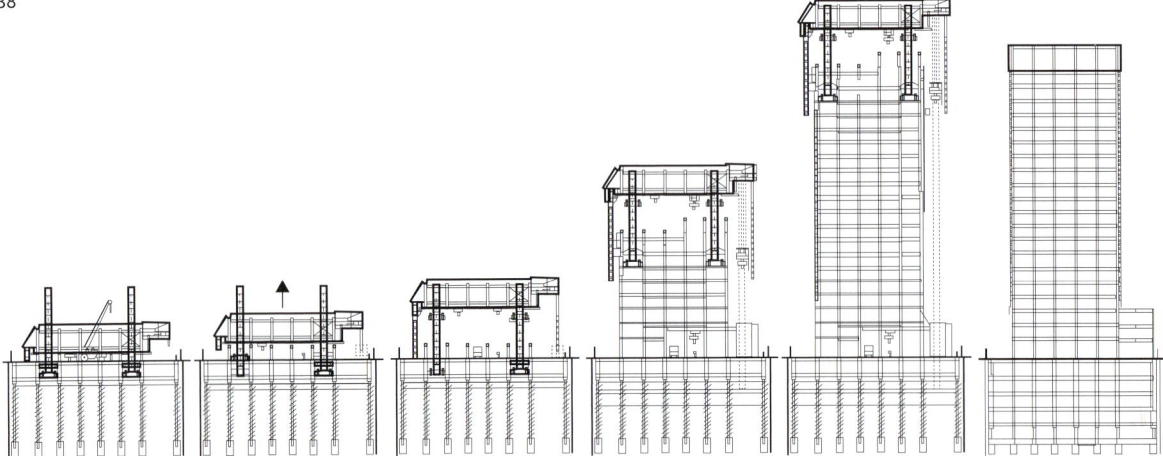

Integrated automation systems automate assembly operations. Achieved by building a vertical moving factory site – which includes automated logistics, positioning of structural elements, automated welding and real-time process monitoring – the system can be located on the highest floor of the building and moves upwards during the construction process. This construction technique is suitable for medium-rise and high-rise construction in tight urban areas, where construction sites are limited.

ROBOTICS IN CONSTRUCTION
Within a relatively short time, industrial robots have turned from exclusive tools for specialised industries to multifunctional machines for a wide range of uses, including architecture and construction. The demands for these applications significantly differ from how robots are used in other industries – such as the automotive industry – since construction requires a wide range of robotic devices, the ability to move within the construction site and the necessity to operate alongside human construction workers and autonomously for different tasks.

The introduction of the first robot that used the now-standard set-up of six electric motor-driven axes was nearly forty years ago. Since then, robots have become faster, more efficient, accurate, affordable and accessible. New interfaces, sensors and strategies that enable accessible programming have also been developed. Currently, robotic construction is used for site excavations, pipe installations, panel handling and installations, painting, concrete plastering, brick handling and laying, curtain-wall installations and demolition.[7]

The Building Realization and Robotics research team at the Technical University of Munich has been investigating the use of robotics for the construction industry. The team leader was also involved in research at the University of Tokyo, related to the solid material assembling system (SMAS), used for assembling reinforced-masonry units. SMAS processes standard building blocks

– consisting of precast concrete blocks and cross-shaped steel bars within each component – to construct structural walls.[8] The building blocks are positioned automatically by the robot and do not require conventional bonding. After the blocks are positioned, steel bars are connected by the robot with mechanical connectors and concrete is grouted from the top of the wall. Experiments have been carried out to test the operation and structural wall construction. The research team leader was also involved in the development of the robot construction system for computer-integrated construction (ROCCO), as part of an EU Esprit project. This mobile robotic system integrates the design and construction of masonry units and enables fully automated masonry construction on-site. It allows for data generation for the prefabrication and customisation of masonry blocks, the layout on the construction site and the automatic robot construction.[9] Based on the CAD representation of the building, the walls are divided automatically into the masonry units. Then, the optimal working positions of the robot are calculated automatically, as well as the arrangements of the blocks. The construction and assembly is automatically performed by the robot; however, controls can still be managed by the construction worker. The user interface is graphically interactive and allows construction workers to partially reprogram robots in order to deal with the uncertainty during the construction process.

Although robotic construction and automation are increasingly used, there are still a lot of opportunities for development and adoption. The primary reason for slow implementation is the lack of economic justification for wider adoption in construction – in the past, the wide use of construction robotic technologies in the building industry was cost-prohibitive. However, the three primary reasons for the use of robotic construction techniques and automation are improved safety, increased productivity and improved quality of construction. As the costs of automated systems and robotic technologies are decreasing, it is expected that there will be wider implementation of these advanced construction techniques. There are two basic methods for wider adoption – integration of robotics with existing construction techniques, and total redesign of traditional methods to adapt them for robots and automated processes.

SMART AND RESPONSIVE BUILDINGS
Smart and responsive buildings respond to different physical and environmental stimuli, and adapt their functioning and behaviour. They have performance characteristics that allow them to sense changes in the environment and adapt accordingly, including real-time sensing, climate-adaptive elements, smart materials and building automation systems. They can adjust and learn over time, depending on the changing environmental conditions (air temperature, humidity levels, daylight levels and solar radiation), preferences of building occupants, energy consumption, and so on. There are two basic categories: the first includes smart and responsive buildings that contain intelligent elements, which act as isolated systems, such as responsive building facade and dynamic shading elements; the second category includes buildings

38 Diagram showing automated high-rise construction.
This diagram indicates the vertical movement of the integrated automation system on a high-rise construction.

39 Solid material assembling system (SMAS).
This system is used for the robotic assembly of reinforced-masonry units.

40 Robot construction system for computer-integrated construction (ROCCO).
This system enables fully automated masonry construction.

that have multiple integrated systems that sense changes in the environment, communicate and adapt as a unified entity. For example, integrated intelligent systems that include responsive building facades, HVAC systems, lighting and BAS that monitor and control the functionalities of all subcomponents are the basis of holistic smart buildings. Over the last two decades, the majority of applications have been within the first category. However, ongoing research and development is currently focusing on the second category, and investments are increasing for technologies and applications that may transform the future of responsive and intelligent buildings.[10, 11]

Responsive building envelopes have seen significant progress, with different systems commercially available. The primary goal for most of these systems is to change and adapt their configuration in response to external environmental conditions, mainly solar radiation, to block solar rays, prevent overheating or glare, or allowing natural light and passive heating. A system consisting of an insulated glazing unit, a series of stacked metal panels with perforated patterns, an actuator and a motor is commercially available, and it creates a dynamic facade element that controls solar heat gain and light as the position of the individual panels changes. Another system is available that is composed of an insulated glass unit with a series of movable transparent panels with ceramic frit. This can be used to control transparency, transmit light, and for solar gain, privacy and views.

The North House project was developed by an interdisciplinary team of researchers and students at the University of Waterloo, Ryerson University and Simon Fraser University for the United States Department of Energy's 2009 Solar Decathlon. One of the primary goals was to investigate design-responsive systems capable of adapting to changing environmental, energy and occupant demands.[12] Also, the objective was to design and prototype a high performance single-family residential building for mass-customised housing, suitable for cold climates. The

41 University of Waterloo, Ryerson University and Simon Fraser University, North House, Waterloo, Canada, 2009.
This building, designed and developed by an interdisciplinary team of researchers and students from several academic institutions, is a net-positive energy dwelling that incorporates a responsive building envelope and advanced control systems.

house, designed to perform as a net-positive energy dwelling, incorporated renewable energy sources as building-integrated and building-applied photovoltaics.[13] The house also had a responsive, high-performance building envelope that adapted to changing environmental conditions. Two systems were used for energy management, automation and control: central home automation server (CHAS) and adaptive living interface system (ALIS).

The north facade primarily consists of opaque elements with high thermal resistance, while the east, south and west facades were built using transparent assembly components with movable exterior shading. The floor-to-ceiling curtain-wall system with custom-designed wood frame and quadruple insulated glazing units provides very high thermal resistance, but also allows passive solar heating. Automated active exterior shading consists of motorised horizontal aluminium blinds, attached by vertical tension members to the structure of the facade. Motorised interior blinds were used to diffuse daylight, and custom fabric diffuser panels installed on the ceiling transmit natural light deep into the interior. PCMs, as a salt-hydrate solution contained in polypropylene panels, were embedded within the floor's timber-frame assembly to provide passive thermal regulation for the interior space by storing latent heat energy and reducing cooling loads.

A customised CHAS was developed to control and manage all building systems, and to enhance energy performance. It optimises available energy flows based on the operation of different systems, sensor readings and exterior and interior environmental conditions. It interfaces and coordinates seven systems: HVAC, domestic hot water, exterior shades, interior blinds, lighting, energy monitoring and the ALIS. Exterior sensors were on the roof, and interior sensors were embedded above the interior fabric ceiling. Both provide continuous real-time data to the CHAS, and a control algorithm allows CHAS to make intelligent decisions based on real-time inputs and previous system states. For example, CHAS determines the operation of the exterior shades as a function of the interior and exterior air temperatures, available solar irradiation, exterior wind speed and the detected position of the sun. Based on sensor readings, the system determines whether solar-heat harvesting or solar-heat rejection modes should be utilised. CHAS also determines the operation of the HVAC system in conjunction with the exterior shades to maximise energy efficiency. Two computers are used for the CHAS: the HVAC system is controlled by an embedded PC (that collects sensor data and coordinates heat pumps, circulation pumps and fans), and a touch-screen panel PC enabling the occupant to prioritise system goals and receive performance feedback in a range of formats, while allowing for system override on demand. Energy monitoring measures energy consumption of all systems, as well as energy production of the PVs, and the data is displayed for building occupants. The ALIS enables building occupants to set predefined operation modes, to override the system and to operate the house according to their needs and lifestyles. It includes intuitive graphical touch-screen interfaces and

42

1 Automated exterior aluminium shades
2 Wood framing
3 Thermally inert rubber mullion cap
4 Quadruple insulated glazing unit
5 BIPV panels
6 Interior shades
7 Floor panels with integrated PCMs
8 Fabric diffuser ceiling

42 University of Waterloo, Ryerson University and Simon Fraser University, North House, Waterloo, Canada, 2009.
A curtain-wall system with custom-designed wood frame and quadruple-insulated glazing units provides very high thermal resistance for the east, west and south facades, but also allows passive solar heating. The automated exterior shading elements are motorised aluminium horizontal blinds. Motorised interior blinds diffuse daylight within the interior space, as well as the custom interior fabric soffit. PCMs are integrated into the floor for passive thermal regulation.

43 University of Waterloo, Ryerson University and Simon Fraser University, North House, Waterloo, Canada, 2009.
CHAS controls and manages all building systems and enhances energy performance. It consists of exterior and interior sensors, control algorithms and energy metering.

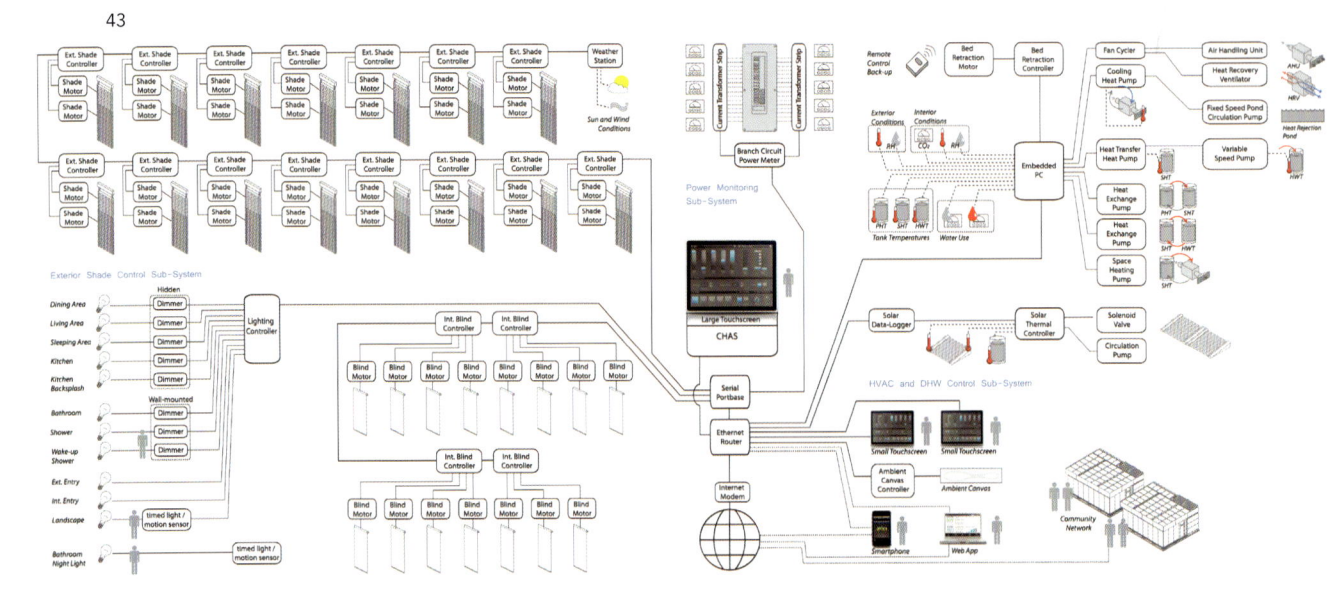

43

Lighting controls   Interior blinds controls   Central controls   ALIS

44 University of Waterloo, Ryerson University and Simon Fraser University, North House, Waterloo, Canada, 2009.

ALIS offers building occupants the ability to set predefined operation modes, to override the system and to operate the house according to their needs and lifestyles. It includes intuitive graphical touch screen interfaces, and allows occupants to monitor building performance, receive feedback and override individual systems.

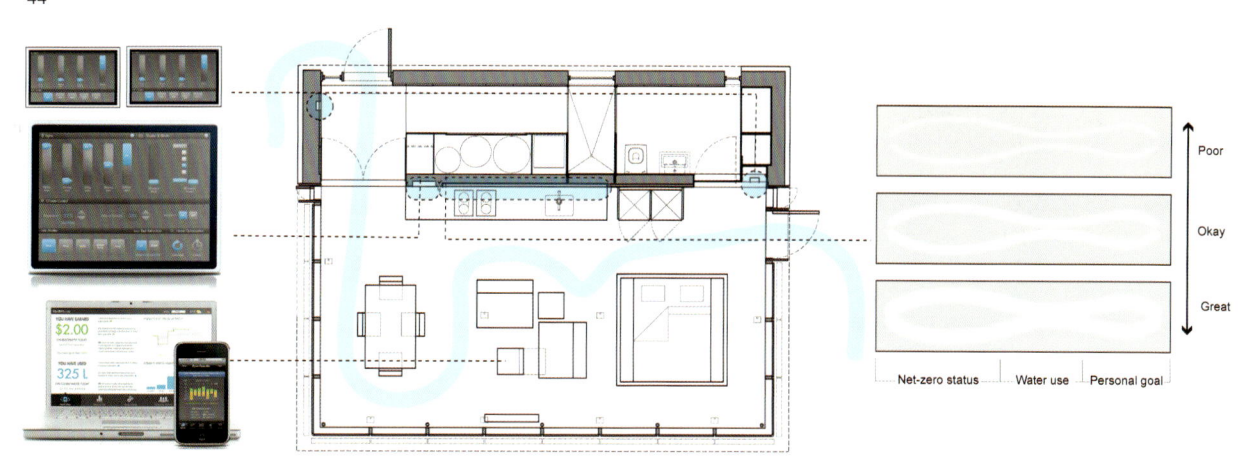

Locations of displays for ALIS and performance feedback

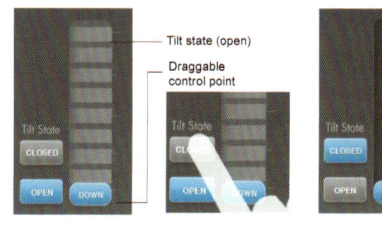

Interfacing and controls

3 TECHNOLOGICAL INNOVATIONS 166-167

functions beyond automated controls since occupants can monitor performance, receive feedback and override individual systems.

CONCLUSION: THE INTEGRATION OF ADVANCED TECHNOLOGIES IN DESIGN AND CONSTRUCTION

As we have seen in this chapter, advanced building technologies and construction methods are having an impact on design processes, delivery methods and building construction. Developments in building systems, facades, HVAC and lighting, and building automation systems are offering new strategies for the design and operation of energy-efficient, high-performance, responsive buildings. Also, prefabrication, modular construction, robotics and automation are influencing the way that building components are manufactured and assembled, as well as whole-building construction techniques. We have reviewed multiple case studies and demonstrations in this chapter, which outline specific design and construction techniques, ranging from innovative facades, building systems and their integration, to robotics and intelligent buildings. The challenges – which many design, engineering and construction firms are currently facing – are to design better performing, energy-efficient buildings that use less in the way of resources, but deliver and construct them faster and cost-effectively. The solutions should be based on smarter design processes, where research, enhanced collaboration between all stakeholders and throughout all stages of the design, and design and construction technologies are utilised to address these challenges. Therefore, the next chapter focuses on the organisation and operation of innovative practices, the role of research in design, integrated project delivery, economic impacts and risk management.

REFERENCES

1 Ajla Aksamija, *Sustainable Facades: Design Methods for High-Performance Building Envelopes*, John Wiley & Sons (Hoboken, NJ), 2013.
2 Ibid.
3 Richard Roger-Bruno, 'Industrialised Building Systems: Reproduction before Automation and Robotics', *Automation in Construction*, Vol 14, No 4, 2005, pp 441–51.
4 Harvey Bernstein, 'Prefabrication and Modularization: Increasing Productivity in the Construction Industry', in John Gudgel, Donna Laquidara-Carr (eds), Smart Report, McGraw-Hill Construction, 2011.
5 Edmundas Kazimieras Zavadskas, 'Automation and Robotics in Construction: International Research and Achievements', *Automation in Construction*, Vol 19, 2010, pp 286–90.
6 Pentti Vähä, Tapio Heikkilä, Pekka Kilpeläinen, Markku Järviluoma and Ernesto Gambao, 'Extending Automation of Building Construction – Survey on Potential Sensor Technologies and Robotic Applications', *Automation in Construction*, Vol 36, 2013, pp 168–78.
7 Chang-soo Han, 'Human–Robot Cooperation

Technology: An Ideal Midway Solution Heading Toward the Future of Robotics and Automation in Construction', *Proceedings of the 28th International Association for Automation and Robotics in Construction (ISARC) Conference*, Seoul, Korea, 2011, pp 13–18.

8 Thomas Bock and Thomas Linner, *Robot-Oriented Design: Design and Management Tools for the Deployment of Automation and Robotics in Construction*, Cambridge University Press (New York), 2015.

9 Thomas Bock and Thomas Linner, *Robotic Industrialization – Automation and Robotic Technologies for Customized Component, Module, and Building Prefabrication*, Cambridge University Press (New York), 2015.

10 Shengwei Wang, *Intelligent Buildings and Building Automation*, Spon Press (Abingdon, Oxon), 2010.

11 James Sinopoli, *Smart Building Systems for Architects, Owners, and Builders*, Butterworth-Heinemann (Burlington, MA), 2010.

12 Geoffrey Thün and Kathy Velikov, 'North House: Climate Responsive Envelope and Controls Systems', in Franca Trubiano (ed), *Design and Construction of High Performance Homes: Building Envelopes, Renewable Energies and Integrated Practice*, Routledge (London), 2012, pp 265–82.

13 Geoffrey Thün and Kathy Velikov, 'North House: Prototyping Climate Responsive Envelope and Control Systems', *Perkins+Will Research Journal*, Vol 5, No 1, 2013, pp 39–54.

IMAGES

Opening image © Rob Ley Studio/Photography by Serge Hoeltschi; figures 1, 10, 30 and 38 © Ajla Aksamija; figure 2 © Greenovate Europe EEIG; figure 3 Courtesy Sean Godsell Architects, Earl Carter; figures 4 and 5 Courtesy Sean Godsell Architects; table 1 © Ajla Aksamija; figure 6 © Dico si Tiganas, photo Cosmin Dragomir and Alexandra Bendea; figures 7 and 8 © Dico si Tiganas, Florin Dico, Alexandrina Kiss, Bogdan Dico, Șerban Țigânaș, Camelia Gâz and Diana Edițoiu; figures 9 and 13 © Arsalan Abbasi; figures 11 and 12 © Snøhetta; figures 14 and 17 © Cesar Rubio, courtesy William McDonough + Partners; figures 15 and 16 © William McDonough + Partners; figures 18, 19, 20, 21 and 22 © Synthesis Design + Architecture; figures 23, 24, 26 and 28 © IDOM, Photographer Aitor Ortiz; figures 25 and 27 © IDOM; figure 29 © YouBIM, LLC; figures 31 and 37 © Perkins + Will, photo Charles Davis Smith; figures 32, 33, 34, 35 and 36 © Texas Health Resources-Owner, Perkins+Will-Architect and The Beck Group-General Contractor; figures 39 and 40 © T. Bock; figure 41 © Geoffrey Thün, 2009; figures 42, 43 and 44 © RVTR/Team North, 2009

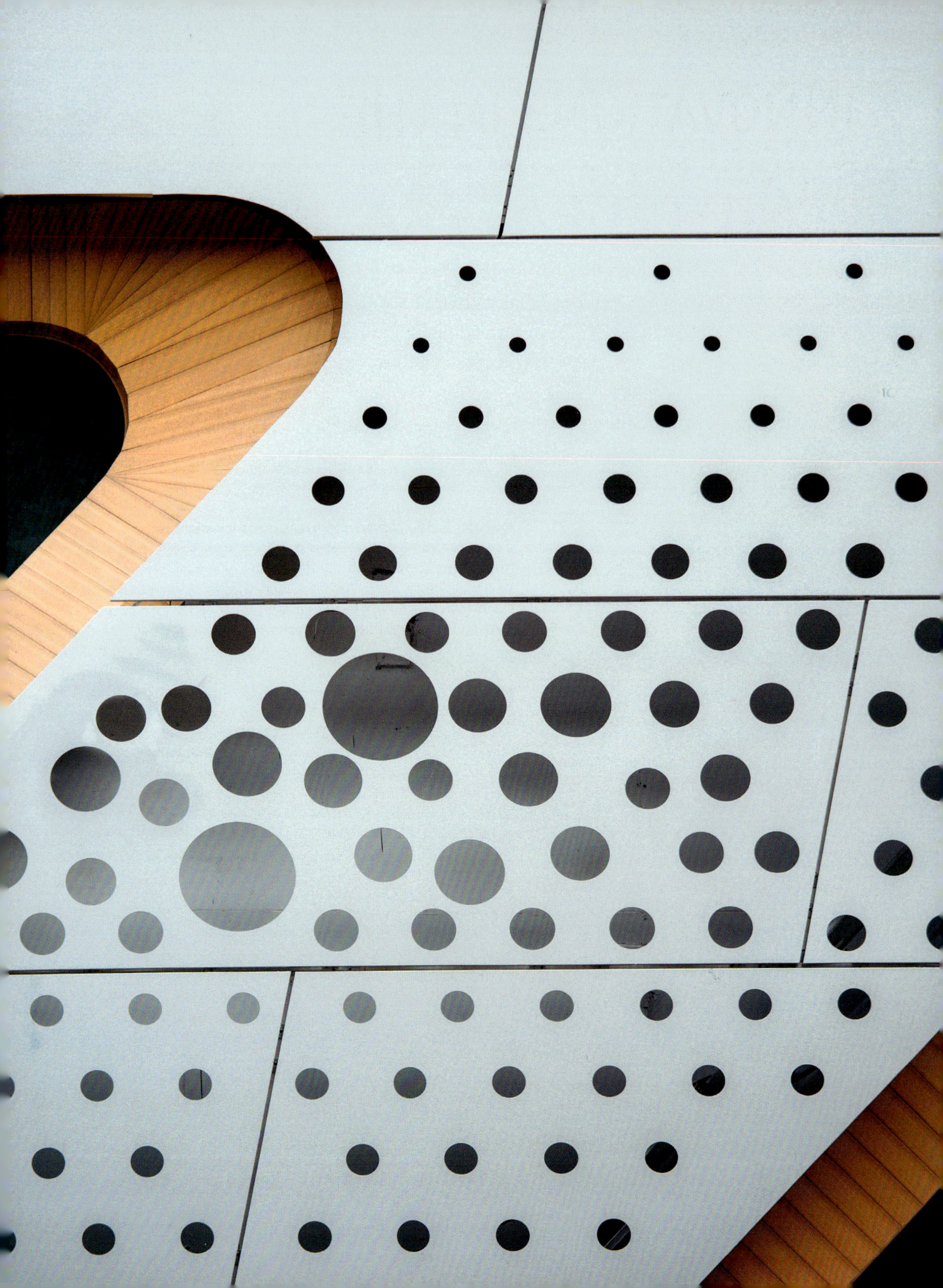

4 INNOVATIONS IN THE DESIGN PROCESS AND ARCHITECTURAL PRACTICE

In earlier chapters, we have seen that innovation affects products (buildings, physical spaces or objects in an architectural context), services (operation, interaction with clients, building occupants and constituents) and process, which refers to the design process and practice. This chapter focuses on services and process, since firms' culture, organisation and operations greatly influence innovation, specifically management, research and development, financial aspects, and risks.

Innovative design practices support organisational change, incorporate integrated design methods, integrate research and development into their operations, embrace technological change, and improve employee performance, thus increasing business performance. The key aspect is that the management must also support innovation, since traditional management of architectural firms is often driven by models whose priority is not creativity and innovation, but the profitability of the firm. Innovative firms should set the context, create a strategy and goals, guide the process of innovation and welcome change. The role of management therefore, becomes essential to providing a work environment where innovation is welcome. But, what are the drivers for innovation? Our understanding remains limited, despite numerous publications over the last few decades.[1] It is essential for every firm and organisation to determine specific drivers, motives and goals in order to stimulate innovation. This chapter provides an overview and recommendations for establishing a culture that supports and welcomes innovation, determining motives and goals, establishing operational models, integrating research and development, considering financial aspects and economics and managing risks in innovative practice.

MOTIVES AND GOALS FOR INNOVATION

Setting up motives and goals for innovative design practice should be a process that every creative firm undertakes. But the following aspects must be taken into consideration and clearly defined to establish a culture of innovation:

- Strategy: the corporate strategy, including mission, goals, vision and core meaning should be determined, where specific components that affect innovative areas of the practice are defined.
- Expression: the identity of the firm and the way that it is

recognised and distinguished from other firms is essential.
- Value: the firm should establish the value of services and design outcomes, both tangible and intangible.
- Engagement: the firm should determine how it engages, internally and externally, with clients and constituents and how its actions and services have an impact on society.

Architectural firms must adapt continuously to complex and changing conditions. They can survive and thrive in changing market conditions only if they are able to respond to change. However, the motives and goals should be identified in such a way that the changing market conditions do not have an impact on the core values and strategy. The skills and services, design processes, project delivery methods and technologies might change and adapt. In order to deliver value, architectural firms should demonstrate the following characteristics within the context of innovation:

- Inquiry.
- Integration of design, methods and technology.
- Analysis.
- Research-based design.
- Technical aptitude.
- Communication and dissemination.

Motives, goals and values should reflect these characteristics and concepts, since they implicitly describe the culture and distinct nature of architectural practices.

ORGANISATION AND ROLES

Creating an environment that fosters innovation, the exchange of ideas, research and development, creative thinking, continuing education and experimentation is essential for innovative architectural practices, regardless of the size of the firm. However, organisational structure has an impact on the culture of the firm as well as its operation. There are three basic categories of firms based on the operational models: strong delivery firms, strong service firms and strong idea firms.[2] These typologies are intensely influenced by a firm's values. The strong delivery firms are organised for efficiency and rely on standard solutions. They tend to have a strong formal structure and stable working environment, and often specialise in specific building types. The design processes and production are standardised. The strong service firms are organised for service and have a highly dynamic internal environment that allows changes to managerial structure. This allows the firms to respond to the different needs of the clients, and they typically cover a wider range of building types. Strong idea firms tend to focus primarily on conceptual processes and design thinking, but the organisational structure is flexible. They provide unique results, and standard solutions are rarely considered since clients typically employ these types of firms for a unique project. Architectural firms fit within these categories, and may operate within two or three categories simultaneously. It is necessary to find a balance between a firm's culture, underlying

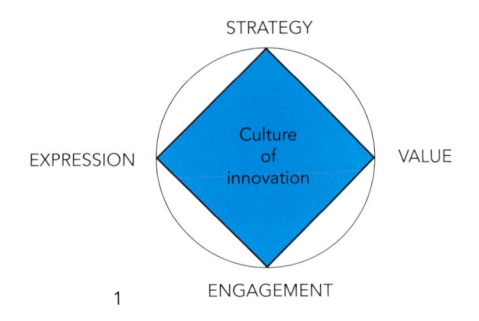

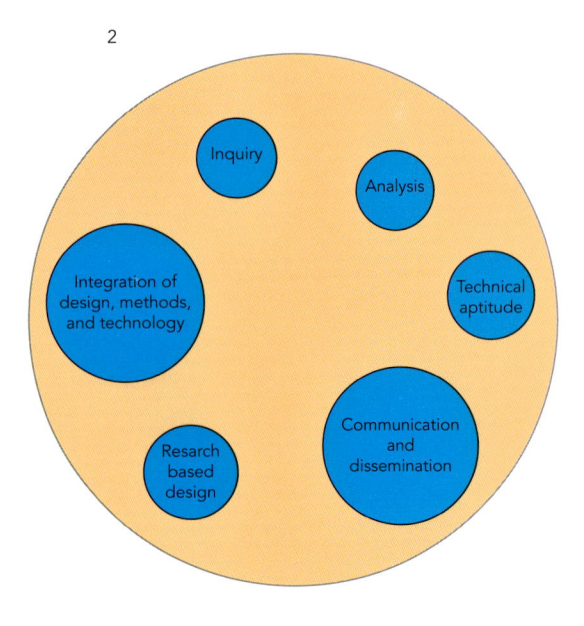

3

Strong delivery   Strong service   Strong idea

1 Culture of innovation.
In order to establish a culture of innovation, firms and organisations must establish and define specific goals and motives, including strategy, expression, value and engagement.

2 Characteristics of innovative firms.
Innovative firms invest in research and development and incorporate the results of these efforts with design, integrate advanced design technologies into their operation, base their operation on analysis, inquiry and technical aptitude and disseminate results.

3 Different types of organisational models for architectural firms.
Strong delivery firms are organised for efficiency and rely on standard solutions. Strong service firms are organised for service and have a highly dynamic internal environment that allows changes to managerial structure. Strong idea firms tend primarily to focus on conceptual processes and design thinking, but the organisational structure is flexible. Architectural firms may operate in two or three categories simultaneously.

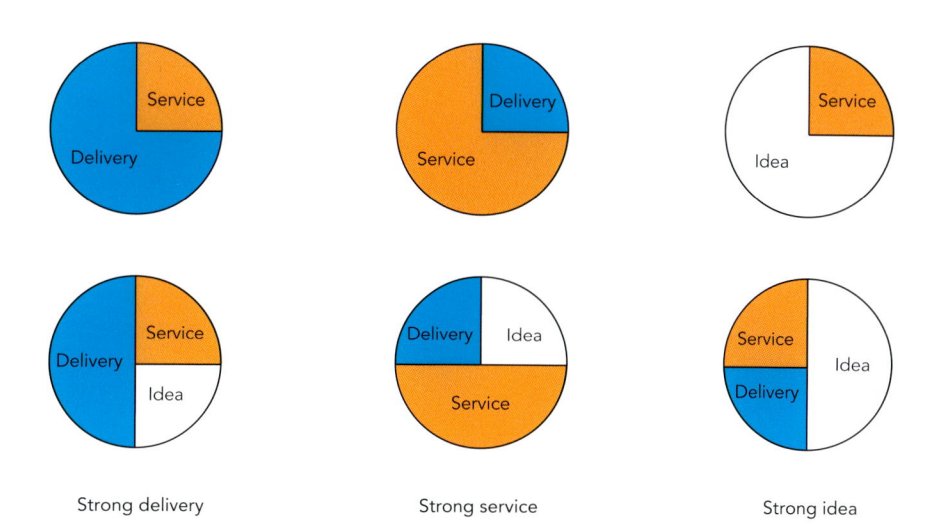

values and organisational model. The cultural environment and organisational model are important to achieve the best design work, but also for attracting and retaining new talents and clients. Innovative firms nurture success, openness and flexibility, internal communication and knowledge dissemination, professionalism, risk-taking, responsibility of employees, appreciation of employees, as well as collaboration. Therefore, the organisational structure and management should cultivate these qualities.

The roles in innovative firms are also shifting. Traditionally, architectural firms have been organised according to the types of activities and project stages. Design, project management and technical teams are the three basic pillars for any project: design teams tend to be primarily involved during conceptual and schematic design phases; project managers are involved from the beginning to the end stages, with varying levels of responsibility during different design phases; and technical teams are primarily involved during design development, construction documentation and construction administration. Changing design processes and technologies are influencing this paradigm, requiring more integration and collaboration during all design phases. Traditional roles are blurred in innovative practices, since improved collaboration between project team members is necessary. Besides internal collaboration, an integrated design process that involves architectural, engineering, fabrication and construction disciplines from the beginning of the project is also a key aspect for innovative practices. The complexity of the projects, economic drivers and technological changes are the principal factors for integrated project delivery.

Besides design and engineering disciplines, innovative firms often involve team members or consultants from other disciplines, including among others computer scientists, material scientists, chemists and psychologists. Interdisciplinary collaboration becomes especially crucial for research and development, since research methods often require input from these specialised fields.

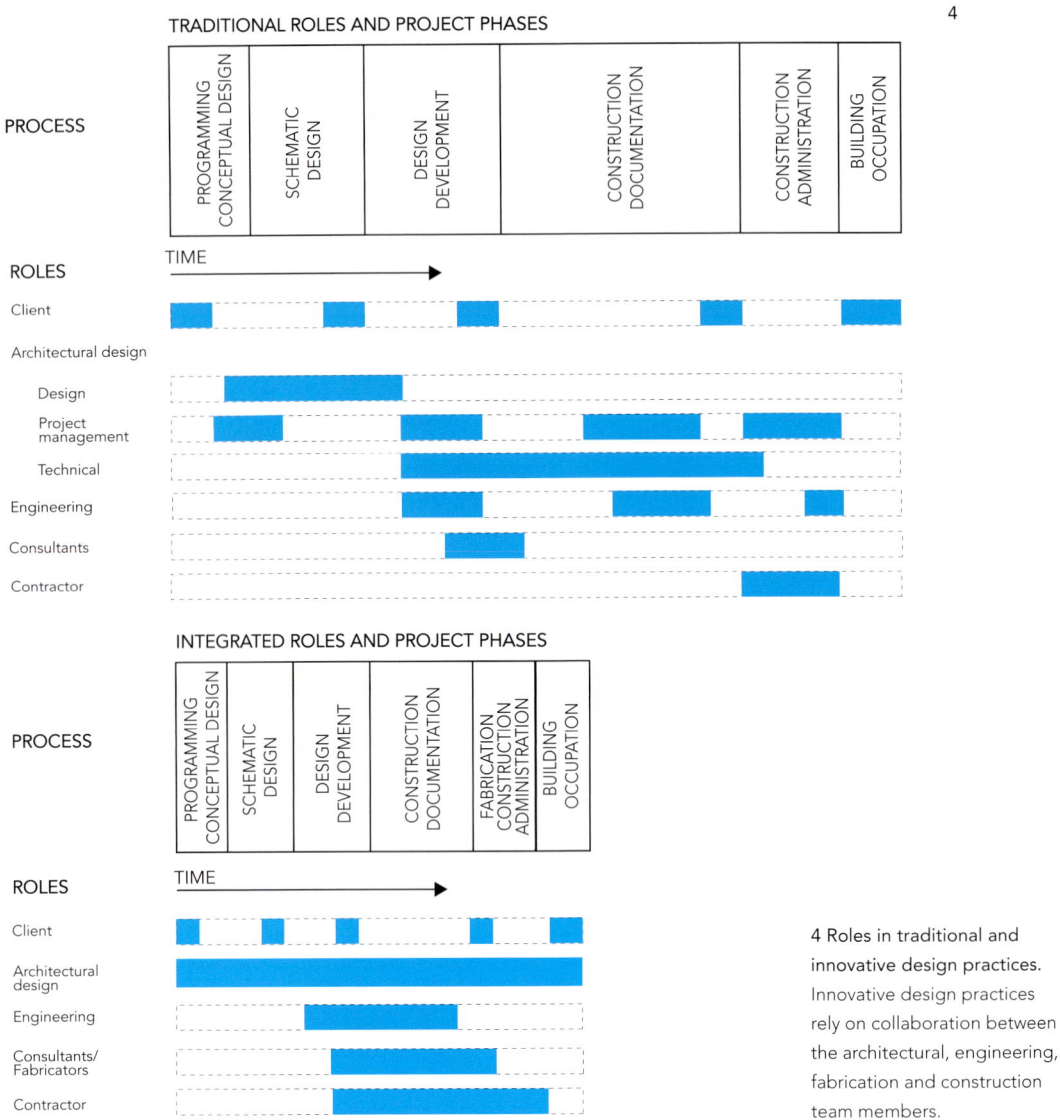

4 Roles in traditional and innovative design practices. Innovative design practices rely on collaboration between the architectural, engineering, fabrication and construction team members.

INTEGRATION OF RESEARCH AND DESIGN PRACTICE

Research in architectural design is not a new phenomenon. Gradual technological changes – such as the development of new materials, construction techniques and design representations – have accelerated the need for research over time. Today, however, research is more important than ever and it is becoming an integral component in design practices. A variety of factors have made designers' jobs more complex, including technological advancements, changing client expectations and new design methods and processes.

Architectural and design research has evolved in fundamental ways during the last 100 years. Prior to the 1950s, the major focus of research related to architectural history and theory. This focus shifted as research broadened to include mass-produced construction, alternative construction materials, and engineering and economics-related topics. During the 1970s, the oil crisis resulted in unprecedented energy concerns, and architectural research expanded to include environmental topics and methods for improving the energy efficiency of buildings. More recently, during the 1980s and 1990s, research expanded to include behavioural research in architecture, focusing on occupants' responses to internal and external conditions (daylight, nature, indoor air quality and so on), and continued to expand with advances in information technologies and digital design.

Over the past two decades, research in architecture has diversified and now often involves interdisciplinary approaches. Topics are wide-ranging, encompassing advanced materials, building technologies, environmental and energy concerns, design computation, automation in construction, management and economics. The true value of research today lies in the evaluation and benchmarking of types of design interventions, including operational efficiency, design effectiveness, building performance and project delivery. The knowledge derived from these investigations helps to inform and propagate a culture of design innovation. The practical value of this knowledge is enhanced by the new direction in architectural research where research originates in practice. Research questions, methods and results are closely tied to architectural projects, design processes and services.

The integration of research and design is essential for innovative architectural practices. Research, in this context, is defined as the systematic investigation and creation of new knowledge and applications, utilising rigorous research methods. Research and development can bring immense value to any organisation for which innovation is important. However, considering the lack of universal models for integrating research with practice, realities of client requirements, schedules and budgets, as well as risks and liability – research in architectural design practices is challenging. Organising and maintaining research departments in architectural design practices can be costly, time-consuming and risky. Therefore, taking a careful and systematic approach to establishing research departments, defining operational models and relationships between research, design practice and business performance are essential. It is necessary to balance and determine different priorities, including short-term goals and long-term strategic focus, alignment with the firm's motives and values, developing internal capabilities or outsourcing and partnering with external research partners. It is also necessary to align research objectives and methods with the objectives of innovation (product, service or process) and the level of innovation (incremental, radical or transformational). The following aspects should be considered when integrating research with design practice:

- How to establish the research arm of the firm, its structure and organisation.

- What are the connections and relationships between the firm's core values, practice and research?
- What are the long-term strategies and objectives of research vs short-term actions?
- How to fund research activities.
- How to translate results of research efforts into practice.

There are several models of operation for research activities within design practices – internal, external and hybrid. These models depend on several factors, including the size of the firm, its dedication to research and development, funding, types of research activities, and so forth. Internal research practices are internally funded by the firm or included as part of the firm's services (so client-driven and funded), where researchers are employees of the firm. Research activities are closely related to the firm's operation, research projects are driven by design projects, and results are directly implemented in practice. External research practices constitute involvement with external partners, where the design firms may fund the activities of various research centres or universities. In this model, researchers are not employed by the firm, but rather act as consultants, or the firm has an impact on the research agenda of the external research centre. Research projects may or may not be influenced by the firm's projects, and the implementation of results strongly depends on the way that the research projects are structured and executed. A hybrid model constitutes a mixture of the previous two types. For example, some design firms are establishing separate non-profit organisations dedicated to research but are strongly influenced by the firm's values, strategies and projects. Part of the research work may be funded by the firm, while other activities may be funded by other sources.

RESEARCH METHODS FOR INNOVATION

The typical steps in research include: identification of a research problem, a literature review to determine the state of the art in current knowledge, identification of gaps in current knowledge, identification of research methods, execution of the study, collection of data and analysis of results, conclusion and implementation of results. Research methodology may

5 Models of operation for research and design. Three basic models for integration of research and design exist: internal, external and hybrid. Firms that have integrated internal research and development departments or teams benefit from their direct involvement in practice. In the external model, design practices fund research work that is executed by other organisations – such as academic and research institutions – which relates to the design practice's interests and goals. In a hybrid model, design practices may initiate non-profit or for-profit organisations that are primarily focused on research.

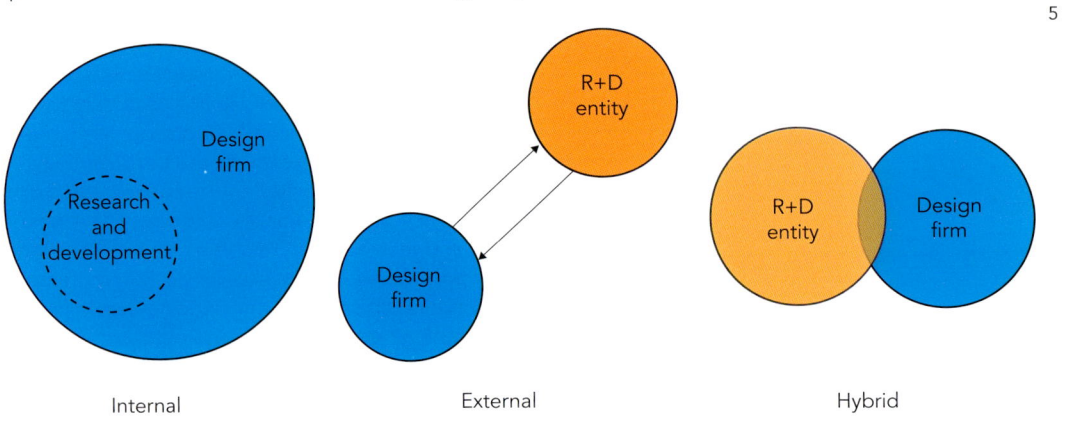

Internal   External   Hybrid

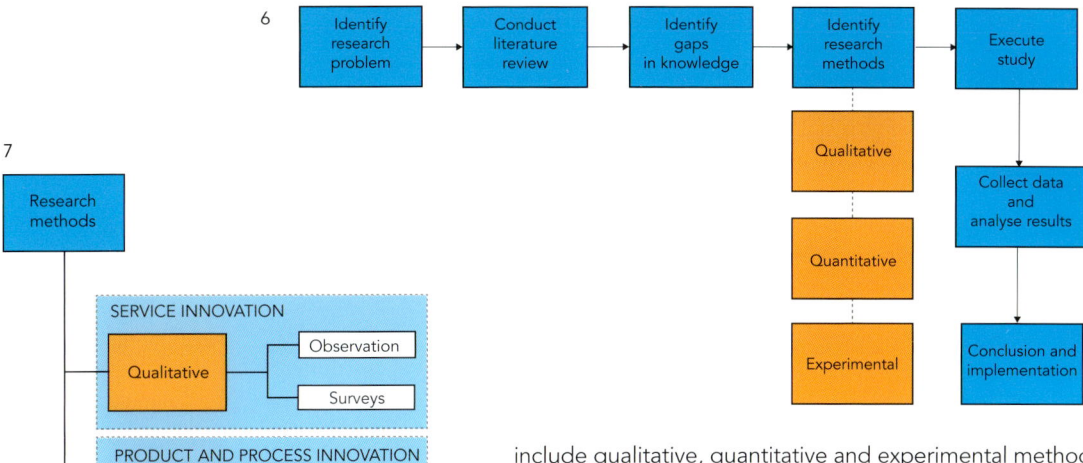

include qualitative, quantitative and experimental methods, and the selection of appropriate methods is heavily dependent on the research questions and problems. Qualitative methods include observations and surveys; quantitative methods include simulations and modelling; and experimental methods include prototyping and testing. Mixed research methods may also be used, where two or more research methodologies are employed to address a certain research problem. For example, in investigating the performance of innovative facade systems, quantitative and experimental methods may be adopted, where simulations and modelling are deployed to investigate heat transfer, structural behaviour and daylight, and mock-up testing is used to investigate physical properties and behaviour.

We have discussed three types of innovation in architectural design practices – relating to buildings, systems and materials ('product'), design services ('service'), and design methods ('process'). Although the selection of applicable research methods is dependent on the specific research problem, research methods can also be distinguished based on their suitability for different types of innovation. For example, quantitative and experimental methods are most suited for 'product' or 'process' innovation, since simulations, modelling, prototyping and experimental techniques can be used to investigate emerging building materials, building performance and energy-efficiency, building systems, design computation, mock-ups and the testing of building components, and so on. Qualitative methods are most suited for 'service' innovation, since surveys and observations are used to determine best design practices, client engagement, quality of design services, and so forth.

FINANCIAL FACTORS AND INVESTMENT FOR INNOVATION

Innovation in architectural design requires investment, including time and resources for research and exploration, financial commitment for short- and long-term innovation strategies, as well as investment in emerging design technologies, such as various computational tools and software programs. Innovative design practices typically employ a systematic collection of ideas, design processes and methods; have strong internal research

6 Research process.
The research process constitutes the following steps: identification of a research problem, literature review, identification of gaps in current knowledge, identification of applicable research methods and execution of the study.

7 Research methods.
Research methods may be qualitative, quantitative and experimental. Qualitative methods include observations and surveys; quantitative include simulations and modelling; and experimental include prototyping and testing. The selection of appropriate methods is heavily dependent on the research problem and questions, but they can also be distinguished based on the suitability for different types of innovation.

and development departments that are closely related to all the firm's activities and projects; provide incentives to employees for innovative projects and design solutions; invest in the firm's infrastructure; and take risks. For all of these aspects, initial investments are necessary and essential, but require a strategic perspective that balances investments and benefits.

Architectural design practices function like many other business enterprises – their operation is based on revenue received for services and overhead costs incurred. Profit is the difference between revenue and overhead costs, and is influenced by many factors, including the billing rates for design services, the costs of operation – the salaries and benefits of employees, office space and equipment, consultant fees and professional insurance – market demands and economic conditions. The establishment of billing rates and the cost of operation are within the direct control of design firms, while market demands and the general state of the economy are the external factors. But, where does funding for innovation come from, and how does it fit within the financial operations of design practices?

All design practices strive to increase profit, while minimising overhead costs. But, innovative design practices should reinvest larger portions of their profit into activities that help them to address innovation strategies, including the development and establishment of research and development departments, employee incentives for innovative projects and results, infrastructure and equipment and marketing. Strategies for increasing profit include:

- Balancing costs of design services, time and rates.
- Providing specific value, satisfying market demands and offering a unique perspective.
- Leveraging capital and effort.
- Controlling design processes through effective management.

Methods for reducing overhead costs include streamlining work processes, the effective management of schedules, controlling the scope of services, employing quality control programmes and financial accountability.

Innovative design practices often categorise investments based on the type of innovation (product, service or process). Service and process innovations should be based on internal funding, where part of the firm's profit is used to advance design services and processes. On the other hand, innovations that are project- or building-specific should be funded accordingly, where contracts are drafted in such a way as to allow integrated design services, including research and development, to be considered as part of the firm's services. For example, if a certain project requires extensive simulations and modelling to investigate building performance, those activities should be included in the contract since they are project-specific.

VALUE OF INNOVATION

Determining reasons for investment in innovation and value is essential for any design organisation. Competitive advantage, market expansion and extension of a firm's services may give financial incentives for the firm to invest in innovation, but there are other intangible benefits, including the improvement of design services and processes. In determining the value of innovation, design firms should establish a value proposition that reflects the core services, market niche and benefits. For example, improving technical expertise and embracing new building and design technologies are tangible benefits of investing in innovation, and directly influence value. Innovative firms should consider the impact of innovation on revenue (as a direct measure) and value (as a measure of all indirect benefits). Investment in research and development requires initial capital, but results have an impact on the activities and practices of the firm, influencing design services and methods. Cutting-edge firms and leaders in innovation create a niche market, increasing the revenue for their services due to increased market demand. On the other hand, late adopters of innovation do not possess value differentiation. Continuous investment and implementation of innovative strategies maintain higher revenues for firms whose core values focus on research and development and the improvement of design services and methods.

INNOVATIONS IN PROJECT DELIVERY

One of the most influential advancements in project delivery methods during the last two decades is the introduction of the integrated project delivery (IPD) method. Project delivery methods for traditional design typically include design-bid-build or design-bid-build with construction management. In these project delivery methods, contractual agreements between the client, architectural/engineering team and contractor are separate. Initially the client contracts the architectural/engineer team to develop construction documentation, and bids are solicited from construction firms after construction documents are complete. In the IPD method, project teams are integrated from the beginning of the design, where contractual agreements are structured to allow maximum collaboration. IPD relies on the early contributions and expertise of all involved stakeholders, effective collaboration, open information sharing, shared risks and rewards and value-based decision-making.

The key characteristics that differentiate IPD from the traditional delivery methods include a multiparty contract, the early involvement of all key stakeholders, collaborative decision-making, shared risks and rewards, value-based compensation that is closely related to project success and improved communication. Using the IPD process requires significant changes in the organisation of architectural and construction projects, and in the relationships between the stakeholders. Early involvement of all stakeholders is a key component in IPD, especially engineers, consultants, contractors and subcontractors. The project stages shift and efficiency is greatly improved in the IPD process. So, instead of

8

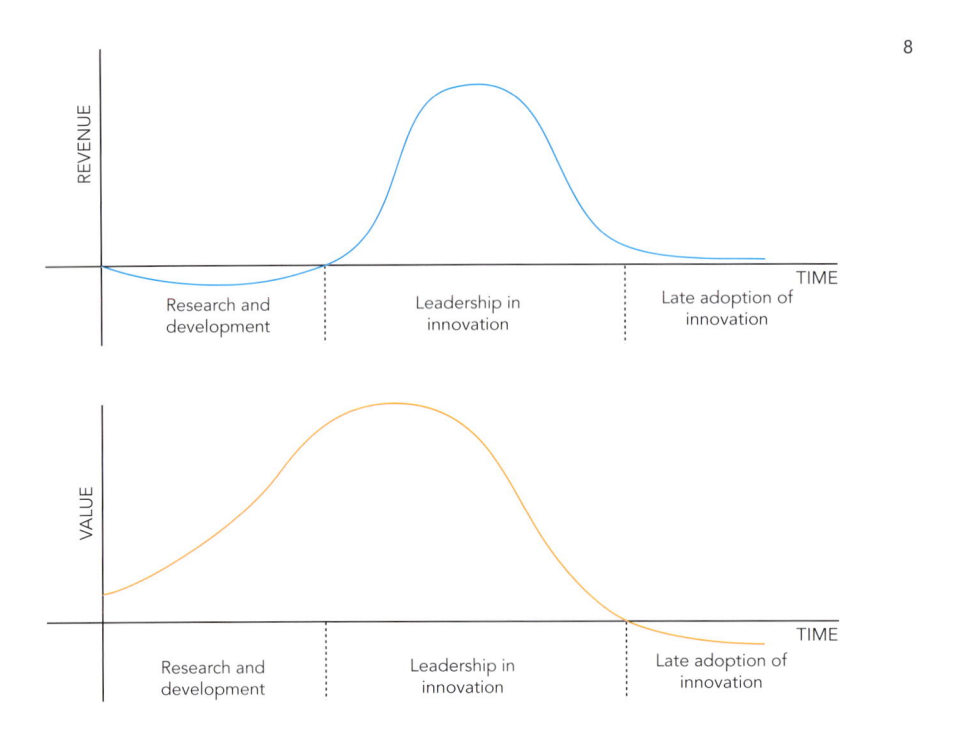

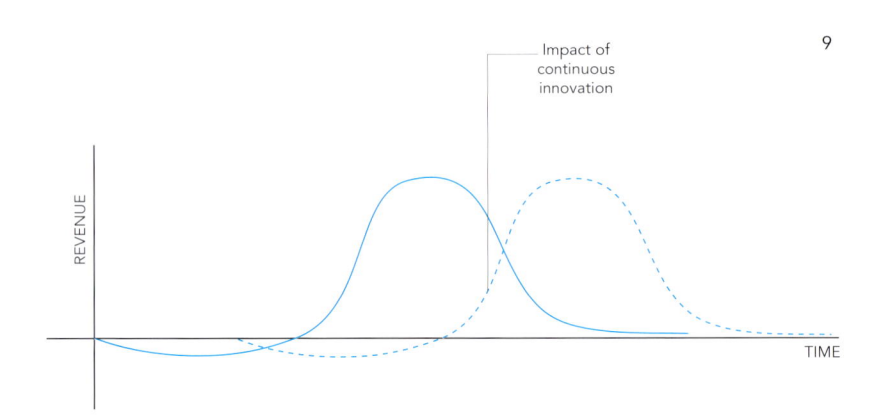

	TRADITIONAL DESIGN	IPD
Teams	Fragmented and hierarchical	Integrated, involving all stakeholders from start
Process	Linear and segregated	Concurrent and collaborative
Contracts	Based on unilateral efforts, allocate and transfer risk	Multilateral, promote collaboration and risk sharing
Communication and technology	Analog, 2D	Digital, virtual, BIM
Risk	Individually managed, transferred	Collectively managed and shared
Compensation and rewards	Individual, first-cost based	Value-based, tied to project services

9

10

8 The impact of innovation on revenue and values.
Innovation requires initial investments (mainly through research and development), but the impact of innovation is that it helps to establish certain values that can create competitive advantages and influence revenues.

9 The impact of continuous innovation on revenue.
Firms and practices that continuously invest in research and development, and focus on innovation, are able to modify their operation and create new markets for their services.

10 The differences between traditional design delivery methods and IPD.
The IPD process involves all project stakeholders from the early stages of the design process, relies on collaborative working methods, promotes risk sharing and instills value-based services.

a typical construction documentation stage, where architectural/engineering and construction roles are completely separated, implementation documents are developed in an IPD model based on the input of all stakeholders. This reduces unnecessary steps during construction administration, minimises the number of change orders and improves quality.

The IPD method relies on effective communication and collaboration, and BIM is essential in achieving effective information sharing and collaboration since it provides a uniform platform for storing and managing design information. Since all key stakeholders are involved in the IPD process (including owners, designers, contractors, subcontractors and facility managers), information sharing, visualisation, code compliance, analysis of design performance, constructability, quality assurance and quality control, construction planning and ultimately facility management are enabled with BIM. Consistency and accuracy of data has a direct impact on the decision-making, and establishing protocols and implementation plans is essential for the effective use of BIM in the IPD process.

RISK MANAGEMENT IN INNOVATIVE DESIGN PRACTICE

Uncertainty is one of the major inherent characteristics of innovation and, as such, it poses risks to firms and organisations engaged in innovative design practices and research. It is important to manage risks and develop management techniques that align with an organisation's strategy and performance measurement system. Major sources of risk in architectural design practices include poor project management; loss of control over costs, changes and time on projects; poor contracts with open-ended commitments; poor budgeting and financial control; lack of quality-control protocols and lack of accountability. However, design practices that integrate innovative design methods face additional risks and must be prepared to manage them effectively.

Risk management is a structured approach for managing uncertainty, and includes several steps: risk identification, risk assessment, risk response planning, risk monitoring and control. The purpose of risk identification is to distinguish risks that may influence the outcomes of various projects and design practices. Risk assessment evaluates the probability of an identified risk, as well as its effect on a project or design practice. Risk response planning identifies appropriate actions that can be taken to reduce potential threats to projects and practices. Risk management strategies should be developed based on these considerations:

- What are the significant risks acceptable to the design practice?
- What are the significant risks that are not acceptable?
- Is there a clear understanding of the magnitude and nature of risks that the design practice is willing to accept to achieve its goals and mission?
- What are the appropriate steps to reduce and manage risks?

TRADITIONAL DESIGN

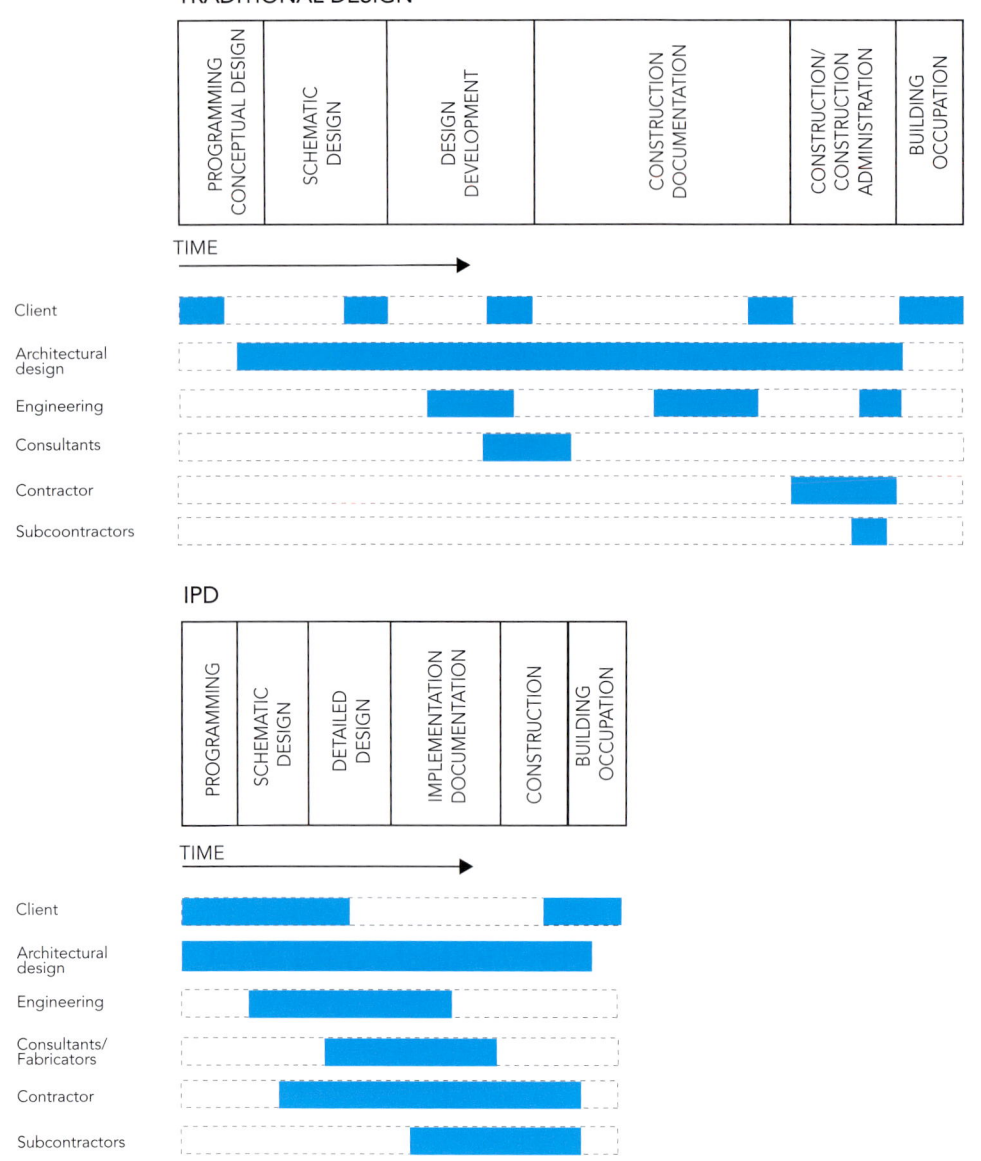

| PROGRAMMING CONCEPTUAL DESIGN | SCHEMATIC DESIGN | DESIGN DEVELOPMENT | CONSTRUCTION DOCUMENTATION | CONSTRUCTION/ CONSTRUCTION ADMINISTRATION | BUILDING OCCUPATION |

TIME →

- Client
- Architectural design
- Engineering
- Consultants
- Contractor
- Subcoontractors

IPD

| PROGRAMMING | SCHEMATIC DESIGN | DETAILED DESIGN | IMPLEMENTATION DOCUMENTATION | CONSTRUCTION | BUILDING OCCUPATION |

TIME →

- Client
- Architectural design
- Engineering
- Consultants/ Fabricators
- Contractor
- Subcontractors

Risk management strategy should not be a rigid set of rules, but rather it should provide guidance for assessing the magnitude of potential threats, as well as methods for reducing, monitoring and controlling those threats, while still engaging in innovation and innovative design practices. It is important to communicate risk management strategy to all employees, develop tools and training materials, implement monitoring and control techniques, but also develop a culture that balances risks and innovation. Risks associated with innovation should not be regarded as negative, rather – they should be understood, assessed and effectively managed.

11 The comparison of different stages and roles in traditional design delivery and IPD. The IPD process saves time and improves the delivery of projects, since all project stakeholders are involved from the early stages and collaborate in decision-making.

CONCLUSION: STRATEGIES FOR INTEGRATING INNOVATION

As we have seen in this chapter, a firm's operation and culture, motives and goals, investments in research and development, collaboration and project delivery methods all influence innovation. To establish a culture of innovation, firms and organisations must evaluate their vision, mission and operational modes, and establish a strategy that specifically addresses these aspects and defines procedures for enabling innovative practice. It should be noted that the identity of the firm is essential in establishing this strategy, since there are a lot of variations in the way they are structured, organised and managed.

The integration of research and development with design is important for innovation. Firms and organisations should establish a plan for integrating research with design, specifically addressing these following aspects: 1) the structure and organisation of the research arm, 2) the relationship to core values and practice, 3) short-term actions and long-term strategies, 4) funding, and 5) the translation and integration of research results into practice. The organisation and operation of research departments depend on several factors, including the size of the firm, economic aspects and funding, types and focus of research activities.

Innovative practice inherently increases risk for design firms. But, that should not be a barrier to embrace change. Firms and organisations should establish risk management strategies that allow a structured approach to manage uncertainty. Specifically, risk management strategies must be able to distinguish acceptable and unacceptable risks, the magnitude and nature of acceptable risks, and the appropriate steps to reduce and control risks. These strategies allow design practices to be explorative and cutting-edge, to adopt new technologies and approaches in their design process, but within a framework that minimises uncertainty.

REFERENCES

1 Josh Lerner, *The Architecture of Innovation*, The Economics of Creative Organizations Harvard Business Review Press (Boston, MA), 2012.
2 Stephen Emmitt, *Design Management for Architects*, John Wiley & Sons (Chichester), UK, 2014.

IMAGES

Opening image © Synthesis Design + Architecture; figures 1, 2, 3, 4, 5, 6, 7, 8, 9, 10 and 11 © Ajla Aksamija

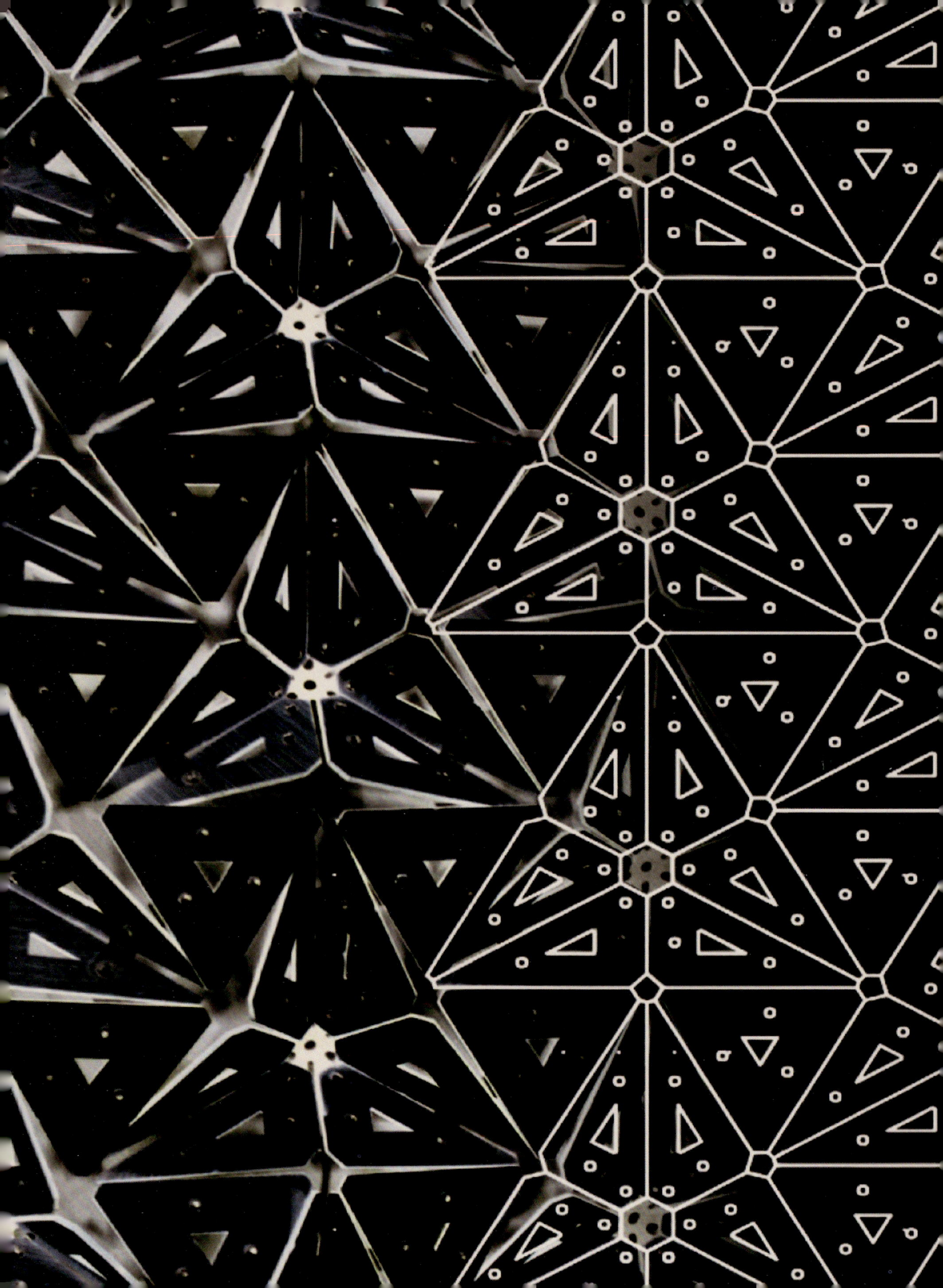

5 BUILDING INTEGRATED INNOVATIONS AND METHODS (CASE STUDIES)

As we have seen in previous chapters, new materials, advances in computational design practices, BIM, advanced building technologies and construction techniques, and the integration of research with design have an impact on innovations in architectural design. Numerous case studies have been presented in earlier chapters to illustrate how specific approaches have been implemented on architectural projects, but this chapter provides several specific case studies that discuss how design and technical innovations are used in an integrated way to improve building performance, collaboration between project stakeholders and design outcomes.

These case studies were chosen to illustrate holistic buildings, rather than isolated design approaches, materials, systems or a technology. These built examples also demonstrate a variety of scales and complexities, from very small to very large buildings, and a variety of building types (small laboratories, academic centres, libraries, museums and commercial buildings). The purpose is to demonstrate how innovative design methods can be applied to any scale and size of project and any building type. Complex building types certainly benefit from certain types of innovations, such as prefabrication and modular construction, but material innovations, computational design methods, responsive and intelligent design, and advanced building technologies can be applied to any building type and scale. It is important to consider the advantages of innovative technologies, materials and systems, as well as their benefits for individual projects. For example, climate-specific design strategies, energy-efficient measures, improved collaboration, streamlined fabrication and construction are valuable for all types of projects, building functions and scales. On the other hand, specific advanced materials, such as aerogel insulation, or advanced building technologies, like double-skin facades, are applicable for certain types of climates. Designers must be cognisant of different properties and characteristics, and the appropriate applications of assorted advanced technologies and architectural innovations, to successfully integrate best practices. The following case studies demonstrate some of the implementations in contemporary practice.

1

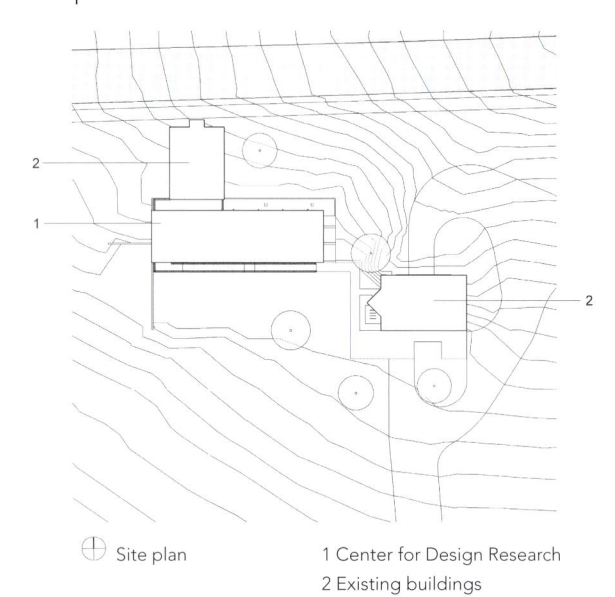

1 Studio 804, the Center for Design Research (CDR), University of Kansas, USA, 2011.
Site plan, showing site context and surrounding buildings.

2 Studio 804, the Center for Design Research (CDR), University of Kansas, USA, 2011.
This building is a research and design development laboratory, focusing on sustainable strategies, material innovation and building efficiency research.

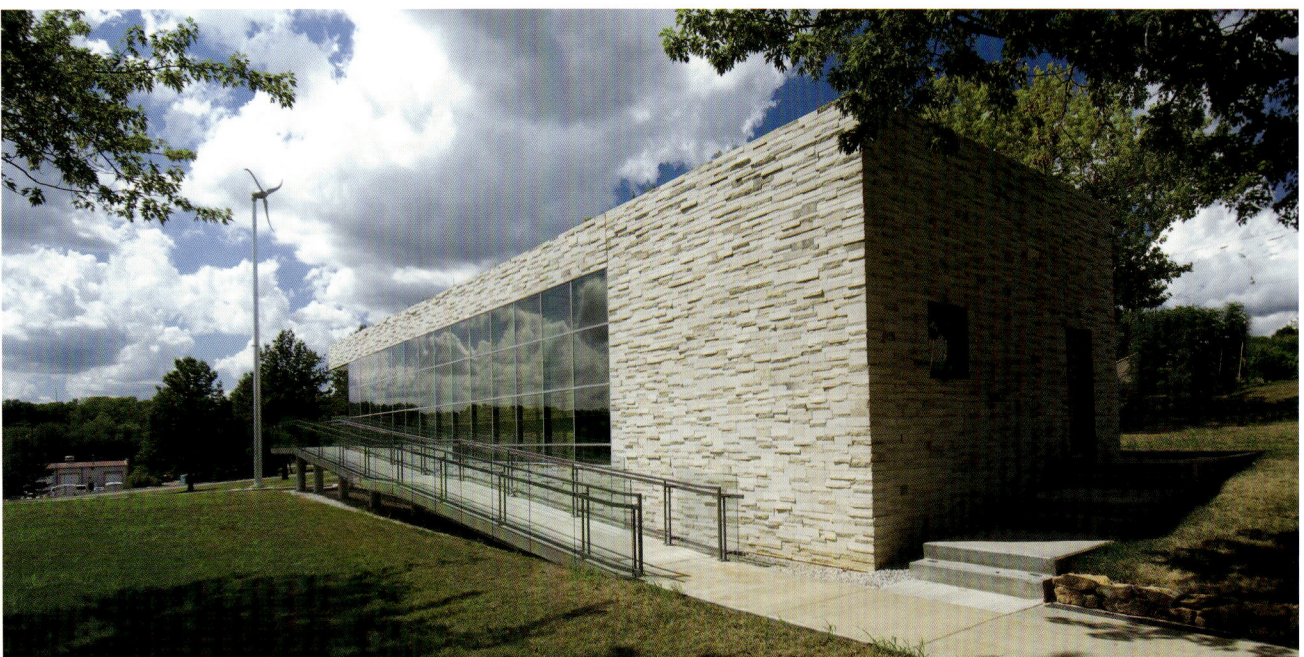

⊕ Site plan

1 Center for Design Research
2 Existing buildings

2

CENTER FOR DESIGN RESEARCH, UNIVERSITY OF KANSAS

The Center for Design Research (CDR) at the University of Kansas was designed by Studio 804. Led by Dan Rockhill, Studio 804 is a non-profit organisation whose participants are graduate students of the University of Kansas's School of Architecture, Design and Planning. The organisation was formed based on the terminal year-long graduate architectural studio, with the primary goal to provide students with an integrated design and construction educational experience.

The centre is a research and design development laboratory, operating under the umbrella of the School of Architecture, Design and Planning, with the purpose of engaging in interdisciplinary research on sustainable design strategies, material innovation and building efficiency. It is on the historic Chamney Farm in Lawrence, Kansas, and was created as an incubator for innovations in building products and services. The site includes two existing buildings that remain from the farm, a stone farmhouse at the north side and a stone barn on the east. The new pavilion includes meeting and presentation space, as well as laboratory components. The structural system includes heavy wood and steel, and each building orientation is treated differently.

The south facade consists of a curtain wall with electrochromic glazing, and stone cladding that was reclaimed from a local quarry as limestone tailings, which were then cut into smaller blocks. Along the south orientation, a Trombe wall is positioned behind the curtain wall and provides passive solar heating during winter. It consists of concrete masonry units and stone cladding. From the exterior, the Trombe wall appears to be a continuation of the building's envelope behind the glass, but on the interior it has a different character. Thick sheets of laminated glass are incorporated horizontally within the joints in the Trombe wall creating transparent areas in the wall. The north facade does not have any openings and the east and west orientations are minimised.

The interior space includes a living wall of ferns irrigated with rainwater collected from the roof. The HVAC system includes an energy recovery system, while LED lighting has been used for interior spaces. A building energy management system tracks energy use, displays real-time energy consumption data to building occupants and monitors energy production from renewable energy systems. Renewable energy systems include a rooftop photovoltaic array and on-site wind turbine with horizontal axis.

This case study is an example of an innovative design process, added to the use of advanced materials and building technologies. The innovation in the design process was that the facility was designed by graduate architecture and design students, providing educational and design experience to these emerging professionals. Traditional architectural education rarely offers opportunities to design and construct actual buildings, and including students in the design of CDR certainly afforded new

3

First-floor plan

1 Entry
2 Trombe wall
3 Electrochromic glazing
4 Green wall
5 Meeting and presentation space

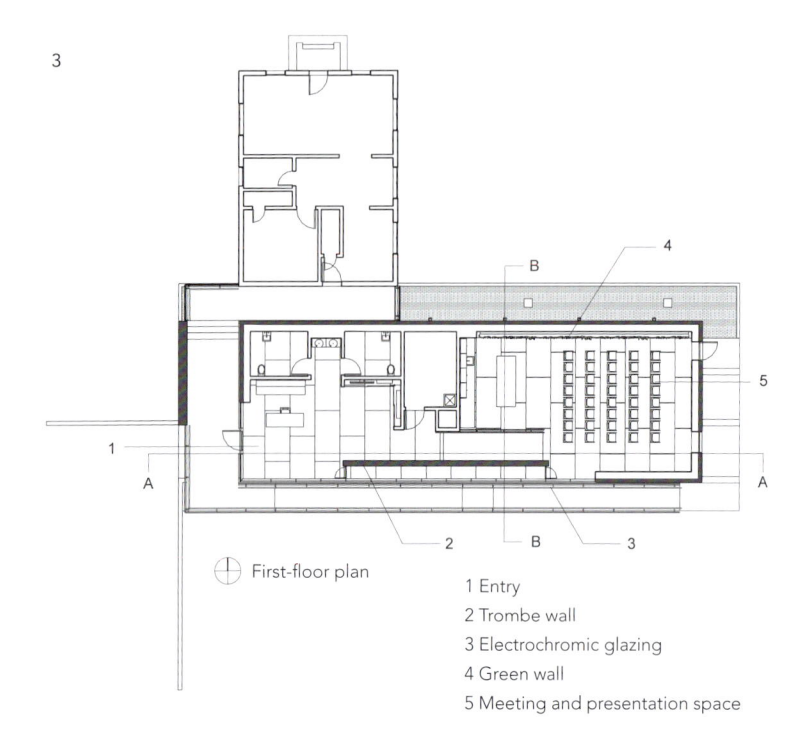

4

3 Studio 804, the Center for Design Research (CDR), University of Kansas, USA, 2011.
Floor plan, showing different spaces and laboratory components.

4 Studio 804, the Center for Design Research (CDR), University of Kansas, USA, 2011.
Exterior views, showing south and north building orientations.

5 Studio 804, the Center for Design Research (CDR), University of Kansas, USA, 2011.
Elevations and sections.

5

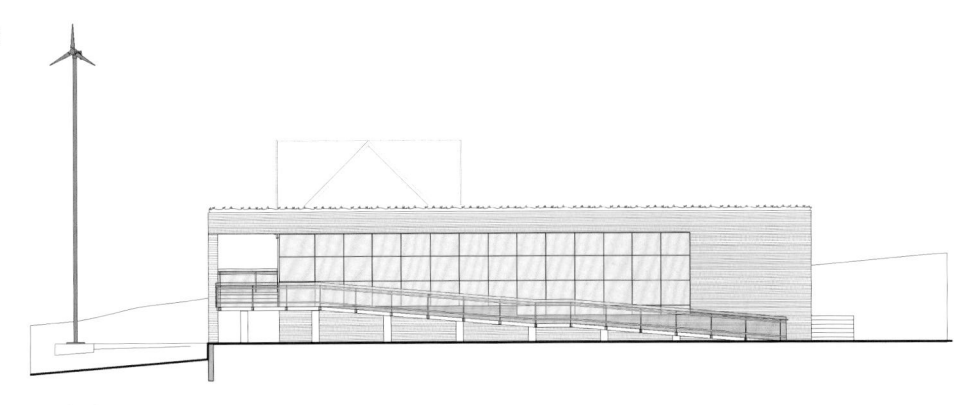

South elevation

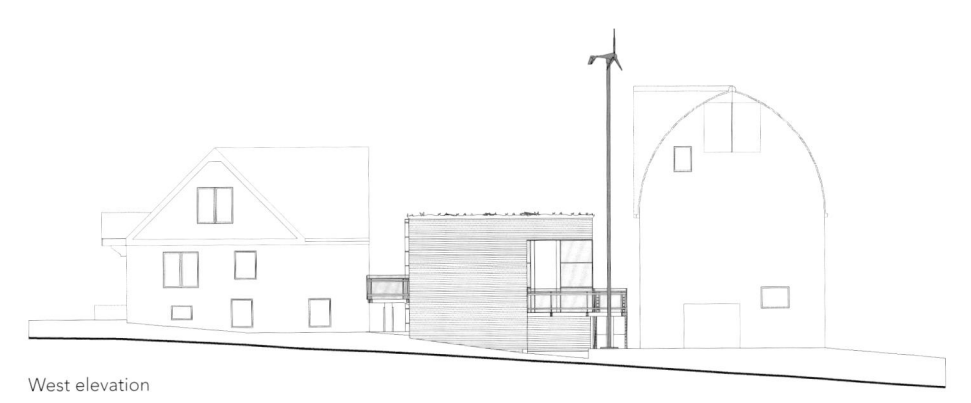

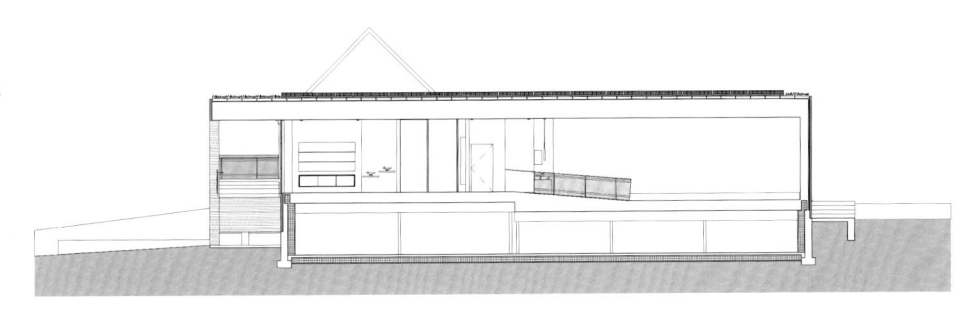

West elevation

Section A-A

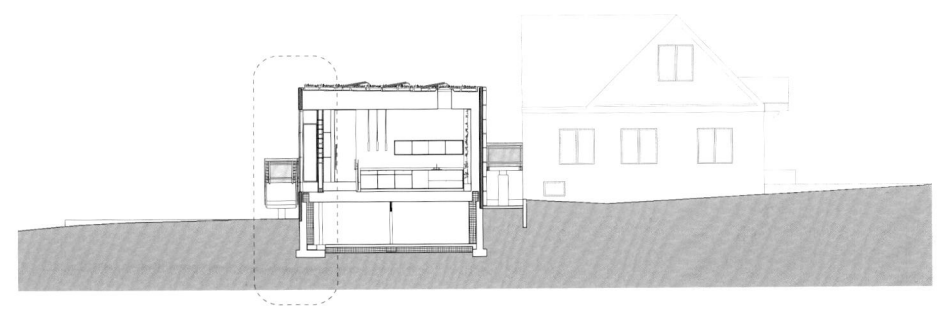

Section B-B

5 BUILDING INTEGRATED INNOVATIONS AND METHODS 188-189

6

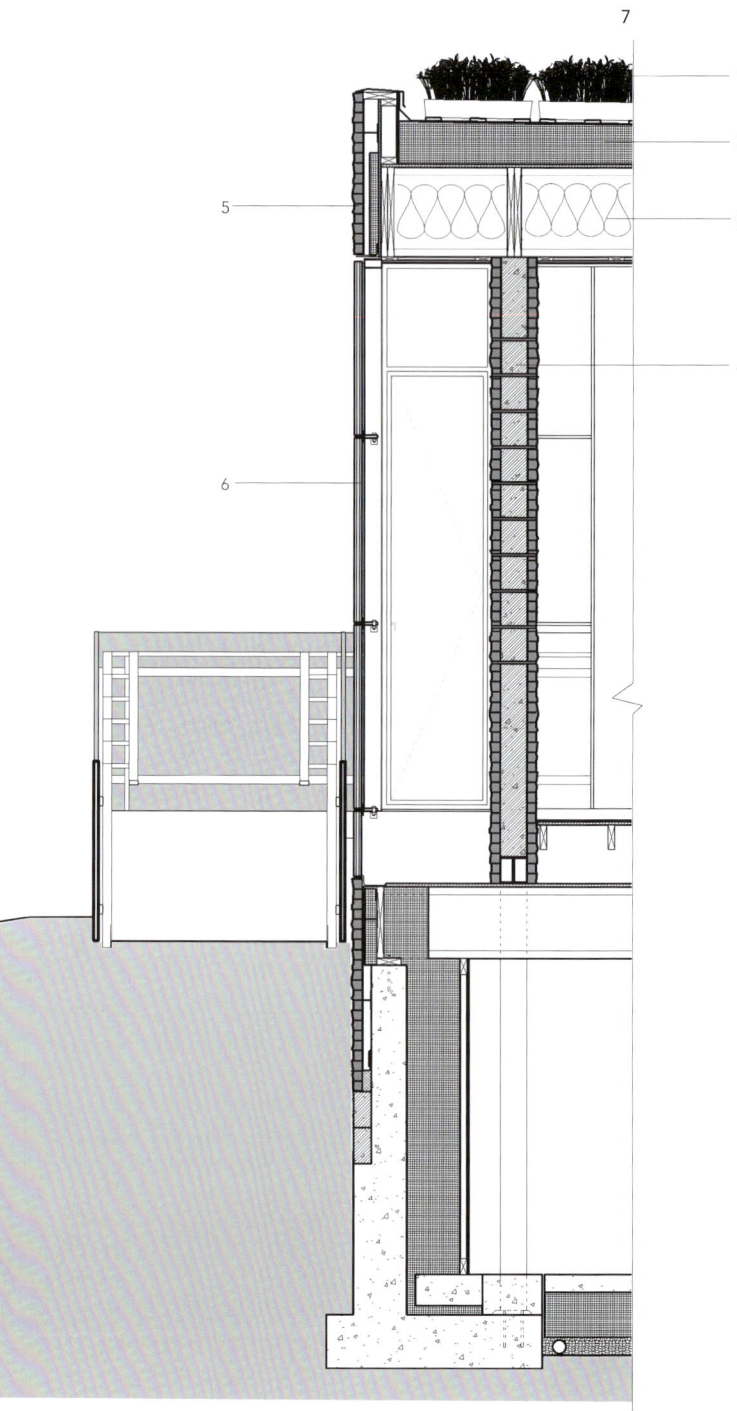

7

Enlarged section

6 Studio 804, the Center for Design Research (CDR), University of Kansas, USA, 2011.
Components of the Trombe wall, which assists in providing passive heating to the interior space.

7 Studio 804, the Center for Design Research (CDR), University of Kansas, USA, 2011.
Section of the south facade, showing electrochromic curtain wall and the Trombe wall.

1 Green roof
2 Rigid insulation
3 Batt insulation
4 Trombe wall
5 Stone cladding
6 Electrochromic glazing

8 Studio 804, the Center for Design Research (CDR), University of Kansas, USA, 2011.
Interior view, showing a living wall and reception area.

techniques for design exploration and experimentation. Moreover, the facility is used as a research laboratory for investigating advanced building technologies, new materials, sustainable design strategies and renewable energy systems. A variety of advanced materials, paired with passive design techniques, have been implemented, such as the electrochromic glazing, the Trombe wall and different types of renewable energy systems. Continuous monitoring of different building systems and the overall energy usage assists in executing the objectives of the CDR, since the building performance is tracked and investigated.

UMWELT ARENA

The Umwelt Arena in Spreitenbach, Switzerland, is an exhibition and event building dedicated to environmental stewardship and sustainability. It is in the industrial area of Spreitenbach, which received the 'Energy Town' label in 2008, which distinguishes communities that pursue sustainable energy policies, promote renewable energy systems, environmentally friendly infrastructure and the efficient use of resources. Designed by René Schmid

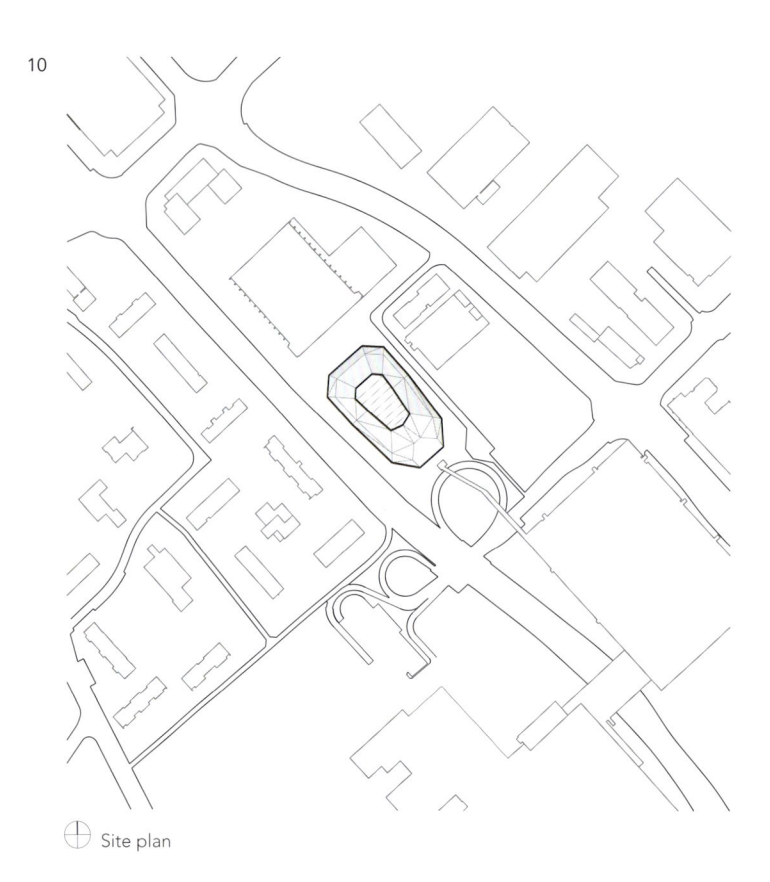

9

10

⊕ Site plan

Architekten, the Umwelt Arena integrates innovative technologies, ecologically sensitive design and advanced building systems to form a positive energy building that produces more energy than it needs for its operation.

The derivation of the building form was, among other factors, based on optimal solar radiation for a vast, roof-integrated photovoltaic array. The building plan is octagonal and includes a large three-storey arena that forms the centrepiece of the building. The building consists of three underground and four above-ground levels, and the programme includes event space, conference and seminar rooms, exhibition space and a restaurant. The arena can hold up to 4,000 people for various types of events, and exhibitions related to energy and mobility, construction and modernisation and renewable energy sources are held throughout the building. The purpose is to allow visitors an opportunity to experience and understand sustainability and environmental technologies, including sustainable retail trade, lighting, domestic appliances, water, recycling, renewable energy sources, public transport, advanced building technologies and building services engineering.

The structural system is a hybrid, consisting of concrete cores, slabs and columns, with glulam columns and wooden trusses supporting the roof. The design team used computational design methods to create the roof structure. The model-based prefabrication of the roof trusses allowed irregular geometries to be produced and then assembled on-site. The building shell consists of a dome, clad in 5,500 monocrystalline photovoltaic panels, of which 1,000 were manufactured in special shapes. This system produces more electricity than is required for the building's operation, with an annual output of 540,000 kWh. There are several other renewable energy systems on the roof, including a solar thermal system, solar absorbers and an energy recovery system.

The building's HVAC system uses six different types of heat pumps, including geoexchange pumps, a heat recovery system, outdoor air and ground water, as well as split systems and reversible heat pumps. Various combined heat and power systems, along with biomass, are used for heating. Concrete core cooling with a thermo-active ceiling is used for heating and cooling. In addition, the supply air can be preheated in case of low outdoor temperatures. Cooling is achieved by using the ground water, a geothermal heat collector and an absorption refrigeration machine that uses solar and waste heat. Two water tanks are used for cold and heat storage. The ventilation system for the arena also makes use of heat recovery. Owing to the size of the building, assorted decentralised ventilation and partial air-conditioning systems are used. The domestic hot water is supplied primarily by a solar thermal system with flat and vacuum tube collectors and hybrid solar collectors. The components of the HVAC system are exposed to demonstrate the latest developments in environmental technologies to visitors to the Umwelt Arena. Different types of sensors are used for the lighting system, including motion and occupancy sensors.

9 René Schmid Architekten, Umwelt Arena, Spreitenbach, Switzerland, 2012.
This exhibition and event building integrates innovative building technologies, ecologically sensitive design and advanced building systems.

10 René Schmid Architekten, Umwelt Arena, Spreitenbach, Switzerland, 2012.
Site plan, showing the location of the arena and the surrounding context.

5 BUILDING INTEGRATED INNOVATIONS AND METHODS

11

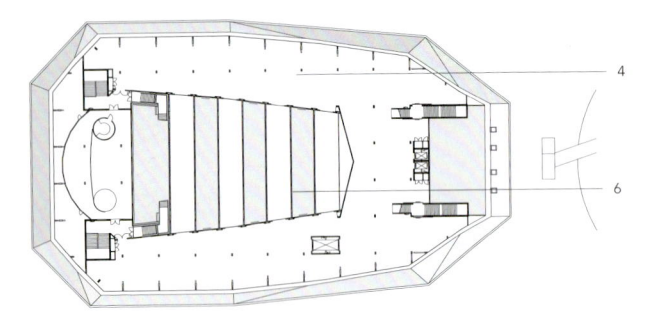

Third-floor plan

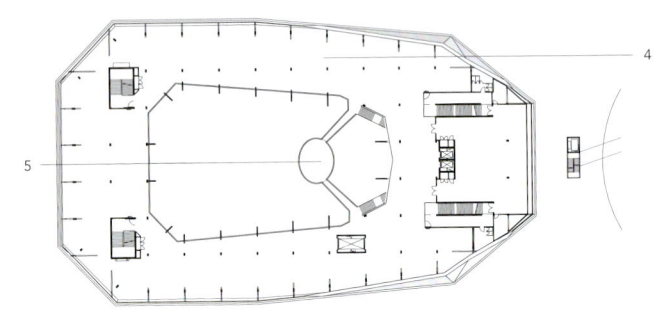

Second-floor plan

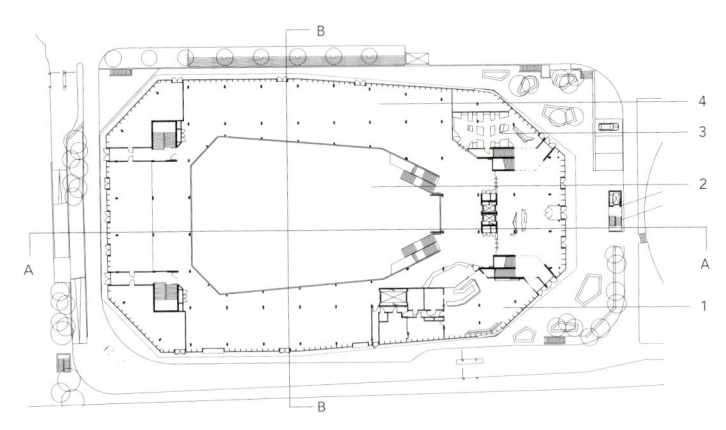

First-floor plan

1 Cafe
2 Arena
3 Gift shop
4 Exhibition space
5 Observation deck
6 Roof

11 René Schmid Architekten, Umwelt Arena, Spreitenbach, Switzerland, 2012.
Floor plans, showing spatial organisation and the interior layout.

12

13

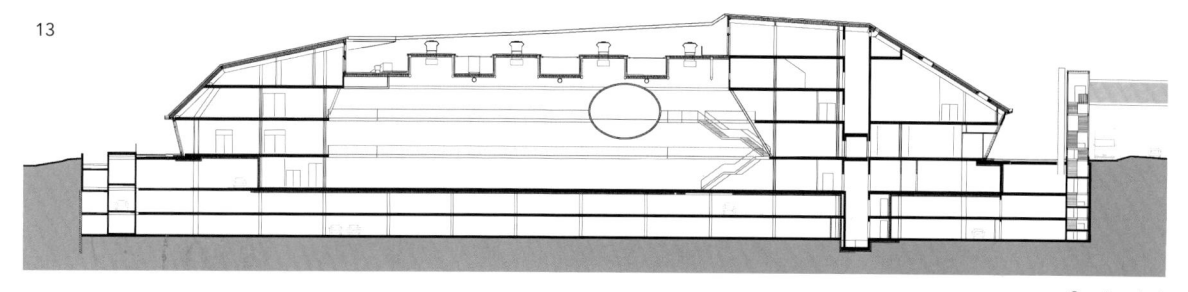

Section A-A

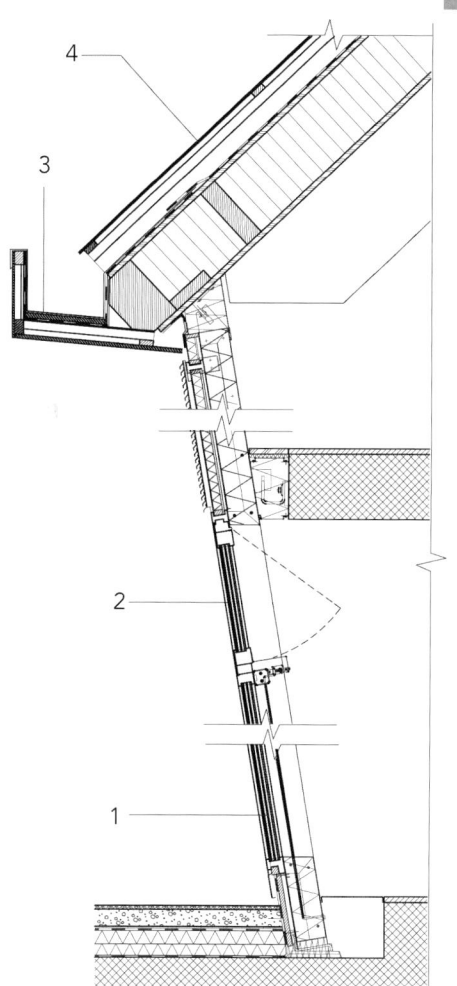

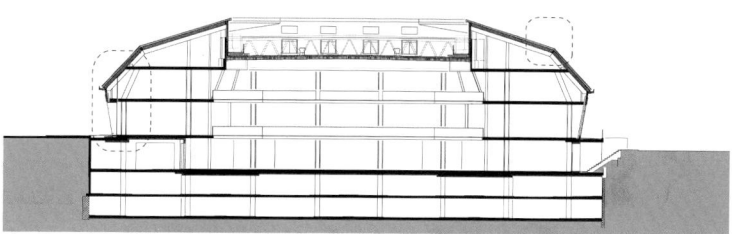

Section B-B

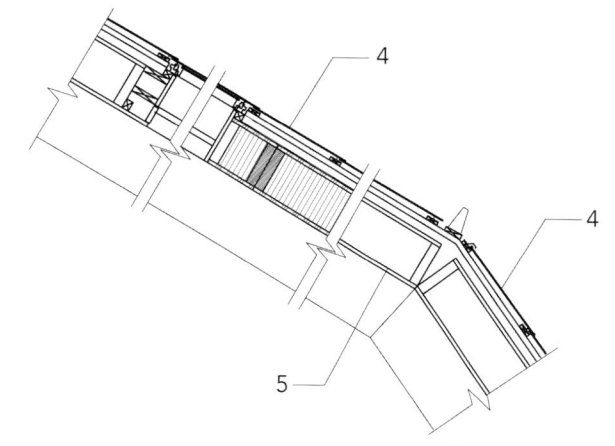

Enlarged roofing section

1 Glazing
2 Operable window
3 Drainage
4 PV panel
5 Framing

12 René Schmid Architekten, Umwelt Arena, Spreitenbach, Switzerland, 2012.
The derivation of the building form was based on optimal solar radiation for a vast, roof-integrated photovoltaic array.

13 René Schmid Architekten, Umwelt Arena, Spreitenbach, Switzerland, 2012.
Sections and technical details of the building facade and roof demonstrate the vertical spatial arrangement and material components. Photovoltaics are integrated in the building envelope, producing a large part of the building's electrical demand.

Enlarged facade section

5 BUILDING INTEGRATED INNOVATIONS AND METHODS 194-195

14

15

14 René Schmid Architekten, Umwelt Arena, Spreitenbach, Switzerland, 2012.
Movable stairs are incorporated within the main arena and an observation deck overlooks the space.

15 René Schmid Architekten, Umwelt Arena, Spreitenbach, Switzerland, 2012.
The interior spaces incorporate multiple material types, colours and textures.

Interior spaces have also been designed using innovative methods. For example, the main arena includes movable stairs that can be transformed and rearranged depending on the requirements and activities taking place within the arena. An observation deck oversees the arena. The interplay of forms, and untreated and raw materials, creates an interesting interior space.

During the construction process, one of the crucial drivers was to minimise the environmental impact as much as possible. Renewable energy sources were used on-site during construction, transportation vehicles used biofuels, and excavation was carried out in stages so that the excavated material could be processed into aggregates in a local concrete factory. These aggregates were mixed with the cement. Recycled steel was used and minimal waste was produced during construction. For example, digital fabrication was used for railings, where flat sheets of metal were cut based on a certain pattern. The remaining pieces were then used in a similar design for outdoor railings, creating a negative image of the interior railings.

This case study illustrates how advanced building materials and technologies can be integrated to drive the form, spatial organisation, structure, selection of heating and cooling systems,

5 BUILDING INTEGRATED INNOVATIONS AND METHODS 196-197

16

17

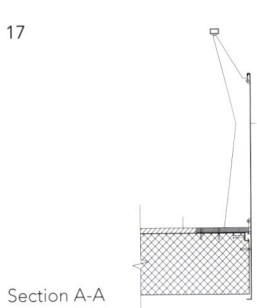

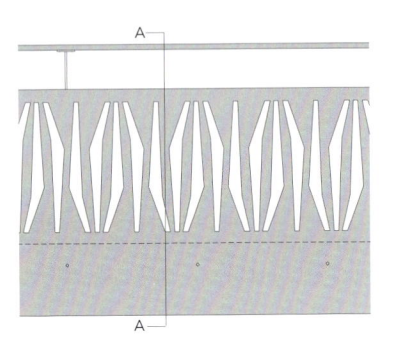

Section A-A

Partial elevation of interior railings

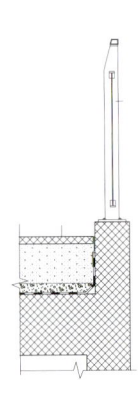

Section B-B

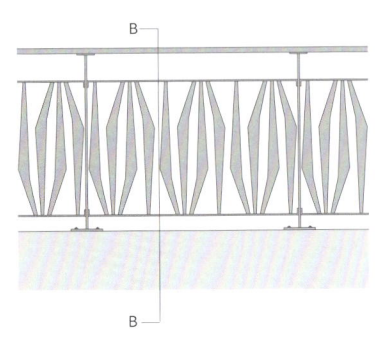

Partial elevation of exterior railings

16 René Schmid Architekten, Umwelt Arena, Spreitenbach, Switzerland, 2012.
The café, gift shop and educational spaces use wood as the primary interior material.

17 René Schmid Architekten, Umwelt Arena, Spreitenbach, Switzerland, 2012.
Details showing railing components. Digital fabrication was used to create custom patterns for interior railings, and remaining pieces were used for the outdoor railings, so minimising construction waste.

18 Gerber Architekten, the King Fahad National Library, Riyadh, Saudi Arabia, 2013.
The site plan showing the urban context, building form, urban plaza and a park.

19 Gerber Architekten, the King Fahad National Library, Riyadh, Saudi Arabia, 2013.
Exterior view showing the new building, facade treatments, urban plaza and a park.

as well as the application of renewable energy sources to create an innovative, high-performing building. The building form and shape were developed based on the integration of photovoltaic panels with the roofing system, taking into account optimal angles to maximise solar radiation and electricity generation. The hybrid structural system – consisting of concrete cores, slabs and columns, glulam columns and wooden trusses – allowed the realisation of the complex building shape. Computational design methods and model-based fabrication and construction were used to determine the overall shape and form, as well as construction and assembly. Since the facility is used to exhibit innovative sustainable technologies, advanced heating and cooling systems were incorporated, which are displayed throughout the building. Building occupants and visitors can observe components and parts of the HVAC system and understand the operation. Innovative construction techniques – which minimised construction waste, recycled excavated materials and applied renewable energy sources – are a remarkable example of how sustainability can drive all design and construction decisions.

KING FAHAD NATIONAL LIBRARY

The King Fahad National Library in Riyadh, Saudi Arabia, was designed by Gerber Architekten. The complex reflects local tradition, encompasses the existing historical building and creates an innovative, climatically and culturally responsive architecture. An urban plaza and park are located in front of the King Fahad National Library, also designed by Gerber Architekten. The park and plaza give pedestrians direct access to the library. The site is bounded by Riyadh's two main traffic arteries.

The plan of the new building is square, surrounding the old library building on all sides. The old building is in an octagonal plan with

Site plan

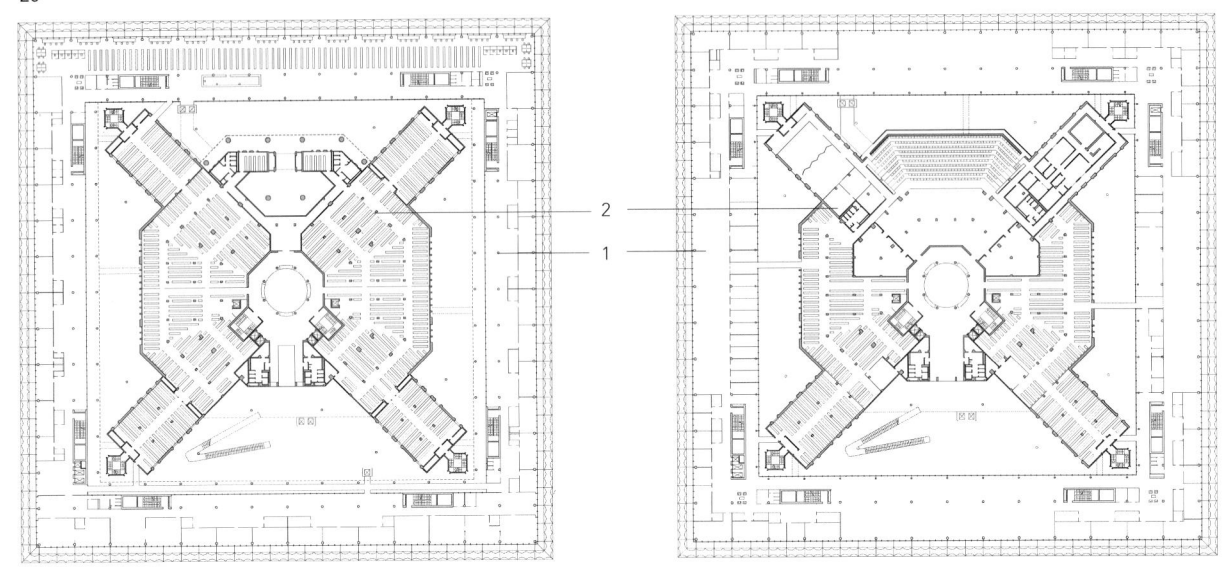

Second-floor plan

Third-floor plan

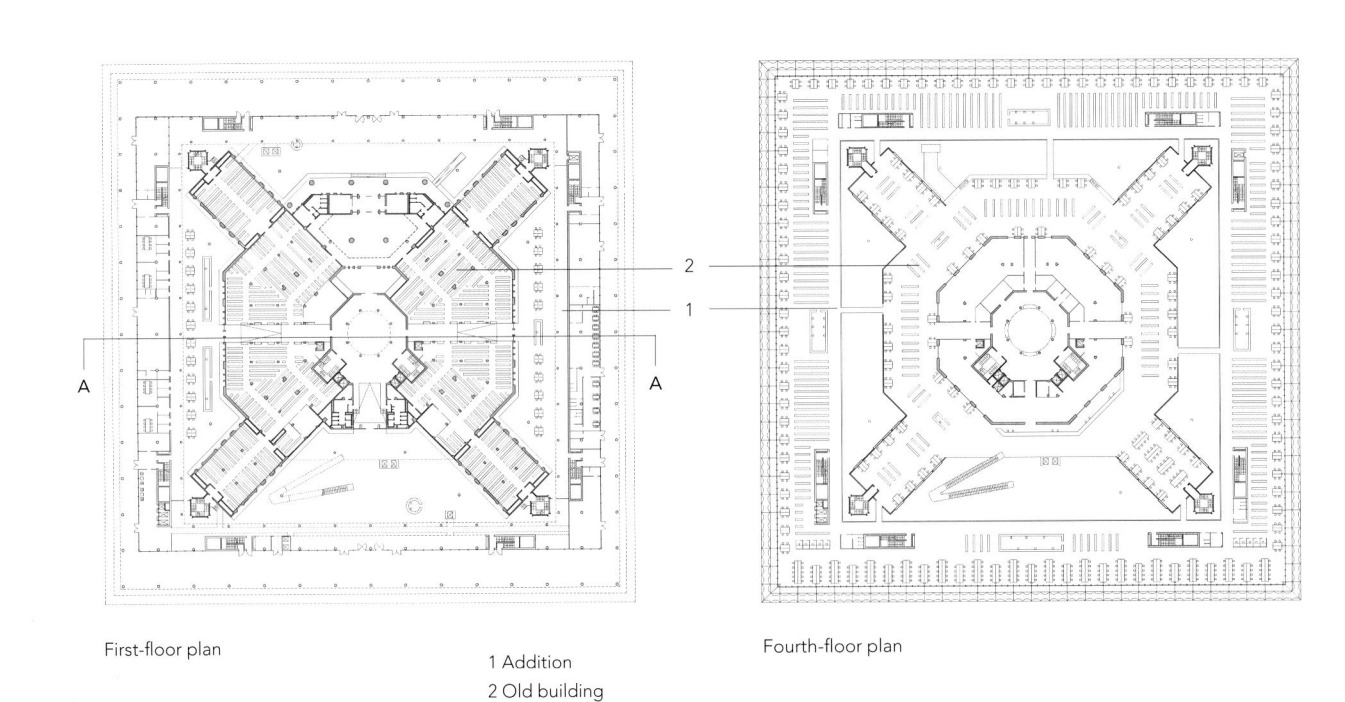

First-floor plan

1 Addition
2 Old building

Fourth-floor plan

21

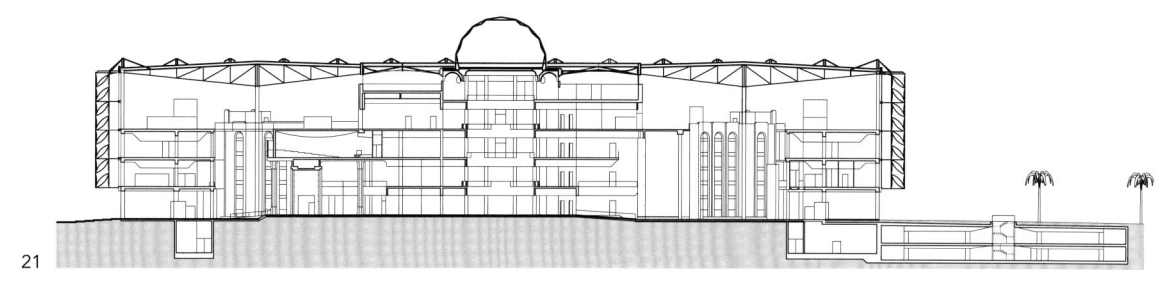

Section A-A

20 Gerber Architekten, the King Fahad National Library, Riyadh, Saudi Arabia, 2013. Floor plans showing the new building and the old, existing building. The new building is square in plan and surrounds the old building on all sides. It contains the reading and circulation spaces, offices and support services. The old building has an octagonal plan and provides the main stacks for the books. Bridges connect the two buildings.

21 Gerber Architekten, the King Fahad National Library, Riyadh, Saudi Arabia, 2013. Section showing vertical spatial organisation, and the new and old buildings. The new structure encompasses the old building on all sides and a new roof system provides daylight to interior spaces. The building facades incorporate shading elements that block unwanted solar radiation. The dome of the old building was reconstructed in steel and glass to increase natural light levels.

four extending arms, with a central dome structure on top, now reconstructed in steel and glass to bring daylight to the centre. A new roof structure unites and covers the old and the new buildings. Skylights are integrated into the new roof to increase natural light levels within the interior space. White translucent membranes are installed underneath, which diffuse and distribute the daylight throughout the interior. The former roof of the old building now provides an interior reading space. It is connected with bridges to reading areas allocated on the top floor of the new building. The old building serves as the main storage for the books and the legal deposits.

The building envelope of the new structure consists of a curtain wall and rhomboid fabric awnings, which shade the facade and create an interesting pattern of revealing and concealing interior space. White fabric membranes are supported by a three-dimensional, prestressed tensile steel cable structure and are inspired by traditional tent structures. This exterior shading system allows only 7% of incident solar radiation, while directing and refracting light into the interior space. The shape of the membranes was optimised based on solar path analysis in order to maximise daylight in the interior space, while providing maximum sun protection. At night, the facade is illuminated, creating a focal point for the urban fabric. The HVAC system includes underfloor cooling and displacement ventilation, which improves thermal comfort and significantly reduces energy consumption.

Retrofitting existing buildings is a growing market in the building industry. Energy-efficiency measures, the adaptation of existing functions and interior spaces, upgrading building systems and building envelope are all driving factors for the renovation and modernisation of existing buildings. The King Fahad National Library is an excellent example of an innovative retrofitting design process, where the new and old parts of the building are seamlessly integrated to form a climate-responsive, and inviting, grandiose structure. The methodology of providing a new outer layer to the building allowed the designers to create a facade that responds to a harsh climate and solar radiation, but also responds to the cultural context, since it borrows design language and patterns from local, traditional architecture and translates them into new forms and applications. The daylight harvesting methods create inviting, naturally lit interior spaces. Even the programme is

22
23

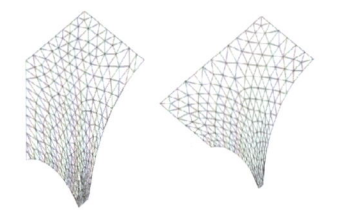

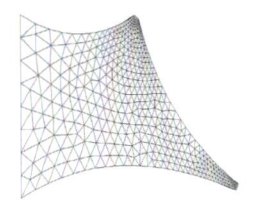

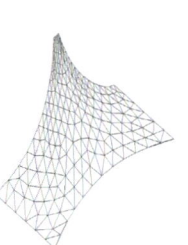

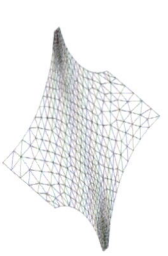

Membranes

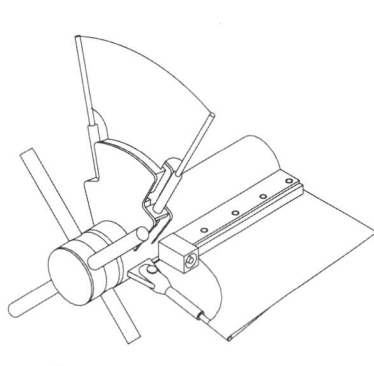

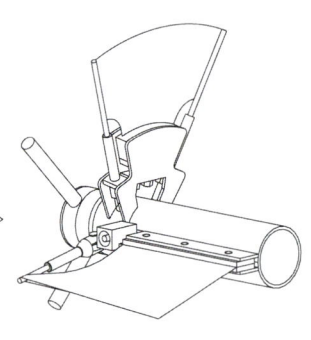

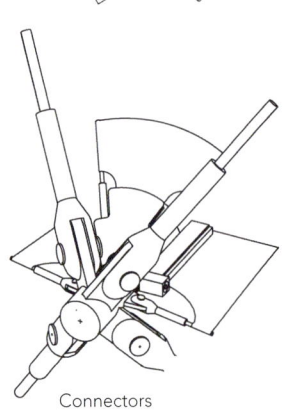

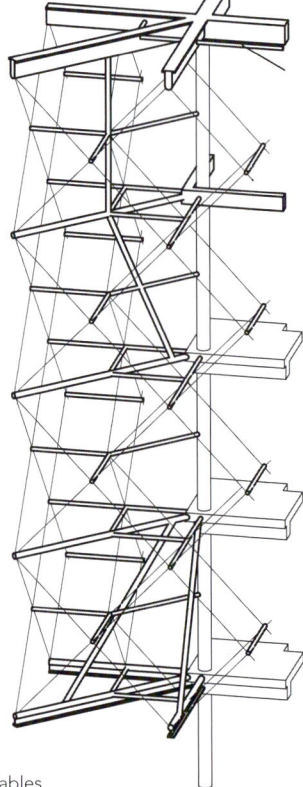

Connectors

Cables

24

25

22 Gerber Architekten, the King Fahad National Library, Riyadh, Saudi Arabia, 2013. Interior view showing the new and old buildings and the connecting bridges.

23 Gerber Architekten, the King Fahad National Library, Riyadh, Saudi Arabia, 2013. A new roof covers the entire area and integrates skylights and white membranes that diffuse daylight.

24 Gerber Architekten, the King Fahad National Library, Riyadh, Saudi Arabia, 2013. Details showing the connectors for steel cables and the shapes of the membranes.

25 Gerber Architekten, the King Fahad National Library, Riyadh, Saudi Arabia, 2013. The building facade integrates the rhomboid fabric shades, which are supported by steel cables.

5 BUILDING INTEGRATED INNOVATIONS AND METHODS 202-203

26 UNStudio, Hanjie Wanda Square, Wuhan, China, 2013. Exterior view showing the building facade treatment.

27

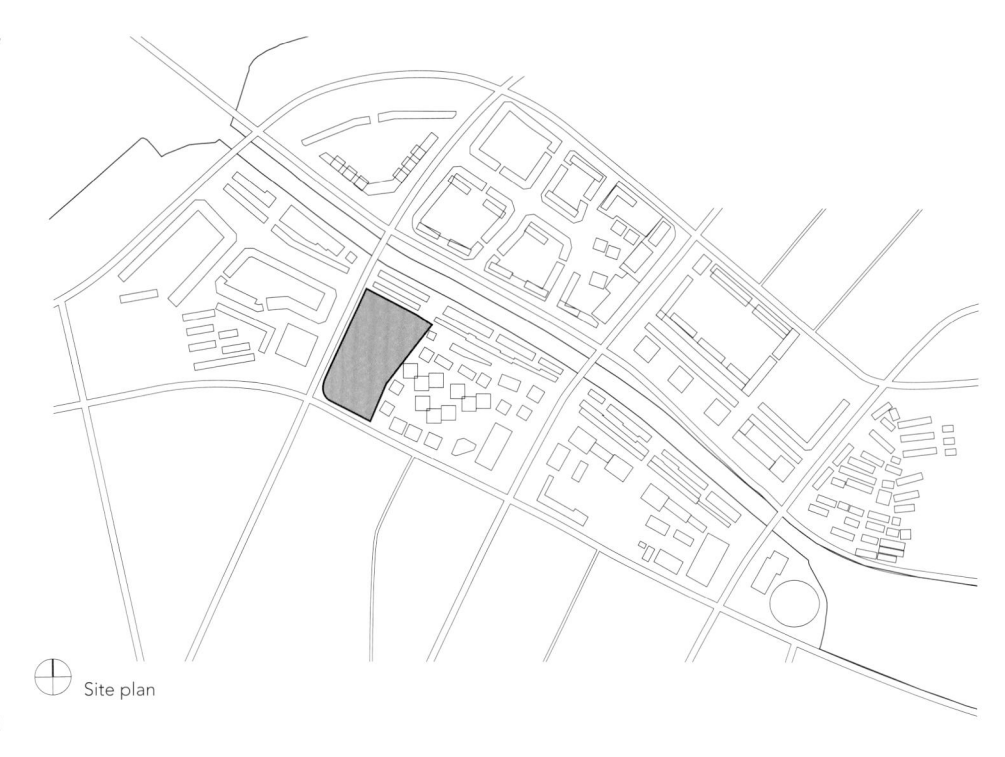

27 UNStudio, Hanjie Wanda Square, Wuhan, China, 2013. Site plan showing the building form and urban context.

Site plan

seamlessly integrated, where the outer, new building serves as an open library and contains reading spaces, offices and service areas, while the old building holds the main stacks. The design methods and techniques are examples of a very successful retrofitting strategy, aimed at improving the building's overall performance, design aesthetics and functionality.

HANJIE WANDA SQUARE

Hanjie Wanda Square is a new shopping centre in Wuhan, China, designed by UNStudio. The building is part of a larger multifunctional masterplan that includes cultural and tourist facilities, commercial, office and residential buildings.

The building programme includes retail spaces, a cinema and restaurants. The building has five above-ground levels. Two large atria are incorporated into the programme (south and north), introducing daylight to interior spaces and forming a central circulation path. The interior layout and design were influenced by circular forms, and the north and south atria were treated differently with variations in geometry, materials and details, creating two slightly different atmospheres. Since the geometry of the elevator shafts and roof within these two atria is complex, structural analysis was necessary to determine the loads and size of structural members. The sizes of structural members vary and correspond to loads. There were two basic types of panel used for the elevator shafts and roof: curved and triangulated. However, the relative dimensions and curvature vary depending on the location of the panels, and detailed modelling was necessary to determine sizes and positions, and to fabricate individual panels, since

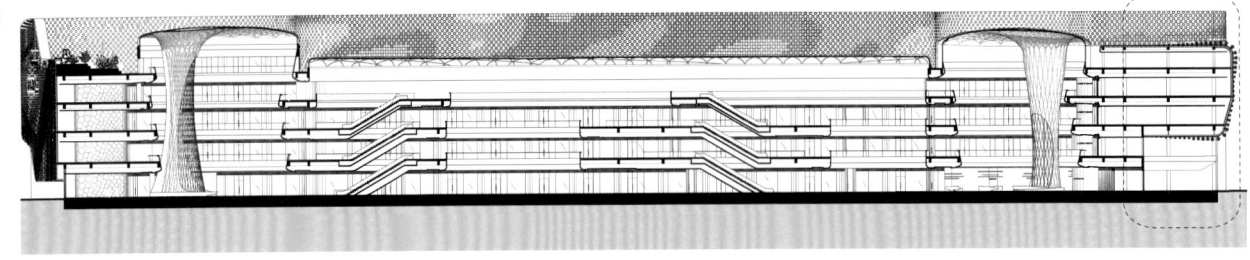

Section A-A

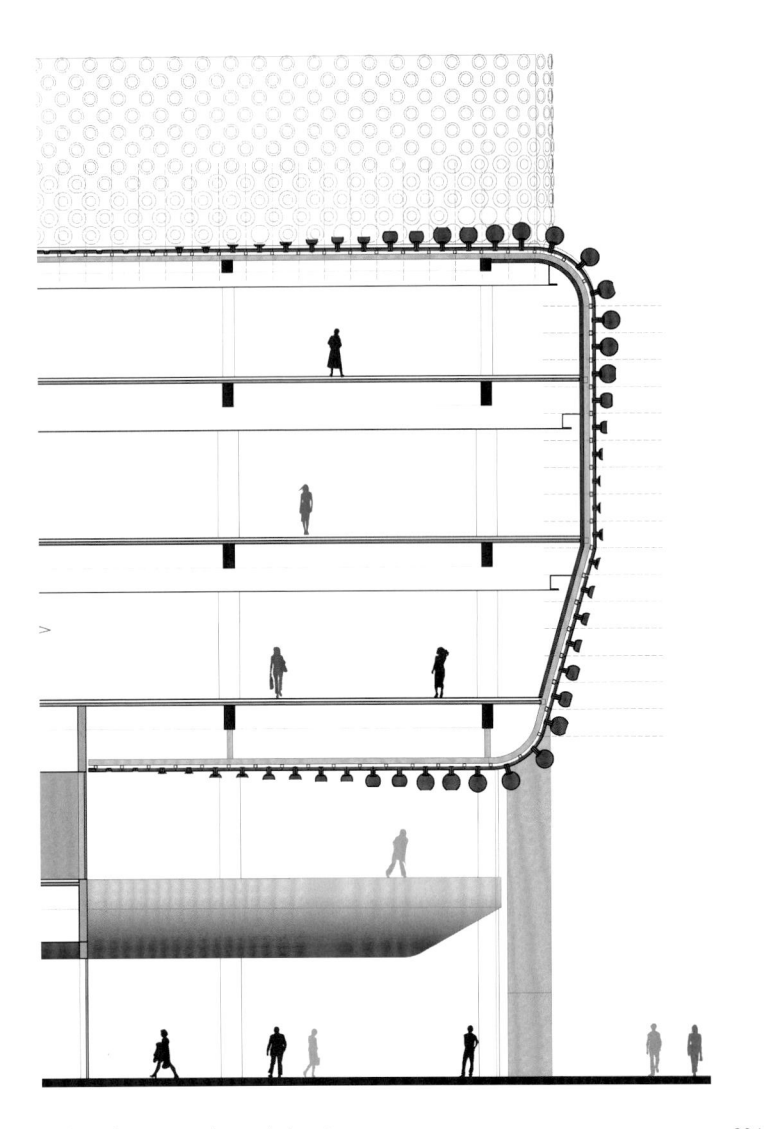

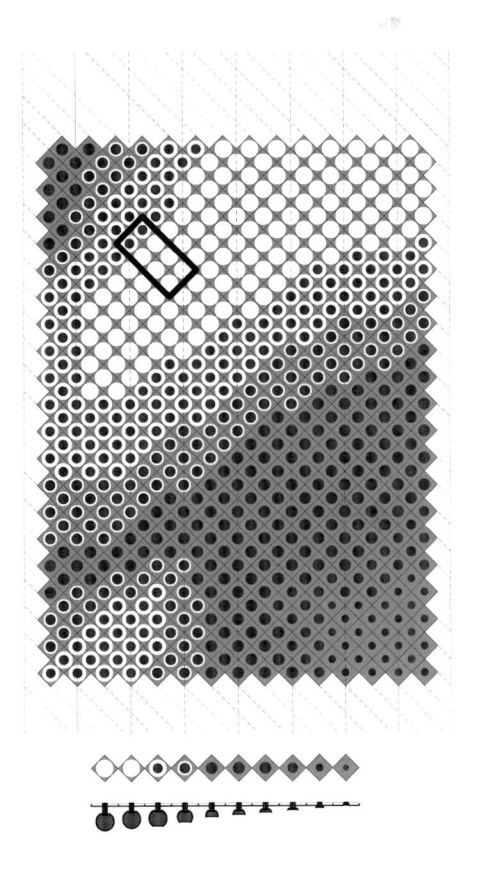

Enlarged section and partial elevation

28 UNStudio, Hanjie Wanda Square, Wuhan, China, 2013.
The sections and partial elevation demonstrate the building facade design and vertical spatial organisation.

29

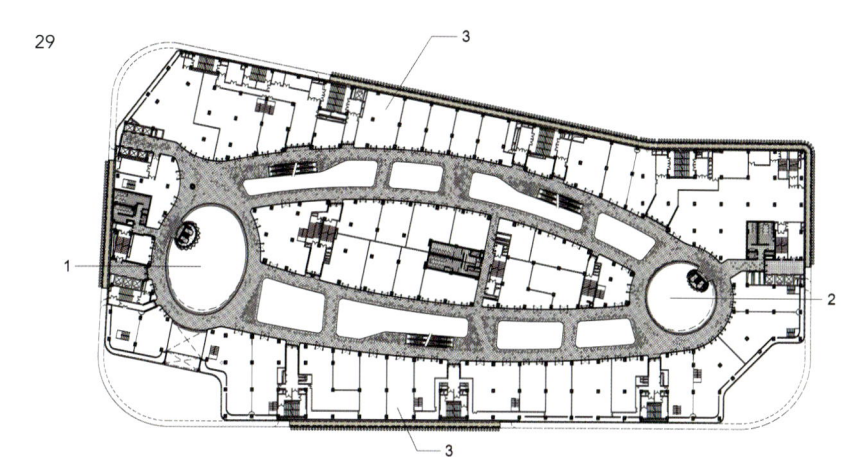

1 North atrium
2 South atrium
3 Retail space

30

Second-floor plan

29 UNStudio, Hanjie Wanda Square, Wuhan, China, 2013.
Floor plan showing the location of the north and south atria, retail and circulation space.

30 UNStudio, Hanjie Wanda Square, Wuhan, China, 2013.
The north and south atria have slight variations in geometry, material and details, but both are influenced by circular forms.

5 BUILDING INTEGRATED INNOVATIONS AND METHODS 206-207

31

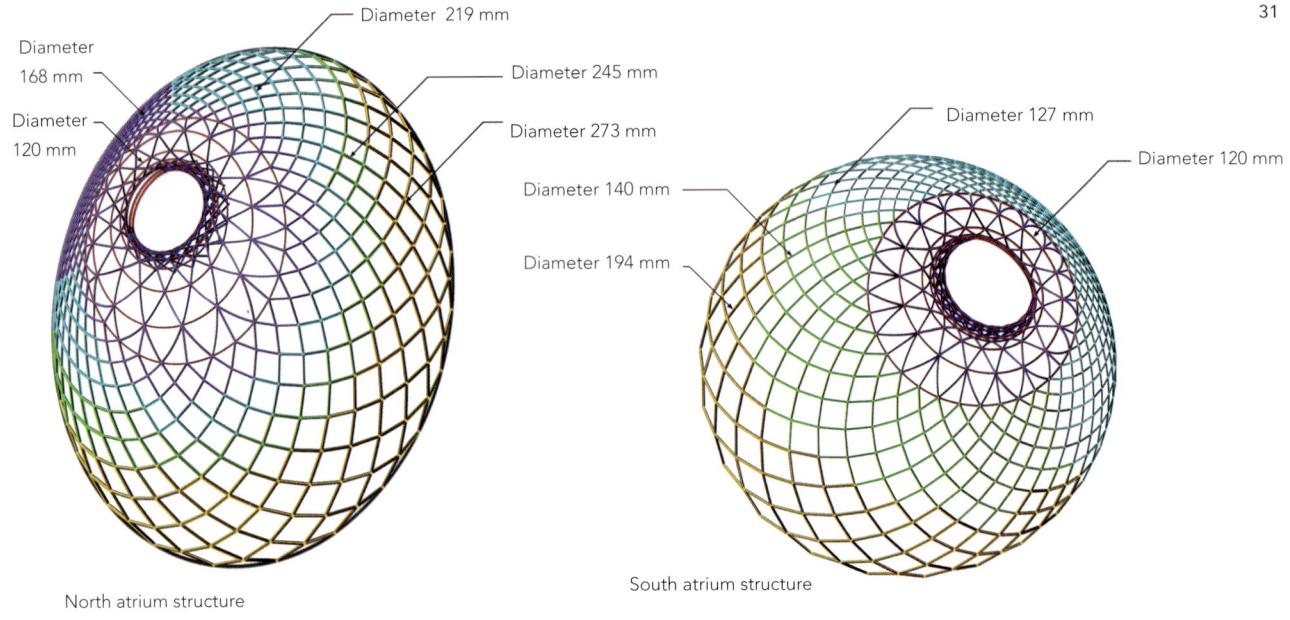

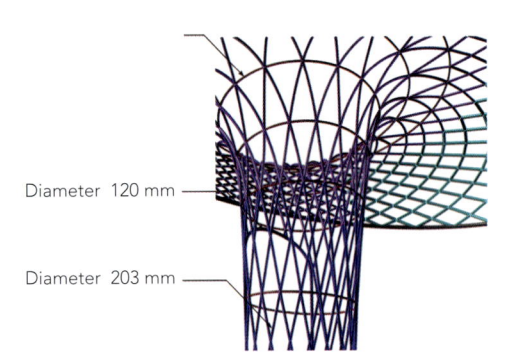

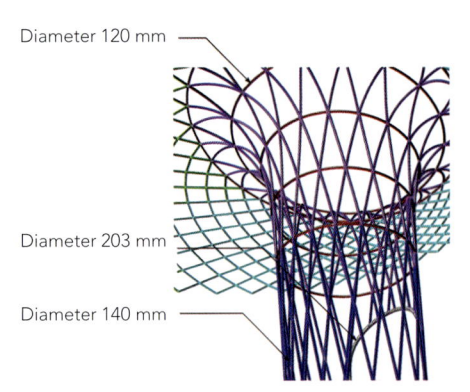

Diameter 168 mm
Diameter 120 mm
Diameter 219 mm
Diameter 245 mm
Diameter 273 mm
Diameter 140 mm
Diameter 194 mm
Diameter 127 mm
Diameter 120 mm

North atrium structure

South atrium structure

Diameter 120 mm
Diameter 203 mm

Diameter 120 mm
Diameter 203 mm
Diameter 140 mm

32

Curved panels (288)
3 to 3.5 m
1 to 1.5 m

Unfolded curved panels

Triangulated panels (1004)
2.5 to 3 m
1 to 1.5 m

Unfolded triangulated panels (skylight)

Unfolded triangulated panels (elevator shaft)

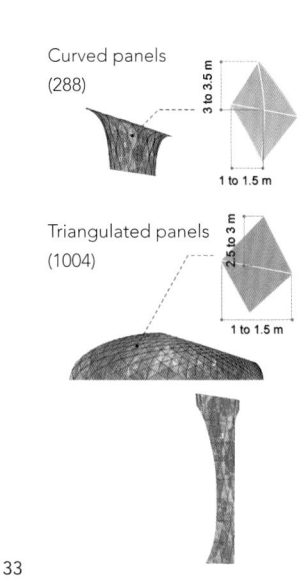

33

31 UNStudio, Hanjie Wanda Square, Wuhan, China, 2013.
Structural analysis was performed to determine loads and to size the structural members of the elevator shaft and skylights in the atria.

32 UNStudio, Hanjie Wanda Square, Wuhan, China, 2013.
Interior views showing material choices, circulation space and a large skylight that introduces daylight into the interior.

33 UNStudio, Hanjie Wanda Square, Wuhan, China, 2013.
Two types of panels were used as cladding material for the elevator shafts and atria skylights: curved and triangulated. Model-based design and fabrication were used to determine the size and position of individual panels, since almost 1,300 panels were used.

almost 1,300 panels were used for these complex shapes. The main circulation space has abundant daylight, since skylights are incorporated in the roof and are clad with ETFE cushions.

One of the most innovative components of the Hanjie Wanda Square is its facade design. It uses two main materials – polished stainless steel and patterned glass. Nine different types of spheres have been applied, crafted using these materials. Their specific location on the facade creates the effect of movement and reflection, where the geometry ranges from full stainless-steel spheres, to a sequence of gradually trimmed spheres, to a hemisphere with an inlay of laminated glass with printed foil. The spheres are mounted at various distances on brushed aluminium panels, which were prefabricated and mounted on-site. The facade system also incorporates lighting, where each sphere contains an LED lighting fixture, and back panels are illuminated with LED lighting too, creating a diffused effect. Various possibilities to combine and control lighting create changing patterns.

This case study is an example of how design, computation and analysis, selection of materials and prefabrication can be integrated to create complex geometries, rationalise and design structural systems and components, construct a dynamic building facade with variable components and create inviting interior spaces. Computational design and structural analysis were essential in rationalising and determining structural components for the atria skylights, elevator shafts and the central skylight, since irregular geometries required non-uniform support and cladding elements. Although the building facade is mostly opaque, the atria skylights and the central skylight introduce daylight into the interior spaces. This was driven by the fact that this location has a humid subtropical climate. Limiting solar heat gain through the facades and providing diffused daylight through skylights is the appropriate method for this climate type. The dynamic nature of the building facade is actually created by the static stainless-steel spheres, which vary in size. The overall design of the building is responsive to climate and the programme, and relied on integrated analysis, prefabrication and the appropriate use of materials to create an innovative retail space.

5 BUILDING INTEGRATED INNOVATIONS AND METHODS 208-209

34 UNStudio, Hanjie Wanda Square, Wuhan, China, 2013.
Facade modules were prefabricated and assembled on-site.

Press-mould forming of stainless steel → Polishing and finishing process → Preassembly and fabrication → Mounting panels on site

35 UNStudio, Hanjie Wanda Square, Wuhan, China, 2013.
The facade system consists of stainless-steel spheres that create the effect of movement and reflection.

Module 1
No lighting

Module 2
No lighting

Module 3
No lighting

Module 4
Frontlight and backlight

Module 5
Frontlight and backlight

Module 6
Frontlight and backlight

Module 7
Frontlight and backlight

Module 8
Frontlight and backlight

Module 9
Backlight

36

36 UNStudio, Hanjie Wanda Square, Wuhan, China, 2013.
Nine different types of sphere have been used for the facade design, constructed of polished stainless steel, glass and lighting. The geometry ranges from full stainless-steel spheres, to a sequence of gradually trimmed spheres, to a hemisphere with an inlay of laminated glass with printed foil. The majority of spheres include front and backlighting.

COLLABORATIVE LIFE SCIENCES BUILDING AND SKOURTES TOWER

The Collaborative Life Sciences Building and Skourtes Tower (CLSB/SKT), designed by CO Architects and SERA, is in Portland, Oregon. CLSB/SKT is a new health sciences education and research building and includes academic and administration spaces for the Oregon Health and Science University (OHSU), Oregon State University (OSU), and Portland State University (PSU). It is located on a 9,700 m² (2.4 acres) site near downtown, adjacent to the Willamette River. The building was conceived as an innovative model of interdisciplinary health sciences education and research, aimed at promoting partnerships among the universities. It expands the universities' teaching facilities, classrooms and learning environments and research activities. Meant to foster collaboration in undergraduate and graduate education among students and faculty members from multiple institutions, CLSB/SKT includes lecture halls, classrooms, laboratories, research centres, offices and underground parking.

The CLSB/SKT consists of a 12-storey north tower, a five-storey south tower and an atrium. The building programme includes medical research laboratories, academic teaching laboratories, medical simulation education spaces, multi-use and multifunctioning classrooms, conference rooms and lecture halls, retail spaces, two levels of underground parking, and academic support amenities. The upper five storeys of the north tower contain the OHSU School of Dentistry and include patient clinical spaces, speciality dentistry, continuing professional dentistry education spaces and faculty offices. The south tower houses the OSU College of Pharmacy and includes a lecture hall, classroom spaces, conference rooms and faculty offices. A clinical medical simulation programme is also in the south tower.

Daylighting was the driving concept for CLSB/SKT, with laboratories open to daylight on two sides. Office spaces are on the east side of the tower, adjacent to the laboratories. Glazed connecting staircases lead to communal spaces or lounges at every other level. The atrium provides ample daylight to the interior through glazed curtain walls and a skylight. The divisible lecture hall is lifted above the ground floor by columns and brace supports, and extends beyond the plane of the curtain wall, as seen in building sections. It is clad in wood-textured panels to create a distinctive exterior visual impression. The learning spaces support team-based learning and include simulation as an essential part of medical education. The fourth floor is flexible and open and can accommodate collaborative clinical training across various disciplines.

Environmental design was considered and integrated into all aspects of the building. Energy-efficient design strategies include high-efficiency lighting, high-performing building envelope, heat-recovery system within the atrium and low ventilation fume hoods in the laboratory spaces. Green roofs provide a native habitat for species and improve storm water management. The rainwater

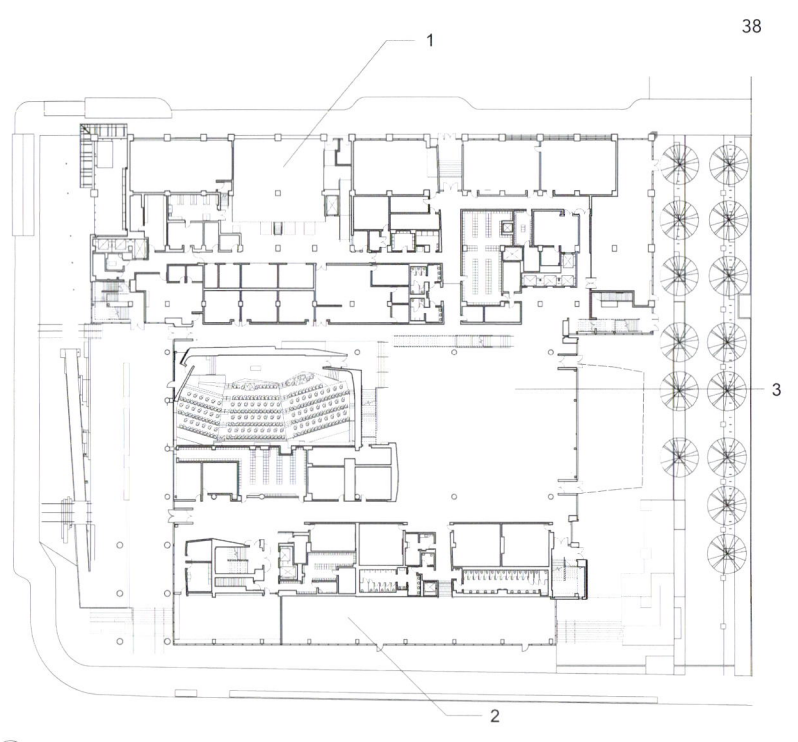

First-floor plan

1 South tower
2 North tower
3 Atrium

Second-floor plan

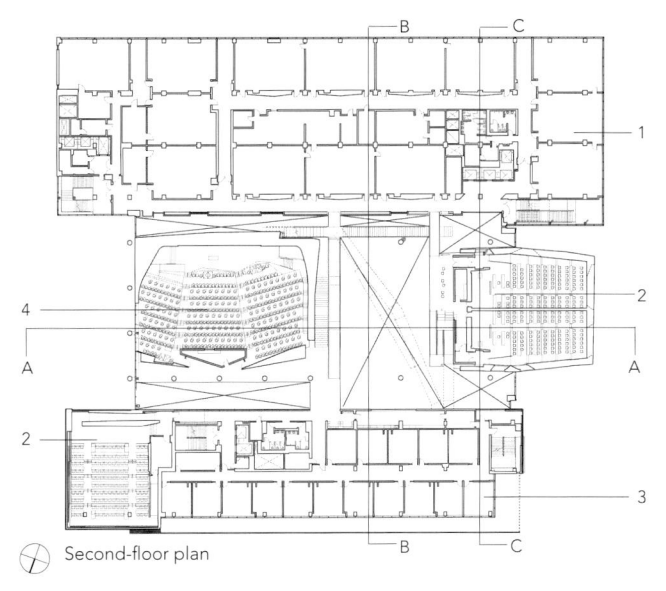

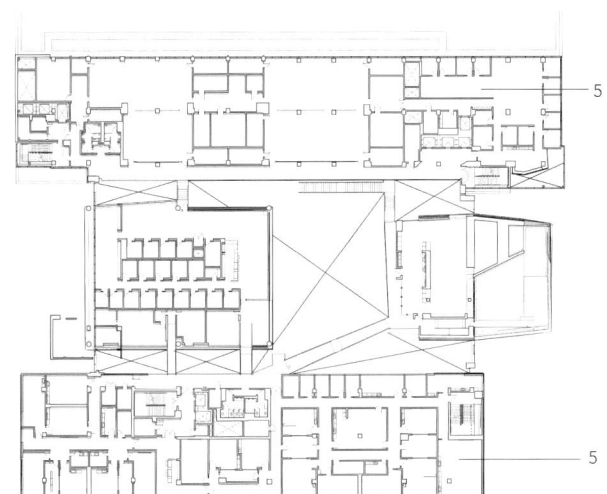

Fourth-floor plan

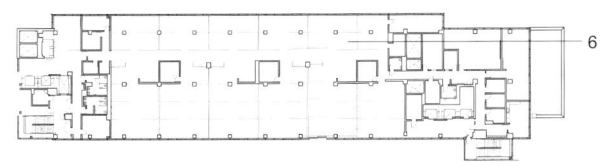

Eighth-floor plan

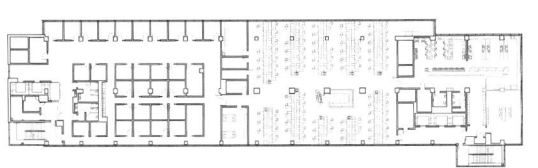

Tenth-floor plan

37 CO Architects and SERA, Collaborative Life Sciences Building and Skourtes Tower (CLSB/SKT), Portland, OR, USA, 2014.
This new integrated health sciences education and research building consists of three major components (south tower, north tower and a central atrium).

38 CO Architects and SERA, Collaborative Life Sciences Building and Skourtes Tower (CLSB/SKT), Portland, OR, USA, 2014.
The first-floor plan shows the relation between the north and south tower, and the central atrium.

39 CO Architects and SERA, Collaborative Life Sciences Building and Skourtes Tower (CLSB/SKT), Portland, OR, USA, 2014.
Floor plans showing the spatial layout arrangement on the upper levels.

1 Classrooms
2 Lecture hall
3 Offices
4 Auditorium
5 Laboratories
6 Flexible learning space

5 BUILDING INTEGRATED INNOVATIONS AND METHODS

Section A-A

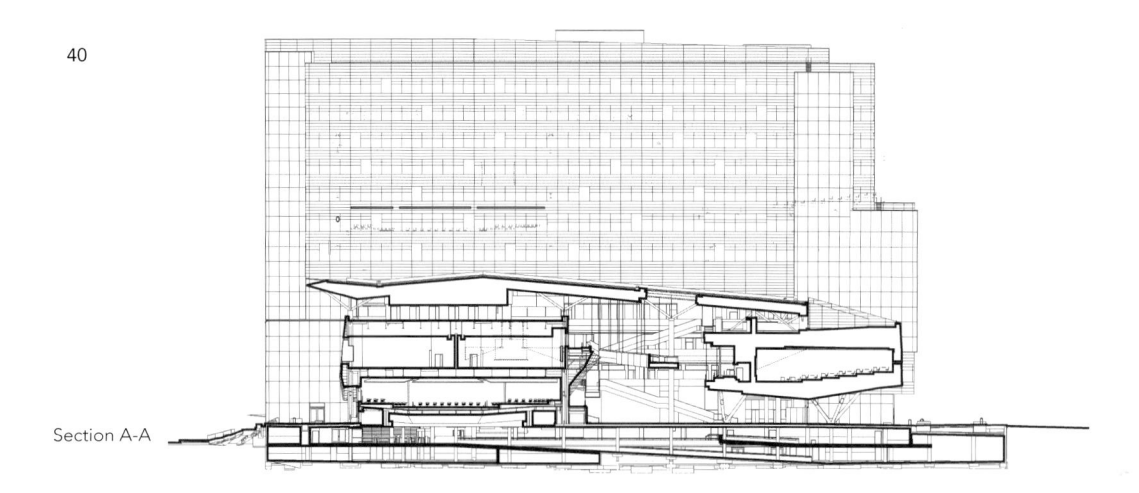

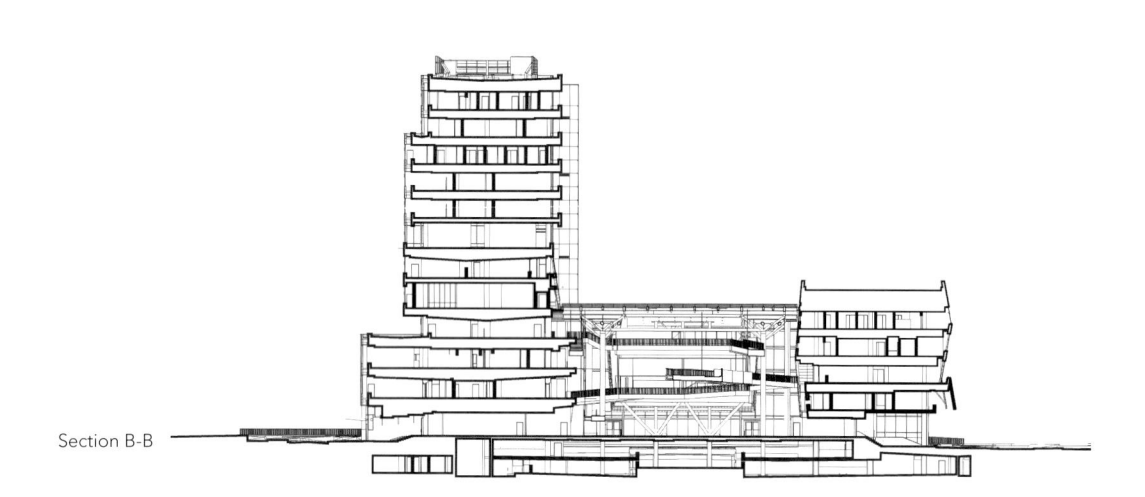

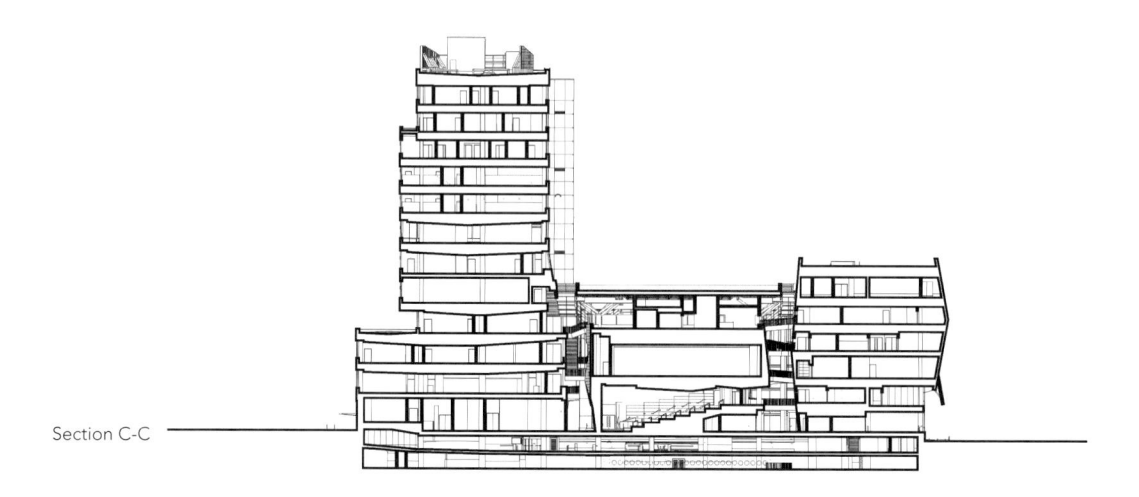

Section B-B

Section C-C

40 CO Architects and SERA, Collaborative Life Sciences Building and Skourtes Tower (CLSB/SKT), Portland, OR, USA, 2014.
Sections indicate the vertical spatial arrangements and relationships between the towers and the central atrium.

41

41 CO Architects and SERA, Collaborative Life Sciences Building and Skourtes Tower (CLSB/SKT), Portland, OR, USA, 2014.
The atrium introduces ample daylight to interior spaces.

collection system is included and provides water for toilet flushing. Innovative design processes consisted of highly collaborative project design and delivery, since the architecture and construction teams were selected simultaneously in the early stages. The building was designed, constructed and delivered in only 38 months with the design and construction teams situated in the same location throughout the design and construction process. This allowed for highly collaborative and interactive design processes, essential for the success of the project.

During design and construction BIM was crucial, as it provided the means to show potential designs, layouts and information for cost modelling within the compressed fast-track schedule. Twenty-three individual models were developed, by the various

5 BUILDING INTEGRATED INNOVATIONS AND METHODS 214-215

42 CO Architects and SERA, Collaborative Life Sciences Building and Skourtes Tower (CLSB/SKT), Portland, OR, USA, 2014.
The divisible lecture hall is clad in wood-textured panels and extends beyond the atrium's curtain wall.

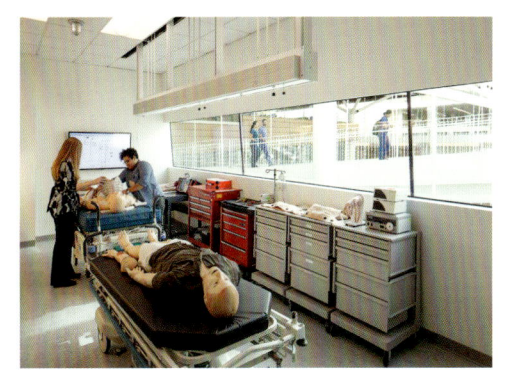

43 CO Architects and SERA, Collaborative Life Sciences Building and Skourtes Tower (CLSB/SKT), Portland, OR, USA, 2014.
Interior views showing the learning and laboratory spaces.

design disciplines, and lined together to form an integrated model. A BIM management plan was developed to establish modelling expectations for the design and construction team members. Clash detection was performed during the later stages of the design to resolve conflicts between different building systems, and during construction in order to resolve any potential conflicts at a finer level.

At each transition point from design to construction, BIM was shared with the contractor and subcontractors for design input, including MEP subcontractors, building envelope and curtain wall subcontractors and the metal cladding subcontractor. The key benefits included the visualisation of all building components and enhanced coordination, which also allowed the prefabrication of certain building elements, such as the plumbing systems and ductwork. The anchors for the MEP and overhead fire-protection systems were cast top-side into the concrete slabs, rather than drilled at later stages. This reduced the project budget, but required coordination, since the location of interior partitions and routing of the MEP systems had to be determined prior to concrete pouring. The coordination was performed using BIM, and 'just-in-time delivery' was possible due to the extensive collaborative efforts and use of technology.

This is an example of an innovative building type that provides a new model for interdisciplinary health sciences education and research. It combines teaching spaces, classrooms, lecture halls

BIM implementation

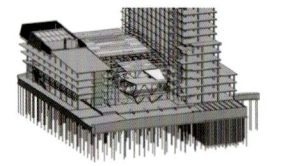

Design visualisation

Building programme and systems

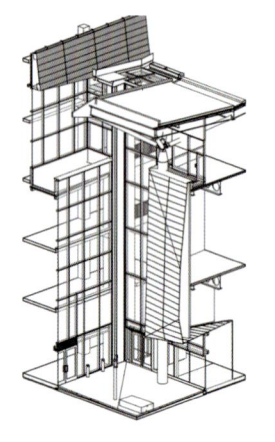

Constructability and coordination

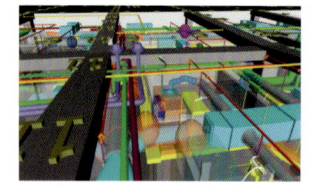

Clash detection

with laboratories and research spaces, and the building is used by several universities. The building form, spatial layout, organisation and circulation respond to the building programme and create an exciting and visually striking complex. Energy efficiency and sustainable design methods were incorporated to improve the building performance. But the primary innovation relates to the design process and project delivery methods – the highly collaborative process included the architecture and construction teams from the early stages of the design. Moreover, BIM was crucial for the successful collaboration and integration of numerous design disciplines. It was used for the architectural design, visualisation, cost estimation, coordination and clash detection, as well as construction planning.

SHANGHAI NATURAL HISTORY MUSEUM

The Shanghai Natural History Museum, designed by Perkins+Will, is a new museum whose shape and building organisation were inspired by the nautilus shell. The building sits adjacent to an urban sculpture park, and the design was influenced by Chinese garden design, mainly through its relationship to the site and nature. A spiralling landscaped plane progresses from the park and wraps around an oval courtyard, which contains a traditional stepped garden composed of rock formations and water features. The pond provides evaporative cooling for the garden, improving comfort conditions in this exterior environment. Rain is collected from the vegetated roof and stored in a tank, filtered and treated, and used to refill the pond if necessary due to water loss from evaporation. Rainwater is also used for irrigation, and for hardscape and roadway cleaning. A geoexchange system has been incorporated for cooling and heating.

The building programme includes exhibition spaces, a 4D theatre, outdoor exhibit garden and a central five-storey atrium. This atrium was incorporated as an organising feature of the museum,

44 CO Architects and SERA, Collaborative Life Sciences Building and Skourtes Tower (CLSB/SKT), Portland, OR, USA, 2014.
BIM was used throughout the design and construction process for design visualisation, coordination, cost modelling and clash detection.

45 CO Architects and SERA, Collaborative Life Sciences Building and Skourtes Tower (CLSB/SKT), Portland, OR, USA, 2014.
Prefabricated ductwork and the BIM model indicate plumbing and mechanical systems.

46 CO Architects and SERA, Collaborative Life Sciences Building and Skourtes Tower (CLSB/SKT), Portland, OR, USA, 2014.
A BIM model was used for the coordination and construction of anchors for the overhead MEP and fire protection systems.

47 Perkins+Will, Shanghai Natural History Museum, Shanghai, China, 2015.
This new museum is dedicated to natural history and is located within an urban park and dense urban fabric.

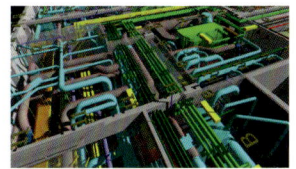

45

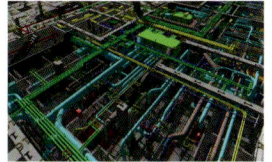

46

and is clad in an iconic, curved building skin that resembles an organic cell membrane, symbolising the basis of all biological life forms. The cell wall functions as a solar sunscreen, the main building structural element and waterproof building enclosure. It consists of three distinct layers: structure, curtain wall and sunscreen. Geometrically, these three layers form offset surfaces with a constant distance from the controlling mesh, which formed a 3D conical shape rather than 2D planar structures. The east facade incorporates vertical vegetation, which improves thermal performance of the building envelope.

Computational design was a key aspect in developing a randomly organic pattern, and extensive research was performed during the design.[1] In order to model the complex form and modules of the atrium, various BIM software programs were explored. The design team ultimately used Rhino3D® modelling software for modelling, prototyping and visualisation to create graphic representations. When beginning the design, parametric solutions were explored using hexagonal cell geometries, which resulted in noticeable repetitions in the cell pattern. Randomised computer-generated patterns produced infinite variations of cell sizes and shapes that

47

5 BUILDING INTEGRATED INNOVATIONS AND METHODS 218-219

Site plan

49

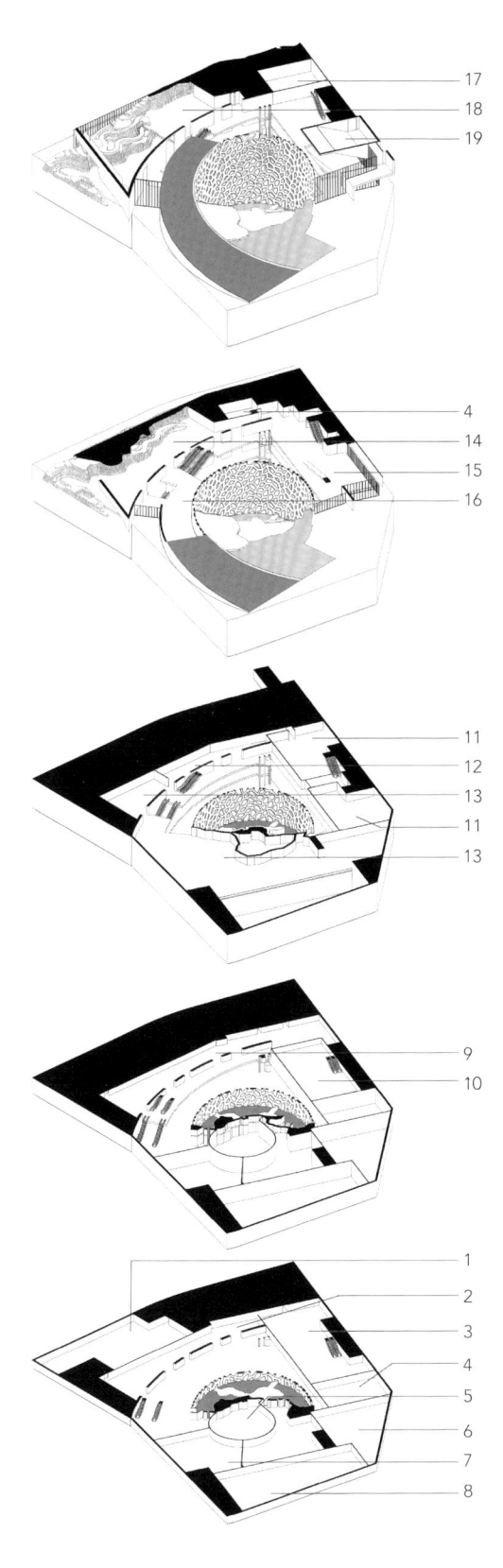

48 Perkins+Will, Shanghai Natural History Museum, Shanghai, China, 2015.
The site plan indicates the location and context of the museum in relation to the surrounding buildings and the park.

49 Perkins+Will, Shanghai Natural History Museum, Shanghai, China, 2015.
The building programme includes exhibition spaces, a 4D theatre, outdoor exhibit garden and a central five-storey atrium.

1 Exploration labs
2 Treasures on Earth
3 Tied to Earth
4 Gift shop
5 Diverse ecologies
6 Colourful lives
7 Survival wisdom
8 Walk into Africa
9 Shanghai story
10 Cafe
11 Temporary exhibit
12 Future pathways
13 The way of evolution
14 River of life
15 Entry lobby
16 Rediscovering nature
17 Lecture hall
18 Mystery of origins
19 4D theatre

5 BUILDING INTEGRATED INNOVATIONS AND METHODS 220-221

First-floor plan

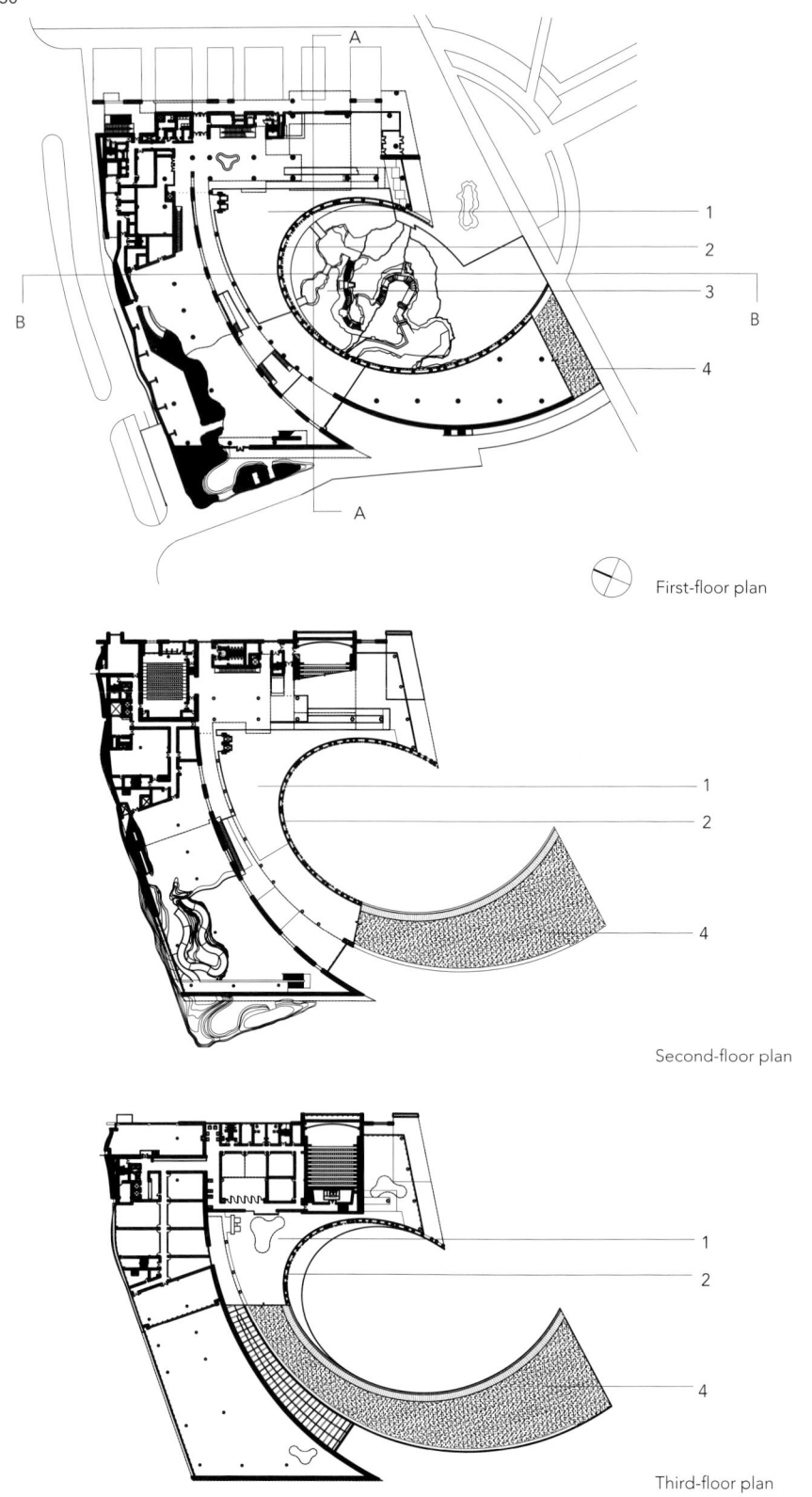

Second-floor plan

Third-floor plan

50 Perkins+Will, Shanghai Natural History Museum, Shanghai, China, 2015. Floor plans showing the spatial arrangement and the building layout. The central garden and atrium provide a focal point, while the curved 'cell wall' provides shading for the atrium. The sloping landscaped plane connects the building roof to the park.

1 Atrium
2 Cell wall
3 Garden
4 Sloping landscaped plane

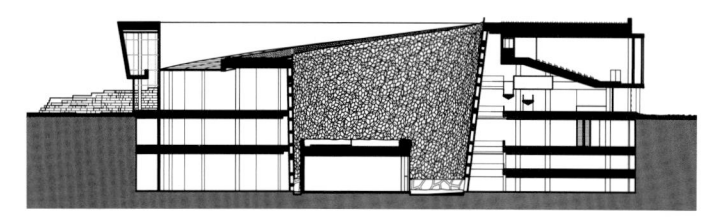

Section A-A'

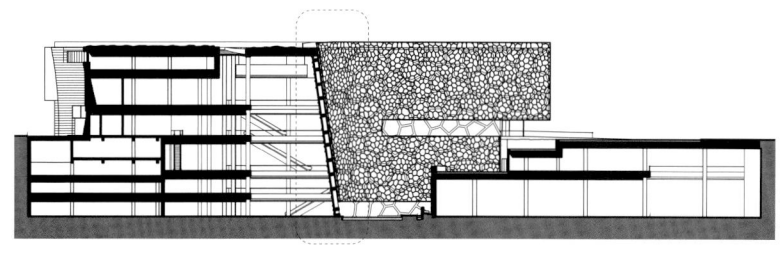

Section B-B'

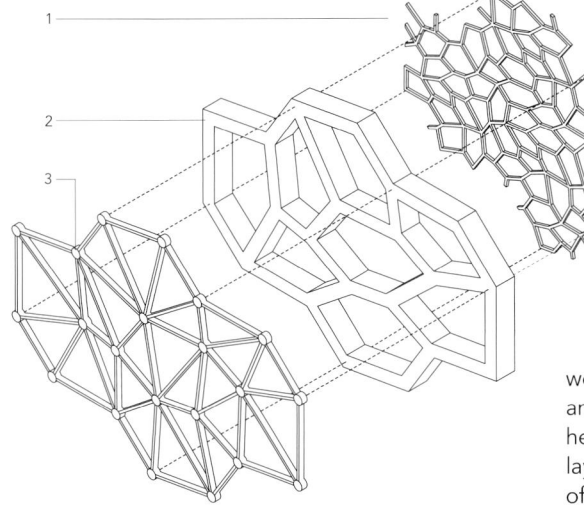

1 Aluminium sunscreen
2 Aluminium clad steel structure
3 Aluminium framed curtain wall

51 Perkins+Will, Shanghai Natural History Museum, Shanghai, China, 2015.
Sections showing the vertical spatial arrangement, central courtyard, atrium and the cell wall.

52 Perkins+Will, Shanghai Natural History Museum, Shanghai, China, 2015.
This diagram indicates the components of the cell wall, which include the curtain wall, aluminium-clad steel structure and the aluminium sunscreen.

were not practical or technically feasible. Instead, manual patterns and generated solutions were investigated, where a mix of hexagonal and polygonal shapes were studied in a conical-curved layout. The overall complexity was controlled by setting the limit of cell-form variations to eight patterns.

Since the cell wall provides the full structural support element for the building, structural engineers were engaged from the start of the design. The cell wall is subject to axial building loads, lateral wind and seismic forces, which had to be analysed and simulated. A finite element method (FEM) analysis was used to study the forces and loads. The structural solution for this complex geometry consisted of welded intersecting steel tubes that formed a solid node. The structural organisation of the nodes was critical for transferring forces and for fabrication feasibility. The structural grid was limited to pentagon and hexagon polygonal shapes, which guaranteed that the intersecting nodes would be limited to three of four intersecting structural members. Steel fabrication methods and on-site construction concepts were investigated, where the 'zipper concept' was envisioned as an approach for steel assembly. The basic steel cell units could be preconstructed in the factory, shipped to the construction site and assembled. The curtain wall

5 BUILDING INTEGRATED INNOVATIONS AND METHODS 222-223

53 Perkins+Will, Shanghai Natural History Museum, Shanghai, China, 2015.
Exterior views and a bird's-eye perspective show the relationship between the museum and the surrounding context, building form and different building facades.

consists of a unitised system, separate and formed independently from the structure, but bracketed from the rear, facing the interior side of the atrium.

The geometric solution for the exterior sunscreen was derived from the patterns developed for the structural wall. It was pinned at the central nodes of the structure. A denser pattern of polygonal cell geometry was developed that would reduce unwanted solar heat gain. Since the curtain wall within the atrium is slightly tilting back and facing different orientations, the density and size of the screen geometry was carefully analysed for the actual solar-shading performance, while also maintaining visual aesthetics and views to the outside.

The innovative design, building form, building envelope treatment and integration with the site and landscape make this building a truly remarkable architectural artefact. The computational design process, integration of advanced technologies, cell wall design, technical detailing and the overall sensitivity to the site and cultural context are the key elements that make this building innovative. The reinterpretation of cultural elements and traditional garden design is evident in the central courtyard, the focal point of the building. The wrapping atrium and curved cell wall, with its intricate design and layers, are technical marvels in terms of geometry, structural support and components, choice of materials and assembly.

54 Perkins+Will, Shanghai Natural History Museum, Shanghai, China, 2015.
The organic pattern of the cell wall and structural support create an interesting, dynamic design.

55

Partial elevations

Enlarged section

Partial plan

56

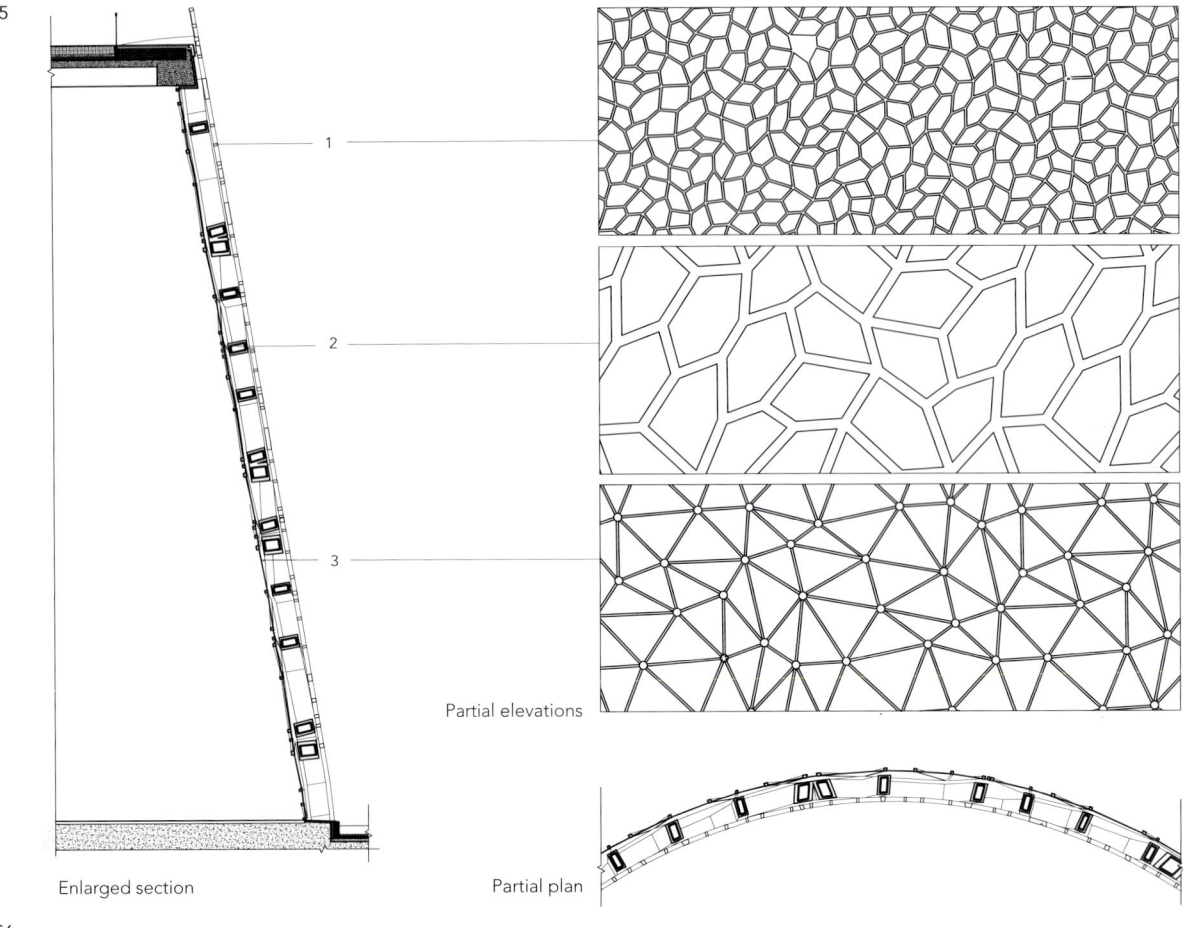

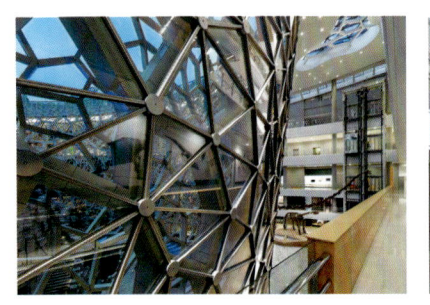

1 Aluminium sunscreen
2 Aluminium-clad steel structure
3 Aluminium-framed curtain wall

55 Perkins+Will, Shanghai Natural History Museum, Shanghai, China, 2015.
Enlarged section, partial elevations and partial plan of the cell wall indicate material components and organic patterns.

56 Perkins+Will, Shanghai Natural History Museum, Shanghai, China, 2015.
Interior views showing the atrium, circulation space, cell wall from the interior and skylights.

57 Perkins+Will, Shanghai Natural History Museum, Shanghai, China, 2015.
The cell wall sunscreen shades the atrium, creating an inviting courtyard.

5 BUILDING INTEGRATED INNOVATIONS AND METHODS 226-227

58 Asymptote Architecture, Yas Hotel, Abu Dhabi, UAE, 2009.
Exterior views showing the complex geometry and components of the building's skin.

59 Asymptote Architecture, Yas Hotel, Abu Dhabi, UAE, 2009.
The site plan showing the building form and surrounding context. The complex is situated along a marina and consists of two oval-shaped buildings, connecting bridge and a vast grid-shell roof structure that provides shading.

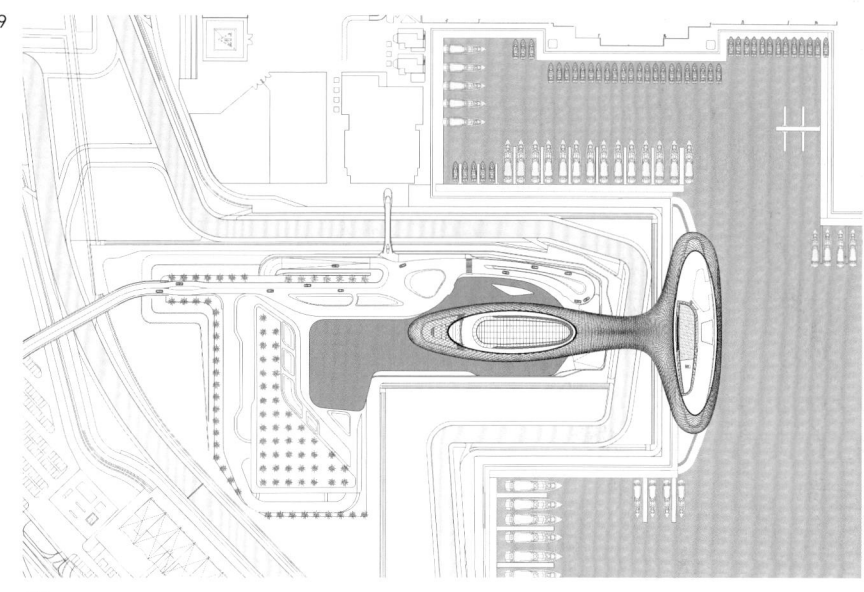

Site plan

THE YAS HOTEL
The Yas Hotel in Abu Dhabi, designed by Asymptote Architecture, consists of two elliptical buildings connected by a curved bridge, and a vast grid-shell structure that provides sun shading and protection. One of the buildings is situated on land, while the other sits on the edge of a marina, surrounded by water. The buildings include 10 levels and 500 hotel rooms, event spaces, services and a Formula One race track that wraps around the buildings. The steel bridge spans and overlooks the race track, while a glass and steel latticework grid-shell structure wraps around the buildings.

The grid-shell is the largest of its kind in the world, and gives this building a recognisable form. It is supported at only 10 points, and is composed of over 5,600 diamond-shaped quadrilaterals, created by the intersection of the structural steel members. The components of the grid-shell structural system include the primary steel-framing and curved steel elements, curved steel rib, cable tension system, integrated framing units that form a rigid mesh and diamond-shaped glass panels. The framing units and glass panels were prefabricated as a unitised system and assembled on-site. Each glass panel is offset and rotated from the primary grid-shell plane by a pivot. The rotation angles vary, and create a flowing effect across the surface. A network of LED luminaires covers the entire building and is optimally positioned on each glass panel, which provides a distinctive effect at night. The diamond shapes are also introduced within the interior spaces.

The structural design, technical detailing and the material components of the grid-shell roof structure demonstrate how technological innovations can influence building design. The primary purpose of the grid-shell is to provide shading for the two buildings and the exterior space between them, since the building

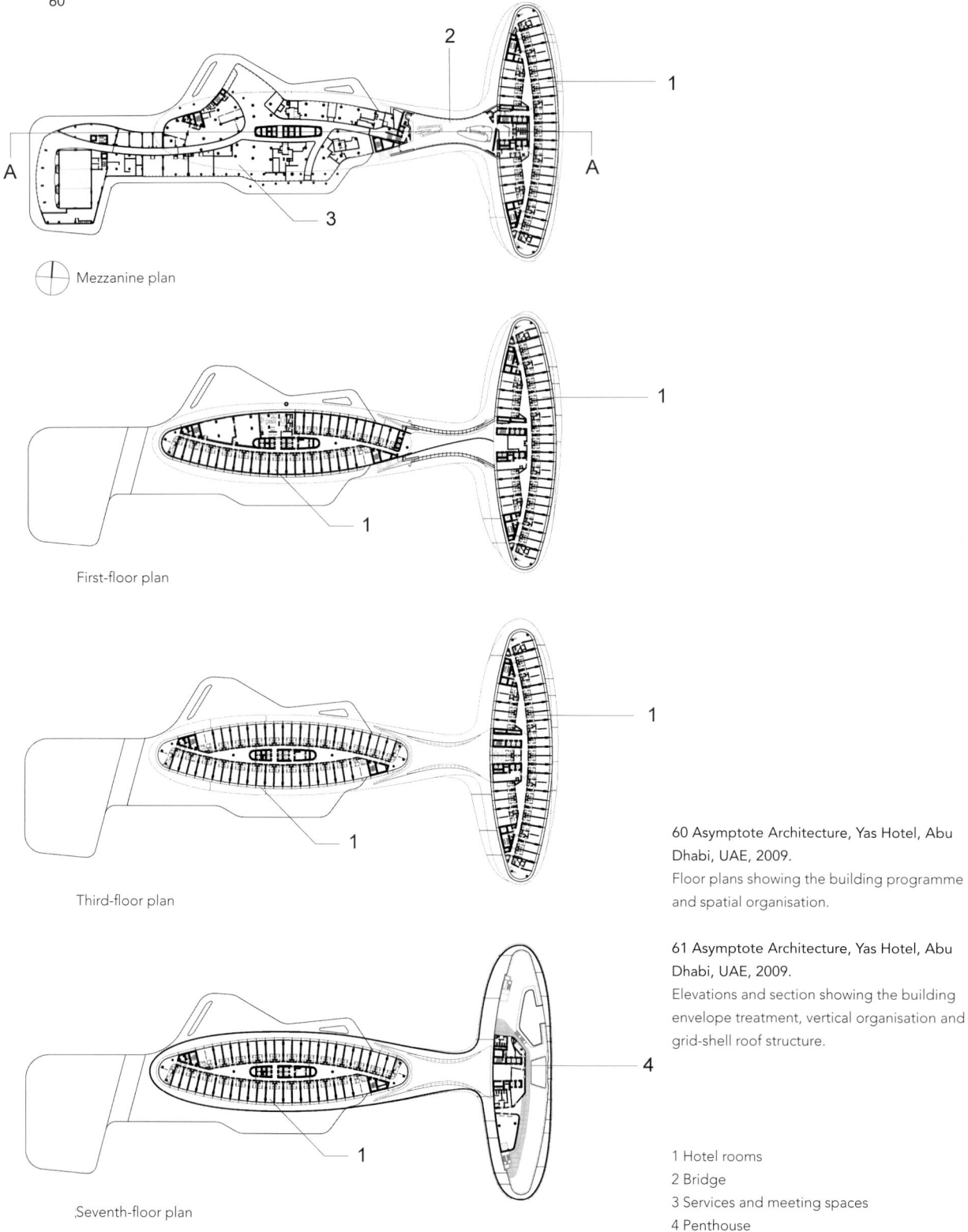

60

Mezzanine plan

First-floor plan

Third-floor plan

Seventh-floor plan

60 Asymptote Architecture, Yas Hotel, Abu Dhabi, UAE, 2009.
Floor plans showing the building programme and spatial organisation.

61 Asymptote Architecture, Yas Hotel, Abu Dhabi, UAE, 2009.
Elevations and section showing the building envelope treatment, vertical organisation and grid-shell roof structure.

1 Hotel rooms
2 Bridge
3 Services and meeting spaces
4 Penthouse

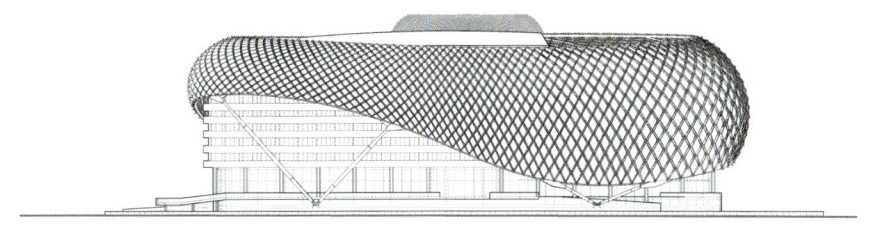

East elevation

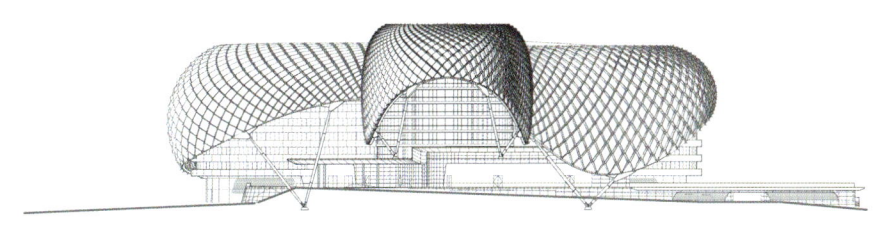

West elevation

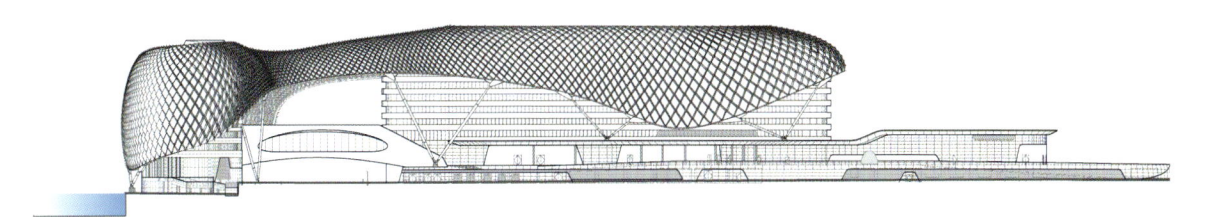

North elevation

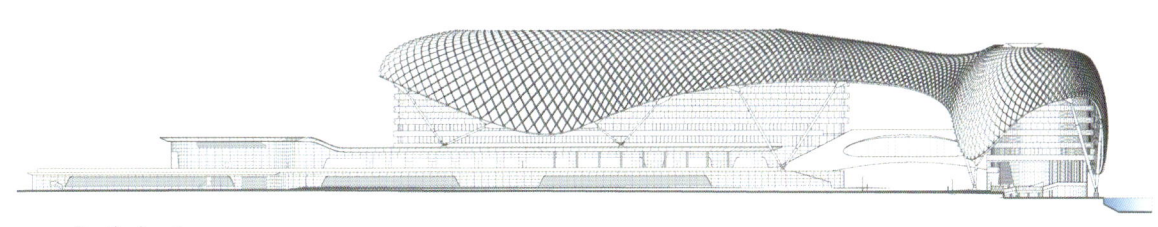

South elevation

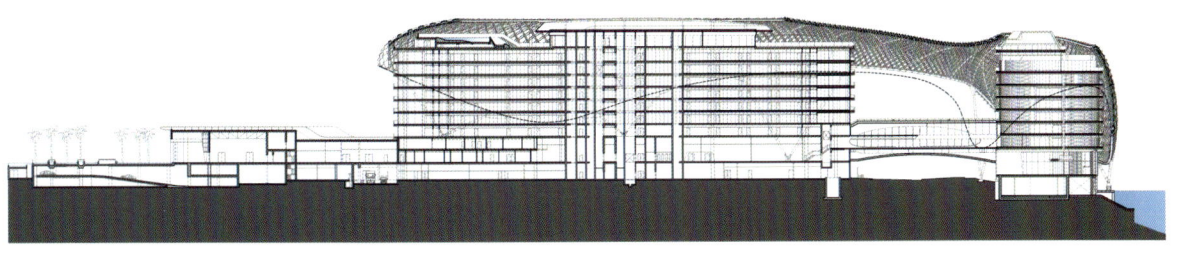

Section A-A

5 BUILDING INTEGRATED INNOVATIONS AND METHODS 230-231

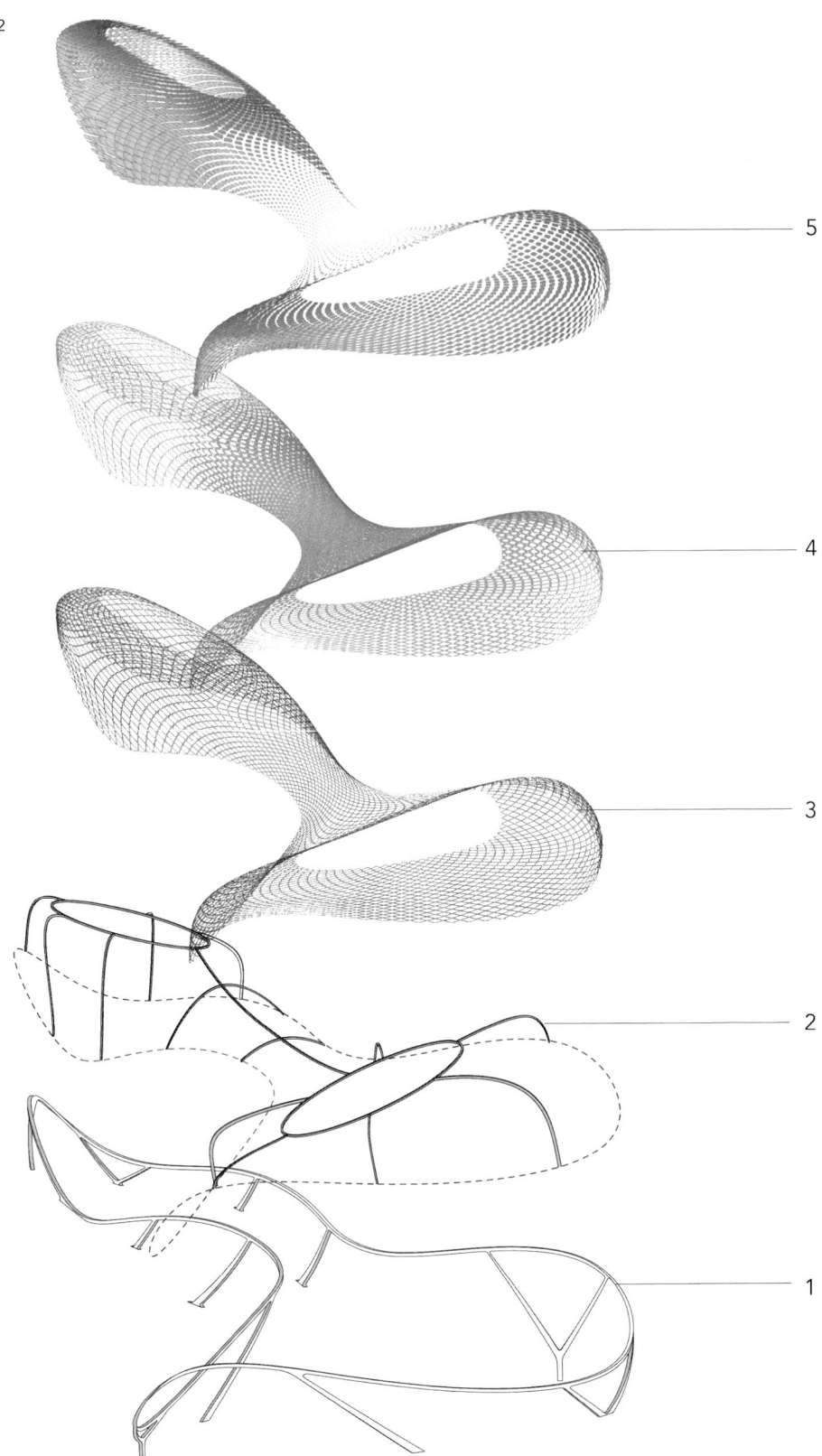

62 Asymptote Architecture, Yas Hotel, Abu Dhabi, UAE, 2009.
Components of the grid-shell structural system.

1 Primary steel framing
2 Steel rib support
3 Cable tension system
4 Integrated framing units
5 Diamond-shaped glass panels

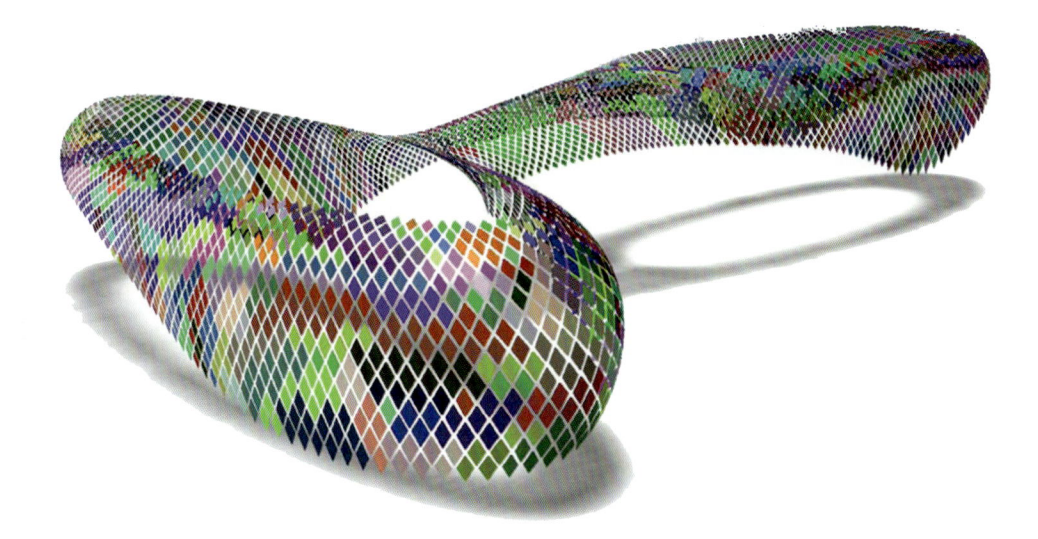

63 Asymptote Architecture, Yas Hotel, Abu Dhabi, UAE, 2009.
More than 5,600 diamond-shaped glazing units are integrated within the grid-shell structure and include LED lighting.

is located in a very hot and sunny climate. It creates a protective secondary skin, but also unifies the complex and establishes a cohesive design language.

HEALTH SCIENCES EDUCATION BUILDING, PHOENIX BIOMEDICAL CAMPUS
The Health Sciences Education Building (HSEB) in Phoenix, Arizona, is a new facility for the University of Arizona College of Medicine – Phoenix and Northern Arizona University. Designed by CO Architects and Ayers Saint Gross, the building provides an integrated and interdisciplinary approach for health sciences education and research. It is part of the inter-institutional campus, and is located within the downtown area.

The building consists of six levels, and includes administration and faculty offices, lecture halls, learning studios, flexible classrooms, student and faculty services, clinical skills suite, simulation suite, class laboratories, learning resource centre, cafeteria, group study rooms, conference rooms and building services. The building's central organising element, known as 'The Canyon', was carved out of the building massing to minimise solar exposure, provide self-shading, allow daylight and provide visual connection to the exterior. There are also two academic wings and a central outdoor space protected by a fabric structure. The desert climate and the need to reduce energy consumption informed the design decisions. The two wings are oriented in the east–west direction, and so the east and west facades are windowless, minimising these orientations and maximising south and north exposures. South facades incorporate horizontal overhangs with perforated screens to provide shading, while vertical fins are used along the north facade.

The design process used BIM right from the initial stages. The architects, client and construction management teams developed a BIM management plan early in the design process. BIM was used

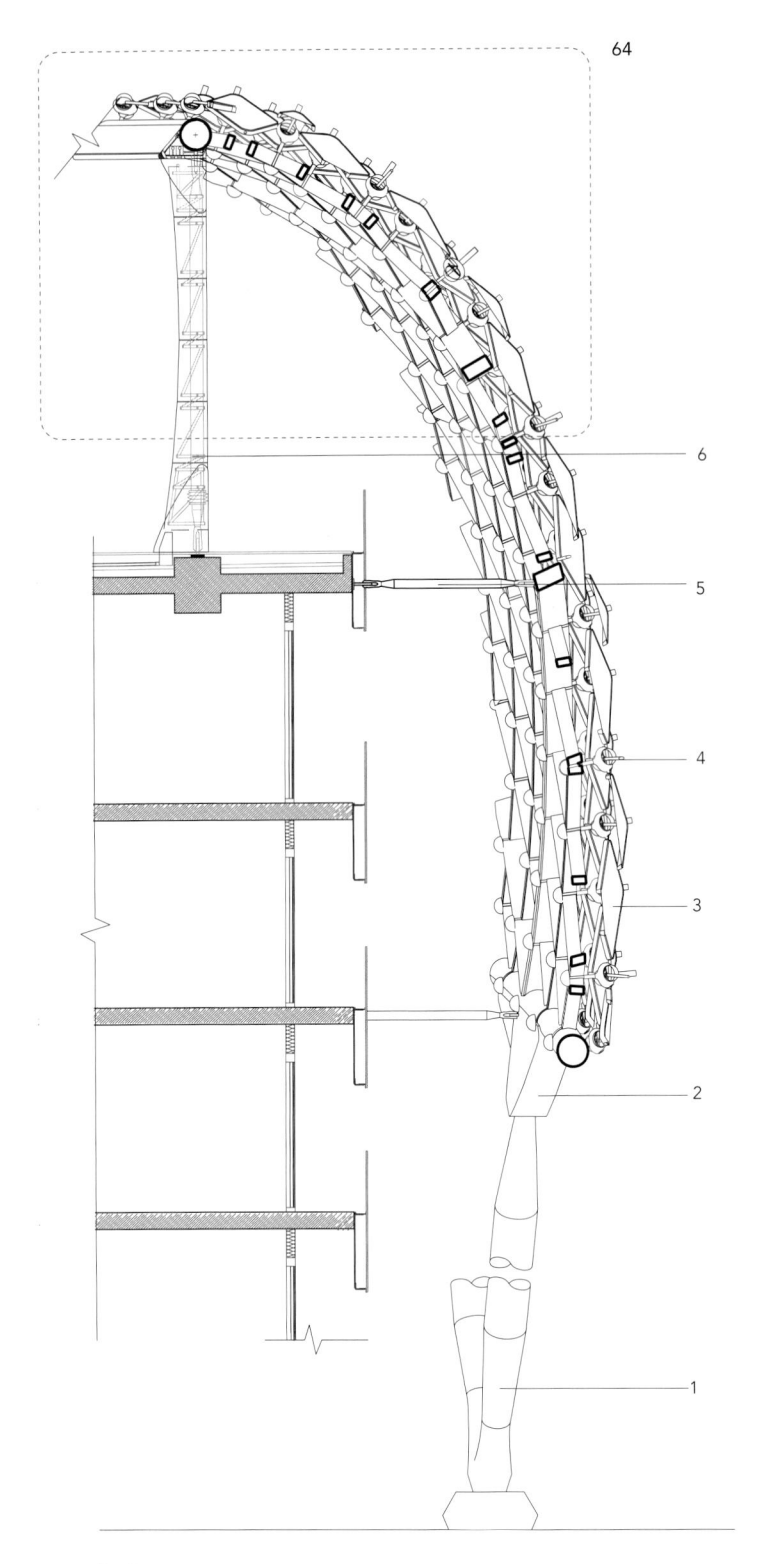

64 Asymptote Architecture, Yas Hotel, Abu Dhabi, UAE, 2009.
Section of the grid-shell system showing components and materials.

1 Lower vertical support column
2 Column to ringbeam connection
3 Glazing panel
4 Glazing panel support pivot node
5 Horizontal support strut
6 Upper vertical support strut

65 Asymptote Architecture, Yas Hotel, Abu Dhabi, UAE, 2009.
The glazing units and framing system for the grid-shell follow the curvature of the building. Glazing units are rotated using pivoting to form a continuous roof surface.

66 Asymptote Architecture, Yas Hotel, Abu Dhabi, UAE, 2009.
Detail of the grid-shell system indicating connections between the framing units and glass panels.

1 Framing unit
2 Luminaire power supply unit
3 Pivoting node housing
4 Ringbeam
5 Glazing panel
6 LED luminaire

Section

65

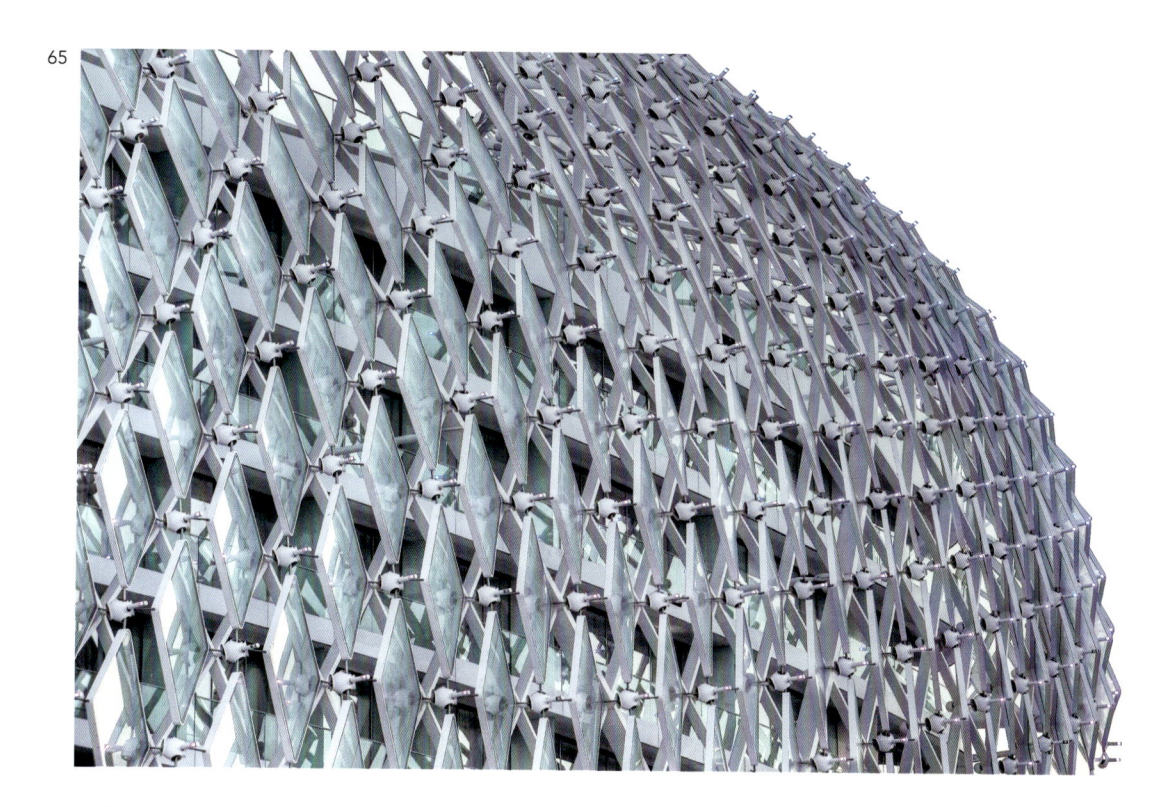

66

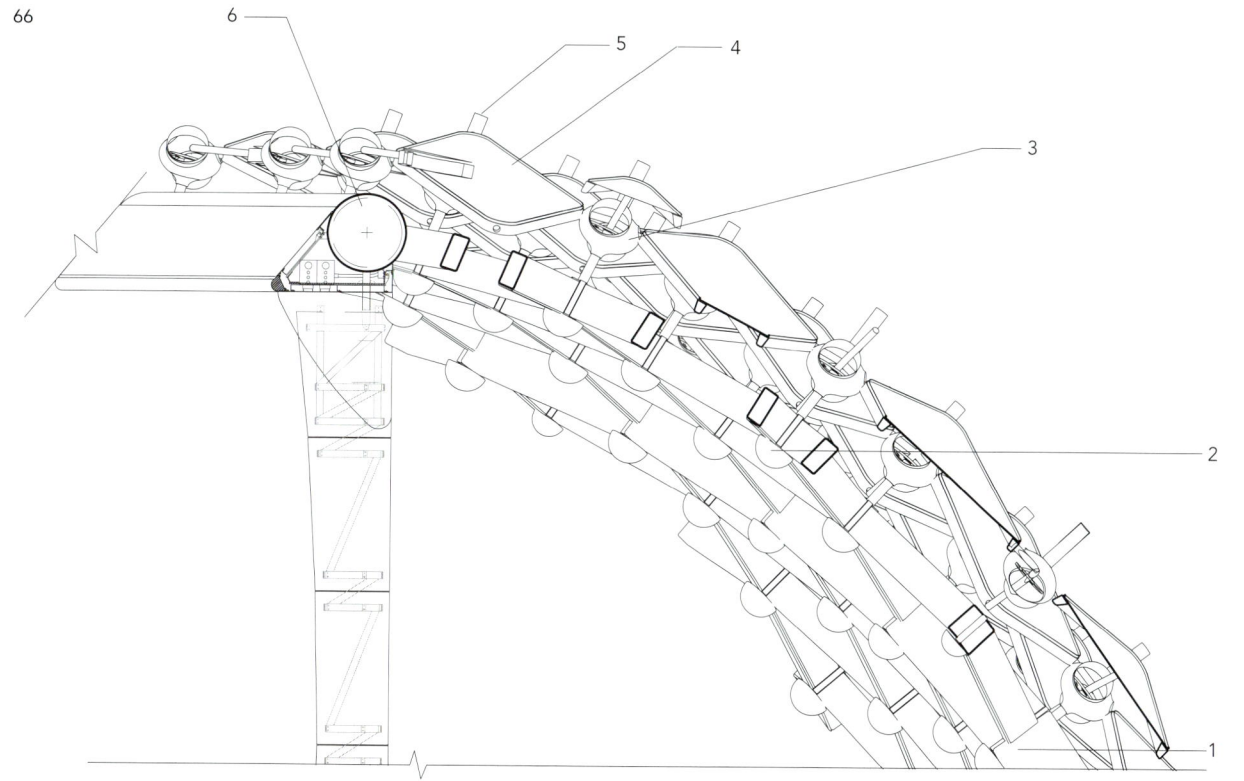

Enlarged section

5 BUILDING INTEGRATED INNOVATIONS AND METHODS 234-235

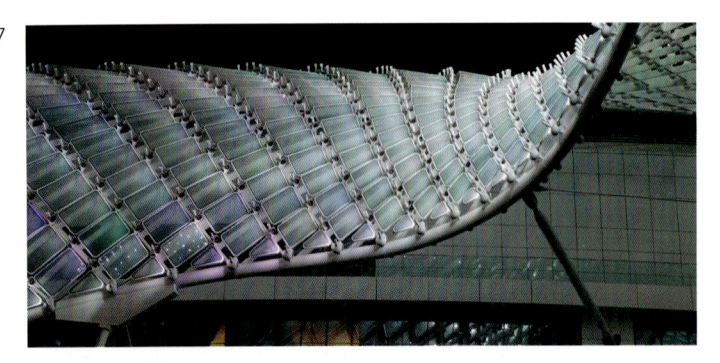

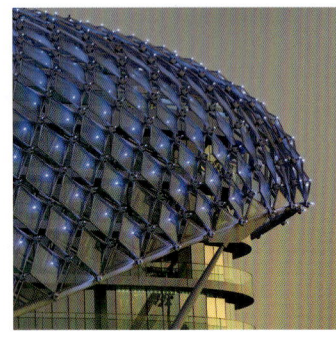

67 Asymptote Architecture, Yas Hotel, Abu Dhabi, UAE, 2009.
Glazing units integrate LED luminaires, providing a striking effect.

68 Asymptote Architecture, Yas Hotel, Abu Dhabi, UAE, 2009.
Interior views showing interior design and materials.

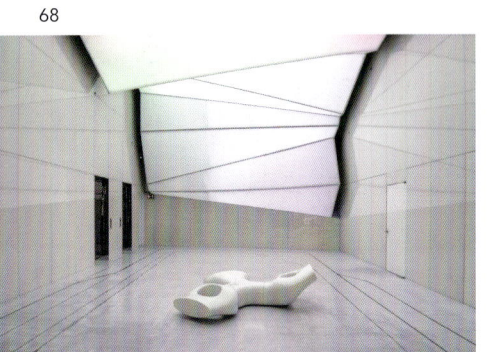

in the programming stage to explore different design options, especially focusing on collaboration spaces. Medical, nursing and allied health representatives were involved in the design process. BIM enabled the development of 3D room diagrams, which allowed a highly visual programming and design process. Virtual reality was used to create immersive environments, allowing the design teams and users to walk through and experience the design. BIM was also used for fabrication and construction, where various trades used BIM for coordination and model-based construction, design visualisation and validation, constructibility surveys, quantity take-offs, cost estimating, virtual prototypes and 4D construction scheduling.

The rainscreen facade at HSEB is clad in copper, a recycled material that was formed, bent and perforated to create the unique design of this building and reference the surrounding mountains and canyons. BIM was essential during the design process of the facade system. The design model, created by the architecture team, was transferred to the metal-cladding contractor who translated the design model into a fabrication model. The patterns of copper panels and their configuration were optimised to create the appearance of naturally occurring random patterns, while using only 13 panel types. The panels were modelled, located and scheduled using BIM. Quantity take-offs were also conducted using BIM. The final copper cladding cost was reduced

69 CO Architects and Ayers Saint Gross, Health Sciences Education Building (HSEB), Phoenix, Arizona, USA, 2012.
Exterior view showing the east building facade treatment.

5 BUILDING INTEGRATED INNOVATIONS AND METHODS 236-237

First-floor plan

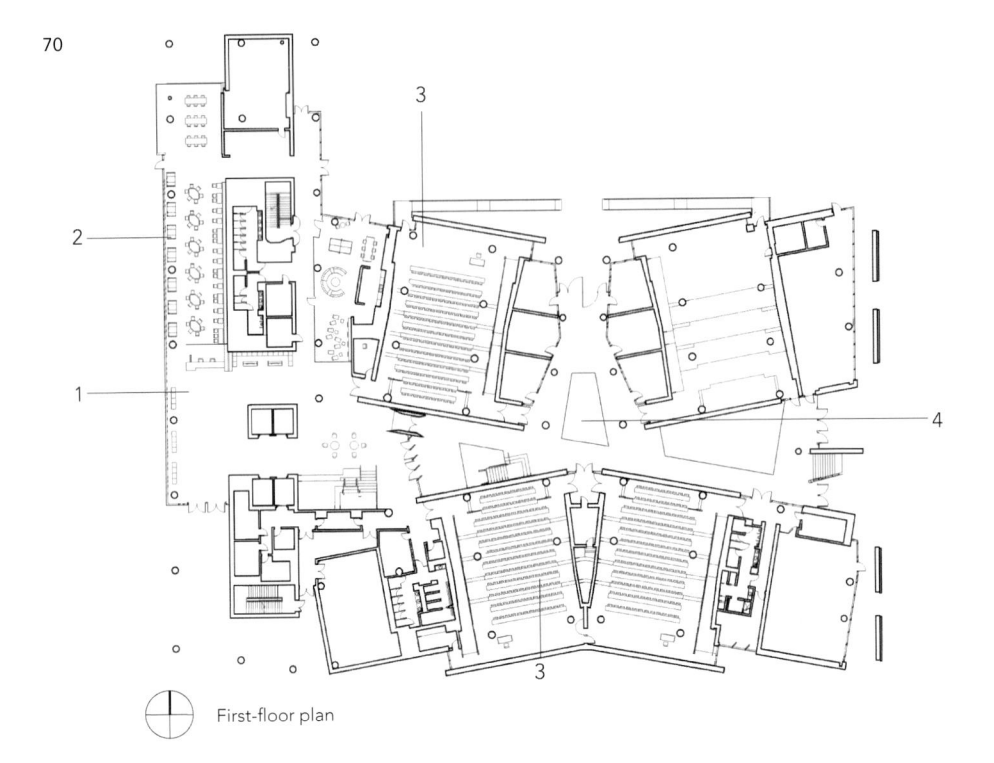

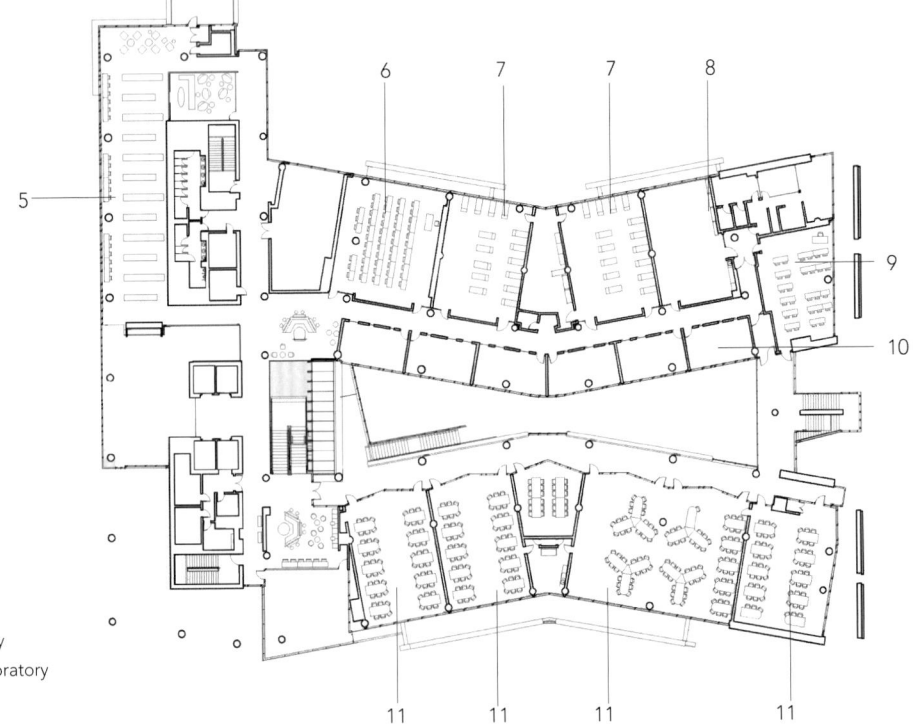

1 Lobby
2 Cafeteria
3 Lecture hall
4 'Canyon'
5 Lockers
6 Computer laboratory
7 Physical therapy laboratory
8 Occupational therapy laboratory
9 Classroom
10 Offices
11 Learning studio

Second-floor plan

71

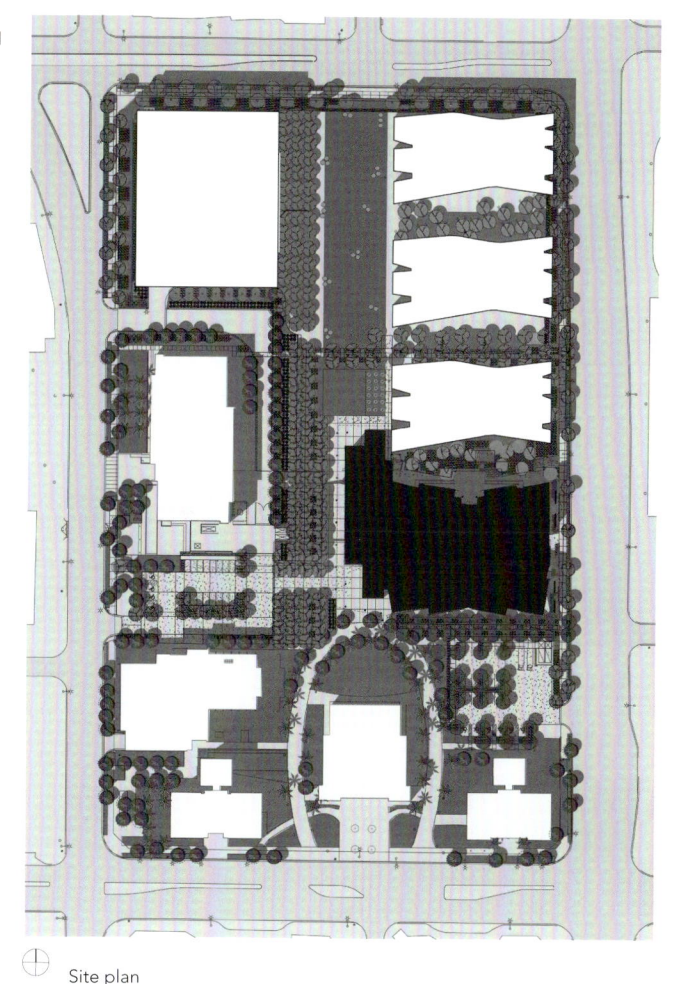

Site plan

70 CO Architects and Ayers Saint Gross, Health Sciences Education Building (HSEB), Phoenix, AZ, USA, 2012.
Floor plans indicating the building programme and spatial organisation.

71 CO Architects and Ayers Saint Gross, Health Sciences Education Building (HSEB), Phoenix, AZ, USA, 2012.
Site plan showing the location of the building and its context.

72 CO Architects and Ayers Saint Gross, Health Sciences Education Building (HSEB), Phoenix, AZ, USA, 2012.
'The Canyon' was carved out of the building massing to minimise solar exposure, provide self-shading, allow daylight and to provide visual connection to the exterior.

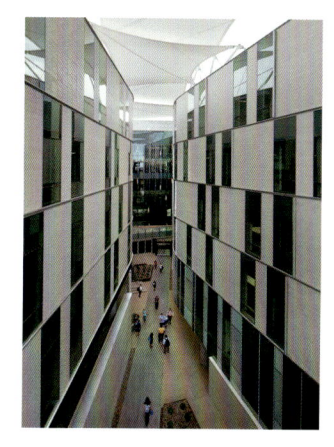

72

5 BUILDING INTEGRATED INNOVATIONS AND METHODS 238–239

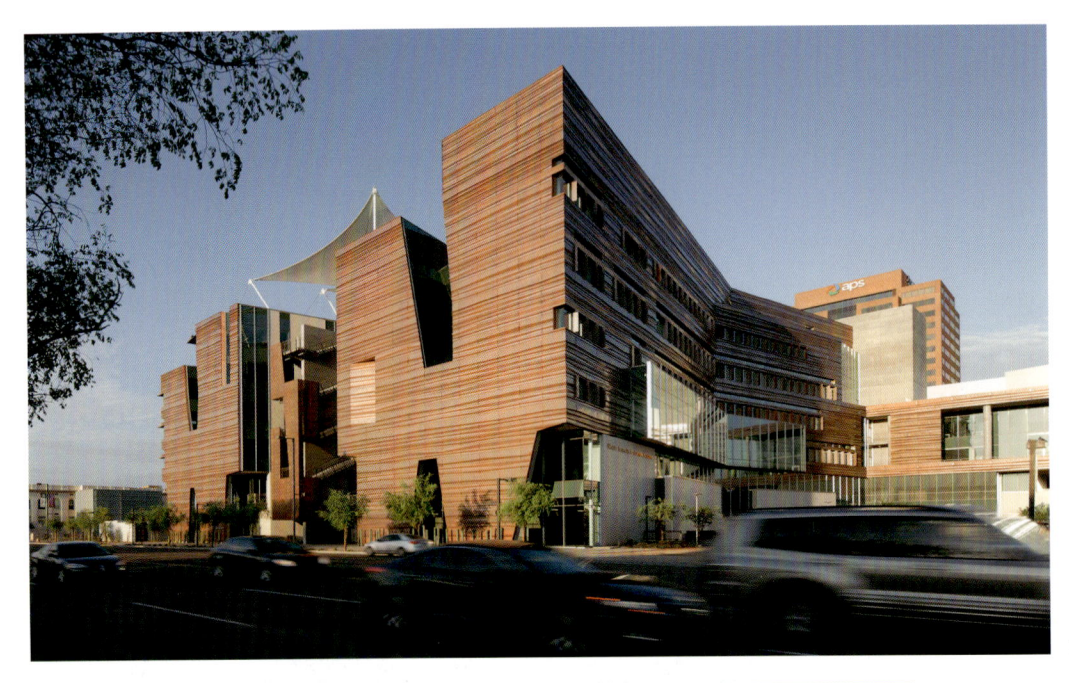

73 CO Architects and Ayers Saint Gross, Health Sciences Education Building (HSEB), Phoenix, AZ, USA, 2012.
East and west building orientations were minimised and do not include glazed elements. The south facade incorporates horizontal overhangs and the north facade includes vertical fins.

by 48% compared with the schematic cost estimate, which was achieved by collaborative design processes, virtual and physical mock-ups, and continuous BIM exchanges among the design, fabrication and construction teams.

During construction, the coordination of different models simplified the installation and detailing of architectural features, including precise detailing of penetrations and openings in exposed architectural concrete walls. Laser scans were conducted prior to concrete pouring to identify any discrepancies, where a point cloud 'as-built' model was overlaid with the coordination model. Prefabrication was also utilised, where the exterior back-up wall was modelled and pre-assembled, improving the quality of construction and increasing productivity. The use of BIM during design, fabrication and construction provided significant cost savings and schedule reduction.

Innovative design processes and construction techniques, collaboration among stakeholders and effective use of BIM for

74 CO Architects and Ayers Saint Gross, Health Sciences Education Building (HSEB), Phoenix, AZ, USA, 2012.
Visual programming was used to determine the flexibility of different spaces, particularly the lecture halls and classrooms.

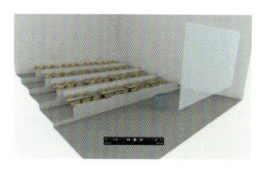

Visualisation and programming of a lecture hall

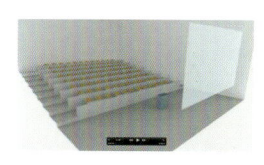

Visualisation and programming of a classroom

5 BUILDING INTEGRATED INNOVATIONS AND METHODS 240-241

Design BIM

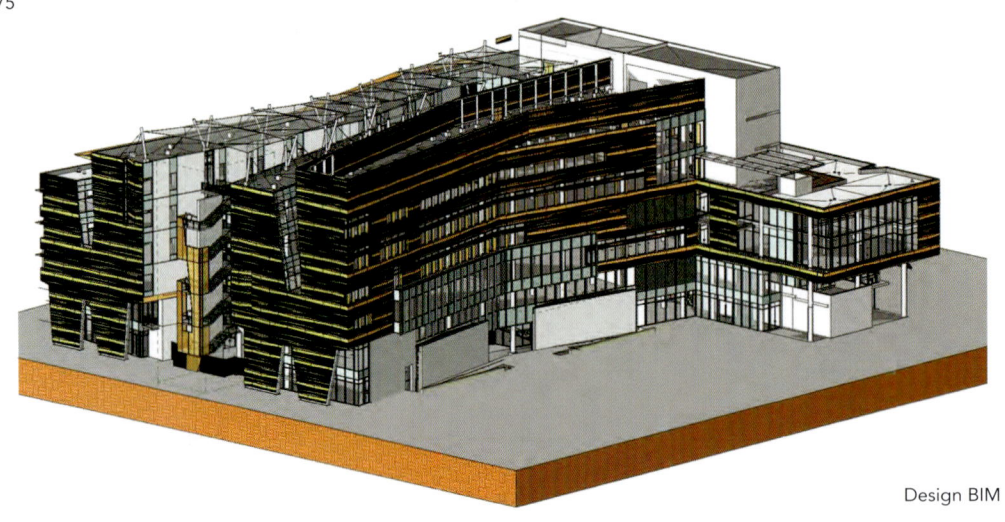

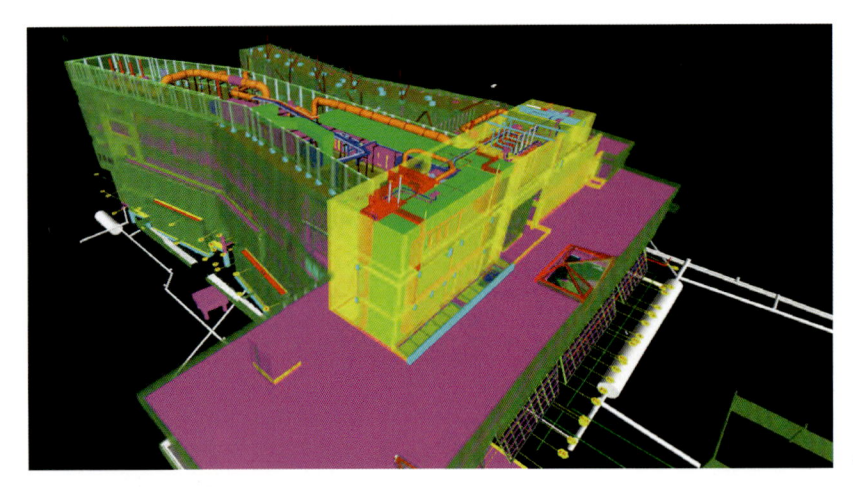

Coordination BIM

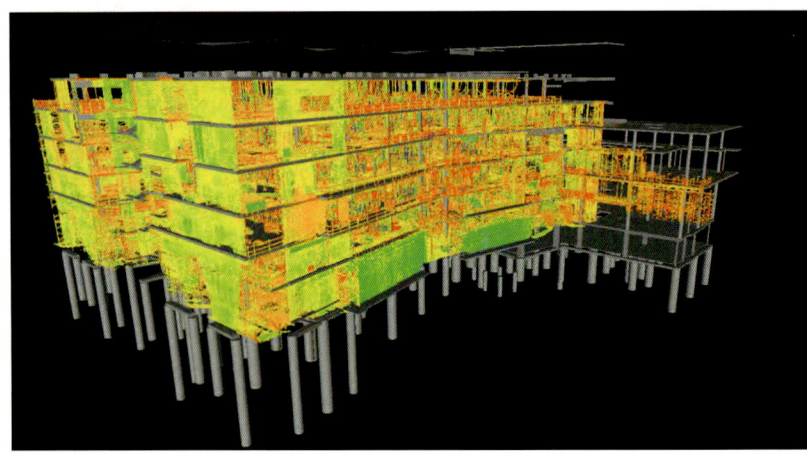

Construction BIM

75 CO Architects and Ayers Saint Gross, Health Sciences Education Building (HSEB), Phoenix, AZ, USA, 2012.
BIM was used for the design, coordination and model-based construction, design visualisation and validation, constructibility surveys, quantity take-offs, cost estimating, virtual prototypes and 4D construction scheduling.

76 CO Architects and Ayers Saint Gross, Health Sciences Education Building (HSEB), Phoenix, AZ, USA, 2012.
BIM was used for facade design, and virtual mock-ups were used to determine the shapes and profiles of the copper-cladding panels to create the desired design effect.

all stages of design and construction, model-based fabrication and coordination are the key characteristics of this case study. Integrated design and digital technologies, collaborative project delivery and advanced construction techniques influenced the design and construction outcomes. The building responds to climate and site, where each building orientation is treated differently to respond to solar radiation. The copper-clad building skin resembles the natural context and landscape, while advanced construction and prefabrication techniques have been used to assemble and construct the building envelope.

CONCLUSION: LESSONS LEARNED FROM CASE STUDIES

The case studies that have been presented in this chapter represent a variety of building types and scale, geographic locations and climates, as well as design and construction methods. We have reviewed small-scale academic buildings, medium-sized commercial and educational facilities, large-scale hotels, libraries, museums, exhibition arenas and academic and research buildings. We have seen how specific design strategies were used for these buildings, and we can conclude that there are a lot of differences between them. But a common thread is that innovative design and construction practices were strategically chosen based on the building type, location and climate, size and complexity, budget and project requirements. Therefore, there is not only one path, method or formula for improving building designs, performance and construction techniques – there are multiple ways and methods. Optimal solutions require

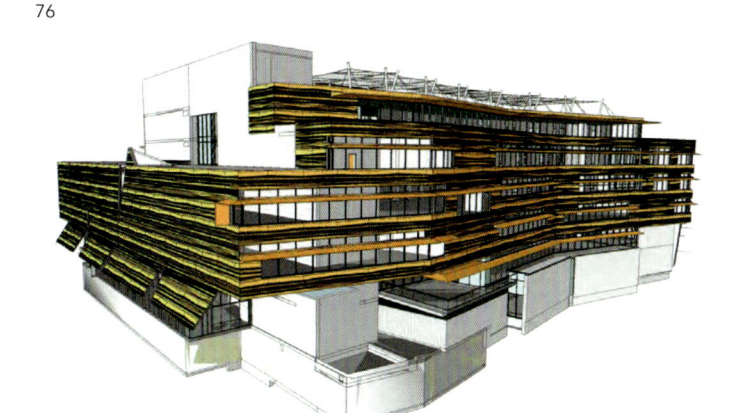

BIM with facade cladding

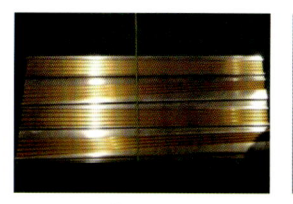

Virtual mock-up

Copper profiles for cladding

77 CO Architects and Ayers Saint Gross, Health Sciences Education Building (HSEB), Phoenix, AZ, USA, 2012.
Physical mock-ups show variations of the copper facade cladding profiles.

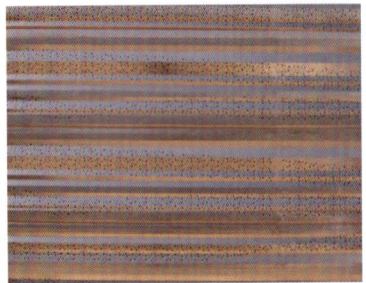

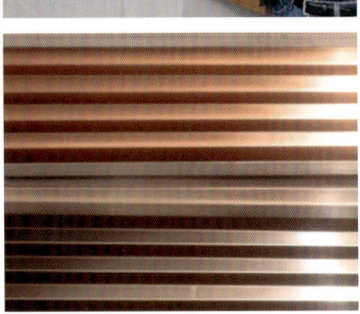

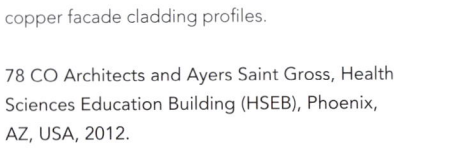

78 CO Architects and Ayers Saint Gross, Health Sciences Education Building (HSEB), Phoenix, AZ, USA, 2012.
Laser scanning was conducted during construction to identify discrepancies between the coordination model and 'as-built' conditions.

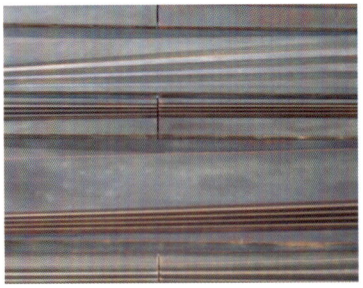

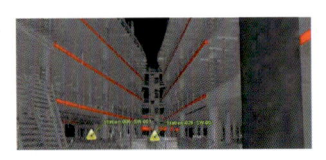

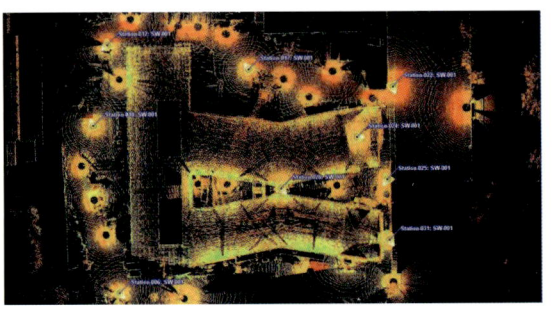

an integrated approach, where innovative design and building technologies, computational methods, construction methods, materials and systems are assessed, evaluated and intelligently applied. Designers must understand the benefits and drawbacks of innovative technologies, materials and systems and their applicability for individual projects. Therefore, the role of research becomes essential and moving forward will become increasingly prominent in architectural design and practice.

REFERENCES
1 Marius Ronnett and Abul Abdullah, 'Cell Wall: Resolving Geometrical Complexities in the Shanghai Nature Museum Iconic Wall', *Perkins+Will Research Journal*, Vol 2, No 1, 2010, pp 7–21.

IMAGES
Opening image © Institute for Advanced Architecture of Catalonia; figures 1, 2, 3, 4, 5, 6, 7 and 8 Courtesy of Studio 804; figures 9, 10, 11, 12, 13, 14, 15, 16 and 17 © Rene Schmid Architekten; figures 18, 22 and 25 © Christian Richters; figures 19, 20 and 21 © Gerber Architekten; figure 23 © Gerber Architekten, Photographer: HG Esch; figure 24 © Bollinger + Grohmann; figures 26, 30, 32 and 35 courtesy UNStudio/ © Edmon Leong; figures 27, 28, 29, 31, 33, 34 and 36 © UNStudio; figures 37, 41, 42 (t) and 43 © Jeremy Bitterman; figures 38, 39, 40, 44, 45, 46, 70, 71, 74 models, 75, 76, 77 and 78 © CO Architects; figure 42 © Bruce Forster; figures 47, 53, 54 and 57 © James Steinkamp Photography; figures 48, 49, 50, 51, 52, 55 and 56 © Perkins+Will; figures 58, 59, 60, 61, 62, 63, 64, 65, 66, 67 and 68 © Asymptote: Hani Rashid + Lise Anne Couture; figures 69, 72, 73 and 74 © Bill Timmerman

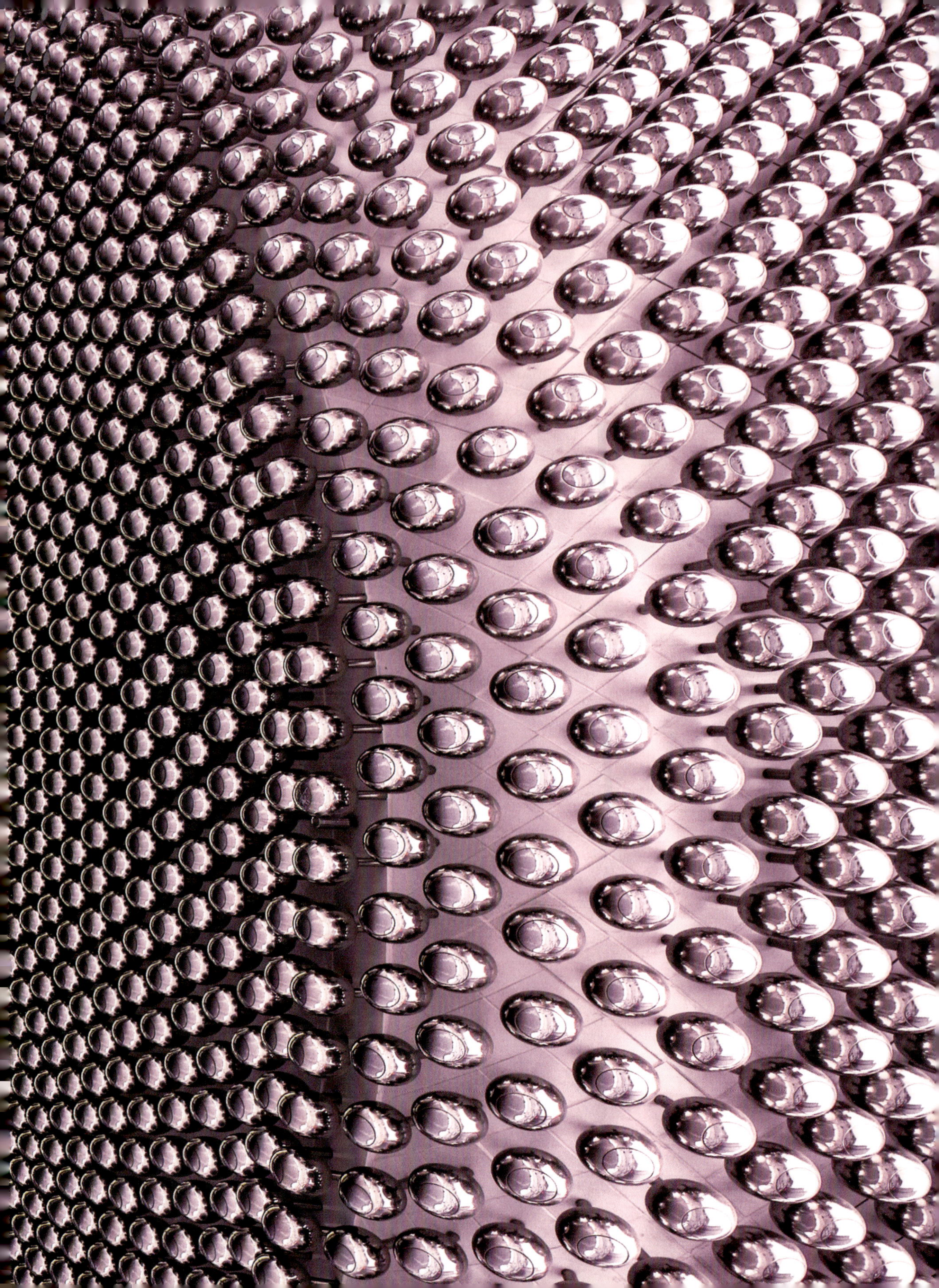

FUTURE OUTLOOKS: CONCLUDING REMARKS

We are entering an era of unprecedented changes in the architectural and building industry. The paradigm shifts that have been initiated in the last two decades, including the wide adoption of BIM, advanced computational design methods, digital fabrication, new materials and building technologies, are all having an impact on the way that architectural and design firms are operating, designing and delivering buildings, collaborating with industry-wide stakeholders and creating the built environment. On the other hand, economic, social and environmental factors are also influencing the building industry, and posing challenges to create better performing, environmentally sensitive buildings, which are designed and constructed faster, cost less, and have a positive impact on the environment, health and productivity of the buildings' occupants. These challenges have caused innovative practices to engage in research and to find novel solutions, since only through systematic investigations is it possible to find optimal answers for often conflicting objectives.

The methods, technologies, processes and techniques that have been discussed in the chapters offer a cross section of cutting-edge materials, building and design technologies, operational strategies for integrating innovation and research in design practice. Technological changes and developments are inevitable, and while we cannot precisely predict what types of new technologies will be developed in the future or how they will influence our lives, we can be quite certain that they will happen. Based on current trends and recent developments in building and design technologies, we can sense a general direction of future advancements. Materials that exhibit advanced properties, smart and intelligent materials and systems, responsive and energy-generating elements, virtual reality in design and construction, robotics and automation – these all warrant more exploration, discoveries and applications in design and construction.

Design firms that embrace change, take charge and create a culture that supports exploration, research, experimentation and innovation establish a competitive edge for their practice, but also nurture techniques that can adapt under various circumstances and an uncertain future, and establish procedures for addressing the challenges that the future might bring. These are the essential qualities of progressive design practices – they respect context, past and history, embrace current innovations and prepare for future changes. As was discussed in the introduction, innovation is a change in a product, service and process, and there are various levels of innovation, ranging from incremental, to radical and transformational. Within the architectural context, the product is the building, physical space, material or object; service refers to the way that we interact with clients, constituents and building occupants; and process refers to the design process. Incremental innovation is a small change that affects certain projects, while radical innovation has an impact on the larger context. Transformational innovation creates a paradigm shift in architectural design and the profession. We have reviewed numerous examples of different types and levels of innovation throughout the book. Each firm and practice must examine their own culture, vision and operation and establish a plan for embracing innovation. The strategies for establishing a culture of innovation are:

- Determine vision and goals as they relate to integrating innovation into design practice, and define specific components that affect innovative areas of practice. Establish the identity of the firm and its expression, which recognises unique aspects of the innovative culture. Determine the value of the services and design outcomes, both tangible and non-tangible. Determine the methods for engaging internally and externally with clients and constituents, and define how the firm's actions and services are having an impact on society.

- Demonstrate these following characteristics: inquiry, integration of design, research and technologies, analysis, technical aptitude, and communication and dissemination of results.

- Establish the research arm of the firm and integrate it with the practice, considering different models and research methods. Determine the structure and organisation of the research arm and funding mechanisms, and define the relationships between research and the firm's core values and practice. Define short-term actions, long-term objectives and strategies for research, and determine methods for implementing and translating results into practice, as well as dissemination to wider audiences.

- Determine risk management techniques that will minimise risk, but still allow innovative methods. For example, these techniques should define acceptable and unacceptable risks, how to determine the magnitude and nature of risks, and appropriate steps for managing and reducing risks.

The aforementioned strategies provide basic steps that can be followed to define specific methods and a culture of innovation, regardless of the firm's size, speciality and location. By establishing specific goals and objectives, methods and procedures that reflect their vision, every firm and organisation can develop and execute plans for integrating innovation into their practice. Doing so would allow us to build an industry-wide culture of innovation piece by piece, and fully infuse innovation into architectural design. We would then be better prepared to face whatever the future might bring, whatever challenges our industry might face, and whatever new technologies become developed.

IMAGES
Opening image of UNStudio/ © Edmon Leong

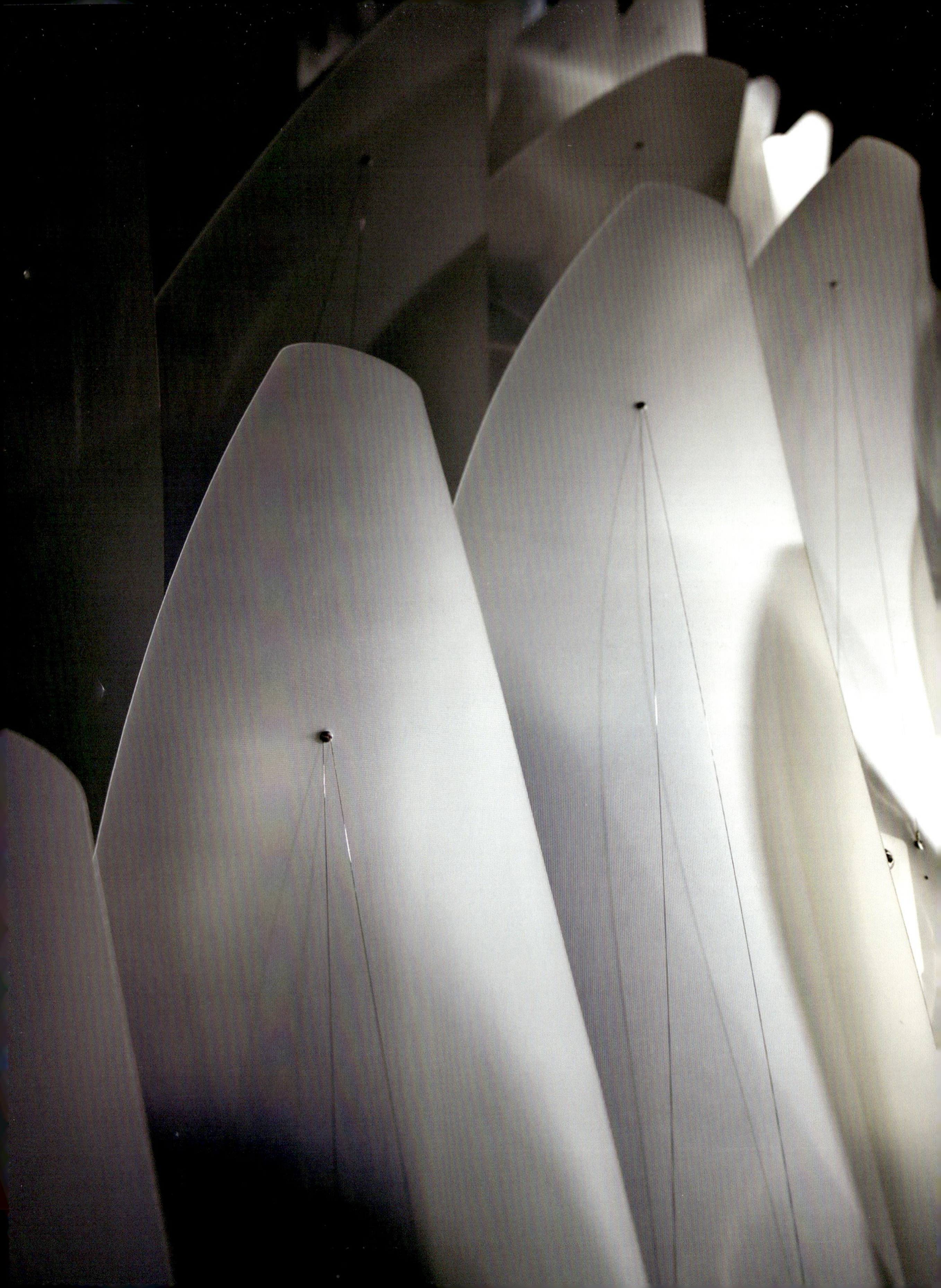

SELECT BIBLIOGRAPHY

- Abecassis-Moedas, Celine and Sihem Ben Mahmoud Jouini, 'Absorptive Capacity and Source-Recipient Complementarity in Designing New Products: An Empirically Derived Framework', *Journal of Product Innovation Management*, Vol 25, No 5, 2008, pp 473–90.
- Addington, D Michelle, and Daniel Schodek, *Smart Materials and New Technologies: For the Architecture and Design Professions*, Architectural Press (Oxford), 2005.
- Adriaenssens, Sigrid, Philippe Block, Diederik Veenendaal and Chris Williams (eds), *Shell Structures for Architecture: Form Finding and Optimization*, Routledge (New York), 2014.
- Akintoye, Akintola, Jack Goulding and Girma Zawdie, *Construction Innovation and Process Improvement*, Wiley-Blackwell (Chichester, UK), 2012.
- Aksamija, Ajla, 'Analysis and Computation: Sustainable Design in Practice', *Design Principles and Practices: An International Journal*, Vol 4, No 4, 2010, pp 291–314.
- Aksamija, Ajla, *Sustainable Facades: Design Methods for High-Performance Building Envelopes*, Wiley (Hoboken, NJ), 2013.
- Aksamija, Ajla, 'Building Simulations and High-Performance Buildings Research: Use of Building Information Modeling (BIM) for Integrated Design and Analysis', *Perkins+Will Research Journal*, Vol 5, No 1, 2013, pp 19–37.
- Aksamija, Ajla, 'BIM-Based Building Performance Analysis in Architectural Practice: When, Why and How', in *Architecture and Sustainability: Critical Perspectives for Integrated Design*, Ahmed Z Khan and Karen Allacker (eds), Sint-Lucas Architecture Press (Brussels), 2015, pp 221–30.
- Aksamija, Ajla, 'Design Methods for Sustainable, High-Performance Building Facades', *Advances in Building Energy Research*, DOI: 10.1080/17512549.2015.1083885, 2015.
- Aksamija, Ajla, 'A Strategy for Energy Performance Analysis at the Early Design Stage: Predicted vs Actual Building Energy Performance', *Journal of Green Building*, Vol 10, No 3, 2015, pp 161–76.
- Aksamija, Ajla, 'Regenerative Design of Existing Buildings for Net-Zero Energy Use', *Procedia Engineering*, Vol 118, 2015, pp 72–80.
- Aksamija, Ajla, Mario Guttman, Hari Priya Rangarajan and Tim Meador, 'Parametric Control of BIM Elements for Sustainable Design in Revit: Linking Design and Analytical Software Applications through Customization', *Perkins+Will Research Journal*, Vol 3, No 1, 2011, pp 32–45.
- Aksamija, Ajla, and Ivanka Iordanova, 'Computational Environments with Multimodal Representations of Architectural Design Knowledge', *International Journal of Architectural Computing*, Vol 8, No 4, 2010, pp 439–60.
- Aksamija, Ajla, John Haymaker and Abbas Aminmansour (eds), *Future of Architectural Research: Proceedings of the Architectural Research Centers Consortium Conference*, Perkins+Will (Chicago), 2015.
- Atkin, Brian and Adrian Brooks, *Total Facilities Management*, Wiley (Chichester, UK) 2015.
- Azman, Mohamed Nor Azhari, Mohd Sanusi S Ahamad, Taksiah Abdul Majid and Mohd Hanizun Hanafi, 'Off-Site Construction Industry: The Common Approach', *Australian Journal of Basic and Applied Sciences*, Vol 4, No 9, 2010, pp 4478–82.
- Barf, Herwig, *Innovative Design + Construction: Manufacturing and Design Synergies in the Building Process*, Detail (Munich), 2010.
- Beorkrem, Christopher, *Material Strategies in Digital Fabrication*, Routledge (New York), 2013.
- Bock, Thomas and Thomas Linner, *Robot-Oriented Design: Design and Management Tools for the Deployment of Automation and Robotics in Construction*, Cambridge University Press (New York), 2015.
- Boswell, Keith, *Exterior Building Enclosures: Design Process and Composition for Innovative Facades*, Wiley (Hoboken, NJ), 2013.
- Brownell, Blaine, *Material Strategies: Innovative Applications in Architecture*, Princeton Architectural Press (New York), 2012.
- Burry, Mark, *Scripting Cultures: Architectural Design and Programming*, Wiley (Chichester, UK), 2011.
- Castilla, Maria Del Mar, *Comfort Control in Buildings*, Springer (London), 2014.
- Cheng, Tao and Jochen Teizer, 'Real-time Resource Location Data Collection and Visualization Technology for Construction Safety and Activity Monitoring Applications', *Automation in Construction*, Vol 34, 2013, pp 3–15.
- Corser, Robert, *Fabricating Architecture: Selected Readings in Digital Design and Manufacturing*, Princeton Architectural Press (New York), 2010.
- Coutelle-Brillet, Patricia, Arnaud Riviere and Véronique des Garets, 'Perceived Value of Service Innovation: A Conceptual Framework', *Journal of Business & Industrial Marketing*, Vol 29, No 2, 2014, pp 164–72.
- Dent, Andrew and Leslie Sherr, *Material Innovation: Architecture*, Thames & Hudson (New York), 2014.
- Descamps, Benoît, *Computational Design of Lightweight Structures: Form Finding and Optimization*, Wiley (Hoboken, NJ), 2014.
- Deutsch, Randy, *BIM and Integrated Design: Strategies for Architectural Practice*, Wiley (Hoboken, NJ), 2011.
- Deutsch, Randy, *Data-Driven Design and Construction: 25 Strategies for Capturing, Analyzing and Applying Building Data*, Wiley (Hoboken, NJ), 2015.

- Dunn, Nick, *Digital Fabrication in Architecture*, Laurence King (London), 2012.
- Emmitt, Stephen, *Architectural Technology: Research & Practice*, Wiley-Blackwell (Chichester, UK), 2013.
- Emmitt, Stephen, Matthijs Prins and Ad den Otter, *Architectural Management: International Research and Practice*, Wiley-Blackwell (Chichester, UK), 2009.
- Fernandez, John, *Material Architecture: Emergent Materials for Innovative Buildings and Ecological Construction*, Architectural Press (Oxford), 2006.
- Fortmeyer, Russell, and Charles Linn, *Kinetic Architecture: Designs for Active Envelopes*, Images Publishing (Mulgrave, Australia), 2014.
- Garber, Richard, *BIM Design: Realising the Creative Potential of Building Information Modelling*, Wiley (Chichester, UK), 2014.
- Groat, Linda and David Wang, *Architectural Research Methods*, Wiley (Hoboken, NJ), 2013.
- Hensel, Michael (ed), *Design Innovation for the Built Environment: Research by Design and the Renovation of Practice*, Routledge (New York), 2012.
- Hensel, Michael, Achim Menges and Michael Weinstock, *Emergent Technologies and Design*, Routledge (New York), 2010.
- Hootman, Thomas, *Net Zero Energy Design: A Guide for Commercial Architecture*, Wiley (Hoboken, NJ), 2012.
- Iwamoto, Lisa, *Digital Fabrications: Architectural and Material Techniques*, Princeton Architectural Press (New York), 2009.
- Jani, Jaronie Mohd, Martin Leary, Aleksandar Subic and Mark Gibson, 'A Review of Shape Memory Alloy Research, Applications and Opportunities', *Materials and Design*, Vol 56, 2014, pp 1078–113.
- Kieran, Stephen, and James Timberlake, *Refabricating Architecture: How Manufacturing Methodologies are Poised to Transform Building Construction*, McGraw-Hill (New York), 2004.
- Kim, Hyunjoo, Kyle Anderson, SangHyun Lee and John Hildreth, 'Generating Construction Schedules through Automatic Data Extraction Using Open BIM Technology', *Automation in Construction*, Vol 35, 2013, pp 285–95.
- Knaack, Ulrich and Tillmann Klein, *The Future Envelope 2: Architecture, Climate, Skin*, IOS Press (Amsterdam), 2009.
- Kolarevic, Branko, and Kevin Klinger, *Manufacturing Material Effects: Rethinking Design and Making in Architecture*, Routledge (New York), 2008.
- La Roche, Pablo, *Carbon-Neutral Architectural Design*, CRC Press (Boca Raton, FL), 2012.
- Lawson, Mark, Ray Ogden and Chris Goodier, *Design in Modular Construction*, CRC Press (Boca Raton, FL), 2014.
- Lerner, Josh, *The Architecture of Innovation: The Economics of Creative Organizations*, Harvard Business Review Press (Boston, MA), 2012.
- Lévy, François, *BIM in Small-Scale Sustainable Design*, Wiley (Hoboken, NJ), 2012.
- Moe, Kiel, *Integrated Design in Contemporary Architecture*, Princeton Architectural Press (New York), 2008.
- Mu, Jifeng, Gang Peng and Douglas MacLachlan, 'Effect of Risk Management Strategy on NPD Performance', *Technovation*, Vol 29, No 3, 2009, pp 170–80.
- Naboni, Roberto and Ingrid Paoletti, *Advanced Customization in Architectural Design and Construction*, Springer (Heidelberg), 2015.
- Oxman, Rivka and Robert Oxman, *The New Structuralism: Design, Engineering and Architectural Technologies*, Wiley (Hoboken, NJ), 2010.
- Peters, Sascha, *Material Revolution II: New Sustainable and Multi-Purpose Materials for Design and Architecture*, Birkhäuser (Basel), 2014.
- Portman, Jackie, *Building Services Design Management*, Wiley (Hoboken, NJ), 2014.
- Prins, Matthijs and Robert Owen, *Integrated Design and Delivery Solutions*, Earthscan (London), 2010.
- Ritter, Axel, *Smart Materials in Architecture, Interior Architecture and Design*, Birkhäuser (Basel), 2007.
- Sacks, Rafael, and Ronen Barak, 'Impact of Three-Dimensional Parametric Modelling of Building on Productivity in Structural Engineering Practice', *Automation in Construction*, Vol 17, No 4, 2008, pp 439–49.
- Schein, Jeffrey, 'An Information Model for Building Automation Systems', *Automation in Construction*, Vol 16, Iss 2, 2007, pp 125–39.
- Sinopoli, James, *Smart Building Systems for Architects, Owners, and Builders*, Butterworth-Heinemann (Burlington, MA), 2010.
- Smith, Ryan E, *Prefab Architecture: A Guide to Modular Design and Construction*, Wiley (Hoboken, NJ), 2014.
- Syed, Asif, *Advanced Building Technologies for Sustainability*, Wiley (Hoboken, NJ), 2012.
- Teicholz, Eric, *Technology for Facility Managers: The Impact of Cutting-Edge Technology on Facility Management*, Wiley (Hoboken, NJ), 2014.
- Teicholz, Paul, *BIM for Facility Managers*, Wiley (Hoboken, NJ), 2013.
- Tschirky, Hugo, *Managing Innovation Driven Companies: Approaches in Practice*, Palgrave Macmillan (New York), 2011.
- Turró, Andreu, David Urbano and Marta Peris-Ortiz, 'Culture and Innovation: The Moderating Effect of Cultural Values on

Corporate Entrepreneurship', *Technological Forecasting and Social Change*, Vol 88, 2014, pp 360–9.
- Wang, Shengwei, *Intelligent Buildings and Building Automation*, Spon Press (Abingdon, Oxon), 2010.
- Weygant, Robert S, *BIM Content Development: Standards, Strategies, and Best Practices*, Wiley (Hoboken, NJ), 2011.
- Yudelson, Jerry, *Green Building through Integrated Design*, McGraw-Hill (New York), 2009.
- Zwaag, Sybrand van der, *Self-Healing Materials: An Alternative Approach to 20 Centuries of Materials Science*, Springer (Heidelberg), 2007.

APPENDIX: CASE STUDIES INDEX

CHAPTER 1

BRUSSELS ENVIRONMENT
Building Size: 19,690 m² (211,941 SF)
Year of Completion: 2014
Location: Brussels, Belgium
Architect: cepezed
Local Architect: Philippe Samyn and Partners
Client: Project T&T NV
Structural Engineer: SmitWesterman
Local Engineer: Ingenieursbureau Meijer
MEP Engineer: Flow Transfer International
Sustainability Consultant: DGMR
Contractor: Van Laere, Zwijndrecht

CASCADE MEADOW WETLANDS
Building Size: 1,459 m² (15,700 SF)
Year of Completion: 2011
Location: Rochester, MN, USA
Architect: LHB, Inc
Client: Cascade Meadow Wetlands & Environmental Science Center
Structural Engineer: LHB, Inc
MEP Engineer: LKPB Engineers, Inc
Civil Engineer: LHB, Inc
Landscape Architect: LHB, Inc
Sustainability Consultant: LHB, Inc
Contractor: Alvin E Benike, Inc

FIRST AID EMERGENCY POST
Building Size: 150 m² (1,600 SF)
Year of Completion: 2011
Location: Galder, the Netherlands
Architect: Frank Marcus

GIANT INTERACTIVE GROUP CORPORATE HEADQUARTERS
Building Size: 23,996 m² (258,300 SF)
Year of Completion: 2010
Location: Shanghai, China
Architect: Morphosis Architects
Local Architect: SURV (Shanghai)
Managing Director: Alexander Moh
Director in Charge: Thomas Chow
Project Manager: Leo Huang, Mel Tang, Jie Zhu
MEP Coordinator: Hai-Tao Hu
Client: Giant Interactive Group
Structural Engineer: Bao Ye, MAA Engineering Consultants (Shanghai) Co Ltd
Thornton Tomasetti (concept design)
MEP Engineer: IBE Consulting Engineers (concept design) MAA Engineering Consultants (Shanghai) Co Ltd
Landscape Architect: SWA Group
Local Landscape Architect: TOPO Design Group
Contractor: China State Construction Engineering Company 3rd Bureau
Design Institute: MAA Engineering Consultants (Shanghai) Co Ltd
Electrical Engineer: IBE Consulting Engineers (concept design) MAA Engineering Consultants (Shanghai) Co Ltd

HEMA BUILDING
Building Size: 680 m² (7,320 SF)
Location: Oosterbeek, the Netherlands
Year of Completion: 2009
Architect: Strategie Architecten bna
Client: Schwirtz & Partners
Structural Engineer: Adams Bouwadvies
Contractor: Tiemessen Bouwprojecten bv

HYLLIE TRAIN STATION
Building Size: 8,500 m² (91,493 SF)
Year of Completion: 2010
Location: Malmö, Sweden
Architect: Metro Architekter (Sweco Architects)
Client: CTP

iCON INNOVATION CENTRE
Building Size: 3,700 m² (39,826 SF)
Year of Completion: 2011
Location: Daventry, UK
Architect: Consarc Architects
Client: West Northamptonshire Development Corporation
Structural Engineer: Terry Collier Associates and Sinclair Knight Merz
MEP Engineer: Synergy
Landscape Architect: Kinnear Landscape Architects
Sustainability Consultant: Udox Solutions
Contractor: Winvic

JOGGINS FOSSIL CENTRE
Building Size: 1,235 m² (13,290 SF)
Year of Completion: 2008
Location: Nova Scotia, Canada
Architect: Architecture49
Client: Joggins Fossil Institute
Structural Engineer: BMR Structural Engineering
MEP Engineer: FC O'Neill, Scriven and Associates
Civil Engineer: ABL Environmental Consultants
Landscape Architect: Vollick McKee Petersmann and Associates
Sustainability Consultant: Architecture49
Contractor: Pomerleau
Site Remediation: Strum Consulting

L'OFFICE 64 DE L'HABITAT
Building Size: 4,264 m² (45,881 SF)
Year of Completion: 2011
Location: Bayonne, France
Architect: Patrick Arotcharen Agence d'Architecture
Client: Office 64 de l'Habitat
Structural Engineer: BET OTCE PAU
MEP Engineer: BET OTCE PAU
Civil Engineer: BET OTCE PAU
Landscape Architect: Sabine Haristoy
Sustainability Consultant: Nobatek
Contractor: Delta Construction
Acoustic Engineer: idB Acoustique
Interior Design: ASA 2002

MORGAN LIBRARY, COLORADO STATE UNIVERSITY
Building Addition Size: 278 m² (3,000 SF)
Year of Completion: 2012
Location: Fort Collins, CO, USA
Architect: Studiotrope
Client: State of Colorado, Colorado State University
Structural Engineer: Studio NYL
MEP Engineer: BCER Engineering
Civil Engineer: Northern Engineering
Landscape Architect: Chroma Design
Sustainability Consultant: YR&G Sustainability
Contractor: Pinkard Construction
AV/IT/Acoustics/Security: Shen Milsom & Wilke

NEW YORK CITY BEACH RESTORATION MODULES
Building Unit Size: 669 m² (7,200 SF)
Year of Completion: 2013
Location: New York, USA
Architect: Garrison Architects
Client: New York City Parks Department and the Department of Design and Construction

NOBEL HALLS
Building Size: 16,258 m² (175,000 SF)
Year of Completion: 2010
Location: Stony Brook, NY, USA
Architect: Goshow Architects
Client: Stony Brook University
Structural Engineer: WSP
MEP Engineer: Goldman Copeland Associates, PC
Civil Engineer: Lockwood, Kessler & Bartlett, Inc
Landscape Architect: AECOM
Contractor: J Kokolakis Contracting, Inc

PGE GiEK CORPORATE HEADQUARTERS
Building Size: 8,300 m² (89,340 SF)
Year of Completion: 2013
Location: Bełch Bełchatów County, Łódź Province, Poland
Architect: FAAB Architektura
  Project Architects: Adam Białobrzeski, Adam Figurski, Maria Messina
  Architectural Assistant: Paulina Filas
Client: PGE GiEK Concern
Structural Engineer: KBil Sieczkowski & Nikoniuk
MEP Engineer: Bema-projekt, SINAP Sp. z o.o.
Landscape Architect: Ogrody Dankiewicz
Contractor: Budus, RAMB

SCHOOL OF BUSINESS BUILDING, UNIVERSITY AT ALBANY
Building Size: 8,918 m² (96,000 SF)
Year of Completion: 2013
Location: Albany, NY, USA
Architect: Perkins+Will
Client: State University Construction Fund / University at Albany School of Business
Structural Engineer: Leslie E Robertson Associates
MEP Engineer: Bard, Rao + Athanas Consulting Engineers
Civil Engineer: Watts Architecture & Engineering
Landscape Architect: Thomas Balsley Associates
Sustainability: Perkins+Will
Contractor: Kirchhoff Consigli

Construction Manager: Skanska
Lighting: Horton Lees Brogden Lighting Design
Acoustics: Cerami & Associates
Audio/Visual: Sextant Group
Cost Estimating: Toscano Clements Taylor
Graphics/Signage: Calori & Vanden-Eynden
Educational Programming: Scott Blackwell Page

SWISSTECH CONVENTION CENTER
Building Size: 41,822 m² (450,168 SF)
Year of Completion: 2014
Location: École Polytechique Fédérale de Lausanne (EPFL), Switzerland
Architect: Richter Dahl Rocha & Associés

TAICHUNG CONVENTION CENTER
Building Size: 216,161 m² (2,326,737 SF)
Location: Taichung, Taiwan
Architect: MAD Architects
  Directors: Ma Yansong, Dang Qun
  Design Team: Jordan Kanter, Jtravis Russett, Irmi Reiter, Diego Perez, Dai Pu, Rasmus Palmquist, Art Terry, Chie Fuyuki

TRINITY RIVER AUDUBON CENTER
Building Size: 2,044 m² (22,000 SF)
Year of Completion: 2008
Location: Dallas, TX, USA
Architect: Antoine Predock Architect PC
Executive Architect: BRW Architects
Client: City of Dallas Park & Recreation Department, Texas Audubon Society
Exhibit Consultant: Lyons/Zaremba, Inc
Structural Engineer: Jaster-Quintanilla Dallas, LLP
Civil/MEP Engineer: LopezGarcia Group Inc
Sustainability Consultant: Rocky Mountain Institute
Contractor: Sedalco

UNIVERSITY OF MICHIGAN CARDIOVASCULAR CENTER
Building Size: 32,516 m² (350,000 SF)
Year of Completion: 2007
Location: Ann Arbor, MI, USA
Architect: Shepley Bulfinch
Associate Architect: Harley Ellis Devereaux
Client: University of Michigan Health System
Structural Engineer: Harley Ellis Devereaux
MEP Engineer: Smith Seckman Reid, Inc
Civil Engineer: Harley Ellis Devereaux
Landscape Architect: Brown Sardina
Sustainability Consultant (Commissioning Agent): Horizon Engineering

Contractor: Barton Malow CoInterior
Landscape: Foley Design
Code Consultant: Sullivan Code Group
Parking Consultant: URS Corporation
Lighting Consultant: Lam Partners
Acoustic Engineer: Acentech

CHAPTER 2

ANAHEIM REGIONAL TRANSPORTATION INTERMODAL CENTER (ARTIC)
Building Size: 6,225 m² (67,000 SF)
Year of Completion: 2014
Location: Anaheim, CA, USA
Architect: HOK
Structural Engineer: Thornton Tomasetti
MEP Engineer: Buro Happold
Civil Engineer: Parsons Brinckerhoff
Landscape Architect: SWA
Contractor: Clark Construction

CASE WESTERN RESERVE UNIVERSITY, TINKHAM VEALE UNIVERSITY CENTER
Building Size: 8,316 m² (89,513 SF)
Year of Completion: 2014
Location: Cleveland, OH, USA
Architect: Perkins+Will
Associate Architect: CBLH Design
Client: Case Western Reserve University
Structural Engineer: Thornton Tomasetti
MEP Engineer: Affiliated Engineers, Inc
Civil Engineer: KS Associates
Landscape Design: Perkins+Will
Sustainability: Perkins+Will
Contractor: Donley's, Inc

ESKENAZI HOSPITAL PARKING STRUCTURE ART FACADE
Year of Completion: 2014
Location: Indianapolis, IN, USA
Architect: Rob Ley Studio
Client: Eskenazi Hospital
Structural Engineer: Nous Engineering Fink Roberts & Petrie, Inc

EXPLORATORY HALL, GEORGE MASON UNIVERSITY
Building Size: 13,940 m² (150,000 SF)
Year of Completion: 2013
Location: Fairfax, VA, USA
Architect: Perkins+Will
Client: George Mason University
Structural Engineer: Robert Silman Associates
MEP Engineer: Integral Group

Civil Engineer: Pennoni Group
Landscape Design: Perkins+Will
Contractor: Donley's, Inc
Integrated Instructional Art Consultant: Larry Kirkland

GANTENBEIN VINEYARD
Year of Completion: 2006
Location: Fläsch, Switzerland
Architect: Gramazio Kohler Architects, ETH Zurich
   In cooperation with: Bearth & Deplazes Architekten, Valentin Beath, Andrea Deplazes, Daniel Ladner, Chur/Zurich
Client: Martha and Daniel Gantenbein
Collaborators: Tobias Bonwetsch (project lead), Michael Knauss, Michael Lyrenmann, Silvan Oesterle, Daniel Abraha, Stephan Achermann, Christoph Junk, Andri Lüscher, Martin Tann
Selected Experts: Jürg Buchli (structural engineer), Dr Nebojsa Mojsilovic and Markus Baumann, IBK ETH Zurich (structural tests)
Industry Partner: Keller AG Ziegeleien

HEYDAR ALIYEV CENTRE
Building Size: 101,801 m^2 (1,095,776 SF)
Year of Completion: 2012
Location: Baku, Azerbaijan
Architect: Zaha Hadid Architects
   Design: Zaha Hadid and Patrik Schumacher with Saffet Kaya Bekiroglu
   Project Architect: Saffet Kaya Bekiroglu
   Project Team: Sara Sheikh Akbari, Shiqi Li, Phil Soo Kim, Marc Boles, Yelda Gin, Liat Muller, Deniz Manisali, Lillie Liu, Jose Lemos, Simone Fuchs, Jose Ramon Tramoyeres, Yu Du, Tahmina Parvin, Erhan Patat, Fadi Mansour, Jaime Bartolome, Josef Glas, Michael Grau, Deepti Zachariah, Ceyhun Baskin, Daniel Widrig
Architect of Record: DiA Holding
Consultants: Tuncel Engineering, AKT (Structure), GMD Project (Mechanical), HB Engineering (Electrical), Werner Sobek (Facade), Etik Fire Consultancy (Fire), Mezzo Stüdyo (Acoustic), Enar Engineering (Geotechnical), Sigal (Infrastructure), MBLD (Lighting)
Contractor: DiA Holding
Subcontractors and Manufacturers: MERO (Steel Space Frame System) + Bilim Makina (Installation of Space Frame System) | Doka (Formwork) | Arabian Profile (External Cladding Panels / GRC & GRP) | Lindner (Internal Skin Cladding) | Sanset İkoor (Auditorium Wooden Cladding) | Quinette (Auditorium Seats) | Zumtobel (Lighting Fixtures) | Baswa (Special Acoustic Ceilings) + Astas (Installation of Ceilings) | Solarlux (Multipurpose Hall Facade Door) | Bolidt (Polyurethane Floor Finish) | Kone Elevators + Ikma (Installation of Elevators) | MIM Mühendisler Mermer (Marble Cladding Works) | HRN Dizayn (Landscape LED Installation) | Thyssen Group (Escalator) | Remak Makina (Fire Doors and Concrete-Clad Doors) | Tema (Gypsum Panel Works) | MIM Mühendislik (Structural Steel) | Elekon Enerji Sistemleri (Main Building Lighting Control System) | NIS Epoksi Kaplama Sistemleri (Epoxy Works) | Light Projects Group (Lighting Fixtures) | Limit Insaat (External Skin Insulations and Structure)
Special Thanks: Charles Walker

IAAC TRANSLATED GEOMETRIES
Year of Completion: 2014
Project Designer: Institute for Advanced Architecture of Catalonia (IAAC), developed in the Master in Advanced Architecture 2013/14 programme
Students: Efilena Baseta | Ece Tankal | Ramin Shambayati
Senior Faculty: Areti Markopoulou
Faculty Assistants: Alexandre Dubor | Moritz Begle
Research Line: Digital Matter | Intelligent Constructions

ICD/ITKE RESEARCH PAVILION 2013–14
Building Size: 50 m^2 (538 SF)
Year of Completion: 2014
Location: Stuttgart, Germany
Project Team: Institute for Computational Design – Prof Achim Menges
   Institute of Building Structures and Structural Design - Prof Jan Knippers
Research Development and Project Management: Moritz Dörstelmann | Vassilios Kirtzakis | Stefana Parascho | Marshall Prado | Tobias Schwinn
Concept Development: Leyla Yunis
System Development and Realisation:
   Winter 2012 – Summer 2013: Desislava Angelova | Hans-Christian Bäcker | Maximilian Fichter | Eugen Grass | Michael Herrick | Nam Hoang | Alejandro Jaramillo | Norbert Jundt | Taichi Kuma | Ondrej Kyjánek | Sophia Leistner | Luca Menghini | Claire Milnes | Martin Nautrup | Gergana Rusenova | Petar Trassiev | Sascha Vallon | Shiyu Wie
   Winter 2013: Hassan Abbasi | Yassmin Al-Khasawneh | Desislava Angelova | Yuliya Baranovskaya | Marta Besalu | Giulio Brugnaro | Elena Chiridnik | Eva Espuny | Matthias Helmreich | Julian Höll | Shim Karmin | Georgi Kazlachev | Sebastian Kröner | Vangel Kukov | David Leon | Stephen Maher | Amanda Moore | Paul Poinet | Roland Sandoval | Emily Scoones | Djordje Stanojevic | Andrei Stoiculescu | Kenryo Takahashi | Maria Yablonina supported by Michael Preisack
In Cooperation With:
   Institute of Evolution and Ecology, Evolutionary Biology of Invertebrates, University of Tübingen – Prof Dr Oliver Betz
   Department of Geosciences, Paleontology of Invertebrates and Paleoclimatology University of Tübingen – Prof James H Nebelsick
   University of Tübingen, Module: Bionics of animal constructions, Winter 2012: Gerald Buck | Michael Münster | Valentin Grau | Anne Buhl | Markus Maisch | Matthias Loose | Irene Viola Baumann | Carina Meiser
   ANKA / Institute for Photon Science and Synchrotron Radiation, Karlsruhe
   Institute of Technology (KIT) – Dr Thomas van de Kamp, Tomy dos Santos Rolo, Prof Dr Tilo Baumbach
   Institute for Machine Tools University of Stuttgart – Dr-Ing Thomas Stehle, Rolf Bauer, Michael Reichersdörfer
   Institute of Textile Technology and Process Engineering, ITV Denkendorf – Dr Markus Milwich
Funding/Sponsors:
   KUKA Roboter GmbH
   Kompetenznetz Biomimetik
   SGL Group
   Sika AG
   AFBW

LOUISIANA STATE MUSEUM AND SPORTS HALL OF FAME
Building Size: 2,601 m^2 (28,000 SF)
Year of Completion: 2013
Location: Natchitoches, LA, USA
Architect: Trahan Architects
Client: State of Louisiana
Structural Engineer: LBYD
MEP Engineer: Associated Design Group

Civil Engineer: CSRS
Landscape Architect: Reed Hilderbrand
Contractor: VCC
Geotechnical Engineer: GeoConsultants
BIM Manager and Technology: CASE Cast Stone Support Steel Geometry and Detailing: Method Design
Cast Stone Support Steel Engineer: David Kufferman PE
Acoustics: SH Acoustics
Waterproofing: Water Management Consultants & Testing
Interior: Lauren Bombet Interior

METROPOL PARASOL – PLAZA DE LA ENCARNACION
Building Size: 5,000 m² (53,819 SF)
Year of Completion: 2011
Location: Seville, Spain
Architect: J MAYER H Architects
 Project Architects: Andre Santer | Marta Ramírez Iglesias
Client/Contractor: Ayuntamiento de Sevilla and SACYR
Structural Engineer: Arup GmbH
Building Service Engineering Team: Salvador Castilla | Alborada Delgado | Marta Figueruelo Calvo | Arup GmbH
Fire Security Consultant Team:
 George Faller | Benjamin Barry-Otsoa | Jimmy Jonsson | Arup GmbH
 Engineers Project Management: Jose de la Peña | Jan-Peter Koppitz | Arup GmbH
Timber Engineer and Detail Design: Finnforest

THEATRE DE STOEP
Building Size: 7,000 m² (75,347 SF)
Year of Completion: 2014
Location: Spijkenisse, the Netherlands
Architect: Ben van Berkel | UNStudio
Architecture Team: Ben van Berkel | Gerard Loozekoot | Jacques van Wijk | Hans Kooij | Lars Nixdorff | Thomas Harms | Gustav Fagerstrom | Ramon van der Heijden Tatjana Gorbachewskaja | Jesca de Vries | Wesley Lanckriet | Maud van Hees | Benjamin Moore | Henk van Schuppen | Philipp Mecke | Colette Parras | Daniela Hake | Mazin Orfali | Selim Ahmad
Client: Municipality of Spijkenisse
Structural Engineer:
 Arup (Design phase)
 IOB (Execution phase)
 MEP Engineer: De Blaay – Van den Bogaard

Contractor: VORM Bouw
Lighting Design: Arup
Theatre Technique: PB theateradviseurs
Acoustics: SCENA Akoestisch Adviseurs
Fire: DGMR
Costs: Basalt Bouwadvies

CHAPTER 3

GROOVE CENTER
Building Size: 12,000 m² (129,166 SF)
Year of Completion: 2013
Location: Bangkok, Thailand
Architect: Synthesis Design + Architecture
Local Architect: A49 Architects
Local Architect: Foundry Space
Client: Central Pattana Pnc
Structural Engineer: Doctor Kulsiri Chadrangsu – Ferrand
MEP Engineer: MITR
Landscape Architect: Trop Design

JAMES B HUNT JR LIBRARY
Building Size: 20,446 m² (220,000 SF)
Year of Completion: 2013
Location: Raleigh, NC, USA
Architect: Snøhetta
Client: North Carolina State University
Structural Engineer: Stewart Engineering, Arup
MEP Engineer: Affiliated Engineers
Landscape Architect: Snøhetta
Contractor: Skanska

MULTIFUNCTIONAL SPORTS HALL
Building Size: 38,500 m² (414,410 SF)
Year of Completion: 2014
Location: Cluj-Napoca, Romania
Architect: Dico si Tiganas architecture and engineering
Client: Cluj-Napoca City Hall
Structural Engineer: SC Plan 31 Ro SRL
MEP Engineer: SC Instal Data SRL
Landscape Architect: Dico si Tiganas architecture and engineering
Contractor: SC Con-A SRL
Photography: Cosmin Dragomir | Alexandra Bendea

NASA SUSTAINABILITY BASE
Building Size: 4,645 m² (50,000 SF)
Year of Completion: 2012
Location: Moffett Field, CA, USA
Architect: William McDonough + Partners
Architect of Record, Landscape Architect of Record, MEP, Structural, Civil: AECOM
Daylighting, Lighting, Energy Consultant: Loisos + Ubbelohde
Contractor: Swinerton
Landscape Architect: Sitework Studios
Materials Assessment: McDonough Braungart Design Chemistry
Cost Estimator: TBD

THE NORTH HOUSE
Building Size: 74 m² (800 SF)
Year of Completion: 2009
Location: Waterloo, Canada
Architect: RVTR Inc: Kathy Velikov, OAA (Architect of record), Geoffrey Thün, Colin Ripley, Zain AbuSeir, Matt Storus, Matt Peddie
Client: University of Waterloo
Structural Engineer: Blackwell Bowick Partnership Ltd: David Bowick, Cory Zurell
Faculty Team: Geoffrey Thün (Faculty Lead / Primary Investigator) | Kathy Velikov | David Lieberman | Dr John Straube (Sustainability and Building Science) | Dr Michael Collins (Solar Thermal) | Philip Beesley | Donald McKay | Rick Haldenby | Dr Alan Fung | Dr Lyn Bartram (Interaction Design) | Ron Wakkary | Dr. Rob Woodbury (Chair, Advisory Board)
Graduate Student Architectural Team:
 Lauren Barhydt (Project Management and Engineering Systems Coordination) | Chris Black (Architectural Design: Envelope) | Chloe Doesburg (Architectural Design: Prefabrication Logics & Contract Administration) | Maun Demchenko (Media and Public Relations) | Natalie Jackson (Landscape Systems & Transportation Logistics) | Jen Janzen (Interior Design) | Bradley Paddock (Construction Logics & Prototyping) | Matt Peddie, Allan Wilson (Ceiling Systems Development) | Andrea Hunniford | Lindsey Nette | David Schellingerhoudt | Kevin Schorn | Sonya Storey-Fleming | Jamie Usas | Eric Bury | Wade Brown | Andrew Haydon | Hayley Isaacs | Chris Knight | Farid Noufailly
Graduate Student Engineering Team:
 Sebastien Brideau (Mechanical) | Brent Crowhurst (Electrical and Controls) | Ivan Lee (Engineering Coordination and Building Science) | Bart Lomanowski (Energy Modelling) | Andrew Marston (Mechanical) | Toktam Saied (Mechanical) | Humphrey Tse (Mechanical) | Fabio Almeida | Aya Dembo | Brittany Hanam

| Raqib Omer Mian | Omar Siddiqui
Interaction Design Student Team: Rob Mackenzie | Kevin Muise | Johnny Rodgers | Davis Marques | Kush Bubbar | Jin Fan | Yin He | Jenny Thai (SIAT)
Responsive Facade Development: Philip Beesley Architect Inc, RVTR Inc
Controls Design: Chris Brandson (Vertech Solutions), Reid Blumell (Embedia Technologies)
Mechanical Consulting: Al Davies (Eco-Options Geosolar) | Steve Davies (EcoLogix Heating Technologies) | Gord Walsh (Slatus Air) | Aaron Goldwater (Goldwater Solar Services)
Electrical Consulting: (Red Electric) Robin Sanders, Dan Pelkman, Nicolas Stroeder
Plumbing: Laurie Johnson | Wladyslaw Iwaniec
Kitchen Systems: (Bulthaup Canada) | Antje Bulthaup | Stefan Sybydlo
Logistics, Fabrication, Installation: MCM 2001 Inc, Gregory Rybak | Sean Baldwin (Owners) | Jacek Debski (Project Manager & Detail Development) | Witek Jasinski (Crew Lead) | Mikola Minzak | Luke Statkiewicz | Lukasz Szczepanek | Maks Matuszewski | Philip Lesniak | Adam Golaszewski | Richard Pelly | Zbigniew Gembora | Ryszard Goryl | Krzysztof Plaza | Krzysztof Banasek | Pawel Noga | Jan Sawczak | Piotr Dabrowski | Oleg Izvekov (Dynamics Design) | Danny Pietrangelo
Photography: Geoffrey Thün

SAN MAMÉS STADIUM

Building Size: 110,000 m^2 (1,184,030 SF)
Year of Completion: 2014
Location: Bilbao, Spain
Architect: César Azcárate (IDOM-ACXT)
Client: San Mamés Barria SA
Structural Engineer: Armando Bilbao, Javier Llarena (IDOM)
MEP Engineer: Álvaro Gutiérrez, Alberto Ribacoba (IDOM)
Project Manager: Alberto Tijero, Óscar Malo (IDOM)
Sustainability Consultant: Francisco Sánchez (IDOM)
Quantity Surveyors: Javier Ruiz de Prada
Planning: Alexander Zeuss (IDOM)
Deputy Architect: Diego Rodríguez (IDOM-ACXT)

ROYAL MELBOURNE INSTITUTE OF TECHNOLOGY (RMIT) DESIGN HUB

Building Size: 13,000 m^2 (139,930 SF)
Year of Completion: 2012
Location: Melbourne, Australia
Architect: Sean Godsell Architects in association with Peddle Thorp Architects
Client: RMIT University
Structural Engineer: Felicetti Pty Ltd
MEP Engineer: AECOM
Civil Engineer: Felicetti Pty Ltd
Landscape Architect: Sean Godsell Architects
Sustainability Consultant: AECOM
Building Surveyor: Phillip Chun & Associates
Quantity Surveyor: Davis Langdon
Facade Contractor: Permasteelisa Pty Ltd

TEXAS HEALTH HARRIS METHODIST HOSPITAL ALLIANCE

Building Size: 16,908 m^2 (182,000 SF)
Year of Completion: 2012
Location: Fort Worth, TX, USA
Architect: Perkins+Will
  Design Principal: David Collins
  Managing Principal: Cary Garner
Client: Texas Health Resources
Structural Engineer: LA Fuess
MEP Engineer: CCRD
Civil Engineer: RLG
Landscape Architect: KENDALL + Landscape Architecture
Contractor: Beck

CHAPTER 5

CENTER FOR DESIGN RESEARCH

Building Size: 169 m^2 (1,820 SF)
Year of Completion: 2011
Location: Lawrence, KS, USA
Architect: Studio 804
Client: University of Kansas Endowment Association
Structural Engineer: Norton & Schmidt
MEP Engineer: Hoss & Brown, Lawrence, KS
LEED: Henderson Engineers
Environmental Consultants: Cromwell Environmental, Lawrence, KS
Contractor: Studio 804

COLLABORATIVE LIFE SCIENCES BUILDING & SKOURTES TOWER

Building Size: 46,451 m^2 (500,000 SF)
Year of Completion: 2014
Location: Portland, OR, USA
Architect: CO Architects
Interior Designer: CO Architects
Executive Architect: SERA Architects
Client: Partnership of Oregon Health & Science University (OHSU), Portland State University (PSU), Oregon State University (OSU)
Structural Engineer: KPFF Consulting Engineers
MEP Engineer: Interface Engineering
Owner's Representative: DAY CPM
Construction Manager/General Contractor: JE Dunn; Wet Mechanical Contractors: JH Kelly; Dry Mechanical Contractors: Temp Control Electrical Contractors: Oregon Electric Group
Metal Panels: Skyline
Exterior Glazing: Harmon
Skylights/Atrium Glazing: DeaMor

HANJIE WANDA SQUARE

Building Size: 30,500 m^2 (328,299 SF)
Year of Completion: 2013
Location: Wuhan, China
Architect: UNStudio
LDI Architecture: CSADI, Central South Architectural Design Institute, INC
Client: Wuhan Wanda East Lake Real State Co Ltd
Structural Engineer: China Construction Second Engineering Bureau Ltd
Funnel Structure: Arup SHA | Shanghai General Metal Structure Engineer Co Ltd, Facade: Arup SHA
Lighting Facade: ag Licht | LightLife | BUME Lighting Design & Engineering Co Ltd
LDI Facade: Beijing JinXinZhuoHong Facade Engineering Co Ltd
LDI Interior: Beijing Qing Shang Architectural Design Engineering Co Ltd
LDI Lighting: BIAD Zheng Jian Wei Lighting Studio
Landscape Design: Ecoland
Facade Construction: FANGDA Design Engineering Co Ltd

HEALTH SCIENCES EDUCATION BUILDING (HSEB)

Building Size: 24,898 m^2 (268,000 SF)
Year of Completion: 2012
Location: Phoenix, AZ, USA
Architect: CO Architects
Associate Architect, Masterplanner: Ayers Saint Gross
Contractor, Preconstruction, Construction Manager at Risk: DPR Construction | Sundt Construction, Inc
Client: Arizona Board of Regents
Structural Engineer: John A Martin & Associates

MEP Engineer: AEI Engineers
Civil Engineer: Dibble Engineering
Landscape Architect: JJR
Lighting Designer: Kaplan Gehring McCarroll Lighting
Climate Engineer: Transsolar Energietechnik
Geotechnical Engineer: Professional Service Industries
Fire Protection/Code Consultant: Rolf Jensen & Associates
Loading/Vertical Transportation Consultant: Lerch Bates
Audiovisual Technology: The Sextant Group
Cost Estimator: Davis Langdon

KIND FAHAD NATIONAL LIBRARY
Building Size: 86,630 m^2 (932,140 SF)
Year of Completion: 2013
Location: Riyadh, Saudi Arabia
Architect: Gerber Architekten
Client: Kingdom of Saudi Arabia, represented by Arriyadh Development Authority
Structural Engineer: Bollinger & Grohmann Ingenieure, in cooperation with SaudConsult
MEP Engineer: DS-Plan in cooperation with SaudConsult
Civil Engineer: SaudConsult
Landscape Architect: Gerber Architekten in cooperation with Kienle Planungsgesellschaft
Sustainability Consultant: DS-Plan
Contractor: Saudi Binladin Group
Translucent Ceiling Membrane: ART Engineering

UMWELT ARENA
Building Size: 11,000 m^2 (118,403 SF)
Year of Completion: 2012
Location: Spreitenbach, Switzerland
Architect: René Schmid Architekten AG
Structural Engineer: Tantanini & Partner AG
Contractor: W Schmid AG, Generalbau

SHANGHAI NATURAL HISTORY MUSEUM
Building Size: 44,517 M^2 (479,180 SF)
Year of Completion: 2015
Location: Shanghai, China
Architect: Perkins+Will
Associate Architect: Tongji University Architectural Design and Research Institute
Client: Shanghai Science & Technology Museum
Structural Engineer: Tongji University Architectural Design and Research Institute
MEP Engineer: Tongji University Architectural Design and Research Institute
Civil Engineer: Tongji University Architectural Design and Research Institute
Landscape Architect: Hoerr Schaudt Landscape Architects
Sustainability Consultant: DHV, JACOBS
Sustainability: HASKONING and Shanghai Educational Engineering (cooperative unit)
Contractor: Shanghai Construction Group
Curtain Wall Consultant: Aurecon
Curtain Wall Contractor: Shanghai Mechanical Construction Group
Atrium/Cell-Wall Contractor: Sinobau

THE YAS HOTEL
Building Size: 85,000 m^2 (914,932 SF)
Year of Completion: 2009
Location: Abu Dhabi, UAE
Architect: Asymptote Architecture, Hani Rashid + Lise Anne Couture
Local Architect: Dewan Architects & Engineers
Client: Aldar Properties PJSC
Structural Engineer: Dewan Architects + Engineers
MEP Engineer: RED Engineering Middle East
Landscape Architect: Cracknell
Facade Consultants: Front Inc

INDEX

Page numbers in *italics* refer to figures.

A

Acciona Infrastructure:
 ETFE-MFM (research project), 131, 133
active chilled beams, 139, *139*
adaptive living interface system (ALIS), 165, 168
additive methods, of digital fabrication, 112, 113
aerogel inserts, 35, *36*, 37
ALIS (adaptive living interface system), 165, 168
aluminium composite panels, 39, *39*
aluminium foam sheets, *36*–37, *37*, *38*
amorphous silicon cells, 51, 53
Anaheim Regional Transportation Intermodal Center (ARTIC), *92, 93, 94, 95,* 96–97
analysis:
 CFD, 105, 109, 111
 computational structural, 103
 energy, 98–99, 101
 structural, *see* structural analysis
Antoine Predock Architect PC:
 Trinity River Audubon Center, *37, 38,* 39
architectural design:
 with BIM, 89
 to fabrication, 121, 125
 innovation in modern, 15–16
 integration of research and, 174–176
architectural firms, roles in, 173, 174
architecture, biomimetic, 41
Architecture49:
 Joggins Fossil Centre, *34*–*35,* 35
ARTIC (Anaheim Regional Transportation Intermodal Center), *92, 93, 94, 95,* 96–97
Asymptote Architecture:
 Yas Hotel, *228*–*236,* 229, 233
atrium, of Shanghai Natural History Museum, 218, 219
automation:
 building automation systems, 49, 151, 156
 central home automation server, 165
 in construction, 159, 162
 in industrialisation, 157, *157*
 integrated automation systems, 162, *162*
Ayers Saint Gross:
 Health Sciences Education Building, 233, 237, *237*–*244,* 241, 243

B

BAS (building automation systems), 49, 151, 156
Belectric:
 ETFE-MFM (research project), 131, 133
BIM, *see* Building Information Modelling
biomaterials, 39, *39*–*43,* 41
biomimetic architecture, 41
Brussels Environment, 55, *56*–*58*
building automation systems (BAS), 49, 151, 156
building envelope(s):
 of King Fahad National Library, 201
 responsive, 164
Building Information Modelling (BIM):
 applications for, 81, 83
 and building automation systems, 151, 156, *156*
 in Collaborative Life Sciences Building and Skourtes Tower, 215, 217
 in computational design, 88–91
 and fabrication, 121
 in facility management, 95, 98
 in Health Sciences Education Building, 233, 237, 241
 and integrated project delivery, 181
 in virtual construction, 91, 93, 95
building performance:
 and BIM, 156
 environmental simulations and energy analysis for, 98
 new approaches to, 84, 85
Building Realization and Robotics research team, 162, 163
buildingSMART initiative, 83–84

C

CAAD (computer-aided architectural design), 77, 81, 83
CAD (computer-aided design), 77, 81, 83
CAM (computer-aided manufacturing), 85, 111–112
Cascade Meadow Wetlands and Environmental Science Center, 31, *32,* 33
case studies, 185–245
 Center for Design Research, *186*–*191,* 187, 191
 Collaborative Life Sciences Building and Skourtes Tower, 211, *212*–*218,* 215, 217–218
 Hanjie Wanda Square, *204*–*211,* 205, 209
 Health Sciences Education Building, 233, 237, *237*–*244,* 241, 243
 King Fahad National Library, 199, *199*–*203,* 201, 205
 Shanghai Natural History Museum, 218–219, *219*–*227,* 223, 225
 Umwelt Arena, 191, *192*–*198,* 193, 197, 199
 Yas Hotel, *228*–*236,* 229, 233
Case Western Reserve University, *108*–*111,* 109, 111
CDR (Center for Design Research), *186*–*191,* 187, 191
cellular aluminium foam sheets, *36*–37, *37*, *38*
Cener (National Renewable Energy Center of Spain):
 ETFE-MFM (research project), 131, 133
Center for Design Research (CDR), *186*–*191,* 187, 191
central home automation server (CHAS), 165
cepezed:
 Brussels Environment, 55, *56*–*58*
CFD (computational fluid dynamics) analysis, 105, 109, 111
CHAS (central home automation server), 165
chilled beams, active and passive, 139, *139*
CLSB/SKT (Collaborative Life Sciences Building and Skourtes Tower), 211, *212*–*218,* 215, 217–218
CMUs (concrete masonry units), 25, *25*
CO Architects:
 Collaborative Life Sciences Building and Skourtes Tower, 211, *212*–*218,* 215, 217–218
 Health Sciences Education Building, 233, 237, *237*–*244,* 241, 243
 coatings, on glass, 29
 Collaborative Life Sciences Building and Skourtes Tower (CLSB/SKT), 211, *212*–*218,* 215, 217–218
commercialisation or implementation stage (of innovation), 16
composite materials, 41, *44,* 45
computational design, 61–127
 advances in, 63–77
 BIM in, 88–91
 and BIM in facility management, 95, 98
 and BIM in virtual construction, 91, 93, 95
 CFD analysis, 105, 109, 111
 design to fabrication, 121, 125
 digital fabrication and methods, 111–113,

115, 121
environmental simulations and energy
 analysis, 98–99, 101
Eskenazi Hospital parking structure art facade,
 67, 68–71, 69
for Hanjie Wanda Square, 209
ICD/ITKE Research Pavilion 2013-2014, 62–64,
 65, 66–67, 67
Louisiana State Museum and Sports Hall of
 Fame, 69, 71, 72–77
Metropol Parasol, 71, 77, 78–80
for Shanghai Natural History Museum, 219,
 223
structural analysis, 101, 103, 105
tools and methods, 77, 81, 83–85, 88
computational fluid dynamics (CFD) analysis,
 105, 109, 111
computational structural analysis, 103
computer-aided architectural design (CAAD),
 77, 81, 83
computer-aided design (CAD), 77, 81, 83
computer-aided manufacturing (CAM), 85,
 111–112
computer applications:
 for design functions, 81
 for environmental simulations, 98–99
concrete, 22–28, 23, 25, 27, 30
concrete masonry units (CMUs), 25, 25
concrete sandwich wall system, 26, 27
Consarc Architects:
 iCon Innovation Centre, 50–51, 51–53
construction:
 automation in, 159, 162
 with BIM, 90
 BIM with virtual, 91, 93, 95
 modular, 156–157, 158–161, 159
 robotics in, 162–163
 of Umwelt Arena, 197
controls, 48–49, 49
control systems, in building automation
 systems, 49
corporate culture, 171–172
culturally responsive architecture, 199, 201
culture of innovation, 171–172, 248

D

daylight harvesting, 149
daylighting, 211
decoupled HVAC systems, 139
dedicated outdoor air system (DOAS), 139
Dico si Tiganas:
 Multifunctional Sports Hall, 134, 135, 136–137
digital fabrication, 111–113, 115, 121
digital production processes, 84

dimming controls, 149
dissemination stage (of innovation), 16
DOAS (dedicated outdoor air system), 139
double-skin glazed facades, 132–134, 133, 135,
 136–137

E

electrochromic glass, 29, 31, 31–33, 33, 45
electrorheological materials, 21, 23
electrostrictive materials, 21
energy analysis, 98–99, 101
energy management, 151, 156
engagement, and culture of innovation, 172
environmental concerns:
 in Collaborative Life Sciences Building and
  Skourtes Tower, 211, 215
 in design innovation, 17
 in Health Sciences Education Building, 233
 in Shanghai Natural History Museum, 218
 in Umwelt Arena, 191, 193, 197, 199
environmental sensors, 48
environmental simulations, 98–99, 101
'ER response,' 21, 23
Eskenazi Hospital parking structure art facade,
 67, 68–71, 69
ETFE (ethylene tetrafluoroethylene) facade
 system, 130, 131, 133
ETFE-MFM (research project), 131, 133
experimental research methods, 177
Exploratory Hall, 99, 100–103, 101
expression, and culture of innovation, 171–172
exterior shading system prototype, 48–49, 49
external research practices, 176

F

FAAB Architektura:
 PGE GiEK Corporate Headquarters, 44–45, 45
fabrication:
 design to, 121, 125
 digital, 111, 113, 115, 121
 prefabrication, 156–157, 158–161, 159
facade cladding materials, 27, 28, 30, 187
facade systems:
 at Center for Design Research, 187
 of Hanjie Wanda Square, 209
 technological innovations in, 130, 131,
  132–134, 133, 135, 136–138
facility management:
 BIM in, 95, 98
fibre-cement composite panels, 44–45, 45
financial factors, for innovation, 177–178
First Aid Emergency Post, 48, 48
formative methods, of digital fabrication,
 112–113

G

Garrison Architects:
 New York City Beach Restoration Modules,
  22–24, 25
Gerber Architekten:
 King Fahad National Library, 199, 199–203,
  201, 205
Giant Interactive Group Corporate
 Headquarters, 27, 28
glass, 27, 29, 30–36, 31, 33, 35, 37
glass-fibre reinforced concrete (GFRC), 23, 23,
 25
glazing (of glass), 27, 29
glued laminated timber (glulam), 41, 42
Goshow Architects:
 Nobel Halls, 36, 37
Gramazio Kohler Architects:
 Gantenvein Vineyard facade, 115, 118–119,
  121
Greenovate! Europe:
 ETFE-MFM (research project), 131, 133
grid-shell structure, of Yas Hotel, 229, 233
The Groove, 148, 149, 150–151

H

Hanjie Wanda Square, 204–211, 205, 209
Health Sciences Education Building (HSEB), 233,
 237, 237–244, 241, 243
HEMA Building, 41, 43
HOK:
 Anaheim Regional Transportation Intermodal
  Center, 92, 93, 94, 95, 96–97
HSEB (Health Sciences Education Building), 233,
 237, 237–244, 241, 243
humidity sensors, 48
HVAC systems:
 technological innovations in, 135, 139, 141,
  142–144, 145
in Umwelt Arena, 193

I

ICD (Institute for Computational Design):
 ICD/ITKE Research Pavilion 2013-2014, 62–64,
  65, 66–67, 67
iCon Innovation Centre, 50–51, 51–53
IDOM-ACXT:
 San Mamés Stadium, 149, 151, 151–155
IGUs (triple-insulated glazing units), 50, 50
incremental innovation, 248
industrialisation, 156–157, 157
Industry Foundation Classes (IFC), 83–84, 99
innovation, 13–19, 171–183
 activities classified as, 17
 Center for Design Research as example of,

187, 191
defining, 13, 15–16
financial factors and investment for, 177–178
in Health Sciences Education Building design process, 237, 241, 243
integration of research and design practice, 174–176
methods for, 17–19
motives and goals for, 171–172
organisations and roles that foster, 172–173, *174*
in project delivery, 179–182
purpose of, 16–17
research methods for, 176–177
and risk management, 181–182
stages in process of, 16
strategies for integrating, 183
transformational and incremental, 248
value of, 179, 180
Institute for Advanced Architecture of Catalonia:
   Translated Geometries (research project), *114*, 115, *116–117*
Institute for Computational Design (ICD):
   ICD/ITKE Research Pavilion 2013-2014, *62–64*, 65, *66–67*, 67
Institute of Building Structures and Structural Design (ITKE):
   ICD/ITKE Research Pavilion 2013-2014, *62–64*, 65, *66–67*, 67
integrated automation systems, 162, *162*
integrated intelligent systems, 163, 164
integrated project delivery (IPD), 91, 179–182
integration:
   in Collaborative Life Sciences Building and Skourtes Tower, 217
   in complex buildings, 185
   in computational design, 84
   of innovation, strategies for, 183
   innovation in, 18, *19*
   of research and design practice, 174–176
intelligent elements, in smart and responsive buildings, 163
interdisciplinary collaboration, 173
internal research practices, 176
investment, for innovation, 177–178
IPD (integrated project delivery), 91, 179–182
ITKE (Institute of Building Structures and Structural Design):
   ICD/ITKE Research Pavilion 2013-2014, *62–64*, 65, *66–67*, 67
ITMA Materials Technology:
   ETFE-MFM (research project), 131, 133

J
James B Hunt Jr Library, *138*, *140*, 141, *142–143*
J Mayer H Architects:
   Metropol Parasol, 71, 77, *78–80*
Joggins Fossil Centre, *34–35*, 35

K
King Fahad National Library, 199, *199–203*, 201, 205

L
LED (light-emitting diode) technology, 145, 149
Level of Development (LOD), 90
Ley, Rob:
   Reef (installation), *46*, 47, *47*
LHB:
   Cascade Meadow Wetlands and Environmental Science Center, 31, *32*, 33
light-emitting diode (LED) technology, 145, 149
lighting, 145, *146–148*, 149, *150*, 151
lighting sensors, 48
light-to-solar-gain (LSG) ratio, 29
LKPB Engineers:
   Cascade Meadow Wetlands and Environmental Science Center, 31, *32*, 33
LOD (Level of Development), 90
L'Office 64 de l'Habitat, 39, *39*, 40
Louisiana State Museum and Sports Hall of Fame, 69, 71, *72–77*
LSG (light-to-solar-gain) ratio, 29

M
MAD Architects:
   Taichung Convention Center, 41, *41*, *42*
magnetostrictive materials, 21
Marcus, Frank:
   First Aid Emergency Post, 48, *48*
material manipulators, 159
materials, 21–59
   biomaterials, 39, *39–43*, 41
   composite materials, 41, *44*, 45
   concrete, *22–28*, 23, 25, 27, *30*
   electrochromics, 45
   glass, 27, 29, *30–36*, 31, 33, 35, 37
   metals, 37, *37–40*, 39
   phase-change materials, 49–51, *50–52*
   photovoltaics, 51, *52–56*, 53, 55
   self-healing materials, 47–48, *47–48*
   sensors and controls, 48–49, *49*
   shape-memory alloys, 45, *45–47*, 47
   thermoelectrics, 55, *57*
   in Umwelt Arena design, 197, 199
McKeever, Sean:
   exterior shading system prototype, 48–49, *49*

mechanisation, in industrialisation, 156–157, *157*
metals, 37, *37–40*, 39
Metro Arkitekter:
   Hyllie Train Station, 27, *30*
Metropol Parasol, 71, 77, *78–80*
mixed research methods, 177
modular construction, 156–157, *158–161*, 159
monocrystalline silicon cells, 51, 53
Morgan Library, 31, *31*
Morphosis:
   Giant Interactive Group Corporate Headquarters, 27, *28*
motion sensors, 48, 149
Multifunctional Sports Hall, *134*, 135, *136–137*

N
NASA Sustainability Base, 141, *144*, 145, *146–147*
National Renewable Energy Center of Spain (Cener):
   ETFE-MFM (research project), 131, 133
New York City Beach Restoration Modules, *22–24*, 25
nickel-titanium (NiTi) alloys, 47
Nobel Halls, *36*, 37
North House, *164*, 164–165, *166–167*, 168

O
occupancy sensors, 48, 149
opaque PV glass, 53
operation models, 176
operations, activities classified as, 17
organisations:
   change embraced by, 247–248
   culture of innovation established by, 248–249
   supporting innovations in, 17–18
   that foster innovation, 172–173, *174*
overhead costs, 178

P
paraffin, in PCMs, 50
parametric modeling, 63, 65, 81, 83
passive chilled beams, 139, *139*
Patrick Arotcharen Agence d'Architecture:
   L'Office 64 de l'Habitat, 39, *39*, 40
PCMs (phase-change materials), 49–51, *50–52*
Perkins+Will:
   Case Western Reserve University, *108–111*, 109, 111
   Exploratory Hall, 99, *100–103*, 101
   research project, *82–83*, 84, *85*, *86–87*
   School of Business Building, *26–27*, 27
   Shanghai Natural History Museum, 218–219, *219–227*, 223, 225

Texas Health Harris Methodist Hospital
    Alliance, 157, *158–161*, 159
PGE GiEK Corporate Headquarters, *44–45*, 45
phase-change materials (PCMs), 49–51, *50–52*
phenolic wood composites, 41, *43*
photocatalysis process, for self-cleaning
    concrete, *24*, 25
photochromic glass, 33
photovoltaics (PVs), 51, *52–56*, 53, *55*
piezoelectric materials, 21
placing and finishing systems, 159
polycrystalline silicon cells, 51, *53*
prefabrication, 156–157, *158–161*, 159
process innovation, 177
product innovation, 177
profits, 178
project delivery:
    innovation in, 16
    integrated project delivery, 91, 179–182
PVs (photovoltaics), 51, *52–56*, 53, *55*

Q
qualitative research methods, 177
quantitative research methods, 177

R
radiant systems, 139, *141*
rainscreen facade system, *27*, *28*, 237, *241*
Reef (installation), *46*, 47, *47*
remote-controlled and sensing systems, 159
René Schimd Architekten:
    Umwelt Arena, 191, *192–198*, 193, 197, *199*
reproduction, in industrialisation, 157, *157*
research:
    integration of design practice and, 174–176
    methods of, for innovation, 176–177
research and development stage (of
    innovation), 16
responsive building envelopes, 164
responsive buildings, *see* smart and responsive
    buildings
retrofitting existing buildings, 199, 201, 205
Richter Dahl Rocha & Associés:
    SwissTech Convention Center, 53, *54–55*, 55
Rickhill, Dan, 187
risk management, 181–182
RMIT (Royal Melbourne Institute of Technology),
    132–133, 135
Rob Ley Studio:
    Eskenazi Hospital parking structure art facade,
    67, *68–71*, 69
robot construction system for computer-
    integrated construction (ROCCO), 163, *163*
robotics:
    in construction, 162–163
    in industrialisation, 157, *157*
roles:
    in architectural firms, 173, *174*
    that foster innovation, 172–173, *174*
Royal Melbourne Institute of Technology (RMIT),
    132–133, 135
Ryerson University:
    North House, 164, 164–165, *166–167*, 168

S
salt hydrates, in PCMs, 50
School of Business Building, *26–27*, 27
Sean Godsell Architects:
    Royal Melbourne Institute of Technology,
    132–133, 135
self-cleaning concrete, *24*, 25, *26–27*, 27
self-healing materials, *47–48*, *47–48*
self-repairing concrete, 25
semitransparent PV glass, 53
sensors, 48–49, *49*
SERA:
    Collaborative Life Sciences Building and
        Skourtes Tower, 211, *212–218*, 215, *217–218*
service innovation, 177
Shanghai Natural History Museum, 218–219,
    219–227, 223, 225
shape-memory alloys (SMAs), 45, *45–47*, 47
Shepley Bullfinch:
    University of Michigan Cardiovascular Center,
    27, *27*
SHGC (solar heat gain coefficient), 27, 31
Simon Fraser University:
    North House, 164, 164–165, *166–167*, 168
simulations:
    applications for, 81, *83*
    environmental, 98–99, *101*
smart and responsive buildings:
    with building automation systems, 49
    in innovation, 17
    technological innovations in, 163–165,
        166–167, 168
smart materials, 21
SMAs (shape-memory alloys), 45, *45–47*, 47
SMAS (solid material assembling system), *162*,
    162–163
Snøhetta:
    James B Hunt Jr Library, *138*, *140*, 141,
        142–143
solar heat gain coefficient (SHGC), 27, 31
solid material assembling system (SMAS), *162*,
    162–163
SPD (suspended particle device) glass, 33, *33*
Stein, Joshua:
    Reef (installation), *46*, 47, *47*
Strategie Architecten:
    HEMA Building, 41, *43*
strategy(-ies):
    corporate, and innovation, 171
    for establishing culture of innovation, 248
    for integrating innovation, 183
strong delivery firms, 172–173
strong idea firms, 172–173
strong service firms, 172–173
structural analysis:
    computational, 103
    in computational design, 101, 103, *105*
    for Hanjie Wanda Square, 209
    for Shanghai Natural History Museum, 223,
        225
Studio 804:
    Center for Design Research, *186–191*, 187, *191*
    purpose of, 187
Studiotrope:
    Morgan Library, 31, *31*
subtractive methods, of digital fabrication, 112,
    113
suspended particle device (SPD) glass, 33, *33*
Synthesis Design + Architecture:
    The Groove, *148*, 149, *150–151*

T
Taichung Convention Center, 41, *41*, *42*
Taiyo Europe:
    ETFE-MFM (research project), 131, *133*
technological innovations, 129–169
    automation in construction, 159, 162
    in building automation systems, 151, 156
    in facade systems, *130*, 131, *132–134*, 133, 135,
        136–138
    in HVAC systems, 135, 139, 141, *142–144*, 145
    in lighting, 145, *146–148*, 149, *150*, 151
    in prefabrication and modular construction,
        156–157, *158–161*, 159
    robotics in construction, 162–163
    in smart and responsive buildings, 163–165,
        166–167, 168
    in Umwelt Arena design, 197, *199*
    in Yas Hotel design process, 229, 233
Texas Health Harris Methodist Hospital Alliance,
    157, *158–161*, 159
thermal sensors, 48
thermochromic glass, 33
thermoelectrics, 55, *57*
titanium dioxide, 25, *27*
tools, for computational design, 77, 81, *83–85*,
    88
Trahan Architects:

Louisiana State Museum and Sports Hall of Fame, 69, 71, *72–77*
transformational innovation, 248
Translated Geometries (research project), *114*, 115, *116–117*
translucent concrete, 25
Trinity River Audubon Center, 37, *38*, 39
triple-insulated glazing units (IGUs), 50, *50*
TU Delft, 48
Tv (visual transmittance), 27, 29

U

UFAD (underfloor air distribution) systems, 139, 141
Umwelt Arena, 191, *192–198*, 193, 197, 199
uncertainty, as risk factor, 181–182
underfloor air distribution (UFAD) systems, 139, 141
University of Cincinnati:
 research project, *82–83*, 84, *85*, *86–87*
University of Michigan Cardiovascular Center, 27, *27*
University of Waterloo:
 North House, *164*, 164–165, *166–167*, 168
UNStudio:
 Hanjie Wanda Square, *204–211*, 205, 209
 Theatre de Stoep, *120*, 121, *122–125*, 125

V

vacuum-insulated glazing units, 35
value:
 and culture of innovation, 172
 of innovation, 179, 180
variable air volume (VAV) system, 139
virtual construction, 91, 93, 95
virtual reality (VR), 93
visualisation:
 applications for, 81, 83
 with BIM, 88
visual transmittance (Tv), 27, 29
VR (virtual reality), 93

W

water mixtures, in PCMs, 50
weathering steel, 37, *38*, 39
William McDonough + Partners:
 NASA Sustainability Base, 141, *144*, 145, *146–147*
wind-tunnel testing, 109
'Winslow effect,' 21, 23

Y

Yas Hotel, *228–236*, 229, 233

Z

Zaha Hadid Architects:
 Heydar Aliyev Centre, 103, *104*, 105, *106–107*